A. Jacobi

Aufsätze, Vorträge und Reden

Band 2

A. Jacobi

Aufsätze, Vorträge und Reden
Band 2

ISBN/EAN: 9783743327245

Hergestellt in Europa, USA, Kanada, Australien, Japan

Cover: Foto ©Paul-Georg Meister /pixelio.de

Manufactured and distributed by brebook publishing software
(www.brebook.com)

A. Jacobi

Aufsätze, Vorträge und Reden

Aufsätze, Vorträge und Reden

VON

DR. A. JACOBI

FÜR SEINE TOCHTER ZU IHREM SECHSZEHNTEN GEBURTSTAGE
AUSGEWÄHLT

ZWEITER BAND

New York
Press of Stettiner, Lambert & Co.
22-26 Reade Street
1893

INHALT.

THE HISTORICAL DEVELOPMENT OF MODERN NURSING.

ADDRESS DELIVERED AT THE FIRST COMMENCEMENT OF THE MOUNT SINAI TRAINING SCHOOL FOR NURSES, MAY 12TH, 1883.

NURSING is as old as the human species. Even among animals, such as they are at present, we find occasional sympathy with fellow-suffering, and meet with efforts for the purpose of relief. We cannot imagine that human beings, in ever so remote prehistoric times, should have lived together, or near each other, without mutual attempts at relief when suffering or sick. But this is presumption only, not history. No book, no tradition refers to facts in regard to the subject until the times of ancient Hellas and its successor in civilization, ancient Rome. Antiquity yields but few proofs of systematic nursing. It is true, hospitality was the pre-eminent virtue of the Greek. The stranger was always welcome; if he was sick, he was twice so. In all Hellas poor sick citizens found ready admission to, and nursing in, the houses of the rich. It may be that the facility of finding private relief on the part of the sick was one of the causes why no systematic and collective efforts for the purpose of attending and nursing the sick were ever made to any extent. That such was the case

1*

there can be little doubt; for the temples of Æsculapius and the adjoining residences of the physicians were probably not hospitals, but temporary
domiciles for those who congregated in large numbers around the homes of the gods. Of the same
nature was the edifice erected by Antoninus Pius
near the temple of the Epidaurian Æsculapius. In
Italy, also, the temple of Æsculapius, on the island
in the Tiber between Rome and the outlet of the
river, was never of much importance as a hospital
or sanitarium. The only real hospitals at all com-
parable with institutions such as we have, existed
in favor of human property and for the benefit of
soldiers. According to the testimony of Columella,
Seneca, and Celsus, the Romans had hospitals for
slaves, warriors, and gladiators. In Greece, also,
as early as the period of Solon, those injured on
the battlefield were attended and nursed at the expense of the community. Of the great Cæsar it is
well known that he had a regular medical service
in his armies.

There is a word in the ancient Greek which has
given rise to the belief that Hellas may have had
hospitals. But, as no facts and reports sustain that
supposition, it is probable that ιατρειον meant a
medical office, a polyclinic perhaps, but not a hospital. Real hospitals were not built by either Greek,
Roman, or Hebrew. The commonwealth of the
latter was hierarchic and intolerant. The stranger
—though he who was permitted to live in Judæa
was to be treated like a member of the community
—was to be exterminated, and must not be spared.
Thus, while there are no proofs of the existence of

hospitals for the friend, a painstaking care in favor of the stranger was out of the question.

Antiquity, however, is not without its humane culture. The reconciling feature in that immense picture of indifference and thoughtlessness is found in Buddhism. We have the reliable report of a genuine hospital founded by a king in Ceylon in the fifth century B.C. One of his successors in the second century B.C. is credited with eighteen hospitals under regular medical superintendence. In the East Indies hospitals are mentioned in the third century. Nor have other civilizations been slow in outgrowing the humane exertions of Hellas, Rome, and Palestine, for Prescott tells us that there were hospitals in Mexico before the Christian Spaniards introduced the blessings of torture, inquisition, and extermination. And when finally the Christians, in the second century after Christ, bethought themselves of the poor and sick and established hospitals, the largest and most effective ones were founded in Asia Minor and Persia, where Buddhism had prepared both means and public opinion— Buddhism, under whose beneficent rules aiding the poor and nursing the sick were two of the religious duties of kings and princes. Nor has Christianity the claim of having the first *large* hospitals. The Arabs had many good and large hospitals about 1200. Cordova, in Spain, sustained fifty within its own walls.

The first information in regard to Christian hospitals dates back to the second century ; other reports go back as far as the fourth, and a few others to the sixth century. In most cases the establishments were not exactly hospitals, but stopping places and dormitories for pilgrims on their way to Rome. To what extent such institutions were necessities is best proved by the order of the so-called "Bridgemakers" (*Hospitaliers Pontifes*), whose original vocation it was to protect pilgrims from the robberies and rapacity of the ferrymen on the large rivers. They existed a long time, became rich and degenerated, and were finally dissolved in 1672 by Louis XIV.

The hierarchic character of the institutions calculated to benefit the poor remained intact until the period of the Crusade wars. At that time Italian and German merchants initiated the great combinations of the several orders of the Hospital Brothers.

Their efforts were not isolated or altogether premature. For there existed a humanistic movement among the better classes of the Occident, on a Christian basis, it is true, but spontaneous. Particularly in the cities societies were formed for the purpose of nursing the sick and aiding the forlorn. Guy of Montpellier, France, established a hospital in that city, *of larger size*, while up to that time all the institutions of a similar character were small and unavailing, and located outside the walls. The new hospital in Montpellier, and seven more French houses, and two under the same direction in Rome, are first mentioned in a bull of Pope Innocent III. in the year 1198. The secular character of the institutions was at that time fully recognized. In connecting four clergymen with them he commanded that they were to attend to spiritual duties only ("*sine contradictione et murmuratione*"), and not to interfere with the office of the superiors. In 1204 the same pope recognized the newly established Hospital of the Holy Ghost, on the old Tiber bridge, in Rome. With the peculiar mixture of ferocity and mildness so common to the mediæval age, the same man who humiliated emperors, dethroned kings, and persecuted the French heretics with fire and sword to extermination, looked for the helpless and sick in the streets and saved illegitimate babies from their watery graves. Guy de Montpellier's creation, the order of the Holy Ghost, did not remain long in its original condition. Pope Gregory X. (1271–76) subjected all the houses belonging to the order to the one located in Rome, the first step in the attempt at depriving the order and its hospitals of their secular supervision. It was finally disposed of by the bull of Pope Sixtus IV. of the 21st of March, 1477. Meanwhile and afterward the order spread over all Europe. With its increasing wealth and power it degenerated in the seventeenth century. Though clerical by name, it was the most secular of all the institutions of dissipation. Grandmaster and officers lived on the fat of the land and their immense income. In vain Louis XIV. attempted to abolish it. The only change French royalty could work was its transmutation into a royal order. In some of the provinces laymen had succeeded, however, in controlling the management. Thus it was in many parts of Germany, where, between 1400 and 1600, several of the institutions belonging to the order were secularized. In Italy, however, the order of the Holy Ghost remained exclusively clerical. As late as in the beginning of the eighteenth century it had great possessions in Europe and the West Indies.

The order of St. Elizabeth was founded in 1225 by Elizabeth, daughter of Andrew II. of Hungary, and wife of Landgrave Ludwig of Thuringia. Women need not complain that domestic virtues do not warm more than their own home, and do not immortally challenge the admiration of posterity. Her name will never die, when many a great warrior's memory will be buried out of sight. She founded two hospitals in Eisenach, and another in Marburg, into which the twenty-two-year-old widow retired. The rule was to nurse the female sick only. But when Francis Joseph and Windischgrätz (*par nobile fratrum*) let loose their Croats over unhappy Vienna in our own times in 1848, the Sisters of St. Elizabeth were in the front ranks, bringing aid and comfort.

In 1171 the orders of St. Protais and St. Gervais were founded in France ; about the same time the houses in Roncesvalles and Burgos. In 1409 José Gilaberto established an order in Valencia for the special purpose of nursing the lunatic.

Those I have mentioned, with several others, were orders founded by the Church, or whose supervision soon became clerical. Those which, though all of them were anxious to submit to the Church for spiritual reasons, succeeded in retaining their autonomy must be credited with more real success in accomplishing their ends. Among the first we have any information of is the order of St. Catherine. Its members nursed poor and strange women and girls three days, and buried those who died in prisons or in the streets. In those good old times to which many dissatisfied hearts of to-day look back with longing eyes, those good olden times with their innocence, simplicity, and piety, this dying in the street was of common occurrence, and the Sisters of St. Catherine had plenty of work. We have not only accumulated seven more centuries, but gained more safety, more comfort, and more confidence in the future of mankind.

In the Hôtel-Dieu, the immense Paris hospital, thirty-eight men and thirty-eight women served as nurses. The places were, in later centuries, filled by Sisters of Mercy.

The Brothers of Mercy were founded in 1534 by Juan di Dios (John of God) in Granada. They were laymen, entered the order at between eighteen and thirty-one years of age, and nursed the sick of every faith and creed. Within a hundred years they possessed 18 hospitals, and there was a time when in Spain and the West Indies they had 138 hospitals with 4,140 beds, and 47,000 sick annually, and in the rest of Europe 155 hospitals, 7,210 beds, and 150,000 sick. Twenty-five years ago they had in Austria alone 29 hospitals, with 20,000 patients.

Of similar character were the Obregons, founded about 1600, with their complicated duties of nursing the sick, praying, and repenting. This multitude of duties must have crippled their efficiency ; they cannot compare with the Brothers of Mercy.

The " Bons Fils " (Good Boys) were founded in Flanders in 1615. They were tradesmen, with the duties of nursing the sick, mainly the alienated, in their homes, and giving elementary instruction.

The Confraternita della Perseveranza was established in Rome, in 1663, for the purpose of caring for the strangers in the taverns.

The order of the Sisters of Mercy was founded in 1617 by Vincent de Paul, a preacher. In a sermon he placed before his congregation the case of a poor and sick family, urging their co-operation and sympathy. Enthusiasm and much zeal were aroused, and a noble and gifted woman, Louise de Marillac, the wife of Legras, the secretary of Mary de Médicis, enlisted herself at once in the service of that family and of many equally indigent. She and her friends worked both in private residences and in hospitals, and were soon recognized as an order. As early as 1636 a house was founded for the care and education of children and women, a foundling hospital was established, and a home for the alienated in 1645. Her order owned, after a single century, two hundred and ninety stations and had fifteen hundred members, who entered between the ages of eighteen and twenty-four, bound themselves for life to the order and the Church, and worked in hospitals and private residences, in the interest of both women and men, in rescuing fallen girls and educating the young. In Rome, mainly in this century, they assisted those taken with infectious and acute diseases who could not be admitted to the public hospitals, and everywhere they attended the chronic cases of sickness of all denominations. Their foothold in Germany dates from this century only. Their greatest adversity was the all-purifying thunderstorm, the French Revolution. Many emi-

grated to England, but during the Napoleonic wars
their services were so much appreciated as to procure for Sister Martha the cross of the Legion of
Honor.

All of the orders mentioned were composed of
Catholics. Not one of them but was intimately
associated with the Church. In this connection it
ought not to be forgotten that all the culture and
knowledge of the mediæval period was confined
within the limits of the Church. Within its fold
the whole progress of mankind, slow though it was,
toward humanistic evolution was developed. Thus
the efforts of the Catholic Church in favor of the
poor and sick must be duly appreciated, the more
so as the so-called "Reformation" party exhibits
nothing but blank leaves in the history of ethical
and humane development. The revolutionary movement prepared by powerful minds for centuries, and
finally carried out by Luther, did not result in any
good to the sick and poor for a long time. Indeed,
the success of the Reformation was in part due to
the greed of German princes, who gained a rich
harvest by appropriating monasteries, hospitals,
and all other possessions of the Catholic Church.
Thus the Lutheran Church, or churches, were left
so poor that if they *had* the will they had not the
power to make any pecuniary sacrifices in the interest of the poor and sick. But *even that will* they
had not, could not have. For the first axiom in
Luther's doctrine was this, that *not work performed,
but faith only*, made the Christian. That doctrine
was a long stride backward; it fired the imagination
of some bigots, chilled the hearts of most men, sus-

tained the egotist, and created dissensions. Never was there a greater failure. The poetry of the Church gone, its efficiency gone, that was the "re-formation." Not until some decades ago did we know of Protestant unions established on the plan of their Catholic predecessors. But the *male* orders never tried to imitate the useful example of the Catholics. *They* did not care for the sick or the poor. *Their aim* was and is "home mission." *They* are replete with faith, distribute Bibles, and glory in the conversion of that Jew who was baptized, once or often, half a dozen years ago for ready cash. The women, as always, have done better. Their hospital orders, mainly the Deaconesses, have done good work this half-century, both in public institutions and in private. During the war times in Germany they and other associations established on similar plans did good work and deserve all the praise bestowed upon them. Their recognition was complete. Princesses joined hands with them—the Archduchess of Baden, Princess Alice of Darmstadt, the Empress Augusta. And not only in military hospitals did they earn deserved praise. Some general hospitals, such as the Augusta Hospital in Berlin, derive great benefit from their incessant and intelligent labors. I do not mean to stint praise, and therefore make this statement of their work, which has been performed under apparently great difficulties. These difficulties are the very rules, for instance, of the Deaconesses of Kaiserwerth, from which I quote for your edification the following introductory paragraph:

"The Christian women who wish to undertake

the office of a nursing sister, as deaconess for the sick and poor, must possess a somewhat advanced Christian knowledge. Mere church membership, mere attendance on Christian assemblies and reading of Christian works of edification, are not enough. The love of reading the word of God, and a diligent use of the same for a long time past, must exist, as well as a knowledge of the more important histories of the Old and New Testaments. There must also be a knowledge of the sinful heart from their own personal experience, as well as experience of the grace of Christ, in order that they may have learned to despair of themselves, and in their weakness to trust only to the strength of Christ. A Christian walk of life must for a long time have adorned such Christian women," and so on, and so on. You will admit that in the face of so much hyper-religious sentiment an active, unselfish modern woman must feel bewildered.

After all I have said it is evident that the cause of humanity was originally not hampered by the efforts of the Catholic Church. On the contrary, many centuries ago it was the only safe deposit, inasmuch as the Arabs lost their importance in humanistic evolution from the fourteenth century for the gradual development of the human feeling. But that human feeling was not fostered and protected because it was human ; the Church had but one purpose—the aggrandizement of the Church. The latter has a meaning in the case of the Catholic Church, which is at least a union and has a uniform standard, which Protestantism never had and never can have. The latter has, in its imitation of the ways and words of the mediæval rules of Catholic orders, proved one truth, and I emphasize that because here is the great difference between church nursing and modern nursing. "Clerical care of the sick is destined, under the rules, to serve the Church, whatever that may mean, while serving the sick ; the main duties and aims in view are ecclesiastical, and not humane, and, instead of a nurse solely given to the performance of her duties, you deal with ecclesiastical officers " (Virchow). And the necessity is clear that whatever organization is deemed advisable in the interest of the sick, that organization ought to be in our times *un*ecclesiastical and unsectarian. I have alluded to the fact that whatever medical knowledge existed in the masses centuries ago did so through the medium of the clergy. That knowledge was but trifling, for the ancient medicine of the Greeks and the more recent labors of the Arabs were sealed books at that time. But then the clergyman was the doctor. Instead of being so at present, we are daily met with the fact that the exact tendency of modern medicine is an unknown territory to the clergy, and that among them the upholders of all sorts of doubtful practices find their most sincere supporters. Medicine is to them a matter of faith, not science. It is not necessary to refer to that Brooklyn impostor whose criminal career has been detailed but lately in the secular press. For no church and no denomination must be held responsible for his methods of fleecing the ignorant and credulous. But the instances where actual clergymen assume responsibilities beyond their clerical powers and

duties are also very numerous, and the protection
by the Church of a regular monk in a Jersey monastery, who, in the church of his own institution,
plies his nefarious trade of laying on hands and
exorcising the devils of disease for cash, these ten
years, proves to what extent faith can be abused
and the essence of religion distorted. We still live
in a time when mediæval ignorance and modern
enlightenment appear to find resting places side by
side. That the latter is getting the upper hand,
after all, this sketch will prove, I hope, for even the
mediæval organizations in the interest of the poor
and sick, which I was anxious to estimate at their
full value, have finally failed ignominiously. Almost every large society of the kind would degenerate in the end. The uniform report concerning
most of them, mainly the male orders, is this, that
with increasing power and wealth the original un-
selfishness of the founder disappeared, the actual
work was left to low servants, the wealth of
the community was accumulated in the Church.
Thus it was that every great calamity sweeping
over the lands was a source of riches to the Church.
Never was divine blessing more visible in the
Church than when half the population of Europe
succumbed under the destruction of the "black
death." Never was more business shrewdness developed by "fathers" and "brothers" than when
a patient sick with leprosy—much less contagious
than was made out by those who had an interest in
exaggerating its dangers—had to give up half his
property before being permitted to bury himself for
life in the out-of-town places provided by the

Church. The omnivorous taste and good digestion of the Church have become proverbial.

The majority of the clerical associations having failed, the seventeenth, and still more the eighteenth, centuries were far behind former periods in regard to systematic nursing. It has taken a long time between the church institutions, which no longer came up to the intentions of their founders, and the spontaneous efforts of free men and women who felt the necessity of appropriate efforts on a different basis. The history of this slow evolution is very interesting ; it is the co-ordinate of the history of a healthy and wholesome individualism in general, after long indifference and chaos.

Schools for training nurses were established in Germany fifty years ago ; in Berlin by Dieffenbach, Kluge, and Gedike, and in Göttingen by Ruhstaat. Books to serve the purpose of instructing nurses and the public in general have been written by numerous men and women, some of them, particularly in our days, by celebrities. Gedike himself published a work, fifty years ago, which is a very readable one even now. Passing by Nightingale, who has proved how to become immortal without enjoying high office, or playing on cannon, or tyrannizing nations, or being borne on a throne, let me allude to but a few illustrious names : Nothnagel, who wrote on the nursing of those sick with nerve diseases ; Billroth, who published a book on nursing in general ; Esmarch, who taught the first aid in emergencies ; and the greatest of the many great men of the century, Virchow, with his many contributions to the literature of the subject, and mainly, in 1869, with a lecture "On the Instruction of Women in Caring for the Sick outside the existing Ecclesiastical Organizations."

This instruction of women in caring for the sick, and the relation of women to nursing as a profession, can be considered from two distinct points of view : first, in its influence upon them ; second, in its effects upon the public.

The first consideration is a very important one. The opposition to women stepping out of their sphere, which was meant to be cooking and washing, knitting and darning, begging alms and taking a daily whipping, also getting married and raising a family, has been overcome by common sense and habit. Common sense ceased to understand why or how every woman could or should cook and wash, knit and darn, beg alms, or get whipped or married. And habits are formed and reformed with such rapidity that opposition becomes changed into favor in a few years. It is but little more than a dozen years since women physicians were recognized by the profession ; not over half a dozen years since you heard of women lawyers. The female part, and, for that matter, the male part of my audience also, are sorry they heard so much of a woman lawyer in a Western town. At all events, the opposition to the attempt at widening woman's sphere, or spheres, has ceased, and the recognition of the principles of equal rights, no matter for what color or sex or previous servitude, is all but universal.

You will not care to go into the question now whether law or medicine will ever be resorted to by women to any great extent. The entire liberty given them has proved already, will prove more in future, that neither law nor medicine is an appropriate vocation for any but an exceptional class of women, and that the opposition to women practitioners of law and medicine will come less from the professions than from the public. For the public will never admit that a person in the practice of a profession should not give his or her entire attention and strength to it, and the women of the country will never admit that the superintendence of a home and the proper raising of a family are not sufficient employments of all the time and all the powers of the most gifted woman. The amateurs are losing ground. Thus it is that the professions will never be overrun, and the fear of undue competition has long died out, even among the most chicken-hearted braves of the professions. But the question is not how many women will avail themselves of the opportunities granted, but whether they are to have those opportunities, and whether these are to be given the women of all walks of life, of all standards of intellect. And the question has generally been answered affirmatively, to such an extent that it is considered self-understood that, while the mediæval ages attempted to help them as much as possible, modern times prefer to give them the power to help themselves. In regard to nursing, attention was called early to the unmarried and poor among the women. The statistics of Berlin of the year 1872 proved that every third woman had to provide for herself. It was remarked with surprise that, of 407 such help-

less and breadless creatures, but a single one went
into nursing as a business. In other Continental
cities it was still worse. In Vienna the shiftlessness of women was still greater ; misery and
poverty reigned supreme, as must be expected
when you learn that a woman who took the making of her own clothing, even *with the aid* of a professional seamstress, into her own hands, was
punishable under the law.

The proportion of but one nurse to 407 women
who had to work for a living is remarkable, it is
true. For are not nursing and caring and attending implanted in woman's nature ? What is the
reason that so few went into nursing as a business,
if not a vocation ? Probably because the women
felt, or the public made them feel, that without
careful preparation no nurse, or *soi-disant* nurse,
can be efficient. We have still the remnants—I
fear numerous ones—of that self-made class of
nurses among us. In my own recollection of far-
away years I remember a great many ; and a great
many, I was told but lately, remember me also,
perhaps too well. Some of you may have seen
them—in other people's houses—wrinkled prematurely, thinned out by temper, contrary by
nature, or for the most part fattened in the course
of their (to them) useful career, complacent and
drowsy while everything was going well, incompetent and snappish when danger required work
and sufficiency, always ready to have their regular
meals served up-stairs by the help of the house,
who breathed freely when they finally left, and always willing to spend their time between rocking a

2*

baby, speaking of their long experience, sleeping
ten hours, talking gossip all day long, and drinking eleven cups of coffee in the twenty-four hours.
This is hardly an exaggeration, for the number of
women who took up nursing as a business, driven
to it by some natural disposition, gifted with some
intellect, modest and willing to profit by superior
knowledge and experience, interested in the welfare of their patients, and never stunted in their
human feelings by the force of habit, was rather
small. But I am glad to say I knew such, too. I
gladly shook their hands when I happened to meet
them on a common errand, gladly recognizing the
diploma they carried in their brains and hearts.
But these exceptions proved the rule, and the rule
conveyed no blessing. It was, it is, a sad fact that
nursing all over the world grew worse in just the
same time when medical science grew more exact
and medical practice more effective.

Relief in this city came none too soon. The president has detailed to you the history of the training schools of New York. Since their time the
practice in hospitals and in private dwellings has
changed wonderfully. After thirty years' work in
the city, after twenty-five years' constant labor in
public institutions, I ought to know the difference.
And I do know and publicly proclaim that the results of the best of physicians have vastly improved
since their cases have been in the hands of trained
nurses. This is so in private dwellings ; it is the
same in hospitals. In the hospitals the difference
can be measured on a large scale. In them the
trained nurse has worked a vast improvement.

Every large hospital ought to perform a double duty. It must give the poor patient, and many rich also, the best possible chance of recovery from sickness. It can afford to accomplish that because of its pecuniary and intellectual means. Though a hospital be poor, there ought to be, there generally are, means enough to fill all the necessities required. And the intellectual means are expected to be, are supposed to be, above the average of the general practitioner. There are a great many reasons why that should be so, why hospital places should be open for the competition of the best material among the medical profession, recognized to *be* the best by the medical profession *itself*, and why family and personal influence should not fill places which are better not filled at all than with indifferent or bad material. A hospital must also grant the best possible nursing—interested, wakeful, careful. All this is due to the single patients.

A good deal more, however, is due to the public at large. A hospital looking for the interest of the single patient only might just as well be a private institution, a *maison de santé* for the benefit of a landlord. The benefit derived from hospital treatment by a sick person is not all the satisfaction due to a public who pay four hundred dollars a year for every bed. Nor are the public paid sufficiently for their sacrifices by the accumulated experiences of a few physicians, who enjoy the large field of observation and the opportunity of utilizing it for the benefit of private patients. Every hospital which neglects to increase the stock of medical knowledge, and to give an opportunity of learning the theory

and practice of nursing and caring for the sick, per-
forms its duties but half, and serves the public
but incompletely. Every large hospital must be,
and will be, a clinical school and a school for nurses.
It will be acknowledged that, as the presence of a
nurse in a sick-ward, who is sent there to learn, is
considered unobjectionable, the presence of a few
physicians observing a case, which cannot be injured by their so doing, is not only not injurious,
but ought to be demanded by the public, who have
a right to expect a physician in their own families
who has seen and knows and understands what he
is called in to treat. I do not see why hospital patients only should have the best that money and service can afford, and why the public at large should
have to fall back in many cases on untried skill.
Thus the people have a right to demand that every
large hospital should have a clinical school and a
training school for nurses. The public, who are
willing to pay for it, may also demand that the expenses of the same, particularly the nurses' school,
should be borne by the hospital. This demand, if
considered theoretical only, must stand as long as a
hospital is, or claims to be, a public institution.
When the board of directors of any institution will
recognize that they are not the administrators of
the dollars of a small concern, but the benefactors
of the public at large, they will also appreciate not ·
only that a few disinterested ladies will open their
pocketbooks and collect voluntary contributions, but
that a generous public will pay more willingly and
more largely.

The demand that a large hospital should be a

clinical school and a school for nurses, and that the expense should or might be borne by the institution, is not valid in the case of city or commonwealth hospitals only. Most of the hospitals of the country are originally private institutions. They obtain the character of being public affairs when an always increasing number of men and women become interested in and contributors to them. An institution with one or two thousand paying members represents ten or twenty thousand families--in fact, represents a city. And what it represents, of that it assumes the rights and duties. And the main duty which the public at large will soon know how to enforce from the directors of every large hospital, is to administer the public domain to the greatest possible advantage for the greatest possible number. The selfishness of an individual adversary, the animosity of evil-spirited persons, will never weigh, ought never to weigh, against the public good; the latter only is the object of those who are placed in trust of money, institutions, and the public welfare, because of their actual or supposed public-spiritedness and superior intellect.

Is it necessary to detail the advantages of the services of a trained nurse over those of an untrained one? The latter class, as a rule, bring to their work no previous education, no theoretical schooling, no technical experience. They come mostly from inferior walks of life, with less intellectual power and less moral force. Only those who come from better stock, and raise themselves to higher ambitions, will spend money and two years of their lives for the purpose of learning, both theoretically and practically, the art of relieving the sick, aiding their comfort, taking responsibilities which sometimes are as difficult as they are life-saving, and obeying orders with intelligence and understanding. That such persons are valuable additions to our hygienic facilities and sanitary progress everybody can conceive. That without them many a case would not recover, in spite of the most competent medical skill, all of you may have experienced. I, for one, know from personal experience that many a case can be, has been saved, first, by the medical orders; secondly, and often mostly, by the execution of orders, such an execution as is rendered possible by combined knowledge and skill only. If I say that we practitioners have commenced to feel safe in regard to many of our cases only since we could rely on the co-operation of a trained nurse, I express but a common observation. I trust that there are households within hearing which know how to appreciate the services rendered them by a trained nurse.

So much only in regard to individual cases. But the service to the public at large hitherto rendered, and constantly increasing, is of a different and still more important nature. Who is nowadays the teacher of the public at large in sanitary matters, in hygienic rules? The knowledge of the Church, when *it* nursed, was faith, and, let us add, in its best times. love. The knowledge of uneducated women was, and is, ignorance driven to actual or alleged work by starvation. The knowledge of a trained nurse is the result of a two years' study under competent teachers, and a constant practice.

Who in the community is her superior in the
knowledge of the facts mostly necessary for the
health and life of your children, and dear ones in
general? The clergyman is no longer the teacher
of the mysteries of life and common sense. The
schoolmaster or schoolmistress knows about the
classics, geography, and arithmetic, but no normal school ever taught them the elements of applied physiology. The educated member of any
profession except the medical has not the slightest
idea of the necessities of the body, the action of
food, the effect of clothing, and the hundred facts
required by different ages, conditions, and states of
health. With the exception of the physician, whose
advice is frequently sought only to repair the
effects of ignorance, the only teacher the public
have, and will have, is *the trained nurse*. Ten or
twenty families may enjoy her presence annually,
ten or twenty mothers will learn simple and important truths, knowledge will increase, and prevention of disease will become a possibility. Enjoyable and useful as the service of a trained nurse
is in an individual case of sickness, her services to
the community are very much greater by virtue of
her theoretical and practical teaching. May I tell
you what a good trained nurse may teach, and can
teach? How to recognize a fever, how to compare
the local temperatures of the several parts of the
body, and how to equalize them; she knows that
ever so many feeble children might have been
saved if but the feet and the legs had not been
allowed to get cold; how to bathe, when, and when
to stop; how to regulate the position of the head—

I remember quite well the case of inflammatory delirium which would always be relieved by propping up the head ; how to treat intelligently an attack of fainting ; how to render cow's milk digestible by repeated boiling, or lime water, or table salt, or farinaceous admixtures ; how to feed in case of diarrhœa ; how to refuse food in case of vomiting ; how to apply and when to remove cold to the head ; how to ventilate a room without a draught ; and a thousand other things. She will also use her knowledge and influence in weaning the public of nostrums, concerning which hardly anything is known except what you have to pay for the promises of the label. She will break the public of the indiscriminate use of quinia, with its dangers possibly for life ; cure you of the tendency of making the diagnosis of malaria the scapegoat of every unfinished or impossible diagnosis ; she will teach you that the frequent and reckless domestic use of chlorate of potassium leads to many a case of ailment, to chronic poisoning, possibly in the shape of Bright's disease, or to acute poisoning with unavoidable death. These are but very few of the things she can do, and but a little of the knowledge she cannot but distribute. With the aid of the class of women who frequent our training schools, the public at large must and will gain in a short time. Let the number of the schools increase, and increase the number of pupils, and every one of them will be a teacher and an apostle of sound information on sanitary and hygienic subjects. And let nobody leave this place to-night without intending to aid an institution as helpful as this.

Will the pupils come? Certainly they will. There is an increasing demand for their services. Many times had I to wait a day or two before any of the schools could accommodate me. There is no fear that there ever will be too many good nurses. There is no fear, either, that many persons of inferior intelligence and morals will present themselves for, or obtain admission to, a school. By attending the suffering, it is true, many a crude or brutal nature is ennobled; but I should not advise to run the risk of admitting that class at the expense of the sick, or of a rising and beneficent profession. The occasional specimens of cold-hearted and arrogant persons one is apt to meet, even among trained nurses, must discourage the admission of any but the very best. These *will* apply. The calling is an honorable one, it promises a competence, it corresponds with the innermost nature of woman. It is not true that the Church alone could raise the enthusiasm for hard work, the performance of arduous duties, and self-sacrifice. One of the first nurses I had in my division in Bellevue Hospital, many years ago, was an accomplished girl, the daughter of a rich man in the far West. After a year and a half it took all the influence and begging of her family to take her away from us and her hard work among the poorest of the poor. The large number of ladies, wealthy and accomplished, who work assiduously and regularly under Felix Adler and in other places, under our very eyes, prove that the very best class of society can be prevailed upon to do the hardest and most beneficent kind of work. And the fact that the *élite* of the women of the city are willing and anxious to undertake the arduous task of founding and supporting training schools, in the face of all sorts of difficulties, proves also that the work is in accordance with the requirements of both woman's nature and humanity. There will be many trained nurses who will work for humanity's sake, as centuries ago they claimed to serve for God's sake. Many a woman who would have buried herself in a monastery centuries ago, driven from the face of the living earth by misunderstood and unsatisfied longing, I believe would nowadays become a nurse, knowing and enthusiastic.

Ladies of the graduating class : The remarks I was expected to make have extended into a lecture. You have been used to lectures, however ; if you had not enjoyed them and profited by them, you would not be here to-night, the most honored and most conspicuous of this assembly. Thus I thought I might be permitted to speak, instead of to you, of you and your chosen calling and its history. From nothing can any profession derive so much advantage as from the history of its development. It is certainly an interesting spectacle to see how your profession depended intimately on the changing conditions of thought and feeling among mankind. You are happy enough to live and work in a time when, while following individual tastes and having individual motives, your labors are given to the suffering for no outside reason, no church command, but from the free choice of free women in the interest of humanity. I had also to allude to several subjects which may to some appear a little

outside the legitimate domain of your ambition and
duties. You know better. An intelligent woman
will not spend two of her young years in acquiring
a certain knowledge without enlarging her horizon
in general. You have chosen a profession as noble
and as deserving as any there is in existence. You
will be the interpreters and right hands of the
physician, and the connecting link between the
physician and not only the single patient but also
the public at large. My opinion of the services you
can render is high, but I trust not exaggerated.
When your numbers will increase and the character of those who are admitted remain of the same
standard, your importance will grow. In your
hands will, to a great extent, lie the opportunity
for removing prejudices, spreading knowledge,
healing and preventing disease. Even those of you
who will not always consent to serve in *other*
people's homes, will, by example and by teaching,
remain in close alliance and co-operation with such
as intend to remain in the ranks forever. As you
now mean to leave us, endowed with the certificate
of the required accomplishments, I can only add,
while offering my best wishes for your future, that
I trust you will never forget the place which gave
you so ample opportunities for perfecting yourselves. You will never forget the gentlemen who
taught you, nor that accomplished young woman
who impressed all of you with the fact that the
charms of womanhood will not suffer from hard
work, from a classical education, and thorough
medical or other knowledge. Do not forget, also,
at the beginning of your independent career, the

ladies to whose care and sacrifices and labors you owe the existence of the school which sends you forth as its first graduates, nor the great charitable institution which, after having given you your practical training, honors you to-night by the presence of many of its officers, and designates its president to deliver to you your diplomas.

INAUGURAL ADDRESS*

DELIVERED BEFORE THE NEW YORK ACADEMY OF
MEDICINE, FEBRUARY 5TH, 1885.

IT has been my privilege to enjoy many professional honors. Whatever favors my colleagues of
both city and State could ever dispose of they have
liberally conferred on me at different times. To-
night I am called upon to acknowledge my indebtedness and express my thanks to you for an extraordinary proof of your consideration and confidence.
I do so from the depths of my heart, my pride in
my elevation to the presidency of the New York
Academy of Medicine being checked only by the
overwhelming sense of the grave responsibility incurred.

In regard to the two highest positions the profession of the city has ever placed me in I have
been both fortunate and embarrassed. For when,
some fifteen years ago, I took the chair in the
Medical Society of the County of New York, my
predecessors were Edmund R. Peaslee and George
T. Elliot. The former was erudite, wise, a celebrated specialist, a renowned writer of great weight
and force. The latter was bright, quick, versatile,
as eloquent as his predecessor, conversant with the
literature of his profession, also a good writer, and

* Transactions of the Academy of Medicine, vol. v.

universally admired and loved for his pleasing
manner and thoroughly gracious bearing. The difficulty of presiding after such men was relieved by
but one all-important circumstance, which was this
—that they had raised the Society to a flourishing
condition such as had never existed before.

Now, as concerns the presidency in this Academy
of Medicine, I believe I am in nearly the same position. If I were more eloquent I should try to do
justice to the president of so many years, in recall-
ing his services in the interest of the literature of
medicine, of the standing of the profession at large,
and of the development of this Academy. To say
that the medical world knows him well, that we,
the profession of the city and the members of the
Academy, are under a great and respectful obligation to him for his untiring care and energy, his
enduring patience, his kindness and urbanity, and
his uniform success in conducting the affairs of the
Academy, is but an incompetent expression of my
feelings. Personally, I add my extreme gratification at the fact that it was under his guidance and
supervision that the Academy could overcome such
dangers and strifes as I hope these walls will never
behold again. As they, however, are things of the
past, I hope I shall have nothing to do but to preside over harmonious scientific meetings only, such
as were contemplated when the Academy was
founded. It will be my ambition and pride to contribute to its success as much as I can, hoping at
the same time that your expectations will not be
measured by Dr. Barker's eulogistic remarks, which
I should be glad to deserve. In regard to them I

will only say that I believe they were made on the principle and for the reason that it is wise to stimulate ambition into powerful efforts for the accomplishment of ends by praising beforehand. The members present I beg again to receive my thanks, my promises, and my request that every one may consider the interests of this Academy under his personal charge. It will then be an easy task not only to preserve its high character, but in the course of time make it the largest and most influential scientific institution in the country.

How this can be accomplished has engaged my thoughts more than once. For the New York Academy of Medicine has been established for more than one purpose :

First. The cultivation of the science of medicine.

Second. The advancement of the character and honor of the profession.

Third. The elevation of the standard of medical education.

Fourth. The promotion of public health.

It has not been founded upon the plans of European institutions bearing similar names. The academies of sciences or of medicine in Europe, established for the promotion of the science and art of medicine, are institutions with a limited number of members, who have peculiar claims for such distinction. In them we find the most representative men only. Every one is a specialist in his way, a teacher, a savant ; most of them are men of reputation, many are celebrities. They are professors in universities, directors of clinical institutes, independent of pecuniary compulsion to practise medicine, enjoying the leisure required for studies of their own. They are governed in part by rules prescribed by the Government, which pays for their services either rendered to a public institution or to pure science.

Our Academy is a democratic institution. It is not limited in numbers ; on the contrary, it is desirable that the many respectable physicians should gather round its flag. Like our political community, it looks for its development and success in the co-operation of the competent and cultured masses. Like the Union, it is a voluntary confederation of peers, who make their own laws, and obey them because they are of their own making. The members have the same interests, both scientific and professional. There are but very few of us who are not engaged in the practice of medicine. When the Academy was founded the members were, all of them, general practitioners : specialists there were but few. This has changed much ; both study and practice have tried to become more profound by circumscribing and limiting their aims. But all of us are active men, not tied down or given up to study only. Thus we perform less laboratory work than they do in Europe, and write fewer monographs on special subjects. But the number of facts closely observed at the sick-bed or in the examining room has increased from year to year. In spite of the circumstance that we are all busy men, the literature of medicine in New York and the United States is no longer mostly parasitical, as Oliver Wendell Holmes was justified in complaining during the session of the second meeting of the American Medical Association. Original work has taken the place, in part, of translations and reprints ; still all the time the connection between the medical men and the public, the doctor and the patient, has not been severed. This is the peculiar feature of American, as it is of British, medicine. Anglo-Saxon medicine has never forgotten that the aim and end of all medical science is the treatment and healing of the sick, and that every special study is but a means to obtain that end.

Thus our Academy is not to be the centre of a select few, who speak to the rest of mankind through their writings only, but of all who love their science and live the lives of respectable practitioners. All ought to be members. I have often been told, however, that the large number of societies prevents men from becoming members in the old and large ones. That is so. There is too much division and subdivision. But that is not the fault of the Academy. Under other circumstances the Obstetrical Society might well have been a section of the Academy ; the laryngologists, otologists, ophthalmologists, dermatologists, might have their own sections under the auspices of the Academy, though under their own rules, their own officers, and, while doing the same amount of good work, not lose their connection with the main body. The large societies, such as the Academy, or the American Medical Association, or the German Association of Physicians and Naturalists, lose by the secession of important branches and their representatives. The unity of medicine is lost sight of, and the interests

3*

of science and the profession are suffering. Instead of one or two, every section of this Academy ought to be flourishing. Let us hope they will. We have been told to-night that there was more than an abundance of papers offered. Our rooms they are welcome to. Though we have to think of some time increasing our facilities, we can still accommodate them, and others besides. Indeed, most of the medical societies of the city would do well to avail themselves of the home the medical profession of the city have found in this hall, and meet here.

The peculiar features of this Academy I have mentioned permit of varied results. The mixture of the best brains of the profession and the modest practitioner is capable of raising the standard of the average professional man far beyond the level of the European medical man, frequently in knowledge, always in industry and ambition and ethics, without interfering with the individual and original labor of the hardest workers and best thinkers. Have we been successful on this side of the Atlantic?

They say we have no John Hunter. All Great Britain, in all its pride, has but one. No Bichat or Laennec. All the glory and elegance of France have but one. No Virchow. All the centuries of toiling and philosophical Germany have produced but one. What we do have, however, is a medical profession with unbiassed minds, clear insight, critical eyes, undaunted industry, and that republican courtesy which recognizes—*suum cuique*—the peculiar advantages and services everywhere, and the democratic tendency of appreciating and appropriating the intellectual accomplishments of the globe, and of utilizing them for the practical necessities of the commonwealth.

Besides, we do not live in the backwoods or in the darkness. As long as the Confederation and the Union have been in existence, their medical men have been, to say the least, marching in line. In what the Anglo-Saxons have known and taught, they have both participated and co-operated. Without the counting in of the original American contributions to science, the history of modern medicine would be incomplete indeed. Let Europe boast of its great names : this young community has the heirloom of the great names of Bard, Rush, McDowell, Drake, Beck, and many others of *past* years. Let the history of this Academy be written —and a grateful and gratifying labor it would be— and the array of great names is such as to astonish many of the young men in this room, who unconsciously and unconcernedly toil over the graves on which are inscribed the names of men great in lite rature, or achievements, or influence, great in mind and character. Let me mention a few of those who have passed away. I have known personally, and conversed and discussed with, John O. Batchelder, George M. Beard, Gunning S. Bedford, Ch. A. Budd, Gurdon Buck, H. D. Bulkley, William H. Van Buren, Freeman J. Bumstead, Henry G. Cox, George T. Elliot, John W. Francis, Edward Delafield, Elisha Harris, Horace Green, Ernst Krackowizer, Valentine Mott, Josiah Clark Nott, Edmund R. Peaslee, Willard Parker, J. Marion Sims, Joseph M. Smith, Alexander H. Stephens, James

Stewart, John Watson, Robert Watts, Isaac Wood, James R. Wood. Many of these names are known wherever medicine is taught and practised ; some of them will never die. This Academy will always cherish the names of its members who contributed to the glory of universal medicine and the American country.

When I, and those as old as I, knew these men, most of them were in advanced years. At that time the proportion of white heads was very much larger than it is to-day. I venture to say that it was for the good of the Academy that that was so. Neither the political republic nor that of science can thrive without the co-operation of all. At that time the number of older and old men was such as to draw forth sometimes the remark of some class of young men that the Academy was the head-quarters of old fogies, and for that reason might be avoided and shunned. Much has been changed in this respect. Curly heads and young faces are plentiful—a good sign indeed for the energy and activeness of the growing generation. Many white beards, however, and bald heads have commenced to stay away for years—a proof indeed of the increased claim on their time and strength, but we fear also, now and then, of listlessness and indifference

This ought not to be so. Neither in politics nor in science does age extinguish citizenship with its rights and duties. Besides, I know that the best trained young minds are modest enough to admit that they are able and anxious to learn from those whose opportunities extend over a long number of years, and that books, brains, and experience are a greater power than books, brains, and inexperience.

These remarks I make for the purpose of requesting the older members of the profession not to withhold their presence and aid. Among them are men widely known in both hemispheres. When they write every one reads, both here and in Europe. Let them not forget that a vast audience is just as anxious to hang on their lips when they either lecture before us or take part in a discussion. Both their teaching and example are wanted by the rising generation of our younger brethren. They will teach them both medicine and modesty. May nobody who neglects his own duty toward them and the profession at large accuse a young man of forwardness. Some of them have indeed reaped a good harvest from living up to their duties as citizens of our republic of science. For if there be a fountain of youth for old men, it is the constant mixing and working with the young. The Nestor of our surgeons, whose face we greet with joy in almost every meeting, and whose voice we are delighted in hearing in our discussions, proves better than any preaching the powerlessness of so-called old age.

The hosts of others, general practitioners and surgeons and specialists, whom we like to boast of and to honor, will always be welcomed by all of us, both old and young, to seats in the front ranks. If they will consent, not only our scientific but also our public aims will be more apt to be reached.

For our position is that of natural advisers in all matters concerning sanitation and health. The larger the number of our members, the more we represent the best minds and all ages in the profession, the more readily the public and its legislators will listen to us. When they know that our advice will be the digest of the best knowledge and the ripe wisdom of the profession, they will not wait until it is forced upon them. In matters of health the two large medical societies of the city ought to be, will be, the authorities. If that be so, it will no longer depend upon a number of ladies only to remove intolerable nuisances from the heart of the city. The simple appeal of the profession will become the protection of the public. The latter will soon learn that it can rely on your knowledge and public spirit, and, as it calls on the bar for legal advice, it will consult the medical profession for sanitary necessities. In this way it will happen that some time the president of the Board of Health will be nominated or appointed by the profession ; that no Board of Education, no Board of Charities, will be complete without a prominent medical member ; medical bills will pass the Legislature, when backed by the whole power of the profession, without either delay or mutilation ; the supervising officers of factories, nurseries, streets, baths, gas houses will be physicians ; aye, the most improbable thing will happen, which is this : that the public will acknowledge that the government of hospitals ought not to be without medical advisers in their boards. In order, however, to accomplish such results, we must unite our numbers, powers, and influence. The public and legislatures will respect and obey the regular medical profession more eagerly than the advice of individuals or societies. It gives me great pleasure, in this connection, to be able to announce to you that the representatives of the profession of the State agreed but yesterday on a bill to be presented to the Legislature, ordering a Board of State Examiners destined to license the practice of medicine. The unanimity of action in this respect on the part of apparently diverging and conflicting interests is a good omen, in this progressive State, for the growing influence of the medical profession. Thus far the State Medical Society has done its part of the work nobly ; now, may everybody see to it that the Legislature of the State be kept well informed and well advised.

The practical tendency of this Academy corresponds with the peculiar nature of the development of medicine in the English-speaking nations from the last century onward. Even the most fragmentary study of that development is of great interest indeed. Altogether, medicine in the eighteenth century exhibits a peculiar character. It is true that knowledge was not widespread, but the heads of the profession were capable, painstaking, searching, cool-headed men, good observers and excellent describers. There was a large number of good monographs, excellent histories of cases, and fair diagnoses of the general condition of the patient. Local diagnosis, it is true, was mostly out of the question, since no sooner than in the second half of that century Morgagni collected in his illustrious work, "De Causis et Sedibus Morborum," all of the only three thousand post-mortem examinations which had ever been recorded in all ages and countries. Their judgment was sound, their therapeutics—though often exuberant—safe. As the scientific language of most of them was the same—Latin—their spirit was not local nor national. The same class of men were found in Germany and the British possessions ; also in Holland and France. In the former we meet the names of Werlhoff, R. A. Vogel, Zimmermann, Lentin, Van Swieten, J. P. Frank. There was also Auenbrugger, who ought not to have been so readily forgotten. In Great Britain there were Mead, Huxham, Fothergill, Pringle, Heberden, Monroe, Home, Cullen ; there was that giant, John Hunter. In America we had Bard and Rush. In France, Levret. In Holland, at an early date, Boerhaave. The only fanatical theorist of all the English writers was John Brown ; the only obscurist, who ought to have had a place in Germany between 1800 and 1840, was Robert Jones with his " Inquiry into the State of Medicine on the Principles of Inductive Philosophy " (1782). When Broussais reigned supreme in France his doctrines were welcomed by a great many in England. But the Anglo-Saxon mind is not easily drawn away by theories, and there is after all more solid work in Broussais than wanton theory only. Thus the English literature of the early part of this century teems with good observations and monographs by many more than those I here mention—Travers, Williams, Crawford, Astley Cooper, Brodie, Bell, Abercrombie, Cheyne, Pitcairn, Bright, Hope, and Carswell.

Of French names I have mentioned but one.

The redemption of France, after a century of al-

most unparalleled corruption and misery, begins
with its great Revolution. Never before did fate
grant to an unhappy nation a larger number of
great spirits, both in politics and science. The
faint impression the freer institutions of the British
Island made on French literature would not have
influenced the development of the country for centuries to the same extent as did the necessities of
the population. In the history of political and
mental development changes more or less sudden
or gradual appear to be the rule ; rise and decline
change off, as the fertility and sterility of a corn-
field. The fertility of France lasted a long time.
While the greatest man in its political world could
not do better than spread all over Europe part of
the results of the French Revolution through violence and murder, a young scientist revolutionized
medical science by genius and hard work. That is
what Bichat did when he studied the physiology
and pathology of the organic tissues. Since that
period France has marched at the head of medical
science for about half a century. Pinel, Corvisart,
Cruveilhier, Biett, Cazenave, Gibert, Laennec, Ri-
cord, Civiale, Guérin, Guislain, Baillarger, Leuret,
Longet, Guersant, Taupin, Valleix, Legendre, Du-
puytren, Trousseau, Rilliet, Barthez, Durant-Far-
del, Orfila, Louis, Broussais, Piorry—what a host
of illustrious names, and by far not the only ones
who will recall the glory of the French nation when
there will be no longer a political France ! It is true
that a decline has set in. The number of really
great men in modern French medicine is but
limited. Charcot's name overshadows the reputa-

tions of all others, and, it appears to me, will live for centuries. Maybe also that Pasteur will be recognized as a fixed star in the scientific sky, if he will succeed in divesting himself of the doubtful attributes of polemical tendencies.

After Bichat there are three French names connected with the history of medical sciences in all countries. Laennec's revolution of diagnosis by percussion and auscultation is not any the less important and precious because Auenbrugger had worked in the same field more than half a century previously, for no other result than complete oblivion. Magendie's experimental physiology and pharmacology have benefited all mankind. His is the introduction of alkaloids, such as quinine, veratrine, strychnine, piperine, morphine, emetine—his the successful admission of bromine and iodine into practical therapeutics. Finally, Broussais, by overthrowing ontologies—though he created one of his own—by localizing disease, by urging prevention and abortive treatment, by studying the anatomical lesions of pathological processes, has substituted a method of anatomical thought in diagnosis for the merely clinical and empirical observation of the sick, and thus been the intellectual author of that method of medical knowledge and reasoning which is best known by the name of the Vienna school. I shall have to consider its representatives shortly, with all its virtues and faults, both of which were learned and loaned from the illustrious Frenchman. For not only did he convey to them his anatomical way of thinking, but he also taught them to be satisfied with coarse local anatomical lesions and with a nominal diagnosis, adding the assurance that those lesions must lead to death; that, indeed, the case is either getting well spontaneously or is absolutely hopeless, and that a treatment of any kind is powerless.

The parallelism of political and scientific conditions which strikes us so admirably in the history of French development, after the impulse given by the Revolution, is sadly illustrated by poor Germany. The country, poor and forlorn, divided into hundreds of shreds, large and small, tyrannized and robbed by hundreds of dukes and bishops, and princelings of all sorts, every one the inferior in mind, but the emulating admirer of the tendencies of that despotic Frederick the Second of Prussia, in whom it requires the equally despotic soul of a Carlyle to find nothing but admirable traits—that country had, about the end of the eighteenth century, one representative in medicine corresponding with the character of the time. Hufeland was a fair observer, a copious writer, an influential man, but weak and accessible to everybody and everything. It was he who admitted the first Hahnemannian gospels to his journal, and who was of the wise opinion that there may be something good in everything. Then came the French, and whipped the Germans out of political existence. Then the wars which expelled the French, bloody, costly, and short, aroused a peculiar romantic fanaticism which pervaded the whole literature of a short decade, and could but have an unfavorable influence on science. Then came decades of brutal political reaction and suppression, the scanty means of the nation being spent on police, military, and dungeons, in which the flower of the country, and particularly of the universities, was incarcerated. During that time German thought had no place in terrestrial parts; even before that time Schiller had proclaimed man "free though he wore chains." This sort of freedom the Germans utilized to become transcendentalists. The principal method of studying nature was imagination. Even Kant, the mathematical thinker, had taught them the art of construing things *a priori*. Then came Schelling with his system of natural philosophy ; and Hegel, who wrote twenty big volumes, and is reported to have said on his death-bed that in all his life he had but one pupil who understood him, and that one did not know anything about him. Under the influence of these philosophical absurdities no medical science could thrive. That was the time of animal magnetism and cranioscopical humbug.

In such a condition of universal intellectual semi-paralysis and revelry in big words and clouded sensations of all kinds, combined with the insensate and murderous character of therapeutics, it was natural that homœopathy could thrive, with its axioms that disease was an enemy from without, the result of psora or of medicines ; that nature was an enemy of man ; that nature will not cure a disease, but a medicine will ; that no medicine will cure which can be shown by any physical or chemical analysis to still exist ; that its dynamical power increases with its attenuation and annihilation. That was the time in which one of the great lights of German medicine defined inflammation as the

condition in which the "electrical essence (or part)
is affected in the dimensions." Marcus never said
that he understood that himself. At that time the
medical literature of Germany was full of such
philosophizing nonsense ; full of contempt of the
unphilosophical foreign countries ; of Bright, with
his British coarseness which studied nature as it was;
of Laennec, whose percussion and auscultation were
declared to be immoral and irreligious. My beloved
teacher, Prof. Fred Nasse, though all his life a be-
liever in and author on animal magnetism, was one
of the first to utilize Laennec's great innovation
and the lessons of foreign teaching. Even Schönlein, though it was he through whose influence
young Virchow, after he had been expelled from
Berlin for his liberal political views, was called to
Würzburg to teach pathological anatomy, could not
free himself from the influence of philosophical doctrines. At that time the science of therapeutics
consisted indeed in nothing but empty words : its
practice, to a great part, in the traditional blood-let-
ting, salivation, and purging. Thus it was that the
fanatical hydropathists and the adversaries of vac-
cination could obtain such rare opportunities and
successes ; thus that, but forty years ago, Rade-
macher could divide all ailments into saltpetre, cop-
per, and iron diseases, for the reason that each one
of these remedies cured one-third of all the ailments
of German kind.

Schönlein and Liebig having prepared the medical minds, and the influence of foreign literature
being gradually felt in Germany and Austria, it so
happened that Vienna had in its faculty of medicine

quite an array of medical genius. Rokitansky,
Skoda, Hebra, have long reigned supreme. Broussais' doctrines, good and bad, were readily accepted ;
his ontological gastro-enteritis was replaced by Rokitansky's doctrine of the crases of the blood, thus
re-establishing the old humoral theory on an apparently firmer foundation. In Rokitansky's opinion
the anatomical changes were the only things in medicine worth knowing. Skoda, for some time, ex-
perimented carelessly and unsuccessfully with remedies ; his ill-success and Rokitansky's teaching
confirmed the nihilism of Broussais, against which
Laennec protested in France, and made the expec-
tant treatment and the nihilistic faith the gospel
of German practice.

" This was the medicine—the patients' woes soon ended,
And none demanded : Who got well ?
Thus we, our hellish boluses compounding,
Among these vales and hills surrounding,
Worse than the pestilence have passed.
Thousands were done to death from poison of my giving;
And I must hear by all the living
The shameless murderers praised at last."

But in Goethe's " Faust " this is said by an incor-
rigible philosophical roué who is ready to give himself up to the devil, and in Germany it had the result that the public, who have a right to desire to
be cured when they fall sick, preferred the homœo-
pathic pill box to the pathologist's post-mortem
case.

Not long after, Oppolzer, whose name ought to
be blessed forever in Prague, Leipzig, and Vienna,
began his influential career. In him Germany pos-

sessed its first great physician in this century, who
knew pathological anatomy perfectly, was a thorough diagnostician, a humane physician and ami-
able teacher, who recognized the social, scientific,
and humane duties of the practitioner, abhorred
preconceived ideas and *a priori* constructions, acknowledged principles and facts only, and no duty
but to find the truth.

It was about that time that Rudolf Virchow commenced to revolutionize medicine. Modern medical science owes its solid foundation and elabora-
tion to him and his followers. The book of medicine
of to-day, and, I trust, of the future, bears the imprint of his genius on every page. We all have
read and admired and praised, knowing that when
we readily place Germany in the first rank of the
medical world to-day, the name of Virchow is in
every mind and on every lip. This brief sketch
cannot do him justice, nor do I desire to elaborate
a theme with which every one is familiar. But one
remark I cannot suppress—viz., that he is not only
great in his revolutionary discoveries and innova-
tions, but in his self-denying conservatism also. If
the bacteriomania of modern times has not been
accepted uniformly as the universal gospel of
modern pathology, if thoughtful hesitation and
healthy criticism is still heard above the noisy
waves of the seas of all-explaining and all-saving
theories which claim to have given, at last, an absolutely solid base to etiology and pathology, that
merit again belongs to a great extent to Virchow.
I speak of it here because I hope that this Academy
may be able to contribute to the solution of ques-

tions of great import by original studies and discoveries.

For there was lately a time, or, rather, we still
live in that time, when a single series of discoveries
lays claim to having changed the aspect of pathology at one stroke, and solved all problems. You
know I speak of bacteriology. In America, also,
all of those who cannot judge of the question by
their own investigations—that is, the practitioners,
either general or special—have readily accepted the
new gospel, with but few exceptions. The new
theories, that infectious and zymotic diseases have
each their own bacillus, are so pleasant and pro-
mised to be so fruitful that it required some
courage to critically resist the flood. On the other
hand, those amongst us who have a right by their
own researches and special knowledge to be heard,
have hesitated to accept the results of microscopical, actual or alleged, discoveries as the sole explanation of everything infectious and zymotic.
Amongst them I shall only name Wood and For-
mad and Sternberg. Into the merits of the case
and the weighing of reasons I cannot go this evening, but it has appeared to me that it would be
well to direct the attention of the Academy to that
subject as one greatly deserving of its attention.

To me, while I readily acknowledge a valuable
increase of pathological knowledge, and the fact
that the spreading of some diseases at least, slow
and gradual and regular, seems to prove the multiplication of cases of disease by the regular mul-
tiplying of its causes, it has always appeared that
purely bacteric etiology has too often begged the

question, and that the answer to the question,
whether organic or chemical poisons are the main
causes of infectious diseases, has by no means been
satisfactorily given. In the course of the last dozen
years organic chemistry has made as rapid strides
as has microscopy. Cadaveric poisons—ptomaines
—have been discovered in great numbers. Most of
them are very destructive. Sudden deaths from
zymotic and infectious diseases resemble much
those produced by these poisons. That the stings
of insects or the poison engendered in putrid corpses
lead to speedy destruction has always been known.
The symptoms are exactly like those produced by
many known poisons. Forensic medicine has a
great many instances already in which it could be
proven that the poison extracted from the body of
the dead was not a vegetable agent introduced during life, but the cadaveric poison. Count Gibbone
was said to have been murdered with delphinine.
Prof. Selmi proved that what was claimed to be
that vegetable poison was cadaveric. In another
case he saved the life of a suspected person by proving that it was not morphine, but ptomaine, which
was found in the body. Besides the poisons named
there is strychnine, colchicine, atropine, coniine,
woorara, nicotine, veratrine, hyoscyamine, nar-
ceine, the symptoms and chemical reaction of
which are the same, or almost so, as the cadaveric
poisons. Lecithine is found in putrid fish ; a very
dangerous chemical poison has been extracted
from putrefying Indian corn and rye. Thus it
is that many cases of poisoning with cheese,
meat, fish, sausage, jelly, and yeast, many of them

4*

resembling acute infectious fevers, may find, and
indeed have found, their ready explanation.

Brieger found quite a number of different varieties of cadaveric poisons—neuridine, neurine, mus-
carine, æthylendiamine, gadinine, and others.
Many of these destroy life in a short time, and with
the symptoms of acute infectious diseases. These
poisons are found, in many instances, in the fresh
dead body, not in that one which has undergone
complete putrefaction. The results of putrefaction
will, after a while, change entirely and become
rather wholesome than injurious. Many years ago
Salkowski examined a vessel full of ascitic fluid,
which he knew to be in utter putrefaction when he
last inspected it. Not only was there no putrefaction any more, but, on the contrary, chemical decomposition had formed phenol. Thus putrefaction
had worked its own destruction and antidote. The
inference, then, is that a poison, even in the course
of the same disease, may not always be found.*

* Would it be so impossible to judge that the bacterium is
an accompaniment of a chemical poison, and may be present
or absent, according to the changed condition of the poison?
Such changes take place all the time in putrefying material,
as Salkowski has shown, and others after him. They probably take place in the living body also, during infectious
fevers. In the incubation they develop, they are most poi-
sonous and vehement during the height of the process; they
gradually change into less dangerous combinations, into an
indifferent state, and finally a really disinfectant material.
Thus it may be that the floating poison may become even
beneficial. Is it for that reason that patients who have out-
lived a serious attack of typhoid fever are endowed with
better nutrition and more vigor afterward than they ever
enjoyed before?

Ptomaines are often met with in the presence of bacteria. Is it the latter which produce them? Do they so decompose the albumen of the tissue that a ptomaine must or can develop? Or is it their own vital change which produces it? Most modern writers—not chemists—believe it. But if the cause of decomposition of the living or dead be not bacteria, but a chemical poison after all, is it necessary to assume that the poison cannot form except through and with the presence of bacteria? And is the bacterium the only poison, or the only source of the poison?

If deadly poison, such as we know to destroy life suddenly, or almost suddenly, and of such virulence as is reported in what was formerly believed to be legendary only, but which may be historical, will almost invariably originate in the dead body, is it so impossible that it may develop in the still living under certain circumstances? Have we not had enough yet of the monthly instalments of new bacilli which are the invariably correct and positive sources of a disease, and replaced by the next man who comes along? Have we not yet enough of the statements that, as for instance, several bacilli are claimed each to be the only cause of diphtheria, by several observers; that there may be several distinct bacilli, every one of which can produce the same scourge? Is it not just as safe to still presume that, when several forms of bacilli are believed to be such sole causes, that the real cause is in neither?

Exactly so, neither in one nor in the other, notwithstanding it all appeared settled. For our journals are replete with the very latest authentic bacterium of diphtheria. This time it is neither Klebs nor Eberth, but Löffler. Reports, discussions, and even editorials carry his name over the world. The very nature of diphtheria is said to be revealed again, as several times before ; still, the discoverer admits that there are cases without the bacterium.

The matter is becoming ludicrous. I begin to fear something like the recent rebellion against piano-playing in a large European city. Is not music a godly art, and the piano a blessing to the musician ? But the playing of fifty thousand beginners in a large city is a nuisance. When bacterio-microscopy in the hands of beginners becomes noisy like piano-playing—noisy in books, pamphlets, and journals—a gentle protest is permissible. That protest is not meant for the masters who know how to wait and to mature. I do not speak against Robert Koch and his peers, who all of them are more modest than their followers. When the kings build, the cartmen are kept busy—and boisterous.

A dozen years ago the coccus of whooping cough was said to be discovered. There was no doubt about it. There was whooping cough, there was a coccus ; what was plainer and more conclusive ? To cure whooping cough, nothing is required but to kill the coccus. Quinine will kill a coccus, quinine cures whooping cough. Since that time there is no more whooping cough in existence ; or, if a case would be malevolent enough to turn up, it could not last longer than until a few whiffs of quinine can reach it. That is ludicrous, is it not ? But it

was preached like gospel, and it was believed.
Many more such have turned up, and will turn up,
for coming years to smile at.

There is a peculiar feature in this bacteriomania.
Its principal impetus it received in Germany at a
time when great changes had taken place in its
political and financial affairs. All at once there
was an Empire, of which historians so much spoke,
youth so much dreamed, romancers so much fabu-
lated. All at once, at the same time and a decade
before, an unusual industriousness, commerce, enterprise, and unwonted wealth, and still more
expectations than wealth; all at once an influx
of five thousand millions of francs, not earned by
honest work, but conquered by war, which could
not but turn the poor heads and unstable the solid
foundations of regular development. From that
time dates that lack of safety and steadiness in
German financial circles. They have even invented
a name for that period of swindling—"gründer-
thum." Speculation was rife—fortunes were made
in a day from nothing but self-assertion and daring,
and lost as quickly.

The moral and intellectual atmosphere created
by these tendencies is never breathed by one class
of people only. If self-assertion can make a for-
tune in finance, why not in science? If a reputation may perhaps be made by a stroke of chance,
why not try that chance? Speculation was rife.
Any young man can look through a microscope—
perhaps he will draw the prize in the lottery of
alleged science. Looking would be all right, if he
would not write. Medical life would be easier if

there were less journal articles containing the latest
infallible discoveries. Thus it has come to pass
that German medicine has a twofold aspect nowadays. The days of her superiority are not over yet;
her greatest men still live, and the toiling thinkers
are at work, but the number of speculators is immense. A great many of the articles printed in the
journals of the last ten years have been prematurely
published, the number of preliminary notices an-
nouncing discoveries under way is very large. The
great embryo cannot wait. He is afraid of having
his celebrity snatched away from him by the next-
door microscopist.

Thus it is that we often find a difficulty in keeping our eye on the great lights, whose rays are always welcome. If learned and thoughtful specialism has its justification anywhere, its field is the
solution of the mooted questions alluded to. Thus
far I claim, however, that in regard to bacteriology
the main questions are before the medical world
still. I firmly hope the Academy will prove the
centre of critical researches by which the problem,
whether bacteric or chemical poison, still a mystery,
will be carried near its solution.

In this expectation I am justified by a reference
to the historical fragments you permitted me to
sketch to-night. There has been no deviation from
the empirical and clinical tendency of Anglo-Saxon
medicine from the beginning. It was so strong
that it gave character to the medicine of the eighteenth century. In the words of the Testament I
might say, Sydenham begot Boerhaave, Boerhaave
begot Van Swieten, Van Swieten begot John Peter

Frank. Sydenham and his generation of followers are the flower of the whole century, and their spirit penetrates everywhere. In those times the senses alone were the diagnostic apparatus. The exact methods of the following decades have sharpened the senses of the English and American medical men, and render their observations more accurate and their results more correct. Live and learn has been their password. No new methods have ever been neglected, only unfounded theories ought not to find root in the regular medical profession. As the best features of all experience and wisdom of all ages and all nations have been utilized in the establishment of our political system, thus the American medical mind has received, appropriated, and critically digested the results of foreign scientific labor and added of its own. It is with sincere pleasure that I have again read that interesting collective volume containing a century of American medical history. In it those of you who have not read it will find many a good reason to be proud of the achievements of our country. It is so modest in its tone and contents that many more names might have appeared in the enumeration of men and labors, not to speak of those who have added materially to our wealth of intellectual productions since. Its perusal will be a revelation to many who are in the habit of looking for everything new and trustworthy, and—that is the technical term nowadays—epoch-making, only abroad. If there is anything which teaches us both justifiable pride and desirable modesty, it is the history of our science

in our own country. For, besides a great many
of the former and present members of this Academy who have accomplished lasting results. there
are a great many other Americans in other States
and cities who stand on a level with the best of
all nations.

From the reading of old journals I learned but
lately that four years before Semmelweiss proclaimed
the contagious character of puerperal fever, against
the protest of the official standard bearers of obstetrics in Austria and Germany, our own anatomist,
our philosopher, our poet, our Autocrat, our own
Oliver Wendell Holmes, taught, it is true against the
ridiculing sneers of Hodge and Meigs, the frequent
transmission of puerperal fever by physicians and
nurses. I might go on a long time, but I do not
stand here to extol America or American medicine.
Still I feel strongly that we may be well satisfied
with what we, not protected by governmental interference, unaided by a slow growth through centuries, have accomplished in a proportionally short
time. The last few decades gave us the library of
the Surgeon-General's Office, the "Subject Catalogue," "The Medical and Surgical History of the
War," standard books, recognized as such in Europe,
great journals, and a goodly array of valuable
monographs, and vastly improved college education:
they have raised great surgeons and clinicians of
universal reputation, and a progressive profession
whose aim and best efforts are directed toward the
improvement of medical training and of the sanitary condition of the people.

All this I firmly believe is true. If it were not, let us make it so. If it be, let us still rise and work, and with all that let every man among us feel what Holmes said forty years ago: "I am too much in earnest for either humility or vanity."

ADDRESS TO THE NEW YORK ACADEMY OF MEDICINE.*

Fellows of the New York Academy of Medicine:

It is a source of intense gratification to me to greet you this evening in the beginning of a new season of co-operative work, after a long vacation. May the labor of the coming months be successful, both for ourselves and for the medical world ! *Ars longa, vita brevis.* Art is so extensive, indeed, and life so short, that we have to concentrate all our efforts to accomplish a certain amount of results.

In behalf of our common interests I crave your attention, first, to a few facts which I consider of great importance in regard to medical progress. They are connected with the session of the International Congress held in Copenhagen from August 10th to 16th, 1884. In a general meeting held on August 14th, upon propositions made by Sir James Paget, of London; Prof. Ewald, of Berlin; Prof. Bouchard, of Paris ; and Dr. Billings, of Washington, the following resolution was passed : That an International Committee be formed for the Collective Investigation of Disease, in connection with the work of the International Congress, and that a certain number of gentlemen do represent their respective countries thereon. The gentlemen desig-

* Delivered Thursday, October 1st, 1885.

nated for that purpose were Trier and C. Lange, of
Copenhagen ; E. Bull, of Christiania : Rauchfuss,
of St. Petersburg : Ewald and Bernhardt, of Berlin ; Schnitzler, of Vienna ; Pribram, of Prague :
Koranyi, of Buda-Pesth ; D'Espine, of Geneva ;
Bouchard, of Paris : Lepine, of Lyon ; Sir William
Gull and Mahomed, of London ; Humphry, of Cam-
bridge ; Sir Joseph Fayrer, for British India ; Guti-
errez-Ponce, for South America ; N. S. Davis, of
Chicago ; A. Jacobi, of New York ; and Isambard
Owen, Secretary-General, of London. The only
changes which have since taken place in the list of
membership have been brought about by the un-
timely death of Dr. Mahomed, and the addition of
Axel Key, of Stockholm, and Runeberg, of Dorpat.

According to a circular distributed by the Secretary-General some time ago, the main objects which
the Committee seeks to attain through the Collective Investigation of Disease are to broaden the basis
of medical science, to gather and store the mass of
information that at present goes to waste, to verify
or correct existing opinions, to discover laws where
now only irregularity is perceived, to amplify our
knowledge of rare affections, and to ascertain such
points as the geographical distribution of diseases
and their modifications in different districts. It
will be its endeavor to place clearly before the
whole profession the limits and defects of existing
knowledge, as well as to stimulate observation and
to give it a definite direction. It will be a not un-
important incidental result of its work should it
tend, as is hoped, to the better training of the
members of the profession in habits of scientific and

practical observation and in systematic methods of recording the facts which they observe.

The age in which we live has seen enormous advances in the sciences on which the fabric of medicine rests, such as chemistry and other branches of physics, physiology, and pathology. Each of these has taken giant strides. It must be admitted, however, that purely medical knowledge has scarcely made proportionate progress. It cannot be expected that it should do so, as it deals with the aberrations of the most complex of organisms, is of all sciences the most difficult, and demands the greatest patience and the largest accumulation of data.

Hitherto the advancement of medical science has been brought about mainly by individual effort. The value of such work in the past we in no way underrate, nor do we desire to lessen the amount of it in the future; but in medical science there is much that defies interpretation from individual experience, and many problems so far-reaching in an ever-widening field, with elements so manifold, that no single man, however gifted and long-lived, can hope to bring the whole within his range. The need, therefore, in medicine, of that combination and concentration of individual work which is adopted in many other branches of science and in commerce, and to which increasing facilities of intercommunication have given so much impulse and so much strength, cannot be questioned. Indeed, it may be said that, resting on individual research alone, medical knowledge can be advanced but slowly and with difficulty. Future progress to

any great extent must be the work, not of units
acting disconnectedly, but of the collected force of
many acting as one. For many to act as one, organization is needed ; that organization it is the
purpose of our committee to supply.

Disease is many-sided, and we wish to include
in our organization those who see it from every
side. All, therefore, whether hospital physicians,
family and school attendants, specialists, medical
officers of the army and navy, and of workhouses
and asylums, will be asked to contribute their
quota of observations to the common fund.

These are both the motives and the propositions
of the committee appointed at Copenhagen. In regard to them, and collective investigations in general, the favorable opinion of the profession has been
expressed frequently. But now and then a voice is
still heard disparaging its utility, and discouraging
the collection of facts on a large scale, for the reason
that the procedure has not yet been demonstrated
to be useful. Indeed it has not, for it has never
been tried to a large extent. We shall hardly insist, however, that the ground stone must not be
laid because the tower is not yet on the edifice ;
that the seed must not be sown because the fruit
cannot be harvested to-day or was not gathered
yesterday.

Hesitation has also been expressed from another
point of view. One of our foremost medical journals (the Boston *Medical and Surgical Journal* of
September 4th, 1884) makes the remark that those
who labor only for personal renown will not enter
enthusiastically into the work proposed by the com-

mittee. But its demands are very trifling indeed ; the questions to be settled by the observations of large numbers are but few and of such a nature as not to expropriate those who are able and anxious to arrive at, and be credited with, scientific results of their own and benefit by the reputation attached to them.

If the remark above quoted were founded on reality, whoever worked for personal reputation only would not even participate in the discussion of a scientific society, for fear lest his remarks, coupled with the essay of somebody else, would miss the opportunity of being listened to as the main topic of an evening's conversation. Now, on the contrary, we are in the daily habit of seeing experience published and ingenuity displayed in just such discussions. Nor do I believe that, as another journal has it (the New York *Medical Journal*, September 4th, 1884), that "the answers coming from a great body of men of diverse views would constitute but a catalogue of raw impressions," and that "when the facts to be observed are of a nature to call for exquisite discrimination on the part of the observers, to multiply the number of the observers is to depreciate the general quality of the work." For the more uncertain the correctness of observations is apt to be, the more numerous they ought to become. Single observations have settled a fact but very rarely. The very existence of large societies proves the instinctive demand for variety and comparative appreciation of observations. Is not every physiological fact known to us as the outgrowth of a number of experiments of

many men, and pathological knowledge the result
of a great many autopsies by different men in
many countries? What is individual experience
but the accumulation of a multitude of facts of a
similar nature by one man? What is science but
the result of accumulated experience, collected and
compared, of many men, countries, and ages? Are
a hundred meteorological stations more efficient,
or less so, than none would be? I do not belong to
that class who believe a problem easy of solution
merely because its solution is anxiously sought for,
nor do I deny difficulties because they are obstacles
to the accomplishment of cherished ends ; but I
know that we are in a better position to serve the
co-operative work of all countries, now that steam
and telegraph have reduced distances, mail and
travel have multiplied intercourse, and we are to-
day as near St. Petersburg as our ancestors were, a
hundred years ago, to Lake Erie or the James River.

Thus it appears evident that the difficulties are
not excessive. As to the usefulness of collective
investigation the opinions will become all but
unanimous. The efforts of the British Medical
Association and the Medical Society of Berlin, and
the fair success of an attempt at solving a problem
connected with the etiology of croupous pneumonia,
made in the Medical Society of the County of New
York during the last year, are sufficiently promising for the collective investigations of the future.
In their interest it is that I propose to make a
further communication and request your co-operation.

The Central Committee on Collective Investigation of the International Congress has selected the following subjects, viz., rickets, chorea, acute rheumatism, and cancer, planned a number of simple questions in regard to them, mainly to their etiology, and expects as simple answers. Being the Secretary of the American Subcommittee, I have gathered all of them in pamphlet form, added a few introductory general remarks supplied by the Central Committee, and present herewith a specimen for your inspection. Those of you—I hope all of you—and those of the profession at large who will learn of this request, are respectfully asked to interest themselves and their friends in behalf of the undertaking, notify me of their desire to be furnished with a copy, and comply with the suggestions of the Committee contained therein. We do not look for immediate achievements. For the complex of sciences and arts called medicine has required thousands of years to arrive at its present condition ; the aggregation of many wills and forces has resulted in a slow evolution only. No single discovery even, nor the first attempts at collective investigation, will effect a revolution in medicine. But what we do hope to accomplish is the gathering of facts on the strength of an improved method, the confirmation of old and the acquisition of new knowledge, and thus to contribute to the success of at least this one Committee. It need not matter how much may have, nay, has been done to mar the success of the next International assembly, and to deprive us of the opportunity, long looked forward to, of greeting the giants of science, the celebrated teachers, the ingenious experimenters, and our literary or personal friends of Europe, on our own soil. For an International Congress will never convene under the roof of a house divided in itself, though the division may be the work of a few sacrilegious hands only.

But this is a sad theme, known to everybody here, deplored by everybody who feels as both a personal grief and a public calamity the humiliation which is involved in the hesitation on the part of the International Congress to assemble in our country.

It is in profound sorrow that I pass by the subject.; I prefer to speak of another topic, which, while it is not directly connected with any of the aims and immediate purposes of this Academy, concerns us as professional men of the State of New York and the Union. I allude to the almost unexpected success on the part of the profession of the State of New York in harmonizing a large majority of the medical men of the United States.

Let me explain. Chapter II., Art. IV., Sec. 1 of the Code of Ethics of the American Medical Association reads as follows : " A regular medical education furnishes the only presumptive evidence of professional abilities and acquirements, and ought to be the only acknowledged right of an individual to the exercise and honors of his profession. Nevertheless, as in consultations the good of the patient is the sole object in view, and this is often dependent on personal confidence, no intelligent regular practitioner who has a license to practise from some medical board of known and acknowledged responsibility recognized by their association, and who is in good moral and professional standing in the place in which he resides, should be fastidiously excluded from fellowship, or his aid refused in consultations when it is requested by the patient. But no one can be considered as a regular practitioner, or a fit associate in consultation, whose practice is based on an exclusive dogma, to the rejection of the accumulated experience of the profession, and of the aids actually furnished by anatomy, physiology, pathology, and organic chemistry."

This paragraph has been so often criticised by both friends and adversaries that it is unnecessary to refer again to its contradictions, its " nevertheless " and " but," and to its implied acknowledgment of modern " homœopathy." For let us not forget that the Code of Ethics of the American Medical Association saw the light forty years ago, and that what they call " homœopathy " nowadays differs from Hahnemannism of those times in everything but the name. They now claim that their practice is not based on an exclusive dogma ; they claim to teach in their schools, and do teach, anatomy, physiology, pathology, and organic chemistry, and thus come up to the requirements of the above article of the Code of Ethics of the American Medical Association. Indeed, if there were no better grounds for their rejection they would to-day be entitled to membership in the Association.

What the Medical Society of the State of New York, in its sessions of 1882 and 1883, adopted in its stead (Transactions of the Medical Society of the State of New York for the year 1882, page 75).

in a code of medical ethics which covers two pages
instead of the eighteen pages of the Code of Medical Ethics of the American Medical Association
(Proceedings of the National Medical Conventions
held in New York, May, 1846, and in Philadelphia,
May, 1847, pages 91–106; Philadelphia, 1846), reads
as follows :

"Members of the Medical Society of the State of
New York, and of the medical societies in affiliation therewith, may meet in consultation legally
qualified practitioners of medicine. Emergencies
may occur in which all restrictions should, in the
judgment of the practitioner, yield to the demands
of humanity."

Compare with these brief sentences the explanatory declaration of the American Medical Association, passed unanimously in its session at New Orleans of April, 1885. Then and there it was

"*Resolved*, That clause first of Article IV. in the
National Code of Medical Ethics is not to be interpreted as excluding from professional fellowship,
on the ground of differences in doctrine or belief,
those who, in other respects, are entitled to be members of the regular medical profession. Neither is
there any other article or clause of the said Code of
Ethics that interferes with the exercise of the most
perfect liberty of individual opinion and practice.

"*Resolved*, That it constitutes a voluntary discon-
nection or withdrawal from the medical profession
proper to assume a name indicating to the public a
sectarian or exclusive system of practice, or to belong to an association or party antagonistic to the
general medical profession.

" *Resolved*, That there is no provision in the National Code of Medical Ethics in any wise inconsistent with the broadest dictates of humanity, and that the article of the code which relates to consultations cannot be correctly interpreted as interdicting, under any circumstances, the rendering of professional services whenever there is pressing or immediate need of them. On the contrary, to meet the emergencies caused by disease or accident, and to give a helping hand to the distressed without unnecessary delay, is a duty fully enjoined on every member of the profession, both by the letter and the spirit of the entire code.

" But no such emergencies or circumstances can make it necessary or proper to enter into formal professional consultations with those who have voluntarily disconnected themselves from the regular medical profession in the manner indicated by the preceding resolution."

After these resolutions had been passed in New Orleans, many of the professional men who always persisted in adhering to the code of the American Medical Association were of the honest opinion that they had, by accepting them, removed every discrepancy of opinion or difference of action on the part of those adhering to either the old or new code. For it is true that the explanatory declaration of Chapter II., Article IV., Section 1 exhibits a great resemblance to the New York Code of 1882. For the Medical Society of the State of New York it must be a source of intense gratification to be convinced, by the passing of that declaration, that a few years have sufficed to so change public opinion as to oblige even the American Medical Association to recognize the justness of most of the New York proceedings. Upon this result the New York State Society can but be sincerely congratulated, and the spirit of equity and justice, as displayed by the Committee drafting the explanatory declaration, must be commended.

The expressions of opinion in regard to the wholesome effect of the New Orleans declaration have been very numerous. I am in possession of several letters containing remarks full of satisfaction and hope. A gentleman well and deservedly known in the profession of both hemispheres, and markedly so with us for his allegiance to the Code of Ethics of the American Medical Association, gave enthusiastic expression to his delight over the satisfaction that declaration must give, and to the hope that the New York Academy of Medicine would give a public utterance in that direction. That would "immediately settle all difficulty about the code, and at once restore peace and harmony in the profession." I had to tell him that the Academy excluded all politics, ethical or otherwise, from its discussions, and that the only societies who could act in the matter were the medical societies of the County and of the State of New York. There the matter then rested, for I believe I was right in excluding it from any consideration in our midst.

Still, while this Academy is no political body, old and new codes, as far as I know, being equally represented with us, we are an integral part of the body medical, and the events in the professional world affect our interests and sympathies intensely. Thus we have to regret that the wording of the resolutions of New Orleans is very apt to obscure their meaning. Emergencies are acknowledged to be binding, but while the New York Code admits that a physician may (not shall or must) consult with a legal practitioner in a case of emergency, the explanatory declaration of the Association insists that such a meeting is not a meeting in the usual meaning of the term, and such a consultation "no formal professional consultation."

The differences are rather slight, it is true. If, in spite of that, the code question is still made a war cry by some, that fact reminds us of the bloody wars and persecutions directed against former friends because of nominal differences of ecclesiastical opinions in the history of the Church. It is also explained by the intense enmity exhibited under all circumstances by those who have been convinced against their will. In a few instances we have to deal with the zeal displayed by converts, who, after they had greeted the birth of the new code with congratulations, were induced by certain external circumstances to change what they call their minds within the period elapsing between the appearance of two monthly numbers; or, what is still more—shall I say surprising, shall I say sad?—there are those who fought the new code because they longed for a fight without caring on what account. A gentleman who edited a sprightly and rattling journal at that memorable time, and voted "the regular ticket." and was by no means gentle toward the new-code men and principles, has convinced and assured me he never read the new code. I believe him. There are others

again—their number has been large at all times—
whose souls and sensibilities are moved by shibbo-
leths, by single words, provided these words are
skilfully handled by shrewd calculation.

> " Just where fails the comprehension
> A word steps promptly in as deputy.
> With words 'tis excellent disputing;
> Systems to words 'tis easy suiting;
> On words 'tis excellent believing;
> No word can ever lose a jot from thieving."
>   BAYARD TAYLOR's *Faust.*

This is the element which in skilful hands deter-
mines for a moment the result of meetings, caucuses,
assemblies. It is the emotional element which is
swayed by sentiment, both false and true, by ges-
ticulating oratory, and by implicit temporary confidence in the veracity and sound motives of its
presumed leaders ; which, therefore, "takes the
specialists of the new-code persuasion by the tops
of their heads and cuts their throats," but after all
is cooled down by common sense, consciousness, and
conscientiousness when left to itself. Such men are
in the majority. They are the waves of the ocean,
always changing, now smooth and smiling, then
turbulent and raving, and still always the same,
steady in their general effects; now and then a disturbance and an injury, but always the eternal
source of healthful development. We never cease
to bless the ocean, even when it is doing its temporary worst. Let us, therefore, not despair of the
future peaceful and blissful development of the
country or the profession in times of turbulent
commotion.

What difference is left unabolished may be left to itself until acrimony is soothed and bitterness replaced by kindness. Greater discrepancies than these have been wiped out. When the actions of men will be weighed, their opinions in regard to dogmatic utterances will be disregarded. When deeds are counted, let creeds be tolerated. But let us have patience, all of us; great improvements in the universal conscience do not take place by hard fighting and refuting. Lecky is right when he says that the greatest errors cannot be annihilated; it takes time for them to fade out.

In the face of the explanatory declaration passed in New Orleans, which in its main aspects, I take it, indorses the New York State Society and the spirit of the new code, the majority of those present in the meeting of the American Medical Association were guided into believing that they must protect a sacred code from infidel invaders. The main complaint was that new-code men had been given offices in the organizations of the International Congress. On page 101 of the *Journal of the American Medical Association* you will find the following complaint: " Directly upon the threshold of the most important part of their work a majority of the original committee practically ignored all allegiance to the Medical Association, and, assuming an entirely independent attitude, at once placed in the front of their ranks . . . one who was well known to have repudiated the National Code of Ethics." And in a voluminous circular addressed to the State and County Medical Societies, composed almost exclusively of editorials of the *Journal of the American*

Medical Association, and signed by the Permanent
Secretary of the Association and four other gentlemen, the following language is used: "The editorials of the *Journal* of the Association present the
case" (the differences in regard to the proposed
organization of the International Congress) "so
clearly that there can be no doubt of the duty of the
friends of the Association, or of the animus of its
enemies. We feel assured that your Society will
indorse the action of the Association and stand
firm in support of the Code of Ethics."

It is, however, fairly understood by this time that
the war of the codes is over. In fact, it has always
appeared to unsophisticated people that the fighting
about the code was not reciprocal at all; for, when the
New York State Society had settled its code question
to its satisfaction and that of the county societies
in affiliation therewith, it appears that in them and
by them the subject was not mentioned again except on strong provocation. You remember that it
took a great deal of emphasis to relieve even this
Academy of the proffered dispute. The code question is dying a great deal more easily than the
bloody shirt disappeared from the politics of the
country. If it is puffed up as the pivot of the organization of the International Congress, everybody
is perfectly aware that this is either a pretext or
a grave mistake. I believe it is both. Europeans,
who were not afraid of admitting laymen and ho-
mœopathists, expected to meet, if ever they would
consent to cross the Atlantic for an International
Congress, the American medical profession. No
International Congress must be caught in domestic

quarrels, or audaciously kidnapped by a society, or a party, or the faculty of a medical school.

We are presenting a sad spectacle. In our first attempt at welcoming the medical world to our shores we have failed. The humiliation connected with this fact we have to submit to; to trace it to all its causes I cannot undertake here. The least we can do is to admit it; if the task we hoped to accomplish was too much for us, let us try to prepare for the future by attending to those duties of our own which we can perform without hindrance or disturbance.

The affairs of the Academy will require our undivided attention. In many respects we have been very successful indeed. The hall and building in which we meet is practically our own and free of debt. Thus we can look forward again to improve our quarters, enlarge our facilities, and think of securing, in some near future, a fire-proof building for our ever-increasing bibliographical treasures. Our income has increased with our membership. Both, however, require additions. There are many desirable men in the profession whom we ought to carry on our lists for mutual advantage.

The hopes I expressed in my inaugural address a few months ago have begun to be fulfilled. Old sections have been revived, new ones have been formed. I may here assure the gentlemen who have undertaken the task of organizing them that whatever aid the President and Council can give them in their labors will be freely offered. The sections will not only contribute to the improvement of their own members, but will enhance the

interest of the general sessions by the communica-
tions coming to them from the sections and the
discussions emanating therefrom.

To enable them to begin their work, Article VI.
of the constitution had to be altered. That change
has been brought about in the manner prescribed
by law some months ago. It has also appeared to
many Fellows that more alterations are required ;
they have given notice of their desire in this respect, but have been unwilling to come before the
Academy with any propositions to make radical
changes, though in the manner prescribed by law.
Now both the constitution and by-laws may be repealed or amended by a three-fourths vote at a
stated meeting, provided notice of the same has
been given in writing at a previous stated meeting.
But it will prove more satisfactory to guard against
any mistake by trusting the work of moving pro-
posals to change our by-laws in the hands of a committee carefully selected for that purpose. Off-hand
legislation is always dangerous ; it often errs, and
always weakens the conservative tendencies which
must underlie any political, scientific, or social structure, if it be expected to last. The President expresses the hope that if such a committee be appointed, it will be slow in considering and quick in
reporting.

If I be at liberty to state a wish of my own, I
should say that one of the articles which require
amending is that which refers to the Committee on
Medical Ethics. This committee is almost powerless ; it has no initiative whatsoever ; in every case
calling for interference or judgment it has to wait

for a charge to be preferred by a Fellow ; the odium
of an accusation falls always on an individual member, whose unselfish interest in the welfare of the
Academy or the profession is at once published, as
it were, by arraying him personally against the accused. To prefer a charge is thus almost rendered
an impossibility. Thus, indeed, our law is more
apt to encourage derelictions of ethical duties than
to prevent or punish them. Now, I am of the opinion that the interest of an accused member must
always be taken into account, but that of the Academy is at least of equal importance. What the
District Attorney and the police are in the political
and social commonwealth, the Committee on Ethics
ought to be in our midst. It ought to be both authorized and directed not to wait for personal
charges, but itself watch over the moral welfare of
our community. If such an authority be established, the ethically weak would know that he is
observed and may be held responsible without a
Fellow being compelled to draw upon himself odium
or revenge.

No society, either political or otherwise, can ever
do without a penal code, old or new ; thus there is no
harm in admitting that the Academy is in need of
a Committee of Ethics like any other society. If
the number of those who necessitate its existence or
interference be but small, so much the better ; but
the few, when not stopped, act as bacilli of moral
putrefaction. Humankind is so organized that disease germs will operate rapidly and persistently. A
Committee on Ethics, endowed with the authority to
warn and censure in time, without any procrastina-

tion, will strengthen the feeble when he feels the
first symptoms of struggling against temptation,
may frighten the man of harder fibre who would
otherwise rely on his facilities and the difficulties on
the part of the committee, and protect the interests
of society and the endangered dignity of the profession.

That I speak of no imaginary evil we all know too
well. What I said a few months ago of the growing tendency of a few to make the public acquainted
with their merits and accomplishments through the
columns of the secular press was considered timely,
and met with the appreciation of many members
of the profession, both old and young, here and
elsewhere. I mean to deserve the respect of my
peers and superiors in the profession by again directing your attention to the fact that the penny-a-
liners of the daily press are being utilized in the interest of, and by, weak-kneed brothers who cannot
stand on their own legs, who mistake cheap notoriety for reputation, and the grin of derision for the
smile of approval. The more power is concentrated
in commerce, the greater the prevalence which is
conquered by trade, the more rampant the spirit of
grasping egotism, which is pathognomonic of modern industrial pursuits, the more is it the domain of
the liberal professions to approximate their aims to
an ideal. Let us not forget that learning by heart
the action of medicines, or the working of articula-
tions, or the proper use of an instrument, does not
exhaust the possibilities of a medical man. The
physician requires all that, but, beyond that, all the
characteristics of a man of principle and intellectual

and moral culture. Neither can be inculcated by the demands of old or new codes. Still, as a corporation and a profession, we are responsible for the existence of these qualities in our members. It is true we cannot supply ideals to order, nor can we make those whose eyes seek the mire raise their brow to the skies. But such as find it difficult to develop those qualities spontaneously must be taught and aided in acquiring them.

As far as I am concerned, I hope there will be no occasion again to refer to the same subject during my term of service. If there be, I shall repeat my warning. For I take it for granted that when you elected me to the highest office in your possession, you did so both in the belief that your candidate would have opinions and principles of his own, and on the condition that he should do his full duty.

THE CHANCES OF AN INTERNATIONAL MEDICAL CONGRESS IN AMERICA.*

It is evident that the work done by the Committee of the International Congress at its secret meeting in this city is an utter failure. The Committee has won over no new friends, but, on the other hand, withdrawals continue to be made. We believe that there is no exaggeration in saying that there are not half a dozen representative men in the profession now who are prominently connected with the organization of the Congress.

The attempt to hold an international meeting under such circumstances seems certainly very wrong, while, if affairs continue on as present, there will be a collapse of the whole affair before the year 1887. It is known that some of the gentlemen who withdrew from the Congress did so partly because they found that they could not get co-operation at home or abroad; they could not organize sections so as to secure successful work; and this difficulty must steadily increase.

Beyond all this, the obstinate conduct of the gentlemen who are trying to arrange the Congress on American Medical Association principles is arousing a constantly stronger indignation among the profession at large. It is clearly seen that their

* N. Y. Med. Record, October 3d, 1885. Editorial.

6*

perversity and disloyalty are bringing discredit
upon American medicine.

Since there are no hopes of a genuine International Congress under the present management
of affairs, the question arises as to what is the best
course to pursue. Either the profession must take
hold of the matter and reorganize anew, or we
must beg our European brethren to withdraw their
invitation. We should greatly regret to be forced
to the latter alternative, especially as American
physicians are very earnestly desirous of having the
International Congress held here.

This being so, it only remains that they strive to
act harmoniously and energetically with a view, at
the next meeting of the American Medical Association, of reconsidering the hasty and ill-considered
action taken at New Orleans. It will only be
necessary, after all, that at the session in St. Louis
next spring, the policy of the original Committee
be adopted and that of the present Committee
rejected. A large part of the detail work needs no
change. Such restorative action might be criticised as inconsistent, but the injury of such criticism would be small indeed compared with that
wrought by a pursuance of present methods. For
it cannot be too often or too emphatically reiterated
that a Congress like the one now being foisted
upon us, a Congress that has been inoculated with
the poison of a foreign and disorganizing issue, will
be practically a failure. The removal of this issue,
even so late as next spring, would still give time for
organization to be effected. While there is yet this
possibility of some change being effected at St.

Louis we will not quite give up the Congress. But meanwhile it will be hardly necessary to say that those who wish well of their profession will carefully keep aloof from all connection with the present Committee on Organization, which might better be called a Committee on Disorganization. This Committee should be vigorously let alone.

THE INTERNATIONAL MEDICAL CONGRESS.*

CONCERNING THE THREATS OF NEW-CODE MEN AT COPENHAGEN—CORRESPONDENCE BETWEEN DR. A. JACOBI, OF NEW YORK, AND DR. J. V. SHOEMAKER, OF PHILADELPHIA.

110 WEST 34TH STREET,
NEW YORK, MAY 3d, 1885.

Dr. J. V. Shoemaker, Philadelphia.

DEAR SIR:—The *Medical News* of May 2d contains on page 494 the following : "Dr. J. V. Shoemaker said new-code men had made threats at Copenhagen in his presence, hence the statement that he had made was true, as men who had made these threats were now on the committee." As far as I know, the only "new-code man" on the General Committee of the Ninth International Congress is myself. It is natural, therefore, that I should be anxious to know if you accuse me of having made threats.

Very respectfully yours,

A. JACOBI, M.D.

PHILADELPHIA, PA., May 5th, 1885.

Dr. A. Jacobi.

DEAR SIR:—The account in the *News* was not

* The Medical Record, May 30th, 1885.

exactly as I made the remarks. As near as I can remember, the concluding sentence was, the statement that I had made was true, as the new-code men were fully represented on the Congress, which was the very best evidence of their recognition by the Committee.

Yours respectfully,

J. V. Shoemaker.

New York, May 7th, 1885.

Dr. J. V. Shoemaker.

Dear Sir :—Besides the *Medical News*, to which I referred you in a previous note, you are reported, in the *Medical Record* of May 2d, to have said that "the Committee . . . yielded to the threat made by the new-code men at Copenhagen, that unless they were recognized they would use their influence to prevent the Congress from coming to the United States."

I cannot but repeat that I must request you—as I am the only "new-code man" on the Committee —to explain what induced you to make the statement you are credited with, or what may have been the cause of the uniform reports in the journals.

Very respectfully yours,

A. Jacobi, M.D.

Philadelphia, Pa., May 9th, 1885.

Dr. A. Jacobi.

Dear Sir :—I stated in my remarks, which have not been fully reported in any of the accounts that have appeared, the predictions made at Copenhagen, which have been verified by the present arrangement of the Congress.

Yours truly,

J. V. SHOEMAKER.

110 WEST 34TH STREET,

NEW YORK, May 11th, 1885.

Dr. J. V. Shoemaker.

DEAR SIR:—The *Boston Medical and Surgical Journal* of May 7th, 1885, page 456, has the following sentence : "Dr. Shoemaker repeated that the new-code men had made threats at Copenhagen."

The *New York Medical Journal* of May 2d, 1885, page 500, writes as follows : "Dr. John V. Shoemaker . . . alleged . . . that the new-code men present " (at Copenhagen) " had openly threatened that they would prevent the acceptance of the invitation unless they received full recognition ; as a consequence, they had been recognized, as was shown by the fact that they had been given some of the prominent positions with reference to the Washington meeting."

These reports agree fully with those I quoted in my previous notes from the *Medical News* and the *Medical Record.*

Thus you will pardon me for saying that your two notes did not answer my questions concerning the language quoted.

Permit me to ask again :

1. Did you say the new-code men had made threats at Copenhagen ?

2. If so. what are the facts supporting such a statement ?

3. If not, what was the remark you made ?

Pardon me for requesting an answer, for I have to repeat again that I am the only " new-code man " on the General Committee who can have been referred to.

Very respectfully yours,

A. JACOBI, M.D.

PHILADELPHIA, PA., May 13th, 1885.

Dr. A. Jacobi.

DEAR SIR:—Your letter of May 11th is before me. It affords me pleasure to assure you that in my remarks at New Orleans I said nothing that was intended to personally implicate you. You need offer no apology for your persistency, as this explanation would be due any gentleman who regards himself compromised.

I infer from your letter that a personal explanation is what you want, and I am glad of this opportunity to place in your hands such documentary evidence as will exonerate you, if you have been wrongfully accused by others.

If you want any further information for public purposes, I have but to add that it will be *forthcoming* at the *proper time* and *place*. You will agree with me that your claim upon me can only personal not all (? A. J.) affecting individuals. So let me again assure you that I shall be most happy to make any explanations that will relieve you of any censure that my remarks may have brought upon you personally.

Yours respectfully,

J. V. SHOEMAKER.

MAY 14th, 1885.

Dr. J. V. Shoemaker.

SIR:—Your note of May 13th convinces me that you mean to persist in evading a straightforward and honest answer. I asked a few direct and intelligible questions, and you refuse to give anything but circumlocution.

When you spoke in New Orleans you knew you said what was untrue. And now that you are called upon for an explanation of your conduct you try to wriggle out of your responsibility.

You are altogether mistaken if you think—which I do not believe you do—that I need or desire any justification or exoneration at your hands. You know that what you said in New Orleans about threats being made was not true, and your letters show that you have not the courage to stand up to it. A. JACOBI, M.D.

NOTE.—A letter of Dr. Shoemaker's, which arrived two or three days afterward, was returned to its writer unopened. A. JACOBI.

VOLKSMEDICIN.

VORTRAG GEHALTEN VOR DEM DEUTSCHEN GESELLIG-
WISSENSCHAFTLICHEN VEREIN VON NEW YORK
AM 11. MÄRZ 1885.

ICH fürchte, dass ich meinem Vortrage einen falschen Titel gegeben habe. "Fragmente aus der Volksmedicin" wäre ein passenderer Name gewesen, denn in dem Rahmen einer kurzen Stunde lässt sich ein Kapitel, dessen Inhalt der Weltgeschichte parallel läuft, nicht zusammenfassen. Ich bilde mir daher nicht ein, Ihnen vielerlei bieten zu können. In der Beschränkung des Stoffes, welche ich mir habe auferlegen müssen, habe ich indessen nicht umhin gekonnt, mir die Frage vorzulegen, was angemessener sei : den Versuch zu machen, Unterhaltendes und Ergötzliches zu bringen, oder Material zum Nachdenken und Behalten zu liefern. Das Letztere habe ich schliesslich vorgezogen. Zum Vergnügen muss Ihnen der zweite Theil des Abends ausreichen. Wenn ich Einigen von Ihnen mit dem Folgenden nützlich sein kann, so muss mein Zweck erfüllt sein. Hoffentlich werde ich nicht zu vielem Tadel dafür ausgesetzt sein, dass ich ein scheinbar specielles Fachthema zu unserer Unterhaltung ausgewählt habe. Thatsache ist es ja doch, dass das Publikum im Ganzen und Grossen sich gern, und mehr als ihm gut ist, mit ärztlichen Fragen beschäftigt. Sie werden es deshalb einem alten Fachmann nicht übel deuten, wenn er sich auch einmal herausnimmt, dieselben zum Gegenstand seiner Betrachtung zu machen.

Volksmedicin und officielle Medicin stammen aus derselben Quelle. Das Bedürfniss, dem Erkrankten und Verletzten zu helfen, hat beide hervorgerufen. Die Beobachtung dessen, was in ähnlichen oder ähnlich scheinenden Fällen früher einmal nützlich gewesen sein mag, giebt die Grundlage für das Handeln in kommenden Krankheiten oder Zufällen. Dabei war es natürlich, dass dieselben nicht gerade als Naturereignisse, als Folgen natürlicher Vorgänge aufgefasst wurden, sondern dass man sie als Schickungen und feindliche Einwirkungen registrirte. Daher kam es, dass man gern sich an solche Personen wandte, von denen man voraussetzte, dass sie über Schickungen und übernatürliche Einwirkungen genau Bescheid wüssten. Das waren die Priester. Noch heute entsprechen die Zauberer der Neger, die Schamanen der Sibirier den Priesterärzten der Griechen, Aegypter und Inder. Nur der Medicinmann der Indianer, welche diesen Titel jedem höher Begabten und Unterrichteten in ihrem Stamme einräumen, da bei ihnen die Gnade der Religion noch nicht zum Durchbruch gekommen ist, gehört nicht zu dieser Klasse.

Mit den Priesterärzten der Aegypter und Griechen sind wir am meisten vertraut. Die Heiligthümer des Serapis in Memphis, des Aesculapius zu Epidaurus und Kos in Griechenland, und Pergamus in Kleinasien waren gesuchte Heilstätten. Die Temple waren an luftigen gesunden Stellen, in Hainen, nahe an Trink- und mineralischen Quellen erbaut. Ohne körperliche und geistige Vorbereitung durfte Niemand der Heilstätte nahen. "Reinen Sinnes muss sein, wer den duftenden Tempel beschreitet." In den Hallen des Tempels legte sich der Kranke ; im Traume nahte ihm die Gottheit und theilte ihm mit, was er zu thun habe, um seiner Krankheit ledig zu werden, Heilmittel sowohl wie Mass-nahmen. Ihm deutete der Priester seinen Traum, für ihn, wenn er mit keinen Träumen gesegnet wurde, legte sich der Priester in die Tempelhallen, träumte für ihn, deutete ihm, und rieth ihm, im Namen der Gottheit. Dem Priester auch gab der genesende oder genesene Kranke die Geschenke, welche entweder als Dankopfer der Gottheit, oder Anerkennung dem Tempel zugedacht wurden. Was aber damals die Gottheit selber leistete, durch ihre irdischen Diener, das wurde später durch deren Stellvertreter, St. Denis, den heiligen Martin, San Jago di Compostella und die Mutter Gottes zu Kevlaar ausgeführt.

Es konnte indessen nicht fehlen, dass im Laufe der Zeit gute Beobachter unter den Priestern em-pirische Kenntnisse sammelten. Von dem, was gesehen und hülfreich befunden war, wurde Notiz genommen. In besonders wichtigen oder merk-würdigen Fällen, wie noch die neulichen Ausgra-bungen zu Epidaurus ergeben, über welche Prof. Merriam von Columbia College in der Academy of Medicine in nächster Woche berichten wird, wur-den Inschriften angefertigt, und dadurch der Schatz wirklicher Kenntnisse allmählich vermehrt. Die Heilkunst wurde damit langsam dem Glauben und

Schwindel entfremdet. Die ältesten chinesischen Bücher über Medicin datiren Tausende von Jahren, der Papyrus Ebers anderthalb Jahrtausende, die indischen Bücher, Susrutas Ayurvedas, zwölfhundert Jahre vor Christus zurück. Um die griechischen Tempel siedelten sich nicht selten Philosophenschulen an, deren Theilnehmer gute Naturbeobachtung und Trieb nach Wahrheit glücklich vereinigten. In dieser Weise wurde es möglich, das Hippokrates von Kos eine so grosse Menge von naturgetreuen Beobachtungen sammeln und verwerthen konnte, dass noch heute, und für alle Zeiten, seine als echt anerkannten Schriften als Vorbild des wissenschaftlich geläuterten gesunden Menschenverstandes und der unverfälschten Symptombeobachtung am Krankenbette gelten können. Um so grösser sind seine Leistungen und um so vielfacher der Dank, welchen die Nachwelt ihm und dem Jahrtausend seiner priesterlichen Vorgänger schuldig ist, wenn Sie bedenken, dass der ganze damalige Fortschritt der Heillehre ohne Kenntniss des Baues und der Lebensvorgänge des menschlichen Körpers gemacht werden musste ; denn Sectionen waren verboten. Galen, der vierhundert Jahre später lebte, erklärt es für ein grosses Glück, dass ihm vergönnt gewesen sei, auf seinen Reisen die Skelette von zwei Mördern zu sehen, welche man in Aegypten habe verfaulen lassen. Menschen seciren war ausser Frage. Seine Anatomie lernte Galen, oder glaubte er zu lernen, an Affen. Selbst Vesal, der grösste Anatom des Beginnes der Neuzeit, gerieth in Lebensgefahr wegen seiner anatomischen Arbeiten, und kaum

hundert Jahre ist es her, seit in dieser Stadt New
York, um das alte New York Hospital herum, aus
derselben Ursache der "Doktors'-Mob" wüthete
und Brutalität und Todtschlag herrschten.

Im Mittelalter wurde die Arzneikunst, wie alles
Andere, zunftmässig ausgeübt. Es gab eine grosse
Klasse von Medicinalpersonen, welche irgend wie
oder wo ihre Kunst gelernt hatten. Physici waren
auf Universitäten gebildet, meist in Italien oder
Frankreich. Sie genossen grosses Ansehen, besonders da ihre Zahl klein war, als Heilkünstler
und Lehrer der Medicin. Ansässig waren sie nur
zeitweilig; sie führten ein Wanderleben, ver-
mietheten sich wohl als Stadtärzte, und stellten
auf ihren Reisen ihr Licht nicht unter den Scheffel.
In ähnlicher Weise lebten und wirkten die Chirur-
gen. Daneben gab es Bader, Barbiere, Feldscherer,
Apotheker und Hebammen.

Dies waren die Regulären. Dazu kamen Hirten,
Schäfer und Jäger. In alten Zeiten hatte man
ihnen grosse Naturkenntnisse zugeschrieben und
übernatürliche Begabung. Jeder District hatte
seinen Lampe. Scharfrichter und Henker—sie
verstanden sich auf Salben für die Wunden, deren
sie so viele machten, und heilten die Knochen-
brüche, welche sie selber verschuldeten. Schmiede
—sie besorgten die Pferde und verstanden sich daher auf die Krankheiten der Menschen. Alte
Frauen—man schrieb ihnen Prophetengabe zu und
die Fähigkeit, welche heute mit Vorliebe den jungen zugeschrieben wird, durch Wort, Blick oder
Zauber Uebernatürliches zu leisten. Sie konnten
ihre Kunst sogar übertragen, aber, trotzdem dass

sie alt waren, nur auf Männer, wie auch heilkräftige Männer ihre geheime Kunst wieder nur auf Frauen übertragen konnten.

Solche Praktiken und Anschauungen entsprechen ganz den Vorstellungen, welche man vom Alterthum her bis in's späte Mittelalter hinein von der Natur der Krankheit hatte. Sie galt vielfach für eine directe feindliche Einwirkung auf menschliche Wesen, und man glaubte daher, dass eben solche Einflüsse zu ihrer Heilung nöthig seien. Daher erklären sich Wunderglaube, Erbauung von Tempeln für bestimmte Krankheitsgöttinnen, z. B. die Febris ; der neuplatonische Glaube an Dämonen ; die gewaltige Wirkung des Wortes Abracadabra, welches der Arzt des Septimius Severus erfand ; der Glaube an die bösen Geister, welche unter dem Christenthum die Stelle der Dämonen vertraten ; an Besprechen, Berufen, bösen Blick, Hexerei ; an Amulette und andere Schutzmittel, wie Processionen und Wallfahrten. Leider können wir das Mittelalter noch immer nicht als abgeschlossen betrachten.

Denn Gebete, Sagen, Besprechungen sind noch heute Heilmittel, denen Viele nachlaufen. In einem Kloster der Nachbarschaft, über den Sümpfen und Mosquitoes des westlichen Flussufers treibt ein frommes Kirchenglied sein Heilgeschäft in dieser Weise. Der Glaube an ihre Wirksamkeit ist sicherlich stark verbreitet. Mehr aber als sie, scheinen Amulette Zug- und Wunderkraft zu behaupten. Ich habe kaum jemals ein irländisches Wesen—männlich oder weiblich—ausserhalb oder innerhalb eines Hospitals getroffen, das nicht an

schmutzigem Bande ein schmutzigeres Amulett
trug. Gold, Silber. Metalle überhaupt, sind selten,
Leder mit unerforschlichem Inhalt, nicht immer
blos nach Knoblauch, Pfeffer, Kampher u. dgl.
riechend, häufiger. Nicht immer sind es blos die
niedrigsten Volksklassen, welche die Träger dieser
Sachen sind. Der reichgewordene Patentbesitzer
von Holman's Liver Pad, Congressmitglied u. s. w.
hat der zahlenden Bevölkerung dieser Staaten eine
neue Art von Amuletten geschaffen.

Eine andere Auffassung der Krankheit bestand
in der Annahme einer geheimnissvollen Beziehung
des Menschen zur Natur, deren Ausdruck in Plato's
Lehre der allgemeinen Harmonie ursprünglich zu
finden ist. Aus ihr entwickelte sich leicht die
Lehre vom Einfluss der Gestirne, der günstigen
Wirkung der glänzenden Planeten Venus und
Jupiter, der verderbenbringenden des rothen Mars
und trüben Saturn, des Horoscopstellens, der Bedeutung der Astrologie überhaupt für die gelehrte
und die Volksmedicin, der Wichtigkeit gewisser
Wochentage, des abnehmenden Mondes für ärztliche Behandlung gewisser Zustände, und daneben
auch für die Ausbeutung der Natur in ihre tiefsten
und schmutzigsten Winkel hinein. Die Sonderbarkeiten der chinesischen Medicin, und die naiven
Abscheulichkeiten von " Paulini's heilsamer Dreck-
apotheke" (1696), finden in dieser Weise ihre Erklärung.

Eine dritte Ansicht von der Krankheit war die.
dass ein concretes feindliches Wesen in den Körper
eindringe und um jeden Preis hinauszuschaffen sei.
Alle Formen der ausleerenden Behandlung sind von

7*

jeher zu dem Zwecke des Hinausschaffens der
Schädlichkeit in Gebrauch genommen, und wenn
zufällig, oder in Folge eines krankhaften Prozesses,
oder einer künstlichen örtlichen Reizung die Kör-
peroberfläche der Sitz einer Ausscheidung wurde,
so war nichts natürlicher als dass man dieselbe
schonte, pflegte und segnete. Was sagt der gute
Onkel Bräsig : " Du kannst Dir mit die Dams erzählen, was Du willst, wirst aber schwerlich 'ne
Antwort kriegen, wenn Du nich von ihre Krank-
heitsgeschichten anfängst, wo oft sie schon Pückeln
über den ganzen Leib gekriegt haben, un Swären
un blinde Dinger ; denn das ist in einer Wasser-
kunst die gebildtste Unterhaltung."
　Im Zusammenhange damit lassen Sie mich ein
Beispiel dieser Art Volksanschauung prüfen, welches zu Erläuterung dessen, was ich beweisen
wollte, von Interesse sein mag.
　Kopfausschläge bei den Kindern werden für eine
grosse Wohlthat angesehen und vielfach sorgfältig
gehütet. Lassen Sie mich ein paar Worte über
diese armen, schmutzigen Kinderköpfe sagen. Der
Schmutz ist zweierlei, richtiger normaler, oder
Krankheitsprodukt. Jener findet sich bei ganz
Kleinen, ein paar Monate alten. Auf Kinderköpfen
sind eine grosse Anzahl Talgdrüsen stark entwickelt ; bevor das Haar dichter wächst, ist deshalb die Kopfhaut, die Stirn, und das Näschen, das
liebe kleine Näschen, fettig glänzend anzusehen.
Oft bekommt sogar der Finger beim Fühlen den
Eindruck der Fettigkeit. Die Absonderung dieser
Talgdrüsen häuft sich in den Drüsen, in den Aus-
führungsgängen und in deren Umgebung an, ver-

mischt sich, wenn nicht abgerieben und entfernt,
mit den oberflächlichen, abschuppenden Hauttheil-
chen und dem von aussen zugeführten Schmutz,
und das Resultat ist die fest anhaftende, dunkel-
braune oder schwarze Masse, welche zuletzt nur
mit Mühe und grosser Sorgfalt zu entfernen ist.
Gewöhnlich wird sie erst weggeschafft, nachdem sie
zu einer Unterbrechung des Haarwuchses und zu
Hautreiz Veranlassung gegeben hat.

Die andere Form ist ernsthafterer Natur und verlangt vielleicht sogar hier ein Wort der Warnung
und Belehrung. Nach der Geburt entwickelt sich
kein Theil des kindlichen Körpers so schnell und bedeutend, wie der Kopf mit seinem Inhalt. Nicht
nach fünf oder sechs Monaten, sondern sofort fängt
dies rasche Wachsthum an. Die Zähne bilden sich
schon vor der Geburt, wachsen schnell rascher und
kommen zu bestimmter Zeit zum Vorschein. Das
Zahnen, die Entwicklung der Speicheldrüsen, die
rasche Entwicklung geistiger Fähigkeiten, der
Haarwuchs entsprechen nur dem Zudrang des
Blutes zu jenen Theilen, in denen die Entwicklung
des Baues und der Kräfte in gleichem Masse vor
sich geht. Die Schnelligkeit dieser Entwicklung
setzt einen sehr ausgedehnten Blut- und Säftezu-
drang voraus, welcher darin seine Erklärung findet, dass das kindliche Herz eine im Verhältniss
zum übrigen Körper bedeutende Massigkeit besitzt,
und die nach aufwärts gehenden Blutgefässe eine
unverhältnissmässige Weite. Nun werden Sie
leicht verstehen, dass dort, wohin eine grosse Blutmenge strömt mit normalen Wirkungen, oder wie
man sich sonderbarerweise gern ausdrückt, zum

Zwecke der normalen Organbildung—als ob Natur-
vorgänge einen beabsichtigten Zweck hätten—auch
sehr leicht ein Uebermass der Blutzufuhr stattfinden kann. Der Ursachen dafür kann es viele geben.
Ein elastisches, lebendiges, von seinem Bau und
dem seiner Umgebung abhängiges Blutgefäss—und
hunderte kommen in Betracht und zur Wirkung—
ist eben keine Bleiröhre, und das Gehirn und sein
Behälter keine Badewanne. Dieses Uebermass
führt zu Stockungen, zu unregelmässiger Ernährung, zu Schwellungen, zu Ausschlägen. Diese
Ausschläge, d. h. Bläschen mit klarem oder eiter-
igem Inhalt trocknen oder zerbrechen ; der Inhalt
gerinnt sofort, vermischt sich mit Hauttalg, mit
Hautschuppen, mit Schmutz von aussen, mit Papier
und Schmier, mit Bandelin und Vaselin, mit ranzi-
gem Fett, wird sorgfältig gehegt und gepflegt—es
ist ja so gut für das Kind, die geheimnissvolle
Krankheit kommt heraus ! Das ist die Manier, wie
das Engelköpfchen allmählich durch die Scala verschiedener Ehren- und anderer Titel zum Grindkopf
herabsinkt. Wenn die Resultate des Ausschlags,
die Schuppen und Borken, frühzeitig entfernt worden wären, hätte man sich Schmutz und gelegentlich Ekel, dem armen Kinde Jucken und Schmerz
und Schlaflosigkeit und zweifelhafte Titel erspart.
Aber noch viel mehr als alles das ! Da es möglich
ist, dass meine Worte beachtet werden, und dass
dieselben sogar über diese Schwelle hinaus gehört
werden, so will ich eine Bemerkung hinzufügen.
Mit dem Ausbrechen des Ausschlags, und seiner
Schonung und—ich möchte sagen—sorgfältigen
Pflege ist der Schatz des Bösen, welcher dem Baby

für sein künftiges Leben gesammelt wird, lange
nicht erschöpft. Jede permanente Reizung irgendwo auf einer Oberfläche hat ihre unmittelbare
Folge. Sie haben oft von Leichenvergiftungen bei
Aerzten gehört. Eine kleine Abschärfung am Finger wird von Leichengift gereizt, ein Minimum
wird in den Blutlauf aufgenommen, und der Mann
stirbt an allgemeiner Blutvergiftung in kurzer Zeit.
Das erste Zeichen der Krankheit ist die Entzündung
der Lymphgefässe den Arm hinauf und die Schwellung der Lymphdrüsen in der Achselhöhle. In
ähnlicher Weise wirkt jede örtliche Reizung, auch
wenn der Reiz nicht gerade giftig ist. Eine wunde
Haut- oder Schleimhautstelle zieht immer benach-
barte Lymphdrüsen in Mitleidenschaft. Sie werden
gereizt, schwellen, entzünden sich, und werden entweder wieder gesund, oder verhärten sich und werden dadurch unbrauchbar, oder gehen in Eiterung
zu Grunde. So kommt es, dass wunde Hautstellen
bei kleinen Kindern, in den Schenkelbeugen z. B.,
fast niemals ohne Schwellung der benachbarten
Drüsen verlaufen, dass jeder Durchfall ohne Ausnahme, wenn er nur ein paar Tage dauert, z. B. der
sogenannte Zahndurchfall, die benachbarten Drüsen
in Gefahr bringt mit möglicher Entartung für Lebenszeit, dass eine laufende Nase bei kleinen Kindern immer nach kurzer Zeit Drüsenschwellung am
Halse bewirkt, und dass Kopfausschläge immer
Drüsenkränze unter dem Kinn, hinter dem Ohr,
um den Nacken herum hervorrufen. Wäre der ursprüngliche Ausbruch sofort beseitigt, wäre das
Alles nicht passirt. Wäre der Durchfall nicht ge-
schont worden, weil die Nachbarfrau der Meinung

war, dass der Nachbarin Kind am Zahnen, oder
am "zweiten Sommer," leidet, so wären die
Bauchdrüsen nicht entartet; wäre der Kopf zur
rechten Zeit gereinigt, so hätten sie sich Drüsen
und Eiterungen und Verhärtungen, mit der le-
benslänglichen Entstellung und dem lebensläng-
lichen Kranksein, erspart, und vielleicht frühen
Tod. Das ist gar nicht übertrieben, und ich will
Ihnen sagen, warum. Die geschwollenen Hals-
drüsen, welche die Folge der Kopfentzündung sind,
kennen Sie nun. Das sind die sog. scrophulösen
Drüsen. Diejenigen am Halse sehen Sie, die andern
aber nicht. An die schliessen sich Reihen auf
Reihen an, Dutzende, Hunderte, in derselben Nachbarschaft, aufwärts, abwärts, in den Brustkorb, an
die Lungen heran, um die Lungen herum. Die
schwellen, entzünden sich, ihre Verbindung mit dem
Lymphsystem der Luftwege reizt zu Congestion,
Catarrh, Entzündung in ihnen. Die chronischen
Husten ganz kleiner Kinder, welche zu wiederhol-
ten Lungenentzündungen, Todesfällen, gelegentlich
zu chronischer Lungenschwindsucht führen, finden
auf diese Weise ihre Erklärung. Aber nicht genug
damit. Die Verbindung der Lymphgefässe und
Lymphdrüsen des ganzen weiten Körpergebietes
ist eine sehr intime. Krankheiten der einen Region
theilen sich der entfernten sehr leicht mit, wie ein
Ferment in kurzer Frist eine weite Strecke durch-
misst. In dieser Weise wird das, was ursprünglich
blos eine örtliche Drüsenschwellung war, leicht zu
dem, was man allgemeine Scrophulose nennt.
Viele Fälle der letzteren sind nicht, was sie schliesslich werden können, eine allgemeine, sondern eine

örtliche Krankheit, welche sich mit leichter Mühe
hätte verhüten, oder heilen lassen können. Ich
hoffe also, dass diejenigen, welche mich hören, und
diejenigen, welche deren Stimme vernehmen, in
Zukunft darauf achten werden, dass örtliche Reiz-
ungen, wie acute oder chronische Catarrhe der Na-
sen, oder des Darmkanals, oder Entzündung der
Kopfhaut nicht länger die Erlaubniss haben, durch
Vernachlässigung den ganzen Körper krank zu
machen. Der Grundsatz muss bald Eigenthum der
Volksmedicin werden ; und die Volksmedicin muss
sich bequemen, dem Beispiele der wissenschaftlichen Medicin zu folgen, und die Verhütung der
Krankheit höher zu stellen, als die vielleicht un-
mögliche Heilung.

Eine Bemerkung, welche ich in diesem Zusammenhange habe fallen lassen, bewegt mich, über
die Frage des *zweiten Sommers*, welcher in der
Volksmedicin eine so grosse Rolle spielt, und die
Gefährlichkeit desselben für das amerikanische,
speciell New Yorker Kind einige Worte zu verlieren. Diese "Eigenschaft" des zweiten Sommers,
unsere Kinder umzubringen, ist allmählich Evan-
gelium geworden, und wird einfach geglaubt. Der
Sommer kann es wohl nicht recht sein, denn der
zweite des einen ist der erste des andern Würm-
chens und der achtzigste des achtzigsten. Also
handelt es sich wohl um die Gefahr des zweiten
Lebensjahres. Es giebt nur *ein* anderes Vorurtheil,
das ebenso komisch ist, wie dieses, nämlich dasjenige, dass ein Siebenmonatskind leben bleibt,
aber ein Achtmonatskind sterben muss. Wissen
Sie, wie ein grosser Professor in Padua diesen

Glauben, den er von den Lippen der Nachbarfrauen der ganzen Welt annahm, erklärt hat? Sehr einfach so, und vergessen Sie es nicht. Im siebenten Monat der Entwicklung des Kindes regiert Luna (Mond). Sie begünstigt die Lebensfähigkeit durch ihre Feuchtigkeit—übrigens ist der Mond herzlich trocken und nur die Nächte sind nass—und das von der Sonne erhaltene Licht. Im achten regiert Saturn. Der hat seine Kinder gefressen und setzt das Geschäft noch immer fort. Im neunten regiert Jupiter, der Lebensspender, und das ist gut für die Kinder.

Wenn die nun geboren sind, leben sie durchschnittlich in guter Gesundheit, doch in grosser Gefahr. Die Uebergang in das neue Leben, die schnelle Wandlung im Blutlauf, der Einfluss wechselnder Temperaturen, die zarte Entwicklung und Unfestigkeit der Organe und Gewebe bedingen häufige Krankheit und frühen Tod. Mit jedem Tage, welchen das Kind sich von der Geburt entfernt, wird es kräftiger und lebenssicherer, die Sterblichkeit nimmt mit jeder Woche, jedem Monat, jedem Jahre ab. Der zweite Sommer kostet weniger Opfer als der erste. Wer Augen hat zu sehen, der schaue in die amtlichen Register und finde den Beweis dafür in den Zahlen. Aber der zweite Sommer kostet mehr Opfer als er sollte. Die Schuld liegt nicht am *zweiten* Sommer, nich an den Kindern—sie liegt an der *Sommerhitze* und an den Eltern. Die Sommerhitze kann immer gefährlich sein, Sommerhitze bei schlechter Nahrung wird vielfach tödtlich. Thatsache ist, dass fast alle Sommertodesfälle bei Kindern von Krankheiten der Verdauungsorgane erfolgen, dass also alle jene Todesfälle vermieden würden, wenn diese Organe nicht erkrankten. Nun ist der zweite Sommer derjenige, in welchem die künstliche Nahrung der Kinder begonnen hat, oder beginnen soll. Verständige künstliche Nahrung ist die naturgemässe für Kinder, welche alt genug, und deren Organe hinreichend vorbereitet sind. Bei guter Fütterung durch verständige Hand erkranken wenige Kinder vom Magen oder Darm aus. Verständige Mütter in guten Wohnungen und selbst ärmlichen Verhältnissen verlieren keine Kinder aus dieser Ursache. Also nicht der *zweite Sommer* ist es, der die Kinder tödtet, sondern die Unwissenheit oder die Unachtsamkeit der Pfleger oder Pflegerinnen. Das ist um so schlimmer, als die Regeln für Kinderernährung so sehr einfach sind, in der That so einfach, dass sie gerade dieser Einfachheit halber nicht befolgt werden.

Indessen soll ich ja nicht über Medicin reden, oder über meine Ansichten, sondern über Volksmedicin wie sie ist, gelegentlich auch, wie sie sein sollte. In Bezug auf Kinderernährung thut nun die Volksgewohnheit das Menschenunmögliche. Zuerst wird alles Mögliche gefüttert, natürlich schluckt das Würmchen alles, was man ihm in den Mund steckt. "Das Aeffchen gar possierlich ist, zumal wenn es vom Apfel frisst." "*It looks so cunning.*" Fragen Sie sämmtliche Dispensary-Aerzte der Stadt um die stereotype Erkundigung bei unterleibskranken Kindern : Was bekommt das Kind zu essen? Antwort : Alles was vorkommt. Oder : Es isst vom Tisch. Oder : Es isst mit uns.

Lassen Sie mich von den Einzelheiten schweigen—
gefärbtem Candy, saurer Milch, frischem Brod,
Wurst, Kaffee und Thee, rohem Obst, Gemüse:
Durchfall-Krankheiten—Tod. Todesursache? Natürlich, zweiter Sommer. Ich sage Ihnen, das Ge-
storbensein ist nicht schlimm für den kleinen
Leichnam. Aber kein Grabhügel vergräbt den
Jammer und das Verschulden der Ueberlebenden.
Aber haben die Ueberlebenden nicht das Ihrige
gethan? Gewiss, als das Kind krank wurde, haben
sie gesagt, das Kind zahnt ja; oder, das kommt
vom Sommer; oder, die Nachbarin sagt, ihr Kind
hat es gerade so. Schliesslich wird das Gesicht-
chen dünn und die Haut welk, und man fragt den
Doktor. Oft wird es gut, die Nahrung wird be-
schränkt, oder geändert. Aber bei manchen heisst
es: "Was? Gerstenschleim? Das Weisse vom
Ei? Dazu hätte ich keinen Doktor gebraucht!
Nicht so viel trinken lassen? Ich lasse mein Kind
nicht dursten!"

Jetzt kommt die Reihe an das, was heutzutage
Volksmedicin geworden ist, käufliche Kindernahrungsmittel. Sie müssen sehr gesund und zuträglich sein; in Deutschland, England und Amerika,
werden hundert verschiedene Sorten gemacht. Sie
sind so zuträglich, dass sehr viele von den Fabri-
kanten sich sehr wohl dabei befinden. Sie haben
auch den Vorzug vor der einfachen und leicht
kenntlichen Kindernahrung, dass sie theuer sind,
denn die Fabrikschornsteine rauchen doch nicht
umsonst—und eine Nahrung, wie Gerste, Hafer
und Kuhmilch, so billig und so einfach, kann doch
nicht das richtige sein. Es wird also "kaiserliches

Granum," und "Nestlé," und "Ridge" neben einander, vor und hinter einander gegeben, und die
Resultate des Unverstandes bleiben nicht aus. Ich
behaupte übrigens nicht, dass alle künstlichen und
käuflichen Kindernahrungsmittel schlecht seien,
ich behaupte es nur von einem Theil derselben, besonders von einem Theil der eben genannten; einige
sind sogar ganz gut. Was ich behaupte, ist vor
allen Dingen dies, dass selbst gute Mittel der Art
eine Versuchung zur Nachlässigkeit und zum
Schlendrian bieten, weil sie zu dem Glauben ver-
leiten, welcher auf den Umschlagspapieren ge-
predigt wird, dass mit dem Verabreichen derselben
nun Alles gethan sei.

Manche der Verkäufer, nebenbei gesagt, sind
sehr eifrige Leute. In einer öffentlichen Rede, vor
einer ärztlichen Delegatenversammlung, habe ich
meine Meinung über diese Gegenstände ausführlich
dargelegt. Ein Händler, welcher dem Publikum
weismachen will, dass er Phosphor, wie er es
nennt, vitalisirt, wenn er das auf oblongen Apothe-
kerschildern behauptet, war so eifrig auf das Wohl
des Publikums bedacht, dass er mich einlud mich
mit ihm abzufinden, und schliesslich mit einer
Klage drohte, in einem Briefe, der mehr un-
orthographisch als elegant war. Ich benutze diese
Gelegenheit ihn an sein Versprechen zu erinnern.
Eine öffentliche Klage der Art würde, wenn auch
nicht mir, doch dem geprellten Publikum der Vereinigten Staaten eine Warnung sein.

Nach diesen Bemerkungen über ein Kapitel der
Krankheitslehre, und eines der Diätetik, die beide
leider für unsere Tage gültig sind, wende ich mich

nun zu einigen Fragmenten über populäre Arznei-
mittellehre.

Die Schnelligkeit des modernen Verkehrs, das
Aufhören des Abgeschlossenseins des ärztlichen
Standes, die Zunahme der Bücher, Journale,
Wochenblätter, Tageszeitungen aller Art haben
eine grosse Summe von Kenntnissen oder scheinbaren Kenntnissen in allen Schichten der Bevölkerung verbreitet. Die vergrösserte Anzahl der
Arzneimittel, und ihre Besprechung in der Tages-
literatur, ferner die wachsende Dichtigkeit der Bevölkerung hat zu einem enormen Verbrauch von
Arzneimitteln geführt. Kaum wurde eine neue
Arznei in ärztlichen Kreisen bekannt, einerlei ob
ihr Ruf feststand oder nicht, so bemächtigte sich
auch das Publikum derselben. Einige haben sich
ein solches Bürgerrecht erworben, dass sie zu Haus-
mitteln geworden sind. Lassen Sie mich nur einige
von denen nennen, welche bei uns in allgemeinem
Gebrauch sind. Vom Opium nenne ich nur Soothing Syrup und Paregoric. Das erstere ist ein unzu-
verlässiges, bald zu mildes, bald zu kräftiges Opi-
umpräparat, deshalb oft wirkungslos, und nicht
selten gefährlich. Aller Warnungen ungeachtet,
wird es viel gebraucht; sein Gebrauch ist Missbrauch. Paregoric ist ein officinelles Präparat,
welches in einer halben Unze einen Gran Opium
enthält. Die Maximalgabe lässt sich daher leicht
berechnen; die meisten Präparate der Art, welche
in den Apotheken zum Hausgebrauch verkauft
werden, sollen abgeschwächt sein, um Unfällen zu
begegnen. Natürlich widerrathe ich den unberech-
tigten Gebrauch. Es ist leicht, Arzneien zu neh-

men und zu geben ; es ist schwer, die Anzeige dafür
zu finden. Lassen Sie mich eine Bemerkung über
Opium aus *Tabernæmontanus'* Kräuterbuch lesen :
"Dieweil auch die Landstreicher und verzweifelte
Juden diesen Saft in stetigem Gebrauch haben und
grosse Wunderzeichen damit pflegen auszurichten,
dieweil sie gar geschwind und behend alle Schmerzen können damit stillen und niederlegen, und
ihnen daselbst mit ein Ansehn bei dem gemeinen
Mann machen, sonderlich aber die lose Juden ; will
ich Jedermann gewarnt haben, dass er solcher
Leute, so gar kein Gewissen haben, müssig gehe,
denn sie nur gedenken, die Schmerzen zu lindern,
Gott gebe, es gerathe hernach, wie es wolle."

Ipecac, die Wurzel der Ipecacuanha, ist vielfach
in Gebrauch. Der Syrup, dessen Bekanntschaft
unsere Kinder frühzeitig machen, verdirbt leicht,
ist aber eben so leicht ersetzt. Er wirkt als Brech-
mittel, in kleineren Gaben als Lösungsmittel für
festen catarrhalischen Husten. Nebenbei verdirbt
er den Magen, macht die Kinder blass, und erspart
manchem Doktor einen Mitternachtsbesuch, den er
einem hustenden Baby zu machen haben würde,
wenn nicht die sorgsame Mutter ihre Angst um die
Natur dieses Hustens an dem rathlosen Baby aus-
liesse.

Der Saft der Meerzwiebel, " *squills*," wird zu ähnlichen Zwecken gebraucht. Er verdirbt das Mägel-
chen noch schneller, als das vorgenannte Mittel,
und sollte ganz gemieden werden.

Unter den Fiebermitteln ist die Aconittinctur und
das Chinin besonders beliebt. Jene wüthet mehr in
angelsächsischen Kreisen. Sie ist eine kräftige Arz-

nei und verlangt daher eine kundige Hand; ich
hoffe, dass sich in den deutschredenden Kreisen
ihre Verehrer nicht vermehren. Der Chininge-
brauch hat sich unendlich gesteigert. Da es die
Temperatur des catarrhalischen und entzündlichen
Fiebers herabsetzt, und da sich aus ärztlichen
Kreisen, in welchen die Bedeutung hoher Temperaturen besser verstanden wird, in die Volkskreise
der Glaube verbreitet hat, dass das Herabdrücken
der Körperwärme in den meisten Krankheiten das
Hauptziel der Behandlung sei, so ist man blind in
das Mediciniren mit Chinin hineingegangen. Das
Publikum wird wohl thun sich daran zu erinnern,
dass gelegentlich grosse Gaben von Chinin ver-
giftend wirken, dass sie Blindheit und Taubheit
machen, und dass auch kleine Gaben für unvorbe-
reitete Verdauungsorgane verderblich wirken können. Der Chininmissbrauch hat noch dadurch
seine besondere Ausdehnung erhalten, dass es das
Hauptmittel in Wechselfieber und anderen Malaria-
krankheiten geworden ist. Der wohlklingende
Name Malaria hat sich nun schneller eingebürgert
als Pocken oder Cholera, und wirkt bösartiger auf
die Geister, als diese Pesten auf die Leiber. Es
giebt heute schon kein Uebel, das nicht in der
Meinung des Publikums seine volle Berechtigung
hat, wenn das geheimnissvolle Wort von den Lippen
der Frau Nachbarin fällt. In diesem Zeitalter des
Zweifels und der Skepsis ist der Glaube an die
Allgegenwart und Allmacht der Malaria eine Macht
geworden, der zu widersprechen heute fast eben so
bedenklich ist, wie es vor Jahren riskirt war zu erklären, dass man zu keiner Kirche gehöre. Die

Dogmen der letzten Jahre heissen Malaria und Bakterien, die Alles erklären und durch welche Alles gerechtfertigt wird. *"Sweet spirits of nitre,"* Salpeteräther—fast hätte ich dich über dem Malariaunfug vergessen! Das Universalmittel einer zahlreichen Schaar von Gläubigen, Fiebermittel, Krampfmittel, Colikmittel, Darm- und Nierenmittel—wie viel Beruhigung hat es schon denjenigen gegeben, welche es anderen verabreicht haben. Es hat noch eine lange Carriere vor sich, denn es lässt sich kaum beweisen, dass es in kleinen Gaben schädliche Wirkung äussert.

Die zahlreichen Arzneimittel, welche Volksmedicinen geworden sind, fallen unter verschiedene Klassen. Manche sind unwirksam oder unschuldig, die meisten aber sind wirksame, gelegentlich gefährliche Stoffe in unpassenden Händen. Der Auffassung der Krankheit als eines Wesens, das man irgendwie aus dem Körper zu schaffen habe, entsprechen die abführenden und Schweiss treibenden Methoden. Nichts ist dem heutigen Staatsbürger einleuchtender, als dass man seinem Körper dadurch wohl und dem Doktor Abbruch dabei thut, dass man ein oder zweimal wöchentlich ein russisches, türkisches oder römisches Bad nimmt. Die Theorie ist, dass einer Krankheit, welche sich irgendwo festgesetzt hat oder festsetzen will, das Quartier gekündigt wird, indem man ihr in der s. g. Eröffnung der Poren der Haut die Stelle zeigt, wo der Zimmermann das Loch gelassen hat. Die gelegentlichen Fälle, in welchen ein Herzkranker seine Thorheit an Ort und Stelle mit dem Tode be-

zahlt hat, werden bald vergessen. Das vermehrte
Herzklopfen bei andern, welche noch nicht ganz
reif zum Selbstmord sind, wird nur als Beweis dafür genommen, dass das Bad gewirkt hat. Dass
ein mächtiges Mittel, wie jene Bäder, bestimmte
Anzeigen hat und ein zweischneidiges Schwert ist,
das gelegentlich die wirkliche oder vermeintliche
Krankheit, gelegentlich aber den ehrsamen Besitzer
trifft, wird übersehen oder nicht geglaubt.

Eine andere Methode Krankheit oder gefürchtete
Krankheit aus dem Körper zu entfernen, ist das
Verabreichen von Abführmitteln. In früheren
Zeiten waren die Quecksilbermittel hier zu Lande
die gebräuchlichsten. Die angelsächsische Medicin
brauchte viel Calomel und *blue mass*. Als dieselben
aus der regulären Medicin zu verschwinden be-
gannen, bemächtigte sich das Publikum dieser
Mittel und führte den Aerzten durch ihren Missbrauch zahlreiche Patienten zu. Nicht bloss wurden sie gebraucht und missbraucht, sie wurden sogar verehrt und mit Rücksicht behandelt. Ein
Mann, der Calomel genommen hat, betrachtet seinen
Leib als zeitweilig geheiligt, und macht Anspruch
darauf, dass sein Nebenmensch diese Situation re-
spektirt. Ich fragte einst einen seit einem Dutzend
Jahren verstorbenen Collegen, dessen sich Manche
von Ihnen noch erinnern werden : ''Was thun Sie,
wenn Sie Nachts nicht ausgehen mögen?'' ''Was
ich thue? In der That, ich thue gar nichts. Ich
rufe durch mein Sprachrohr : *Good gracious, very
sorry indeed, have just taken my calomel.*''

Seit Jahren haben die dringenden Anzeigen der
völkerbeglückenden Importeurs Calomel und *blue*

mass zu verdrängen angefangen. Was sagte Reha-
beam : "Mein Vater hat Euch mit Peitschen ge-
züchtigt, ich aber werde euch mit Scorpionen züch-
tigen." An die Stelle jener Mittel, welche von Zeit
zu Zeit genommen wurden, sind böhmische, un-
garische, bairische Bitterwasser mit täglichem Gebrauch getreten. Leben und leben lassen, ist,
wenn nicht die Absicht, doch die Praxis der Salz-
eifrigen. Die Gewohnheit hält sie beschäftigt, und
die Doktorenmühlen der medicinischen Schulen des
Staates New York allein liefern jährlich ein halbes
tausend Aesculape, denen die leidenden selbstge-
lieferten Artefacte willkommene Kunstgegenstände
werden.

Statt dieser täglichen oder wöchentlichen Selbst-
kasteiungen gab es, giebt es zum Theil noch, Frühjahrskuren, welche einen wesentlichen Bestand-
theil der Volksmedicin ausmachen. So regelmässig,
wie der brave Bürger seine Steuern auf dem Amt
abliefert, so lieferte er sich in früheren Zeiten dem
Barbier zum Aderlassen oder Schröpfen in die
Hände. Ich erinnere mich ganz gut der Zeit, in
welcher die Bauern und Bäuerinnen meines Dorfes
haufenweise in die Stadt zogen, zum "Lassen";
oder zum Dorfschneider, der das Schröpfen be-
sorgte. Das war das Frühjahrsopfer. Es hat lange
aufgehört, sogar, wie es scheint, in Italien, seitdem
der grösste Italiener des Jahrhunderts, Cavour, mit
Aderlassen umgebracht worden ist. An dessen
Stelle traten die Frühjahrskuren, welche in der
Verabreichung eines tüchtigen Abführmittels bestanden. Nicht immer war die Praxis schlecht.
Die Unbeweglichkeit und der Hausaufenthalt eines

8*

langen nordischen Winters, besonders bei Leuten,
welche das übrige Jahr hindurch an energische
Leibesbewegung gewöhnt sind, machen eine Kur
der Art gelegentlich wünschenswerth. Gar wohl
habe ich mich eines alten Sprichworts oft mit
Nutzen erinnert: "Wer gut abführt, der gut
kurirt." Aber keine Praxis der Art, welche nicht
mehr Unterschied macht, als Regen oder Sonnen-
schein bei Gerechten oder Ungerechten, und welche
so weit ausgeartet ist, dass unter der sogenannten
Blutreinigung nur Abführmittel verstanden werden, ist gerechtfertigt.

Die Frühjahrskuren mit einfachen Abführmitteln erinnern mich schmerzlich an eine andere, die
Wurmkur. Es ist nun fast ein halbes Jahrhundert
her. Meine gute Mutter hatte ihre jährlichen persönlichen Erfahrungen mit dem handfesten Jungen
gehabt und ihre Bemühungen aus guten Gründen
aufgegeben. Weiss Einer oder Eine von Ihnen,
was Wurmsamen mit Syrup bedeutet? Wenn Sie
das wissen, so wird es Ihnen auch begreiflich, vielleicht aus Ihrer persönlichen Erfahrung begreiflich,
dass drei handfeste Bauern kaum genügten, um
dem armen Würmchen jährlich zu seiner Wurmkur behülflich zu sein. Aber die Kur erreichte immer ihren Zweck, ich wurde gedemüthigt und meine
Mutter war beruhigt. Sie hatte Recht und ich
hatte Unrecht. Denn zu jener Zeit dämmerte erst
der Medicin das Bewusstsein auf, dass es mit der
Nothwendigkeit der regelmässigen Wurmkur, noch
dazu bei abnehmenden Monde, doch wohl nicht so
ernst sei. Nur die alte Medicin aber glaubte baum-
fest an die universelle Schädlichkeit der Würmer

im Darmkanal, welche alle möglichen Krankheiten verursachten. Als die Medicin diese Thorheit all mählig aufgab, zog die Volksmedicin das alte Kleidungsstück mit Freuden an. Bis auf die neueste Zeit, trotzdem dass bessere Nahrung der Kinder die Würmer im Darmkanal bei uns zu einem verhältnissmässig seltenen Vorkommen gemacht, ist der Glaube an die Entstehung fast aller Kinderkrankheiten vom Zahnen und von Würmern noch lebendig in den mütterlichen Gemüthern. "Aber ich sage Ihnen doch, Herr Doktor, es kratzt sich immer an der Nase." Dann hauen Sie es gelinde auf die Finger, oder reinigen Sie das R—näschen mit etwas dünnem Salzwasser, oder gebrauchen Sie etwas ungesalzenes Fett, oder Olivenöl, oder Vaselin, aber nicht auswendig, wie das beliebt ist, sondern wirklich inwendig.

Wie ich sagte, fangen die Würmer als Krankheitsursache an, ihren Credit unter uns zu verlieren. An die Stelle der Würmer ist die Malaria getreten, wohlklingend, geheimnissvoll, vielsagend, nichts sagend, nichts bedeutend. Darüber rede ich wohl noch ein anderes Mal mit Ihnen.

Das Zahnen aber hat von seiner Bedeutung noch nichts verloren. Was wäre die gute liebe Volksmedicin ohne das Zahnen? Zahnen nicht alle Kinder? Und sind nicht alle, oder die meisten Kinder einmal krank? oder unpässlich? oder sterben nicht eine Anzahl? Nichts kann einfacher sein, als dieser Zusammenhang. Auch dies interessante Kapitel kann ich nicht weiter berühren. Ich will meine Ketzerei nicht weiter treiben, als dass ich wiederhole, was ich hundertmal gesagt und geschrieben

habe, dass nämlich das Zahnen an Hirnentzündun-
gen, Lungenentzündung, Sommerdiarrhoe, krum-
men Beinen, dicken Knochen, Verkrümmungen
des Rückens, Lähmungen, sogar an Mundentzündungen unschuldig ist. Vielleicht ist mir noch einmal vergönnt, auch vor gemischtem Publikum die
Irrlehre von der Gefährlichkeit des normalen
Zahnens zu bekämpfen.

Das letztgenannte Uebel, die Mundentzündungen,
führt mich übrigens zu dem Thema der zu Haus-
mitteln gewordenen Arzneien zurück, von dem ich
ausgegangen war. Das chlorsaure Kali, oder besser
Kalium, fälschlich Chlorkalium genannt, englisch :
Chlorate of Potassa oder *Potassium*—(gelegentlich
auch das Natrium oder Sodiumsalz der Chlorsäure)
—ist seit etwa dreissig Jahren in der Medicin vielfach verwandt worden. Es ist ein gutes, wahrscheinlich das beste Mittel in den gewöhnlichen
Formen catarrhalischer und geschwüriger Mund-
und Halsentzündung, welche ihren Ursprung der
Reizung durch plötzlichen Temperaturwechsel, Un-
reinlichkeit, faulige Zersetzung von Nahrungsres-
ten und Quecksilberarzneien verdankt. Es ist auch
als Beihülfe zur Behandlung der gewöhnlichen
Formen der Halsdiphtherie vielfach empfohlen
worden. Die grosse Häufigkeit dieser Krankheitsformen, besonders in den letzten fünf- oder sieben-
undzwanzig Jahren, hat sowohl Namen als auch
Gebrauch dieses Mittels im Publikum bekannt und
sehr populär gemacht. Die Folge davon ist gewesen, dass es zum Range eines sogenannten Haus-
mittels in des Wortes verwegenster Bedeutung ge-
stiegen, oder gefallen ist. Ich sage wohl nicht zu

viel, wenn ich vermuthe, dass unter zwei hier Anwesenden wenigstens Einer, oder Eine, ohne ärztliche Anweisung oder Verordnung sich des Mittels
bedient hat. Wenig Familien mag es geben, in
denen die sorgsame Hausfrau nicht eine Schachtel
oder ein loses Papier mit den bekannten weissen
Krystallen zu etwaigem künftigen Gebrauch besitzt.
Nun ist aber nicht einmal das Aufbewahren des
Mittels ganz ohne Gefahr. Trocken und pulverisirt
reicht ein Stoss gelegentlich hin, um es explodiren
zu machen. In meiner eigenen Erfahrung hat das
Schütteln einer Flasche mit dem ausgetrocknetem
Pulver ein Unglück angerichtet. Das ist aber nicht
einmal das Schlimmste, wovor gewarnt werden
muss. Innerlich genommen, wird das Mittel leicht
giftig. Es passirt die Verdauungsorgane und das
Blut, in welches es eindringt, ohne sich zu verändern. Es verlässt den Körper in derselben Gestalt und Lösung, in welcher es eingeführt worden
ist. Dabei verändert es in grösserer Gabe die Beschaffenheit des Blutes und Blutfarbstoffs physi-
kalisch und chemisch. Es bilden sich gelbbraune
Schollen, welche den eingeathmeten Sauerstoff
nicht mehr verwerthen und sich in den kleinsten Gefässen, besonders der Nieren, festsetzen. Die Folge
davon ist Unterbrechung der Nierenthätigkeit und
schneller Tod, in derselben Weise, wie derselbe in
der acutesten Form der sog. Bright'schen Nieren
entartung auftritt. Vor vielen Jahren gab ich
einem Erwachsenen ein und ein halb Unzen (fünf-
undvierzig Grammes) des Mittels mit der Weisung,
dasselbe in einem Quart Wasser aufzulösen und im
Laufe von einigen Tagen als Mundwasser zu ge-

brauchen. Er trank die Masse im Laufe eines
Nachmittags und war in drei Tagen eine Leiche.
Dasselbe Verfahren mit demselben Resultate ist
sonst seither beobachtet worden. Vor drei Jahren
sah ich in der oberen Stadt einen kräftigen Schul-
knaben von fünfzehn Jahren, dessen Geschichte
die folgende war : Seinem Schulvorsteher klagte er
über Schlingbeschwerden und bat um Urlaub, um
zu seinem Doktor zu gehen. Jener erklärte, das
sei unnöthig, er wisse vom Hals soviel wie der Doktor. Er solle Chlorate of Potash kaufen, und fleissig damit gurgeln und davon trinken. Der ver-
trauende Knabe that wie ihm geheissen war. Nach
sechs Tagen traf ich ihn sterbend von dem Gifte,
von dem er, wie der Arzt sorgfältig herausgebracht,
fünf Tage lang fleissig äusserlich, und innerlich
täglich etwas mehr als drei Drachmen (zwölf
Grammes) gebraucht hatte. Ich würde froh sein,
wenn dies die einzigen Fälle der Art wären. Seitdem
ich zuerst die Gefahr des Mittels—nicht im Jahre
1860, wie in seinem kürzlich erschienenen Buche
über den Gegenstand Mehring mir zuschreibt—
im Anfange der siebenziger Jahre, dann wieder in
1877 in Gerhardt's Handbuch der Kinderkrankheiten, und in einer eigenen Arbeit im Jahre 1879, bekannt gemacht habe, vermehrte sich die Literatur
über Fälle von ähnlichen Vergiftungen in er-
schreckendem Masse. Zwanzig Gran für ein ein-
jähriges Kind im Laufe eines Tages, neunzig Gran
für einen Erwachsenen in derselben Zeit sind eine
reichliche Gabe. Was darüber ist, das ist vom
Uebel und eine grosse Gefahr. Wenn ich Ihnen
nun vor diesem beliebten "Hausmittel" einen

Schrecken eingeflösst habe, so ist das ein heilsamer und mein Zweck erreicht, welcher darin besteht, Sie vor dem Vertrauen auf sogenannte Hausmedicinen und populäre Medicin zu warnen. Ob manche alten Prozeduren heilsamer sind, ist fraglich ; aber sie sind nicht gefährlich. In Mitteldeutschland braucht man eines von zwei Dingen bei der Mundfäule des Kindes. Entweder man braucht eine Borax-Auflösung, oder man zieht dem Kinde den Schwanz einer schwarzen Katze durch den Mund. Wahrscheinlich hat man oft die beiden Heilmittel combinirt. In Frickenhausen am Main und in Ochsenfurt heilt man dieselbe Krankheit mit dem folgenden Segen, den man dreimal über den Mund des Kindes spricht, mit dreimaligem Hineinhauchen : ·"Job, Job ging über Land. Er trug ein Stäblein in der Hand. Da bequam ihm Gott der Herr. Gott der Herr sprach : 'Job, Job, warum trauerst Du so sehr?' 'Herr, warum soll ich nicht traurig sein, Es will meinem Kind sein Zung und Mund verfaulen.'"* Das kurirt. Wenn man auch noch den Doktor fragen will, so kann das nicht viel schaden.

Die Reihe der officinellen Arzneien, welche mit Recht oder mit mehr Unrecht, sogenannte Volksmittel geworden sind, ist damit noch lange nicht erschöpft. Ich habe nur darauf aufmerksam machen wollen, dass nicht in jeder Hand ein Werkzeug seinen Zweck erfüllt. Man bekämpft eine Krankheit nicht glücklich, wenn man nicht vorher deren Natur und Wesen kennt, und man bedient

* G. Lammert, " Volksmedicin und medicinischer Aberglaube in Bayern," Würzburg, 1869.

und heilt auch nicht eine Krankheit, sondern den Kranken, je nach seiner Individualität. Wenn man es doch jemals fertig brächte, diese zwei einfachen Sätze den Menschen klar zu machen. Dieselben Wesen aber, welche sich empört wundern würden, wenn man ihnen zumuthen würde, eine Nagelbürste oder einen Apfelkuchen zu construiren, weil man das doch erst gelernt haben muss, finden es ganz begreiflich, bis an die Ellenbogen in chlorsaurem Kali, Chinin oder unerforschtem Soothing Syrup zu arbeiten, wie die gichtischen und rheumatischen Bauern am Rhein in den Eingeweiden frisch getödteter Thiere.

Von Patentmitteln, Nostrum's aller Art, kostspielig annoncirten Mitteln is dabei noch gar nicht geredet worden. Es ist wohl auch nicht nöthig, denn nichts ist leichter zu verstehen als dass die grosse Alliteration R. R. R.—nicht "*rum, rheumatism and rebellion*, sondern Radway's Ready Relief ; dass Witchhazel, dass erst recht, meine Damen—und Herren auch—Pond's Extract Alles kurirt. Alles ohne Ausnahme, meine ich, äusserlich und innerlich. Man sieht gar nicht ein, wie irgend Jemand daran zweifeln kann. Es ist so albern, dass man es glauben muss. Man kann ja doch auch glauben, wenn man nur will, dass ein Ring an jeden Finger passt, eine Schraube in jedes Loch, eine Kugel in jedes Gewehr, ein Rock an jeden Leib, ein Hinterwäldler in jedes Amt. *Credo quia absurdum est.* Ich will es mit meinen Freundinnen nicht verderben : ich glaube an Pond's Extract, und bis zu einem gewissen Grade, an andere Curiosa auch. Man kann sich freilich nicht vorstellen, aber man kann es ja glauben, dass die Dose Gerbstoff, welche in Pond's Extract enthalten ist, alle Leiden hebt. Glauben Sie nicht, Herr Präsident, dass ich persönlich an Curiositäten etwas auszusetzen habe. Eine solche ist unter den vielen Quacksalberbrochüren eine, welche Sie mir vor einigen Tagen einhändigten. Unter dem für Befangene und Ununterrichtete bestechenden Namen des Naturheilverfahrens hat sich bei einer Reihe von unverfrorenen Geschäftsleuten seit dreissig Jahren ein Artikel eingebürgert, der den Vortheil hat, sehr wohlfeil zu sein. Er kostet Nichts, kein Wissen, keinen Verstand, und keine Achtung vor dem Publikum, nur die Schlauheit des Kleinbürgers, *who means business*. Die Brochüre, natürlich im Selbstverlag herausgegeben, entwickelt die gewöhnliche paradiesische Nacktheit von allem Wissen, für das sie die beliebte Verachtung heuchelt. Das Weir Mitchell'sche Bettliegen, sein "rest treatment," wird mit Tabackspfeifen-Gemüthsruhe und deutscher Biederkeit von dem Propheten einfach annektirt, und mit kalter Milch combinirt. Bettliegen und kalte Milch kuriren Blindheit, Taubheit, Lähmung, Rückenmarkserweichung, Lungenkrankheiten, Sängerinnen, Blutsturz, Diphteritis (also unorthographische Diphtherie), Scrophulose, Syphilis, Krebs, Frauenkrankheiten natürlich "aller Art," Blutarmuth, Bleichsucht, Menstruationsstörungen allen Grades, Krämpfe, Migräne, schauerliche Zustände aller Art, Pilzvergiftung, Wahnsinn, Somnambulismus, Unterleibsgeschwülste.

Dieser Art ist das Futter, das dem Esel aller Zun-

gen, besonders dem deutschen, in der Krippe ge-
schoben wird. Diese Sorte Literatur ist sehr gross,
und zwar in allen Ländern. Diese Büchelchen
sehen einander auf ein Haar ähnlich : dieselbe
Verachtung vor dem Wissen, der Wissenschaft, der
deutschen Sprache ; dieselbe Selbstverherrlichung ;
die kurzen Sätze und Absätze.

Nur ist ein Unterschied in der Bearbeitung derselben ganz auffallend. Sie werden finden, dass
ein englisches oder amerikanisches Buch, das für
Reclame irgend eines Schwindels gemacht wird,
wissenschaftliche Thatsachen oder Sätze irgend
welcher Art zu Grunde legt, um darauf ein trügeri-
sches Gebäude zu errichten. Die Verfasser dieser
Dinge bekunden damit einen gewissen Respekt vor
dem Publikum, das sie gewinnen und täuschen
wollen. Nicht so der deutsche Apostel. Er hat so
wenig Achtung vor denjenigen, welche er anredet,
dass er plumperweise weder Kenntnisse noch Intelligenz bei ihnen voraussetzt, und ausdrücklich von
sich selber ausposaunt, dass die Resultate dessen,
was Jahrtausende ehrlicher Geistesarbeit errungen
haben, ihm unbekannt und gleichgültig sind.

Es giebt natürlich bessere Bücher als diese un-
würdige Klasse, und auch die Zahl dieser besseren,
welche für das grosse Publikum bestimmt sind und
die gesammte Diätetik und Medicin oder einige
Theile derselben behandeln und mundgerecht machen sollen, ist enorm. Der Wohlthäter dieser Art
giebt es sehr viele, die Wohlthaten aber sind karg
gemessen. Thatsache ist, dass fast alle diese
Schriftsteller über das Ziel hinausschiessen. So
angemessen die Grundkenntnisse vom Bau und

Leben des Menschenkörpers für jeden unterrichteten Menschen sind, so unzweckmässig ist der Versuch, Spezialkenntnisse in kürzestem Rahmen und
noch kürzerer Zeit beibringen zu wollen. Thatsachen, deren Erlernung und Verständniss dem
Studierenden oder Arzte nur nach langen Jahren
gelingen, werden mit der Schnelligkeit des Lichtes
dem unvorbereiteten Lesekundigen für wenige
Thaler in kürzester Frist eingetrichtert, nach dem
Grundsatze des alten pensionirten Feldwebels, den
ich als Knabe kannte. Der lautete : " Mein Junge,
ich weiss nämlich Alles. Ich brauche blos in meine
Bücher zu sehen."

Eines der anspruchsvollsten der Art von Büchern
ist "das Buch vom gesunden und kranken Menschen," von Bock, dem ich eine kurze Betrachtung
widmen will, weil ich vermuthe, das von den einundeinhalb Dutzend Auflagen, welche dasselbe er-
lebt haben soll, eine Anzahl Exemplare in die
Häuser friedfertiger und argloser Familien eingedrungen sind. Zu sagen, dass das Buch, von wis-
senschaftlichem Standpunkte betrachtet, durchweg
schlecht, würde eben so unrecht sein, als behaupten
zu wollen, dass es in gutem Deutsch geschrieben
sei. Beides ist nur bis zu einem gewissen Grade richtig. Wenn ich aber einen Anspruch an ein solches
Compendium erhebe, so ist es derjenige, dass dasselbe brauchbar und richtig sei. Das wissenschaftlich noch so korrekte ist Ballast, wenn in unpassenden Händen, und das denkbar pikanteste und
witzigste verfehlt seinen Zweck, wenn es falsch ist.
Von diesen beiden Standpunkten aus ist das Buch
ein schädliches. Es will zu viel geben und verliert

dadurch an Werth. Der erste Band enthält gutes
Material aus der Anatomie, Physiologie und Diätetik. Der zweite Band enthält eine ausgedehnte
Krankheitslehre. In demselben finden Sie in der
letzten Auflage Behauptungen aufgestellt, welche
noch lange nicht erwiesen sind, z. B. dass Lungenschwindsucht blos von eingeathmeten Bacillen
stammt. An anderer Stelle eine minutiöse Beschreibung und Behandlung der allerverschiedensten Ver-
giftungsformen, Abhandlungen über krankhafte
Neubildungen und Geschwülste mit griechischen
Namen, unter denen ich den unvorbereiteten und
nichts Böses ahnenden Anwesenden zu Cystomen,
Hygromen, Enchondromen, Fibromen, Sarkomen,
Exostosen u. s. w. ganz besonders Glück wünsche.
Wieder an einer andern, zum Hausgebrauch, eine
Aufzählung ausländischer Krankheitsformen als
da sind, Lepra, Aleppobeule, Elephantiasis, Fram-
bösia.

Grobe Irrthümer giebt es dabei in Menge, selbst in
Bezug auf Gegenstände, welche dem einfachst unterrichteten Arzt geläufig sind. Was der Verfasser
über die häufige Krankheit der spinalen Kinder-
lähmung sagt, ist meist falsch. Wenn er die
Rhachitis der Kinder die Folge ungenügender Kalk-
zufuhr in der Nahrung nennt, so behauptet er, was
genügen würde, einen Kandidaten durchfallen zu
lassen. Wenn er vom grossen Veitstanz als einem
häufigen Vorkommen spricht und Regeln für seine
Behandlung angiebt, so weiss er eben nicht, dass er
wahrscheinlich nie einen gesehen hat, eben so
wenig, wie tausend andere Aerzte, welche ein reich-
liches Quantum Arbeit liefern, ohne jemals einem

Fall von grossem Veitstanz zu begegnen. Diese
Proben sind ehrlich citirt, aber nur auf's Gerathe-
wohl genommen. In meinem Durchblättern bin
ich auf manche ebenso löcherige Behauptungen ge-
stossen. Grobe Verstösse wie diese, sollten auch
den einfachsten Beobachter kopfscheu machen, sobald der Verfasser sich darauf verlegt, Rathschläge
zu geben. Gelegentlich räth er, einen rationellen
Arzt kommen zu lassen. Wie der Leser aber einen
rationellen und gewissenhaften Arzt erkennen soll,
bleibt ungewiss, es sei denn, das es einer ist, der
unter keinen Umständen "Giftstoffe" aus der
Apotheke verschreibt. Die helfen nun einmal gar
nichts. So hat z. B. "die Behandlung des Schar-
lachs mit Arzneimitteln bis jetzt wohl noch nie
etwas Gutes, gewiss aber schon viel Schlimmes bewirkt." Es wird gut sein, die Abschwächung des
prophetischen Diktums durch "bis jetzt wohl noch
nie" und "gewiss aber schon" zu beachten. Natürlich spielt die "Naturheilkraft" eine grosse
Rolle. Sie entfernt z. B. Splitter durch langsame,
vielleicht wochenlange Eiterung—andere Leute
ziehen die sofortige Entfernung mittelst einer
Pincette, sogar das Herausschneiden, entschieden
vor—Blutung, Schlagfluss, Schwindsucht, Lungenentzündung; natürlich alles Andere. Ich glaube
indessen, dass bei Blutung, Schlagfluss, Schwindsucht und Lungenentzündung die meisten seiner
eigenen Jünger vorziehen, zum Arzt zu schicken.
Von der letzten Krankheit sagt der Verfasser wört-
lich : "Hinsichtlich der Behandlung ist zu betonen,
dass die Lungenentzündung in den allermeisten
Fällen bei zweckmässiger Pflege günstig verläuft

und in Genesung übergeht." Ich habe indessen
noch Niemand getroffen, der mit dem statistischen
Resultate zufrieden war, dass die meisten andern
Leute genesen, falls sein eigenes Leben in Gefahr
ist. Uebrigens brauchen die Kranken nicht zu ver-
zagen. Falls sie nämlich wissen sollten, dass sie
an einer Lungenentzündung leiden—dass sie ihren
Zustand erkennen, setzt der gütige Schriftsteller
voraus—versieht sie der arztfeindliche Verfasser
mit einer langen Reihe von Regeln. "Sehr heftige
Brustschmerzen werden durch Eisumschläge, Senf-
teige, oder Schröpfköpfe gemindert." Sie haben
also die Wahl. "Gegen drohende Herzschwäche
sind kräftige Reizmittel anzuwenden." Jetzt weiss
der Kranke Bescheid. Natürlich weiss der Kranke
oder seine Umgebung, wann Herzschwäche droht,
was ein kräftiges Reizmittel ist und wie es an-
gewendet werden soll, nämlich folgendermassen :
"Stärkung der Nerven ist *natürlich* nicht durch
Arzneistoffe, sondern nur auf diätetischen Wege zu
erreichen"; d. h., der Verfasser des vielgelesenen
Buches räth Ihnen, wenn Ihnen ein Kind oder eine
Mutter oder Schwester an Herzschwäche in einer
Lungenentzündung zu Grunde zu gehen droht,
keinen Aether, oder Kampher, oder Moschus, oder
Cognac aus der Apotheke zu benutzen, sondern
diätetisch zu verfahren. Was das heissen soll, ist
mir unklar. Vielleicht soll man Biersuppe kochen,
oder Chamillenthee, oder Trost zusprechen. Und
solche Leute nimmt das Publikum ernsthaft, blos
weil sie sich, wie Heine sich ausdrückt, ihre Unwissenheit selber erworben haben.

Nehmen Sie noch ein Beispiel, das Ihnen bewei-

sen wird, wie der Rath des Predigers in der Wüste
Ihnen so gar nichts nützen würde. Der Verfasser
sagt an einer Stelle: "Die Behandlung im Mi-
gräneanfall" (vom Patienten oft besser als vom
Aerzte gekannt) "besteht in Ruhe, horizontaler
Lage mit erhöhtem Kopf, Dunkelheit und Fasten;
Manche werden durch einen starken Aufguss von
ungebrannten Kaffee oder chinesischem Thee, durch
Erbrechen, Klystiere, Brausepulver, Druck durch
Binden des Kopfes, wohl selten durch äussere, dem
Kopf applicirte Mittel erleichtert. Die radikale
Kur ausser dem Anfalle" (er will natürlich sagen,
ausserhalb des Anfalles) "kann sich nur auf Regu-
lirung der Lebensweise beschränken; übrigens
kann man bei der Behandlung der Migräne nicht
genug vor dem Missbrauch der Medikamente auf
der Hut sein."

Worauf die Bock aller Zungen so viel Werth legen,
ist der Umstand, dass die Aerzte nach ihrer Aussage gelegentlich das Unzweckmässigste oder Falsche thun oder thun können. Der Unterschied
zwischen den armen Aerzten und den Kritikern ist
der, dass jene, wie gesagt wurde, gelegentlich das
Falsche thun, diese aber immer. Denn das Nichtsthun ist immer falsch, und das Nichtsthun predigen
ist Impotenz oder Sünde. Die Hypokrisie dieser
sich vordrängenden Kritik läuft immer darauf hinaus zu behaupten, dass Andere unter dem Thun das
Receptverschreiben verstehen.

Wie der grosse Diätetiker seine Aufgabe versteht,
will ich Ihnen noch an einem einzigen Beispiele
zeigen. Wenn es nämlich irgend einen Gegenstand
giebt, welcher einem Volksdiätlehrer Gelegenheit

geben könnte, werthvolle Vorschriften und Erklä-
rungen zu geben, so ist dies das Kapitel der Haut-
pflege, aber unter den zwölfhundert Seiten füllt
dieser Abschnitt nur zwei. Auf diesen zwei Seiten
sind abgehandelt : Allgemeine und örtliche, heisse,
laue und kalte Bäder, Sturzbäder, Uebergiessungen,
Arzneibäder, Soolbäder, römische Bäder, Abwasch-
ungen, Einpackungen, warme Umschläge, unter-
brochene Berieselungen. Dahingegen haben sie
achtzehn enggedruckte Seiten von Verletzungen
und deren Bedienung, die manchen Ballast enthalten, aber auch manche guten Sachen, unter
denen z. B. die Behandlung des Krankenzimmers,
die diätetische Pflege des Hustens, und die zehn
Seiten über die Behandlung der Bewusstlosen und
Verunglückten eine rühmende Erwähnung verdie-
nen.

Nichts kann dem Kritiker, welcher an dem Wohl
und Wehe des Nebenmenschen Antheil nimmt, an-
genehmer sein als der Umstand, zu solcher Anerkennung berechtigt zu sein. Leider kann sie nicht
oft gezollt werden. Die Sindfluth von Schriften,
welche den Anspruch erheben, populär zu sein,
sind entweder von solchen geschrieben, welche den
Druck als Annoncirmittel missbrauchen, oder sie
sind des Vergnügens halber veröffentlicht, welchen
es gewährt, seinen werthen Namen gedruckt zu
sehen, oder sie setzen zuviel voraus oder wollen zu
viel lehren. Viele von ihnen machen dabei Anspruch auf unverdiente Originalität. So z. B. hat
die sogenannte Volksmedicin, in Gestalt des Naturheilverfahrens, der Hydropathie u. s. w., vielfach
den Anspruch erhoben, die Entdeckerin neuer Prin-

cipien in der Empfehlung der Kälte und besonders
des kalten Wassers zu sein. Kein Anspruch ist un-
gerechtfertigter. Auch hier ist wieder der Beweis
geliefert, dass die Volksmedicin hinter der wissenschaftlichen Medicin sich entwickelt, und nach-
hinkt. Jene Behauptungen wurden zu einer Zeit
aufgestellt, in welcher speziell in Deutschland die
Arzneikunst sich eben erst von der Vielverschrei-
berei, und die Wissenschaft von dem Dunkel der
Naturphilosophie zu erholen anfing. Die Hydropathie wurde dadurch schnell populär, mit allen
ihren Uebertreibungen und Sonderbarkeiten bei
ihren eignen Jüngern. Als eine solche ist mir aus
meiner frühesten Jugend erinnerlich, dass ein Professor an meinem Gymnasium ein grosser Wasser-
anbeter war. Zu jener Zeit gab es einen Gesund-
heitsapostel, der von Stadt zu Stadt zog, um
Naturzustand, Wasser, Eis und Röcke ohne Knopf-
löcher zu predigen. Der hiess Ernst Mahner—der
ernste Mahner—dem leider die apostolische Carriere
später durch die Coblenzer Polizei verdorben wurde,
welche das einfache Naturkind beim Löffelstehlen
erwischte. Die beiden Wasserverehrer erzürnten
sich gründlich über eine heikle apostolische Frage,
indem der Eine behauptete, in einem rohen Apfel
sei Wasser genug, der Andere, man müsse zu einem
rohen Apfel noch Wasser trinken. Aber ich ver-
gesse, dass ich nicht Anekdoten erzählen, sondern
das geschichtliche Verhältniss der Hydropathie zur
Medicin an einfachen Beispielen darlegen wollte.
Aus den Lehrbüchern der Geschichte der Medicin
lässt sich dasselbe leicht erläutern ; Ihnen erlaube
ich mir nur, ein paar alte Belege aus der Literatur
9*

selber vorzulegen. Die vier Bücher, welche ich Ihnen
hier vorlege, sind sämmtlich zwischen den Jahren
1734 und 1811 geschrieben. Der Einblick in dieselben, und der Anblick der reichlichen Citate wird
Ihnen beweisen, dass die Literatur über diesen Gegenstand schon in jener Zeit eine sehr ausgedehnte
war. Nun ist statt des kalten Wassers kürzlich, d. h.
seit einem Dutzend Jahren, das warme Wasser,
oder vielmehr das heisse, Mode geworden. Es ist
nicht mehr nöthig, sich mit dem Essen in Acht zu
nehmen. Iss was du willst, schädlich oder nicht, süss
oder sauer, langsam oder schnell, mässig oder nicht,
dein Magen wird unfehlbar gesund, wenn du früh
Morgens ein Glass heissen Wassers trinkst. Dem
Arzt, welcher fragen wollte, ob nicht unter den
Umständen, wenn doch einmal heiss getrunken
werden muss, ein aromatischer Thee, wie Fenchel
oder Anis, besser schmecken dürfte, antwortet
man mit einem mitleidigen Lächeln. Was dem
Kanonenstiefelstudiosen der saure Häring, ist dem
Philisterthum das heisse Wasser. Zu fragen weshalb, ist nicht nöthig; zu antworten, noch viel
weniger. Das heisse Wasser ist die Reaction gegen
das Eiswasser. Hat man endlich einmal gelernt
oder gehört, dass der übermässige Genuss des Eis-
wassers gesundheitsgefährlich ist, ei, so fällt man
in's andere Extrem und glaubt, die Sünden des
Tages durch ein Heisswassermorgengebet abspülen
zu können. Unter den Tausenden, welche der
Mode huldigen, mögen wenige sein, welche versucht
haben, sich die Gründe für irgend etwas klar zu
machen, was sie ihrem Leibe Gutes oder Böses an-

thun. Diese und andere Moden, welche durch das Haften an gesundheitswidrigen Gewohnheiten und das Haschen nach neuen Methoden und Mitteln sich kennzeichnen, sind eine trübe Erfahrung für den gewissenhaften Arzt, welcher gern sich auf die Intelligenz der Rathholenden stützt; freilich auch eine Quelle des Erwerbs für das ärztliche Geschäft, dem durch jede frische Raserei neue Kunden zugetrieben werden. Ich glaube nebenbei gefunden zu haben, dass diejenigen, welche ihren Nachbarn und Geschäftsfreunden vom Doktor ab-, und zum heissen Wasser zurathen, die fleissigsten Besucher des eigenen Arztes sind.

Um sich über diese und ähnliche Fragen ein Urtheil zu bilden, dazu gehört nicht gleichsam religiöser Glaube und der in Glaubenssachen geübte Fanatismus, sondern der gesunde Menschenverstand, der in die Schule gegangen ist. Etwas positives Wissen gehört dazu, um Fragen der Diät und der einfachen Medicin verstehen und entscheiden zu können. Dieses Wissen fehlt; unsere Schulen geben die Vorbildung nicht. Die meisten unserer Kinder leiden schon an der Hitze und Enge der Schulstuben, dem Luftmangel, dem Krummsitzen, zu viel, um noch mehr Lehrgegendstände ertragen zu können. Eine Aenderung in denselben thut noth. Auswendig gelernte Sätze aus der Moralphilosophie kann ein gut erzogenes Kind schon entbehren, einem schlecht erzogenen sind sie ohnehin Ballast. Aber entbehren lässt sich nicht einige Kenntniss des Menschenleibes und seiner Organe und deren Lebensverrichtungen. Die Grundsätze derselben lassen sich von jedem Schulkinde so leicht

erlernen, wie Rechnen und Schreiben. Wichtig
genug ist es, denn die Zukunft der Nation und des
Menschengeschlechtes hängt von der Kenntniss der
Grundsätze und der Befolgung der Gesetze ab, wie
in der Politik, so in der Diätetik.

MEMOIR OF AUSTIN FLINT, M.D., LL.D.*

THE life of Dr: Austin Flint, one of my most distinguished predecessors in the presidency of the New York Academy of Medicine, was singularly fortunate. We may say that, now that he has passed away and avoided the dangers incident upon any human existence. These incidents made the Greek philosopher exclaim that nobody must be called fortunate before he died. His birth, his life, and finally his sudden and painless death must be considered peculiarly happy.

In the year 1638 Thomas Flint emigrated from Derbyshire, England, to Concord, Mass. Thus the family, of Puritan stock, is one of the oldest in the country. Austin Flint's father, grandfather, and great-grandfather were physicians in Massachusetts. Thus both the number of ancestors and their labors and culture constitute what even in this our country we may claim as genuine aristocracy.

This term I do not wish to be taken in anything like its usual European meaning. The aristocracy of the Continent of Europe, hundreds of years ago. was composed of the men who spent their days in idleness, robbery, and violence. Their right consisted in the strength of their swords and the elasti-

* Read before the New York Academy of Medicine, at the stated meeting, April 15th, 1886.

city of their consciences. It required the invention
of powder and guns to make their castles useless,
change the hitherto unprotected into dangerous
adversaries, and thus render the aristocrat virtuous. This compulsory virtue changed them into
willing servants of the princes, whom they obeyed,
either on the battlefields or in the waiting rooms.
They and their offspring, unless they have consented to take part in the physical or intellectual
labors of the world, have contributed nothing to the
development of morals and culture.

This is not what we may designate aristocracy in
America. Our country has the advantage of not
suffering from the evil inheritance of the mediæval
period. What it has grown into being, it has
become by hard work both of hands and brains.
That kind of aristocratic family was the one Austin
Flint hailed from ; in it he might well have rejoiced,
though pride would never be pardonable in anything accidental and not accomplished by one's
own efforts:

With such hereditary advantages he was born in
Petersham, Mass., on October 20th, 1812. They
were followed by those resulting from a liberal education in Amherst, and in Harvard, where he
graduated in medicine in 1833. Since that time,
without any interruption, he has been in the practice of his profession, adding to the daily practical
labors much and varied literary work, and for the
last forty years constant services as a teacher of
medicine in six different colleges.

In Northampton and Boston he practised three
years until he moved to Buffalo, N. Y., in 1836.

Here he resided sixteen years, with the intermis-
sion of a short period in 1844 in which he taught
clinical medicine in Rush Medical College, Chicago.
He founded the *Buffalo Medical Journal* in 1846,
and edited it through a course of ten years ; he organized, in connection with Frank H. Hamilton
and James P. White, the Buffalo Medical College
in 1847, but left Buffalo in 1852 to take charge of
the chair of clinical medicine in the University of
Louisville. Thence he returned to Buffalo in 1856,
spent the winters of from 1858 to 1861 in New
Orleans, teaching medicine and attending Charity
Hospital, and settled in New York in 1859. His
position as the teacher of clinical medicine in the
Long Island Medical College he resigned in 1868 ;
the same chair in the Bellevue Hospital Medical
College he retained to his end. Its last Commencement took place while he lay dead in his
house, and a day before he was carried to his last,
silent home.

As a teacher he was eminently successful. Thousands of the present practitioners of the United
States were his pupils ; there is no county but has
those who listened to his lectures ; and there is
none but who gratefully remembers the breadth of
his knowledge and the systematic clearness and
elegant simplicity of his diction.

Whoever has not listened to him in the lecture
room has made his acquaintance by his writings.
For forty years he has contributed largely and
worthily to the medical literature of the country.
Many of his first papers appeared in the *Buffalo
Medical Journal,* which owed the high regard in

which it was held mainly to his contributions. From 1848 to 1850 he published articles on diabetes. the pathology of typhoid fever, on the epidemic of cholera in Buffalo, on serous effusions into the arachnoid cavity, on pleuro pneumonitis complicated with pericarditis, and on fifty-two cases of typhoid fever. These essays were followed, in 1852, by clinical reports on continued fever and on variations of pitch in percussion and respiratory sounds, and their application to physical diagnosis : in 1853, by clinical reports on dysentery and on chronic pleurisy ; by (1856) his physical exploration of the chest and the diagnosis of diseases affecting the respiratory organs, and (1859) his practical treatise on the diagnosis, pathology, and treatment of diseases of the heart. In 1865 he wrote his compendium of percussion and auscultation, and of the physical diagnosis of diseases affecting the lungs and heart; and finally. in 1866, his treatise on the principles and practice of medicine.

It is not necessary to enumerate his many essays and papers before and after that time. The publications of the United States Sanitary Commission and the better journals of the country bear evidence of his ever-increasing experience, willingness to contribute to the common stock of knowledge, and the eagerness of the journals to print his papers.

His literary reputation was deservedly a very great one. Some of his works have been translated ; his treatise had an immense sale. The method and mode of his writing is characteristic and instructive ; if some of the modern writers

would imitate him it would be better for them and
for literature. It is apparent that for many years
he wrote nothing but clinical reports and studies.
They were papers replete with careful observations
plainly described, with their immediate results.
These were followed, when his experience grew
and his judgment became matured, by monographs
on special subjects. He was fifty years old, and
already a celebrity, when he published a treatise on
the whole subject of internal medicine. It was the
work of a man who had given two dozen years and
more to the study of his subjects before venturing
before the profession with his great book. Let the
young manufacturers of text books of nowadays,
who collate the pigeon-holed pilferings from the
older books of better men into a volume and try to
build up a reputation with its hoped-for pecuniary
advantages, learn from Austin Flint the period of
life in which a man may be expected to write a
text book for the use of either the student or the
physician.

In his writings nobody ever was more straightforward and honest. What he did not know he
would not state. When he felt that the latest edi-
tions of his text book could be made more scientific
and serviceable by elaborating the pathological anatomy of his themes, he selected William H. Welch
to write the required chapters, and gave him full
credit for his work in his preface. As he was modest in his writings, so he was in discussions. He
was always as anxious to be taught as capable to
instruct. Some may remember a discussion on
pepsin in the American Medical Association many

years ago. When, the next day, he received a note
from one of those present, in which the necessity
was urged to add muriatic acid to the doses of pepsin he had advised, he called in person to express
his appreciation of the, then new, suggestion and
the letter containing it. There was, however, one
thing he was jealous of, viz., the honor of his
country. When, in a discussion, he once complained of the oblivion of Carr's name in connection
with the causation of the crepitant râle, and the pre-
eminence attributed to foreign authors in regard to
the explanation of respiratory sounds, he was rejoiced and proud when he was shown the page on
which Winternich gives full credit to the American
practitioner. Vanity and exalted opinion of himself were not his faults. He would never have accepted the eulogistic exaggeration proclaimed in a
recent obituary, in which it is claimed that nobody
in this century has done so much as he, or more
than he, for the diseases of the respiratory organs.
He would have urged that friendship and esteem
must never go so far as to obscure the names of
Laennec the Frenchman, Skoda the Austrian,
and Stokes the Briton.

Still, he was original in many things. His discussions on pitch and resonance will always be read
with pleasure and profit. Though we owe to him
no great discoveries, we and our successors shall
always admire his clear way of dealing with known
facts and new observations, and of popularizing for
the medical mind the latest evolutions of medical
thought and the most mature fruit of scientific research.

The peculiar qualities displayed by Austin Flint the writer he would also exhibit as a teacher, both didactic and clinical. He taught general medicine, and preferred to study, and give particular attention to, the diseases of the systems of respiration and circulation. He was clear, painstaking, and accurate. He occupied a chair in which there are, to the average student, no amazing features or feats. The student who applauds when a bone is sawed through, or a spouting artery is caught by a dexterous hand, or the actual cautery sends fumes and odor through the amphitheatre, is quite apt to gaze with sleepy indifference at the master whose lips utter the finest points of a difficult diagnosis, or whose brain is exercised over the greatest intricacies of pathological physiology. In the teachings and the daily work of the practitioner there is rarely anything surprising, amazing, or brilliant. In spite of that, it did not take long for Austin Flint to make a great and ever-increasing reputation as a teacher. Let our young men never forget, and let them learn from the example of the illustrious dead teacher, that a good preliminary education, systematic work, earnestness, and solidity are the corner-stones on which alone a teacher and an author can build up a name worthy to be enjoyed and capable of being handed down to posterity. What Flint's importance as a teacher has been, and will be, can be best proven by his thousands of pupils. Still, even as fortunate and successful a man as he was, has his disappointments and curtailments. One ambition of his life was never fulfilled.

Look at this fact : At the meeting of the American Medical Convention, since called Association, at New York, on May 5th, 1846, he was appointed on a committee to report on a resolution, offered by Dr. Isaac Hays, for a uniform and elevated standard of requirements for the degree of M.D. in all the medical schools of the United States. The report is signed by R. W. Haxall, Chairman, and can be found on pages 63-77 of the Proceedings of the National Medical Conventions, held in New York, May, 1846, and in Philadelphia, 1847 (Philadelphia, 1847). The very first of the ten resolutions embodied in that report is this : " That it be recommended to all the colleges to extend the period employed in lecturing from four to six months." And it is true what a late number of a journal* says, " that that report is still to-day a most interesting, applicable, and valuable document." But, alas ! the slowness of spontaneous evolution, and the predominance of circumstances, and the weight of impediments are such as to cripple even a strong man like Austin Flint, who, though his life was spared long, never saw the hopes of his younger years fulfilled.

His successes as an author and a teacher were equalled by those accomplished in his consulting practice. In those special branches to which he had given so much of his time and attention his counsel was frequently requested. No matter whether he had anything new to say, or had only to confirm the diagnosis or fortify the position of the practitioner, everybody here knows that he was always kind, mild, and modest. There is nobody here but has often either admired his superior

* Journ. of the Am. Med. Assn., March 27th.

knowledge and experience, or blessed his pleasing demeanor and generous words. He was an eminently just man, and, for that reason, could afford to be mild and generous.

These qualities he exhibited in a period which has been a critical one in the development of the last few years in the life of the medical profession. During the first successful year of preparations for the International Congress he was true to the *bona fides* entered upon in Copenhagen. From the very beginning he was, like all the greatest and wisest men in the profession of both this country and Europe, earnest in excluding medico-political differences and difficulties from the organization of the Congress. In regard to the latter there was to him no code question at all. I have good reason to believe that the demoralization and disorder in the ranks of the profession, growing out of these differences, caused him the greatest possible pain and many of the most unhappy days of his life. It is a great satisfaction, however, to know that everybody wished to distinguish and honor the man who had served the profession half a century, to his credit and to the advantage of his fellows.

In regard to important moral and ethical questions, it is of graver import to study a man's own words than to listen to what others would wish us to believe; and when that man is Austin Flint, that mode of inquiry is still more indicated. Not that the code question is so grave as some would have it. Indeed, it has begun already to have a historical interest only.

But some time ago everybody took sides in regard to the code question. So did you, so did I, so did Austin Flint. But to belong to a party does not mean to be an offensive partisan. And if ever a party man—so I believe—was impartial, that man was, or tried to be, Austin Flint, whom we honor as much for his words as for his actions. When a man works himself up into celebrity, his memory must serve the surviving as did his life. His opinions ought to be learned from his own papers published in the *New York Journal*.* Read them as if he were still among you. He is among you. For those who have lived a life worth living do not die. I am willing to abide by the platform laid out in those essays. They contain the same thoughts expressed by your presiding officer in an address delivered from this place on October 1st, 1885. Two days afterward that address appeared in print. Two days after its publication I received from the great and good man who is now gone a letter which I shall be proud of preserving as a legacy. I hold in my hand this note of Austin Flint's, which begins with the words: "I have read your address with pleasure"—and finishes with these: "How beautiful, lovely, and salutary it is to promote peace, harmony, and brotherhood!"

On the evening of his inauguration as President of the Academy, in 1871, his predecessor, one of the most illustrious types of American erudition and versatility, Edmund Peaslee, had a right to say to him: "We have always found you the high-minded and sympathetic man and the genial

* April, 1883. Also in his Presidential address of 1884.

gentleman, as well as the finished scholar, the distinguished author, and the skilful practitioner."

All that he proved during his presidential term, which extended over the two years from 1871 to 1873. The routine work performed during that time did not differ much from that of many other years or terms, but some of the papers were of unusual excellence. It would be improper to go into the merits of the essays read and discussed. They were by Allen S. Church, Charles A. Leale, William Detmold, Alfred L. Loomis, Samuel S. Purple, Charles P. Russell, Gouverneur M. Smith, J. Lewis Smith, Frank P. Foster, Gurdon Buck, Ernst Krackowizer, J. C. Dalton, Lewis A. Sayre, E. C. Seguin, Salvatore Caro, and Allan McLane Hamilton.

Flint's contributions to the scientific work of the Academy were not numerous, but their character was high. Amongst others, "The Management of Pulmonary Tuberculosis, with Special Reference to the Employment of Alcoholic Stimulants,"* June 3d, 1863; "Discussion of Dr. Leaming's Paper on Pleuritis,"† March 17th, 1870; "Discussion on the Etiology and Pathology of Bright's Disease,"‡ October 1st, 1862; "Discussion on Dr. Loomis' Paper on Typhus Fever,"§ February 15th, 1865; "Last Illness of Valentine Mott, M.D.,"‖ May 3d, 1865, will always be referred to with sincere pleasure.

---

* Transactions, vol. ii., p. 353.
† Bulletin, vol. iv., p. 48.
‡ Bulletin, vol. ii., p. 1.
§ Bulletin, vol. ii., p. 388.
‖ Bulletin, vol. ii., p. 434.

His membership in the Academy ceased a few weeks before March 13th, on which he breathed his last. You remember the universal reluctance on the part of those present to accept his resignation, and the silence with which the remarks of the presiding officer were listened to. *Malevolence only could misconstrue, and has misconstrued, into their opposite his words of appreciation and regret.* There is one great gratification even in that resignation of his. His good-will toward the Academy is best exhibited by his staying as long as he did, under rather peculiar circumstances; and, moreover, we shall know, by the gift of his library which he bequeathed to the Academy, that the latter was dear to his heart. For the Academy not to speak words of praise and remembrance in behalf of his memory, in this hall which he graced and in which he taught, in spite of suggestions and even demands to the contrary of a personal character; not to keep his memory green among us, is an impossibility. As it is for us, so for the medical men of the country. His name and reputation form part of the history of our profession, and this Academy means to honor its dead who have gone into history.

In listening to or reading the eulogies of the dead, I have often been struck with the well-meant but still obtrusive exaggerations of their characters and services. It then appeared to me that the writer buried the memory of the friend under an oppressive weight of high-strung flatteries. It reminded me of the manner in which an inconvenient beggar is forever cast aside by buying him off with a large sum. That plan may do well enough for the mediocre, who never excelled, and therefore is extolled for once. But if there be any among us who rise above mediocrity and average, or those even whose intellectual stature fills a large space between the soil on which their feet walk and the skies to which their brows are turned, let them while they live harbor the ambition, or when they are dead enjoy the honor, of serving mankind even after and through their very deaths. To accomplish that let the truth be stated, and the truth only. Thus it was the truth only I aimed at in this brief sketch. As its object was great, I found it an easy task to omit the trite platitudes of a commonplace eulogy.

Austin Flint had great advantages, and developed and utilized them for the benefit of the many. Born with an enviable inheritance, he enjoyed a thorough general and special education. He had great physical endurance and uniform health, an imposing presence, pleasant manners, and an equable temperament. With physical and intellectual powers he combined indefatigable love of work, which he performed systematically and energetically. He was a thoroughly modest man, who knew how difficult it is to master the depths of knowledge. Thus he had an unusual degree of common sense, which limits aspirations and aims. Thus he became thorough in what he undertook to practise and to teach. Thus he was successful in practice and enjoyed the confidence of both the profession and public. As a teacher he is remembered by thousands; his pupils loved him and his

10*

colleagues honored him. His writings obtained for
him a national and international reputation. There
was no place of honor in the possession of the profession of the city, State, or country which he has
not filled. The profession of Europe was anxious
to show its respect for him. Thus he lived and
worked to an advanced age, disturbed by but few
symptoms of evanescing powers, and when the
time came he ceased to labor and live on the very
same day.

As a profession let us hope that we shall have
many like him.

DOCTOR JACOBI HAD HIS WAY.*

MEMORIAL MEETING TO THE LATE DR. AUSTIN FLINT.

Why his Widow objected to Honors paid him by the Academy of Medicine—Her Wishes Not Heeded.

IN a memorial address to the late Dr. Austin Flint, delivered before two hundred physicians of the New York Academy of Medicine last night, Dr. A. Jacobi used this language :

"His membership in the Academy ceased a few days before the 13th of March, on which he breathed his last. You remember the universal reluctance on the part of those present to accept his resignation, and the silence with which the remarks of the presiding officer [Dr. Jacobi] were listened to. Malevolence only could misconstrue, and has misconstrued, into their opposite his words of appreciation and regret. His [Dr. Flint's] good-will toward the Academy is best exhibited by his staying so long as he did under rather peculiar circumstances, and forever we shall know, by the gift of his library which he bequeathed to the Academy, that the latter was dear to his heart. For the Academy not to speak words of praise and remembrance to his memory, in this hall which he

* From the New York Times, April 16th, 1886.

graced and in which he taught, in spite of suggestions and even demands to the contrary of a personal character ; not to keep his memory green
among us, is an impossibility. As it is for us, so
for the medical men of the country. His name and
reputation are part of the history of our profession,
and this Academy means to honor its dead who
have gone into history."

These remarks had a peculiar significance to
many of the physicians in the room. They knew
that while Dr. Jacobi was uttering them he had in
his coat pocket correspondence from the widow of
Dr. Flint, urgently requesting him not to deliver
the memorial address. This correspondence had
been an open secret in the profession for a few days
past, and there was some curiosity to see what Dr.
Jacobi, as President of the Academy, would do
about it. When Mrs. Flint first heard that Dr.
Jacobi had nominated himself to deliver a memorial
on her husband, she wrote him a request not to do
so, insisting on her right as a widow to name the
person who should perform a service so personal to
her, and mentioning that she had already made up
her mind as to who this person should be.

To this communication Dr. Jacobi made a reply,
in which he asked to be informed who it was that
Mrs. Flint had selected to memorialize her late husband before the physicians of the Academy. Mrs.
Flint thereupon informed the President of the Academy that she did not desire a memorial of the
doctor to be read before it at all ; the doctor was
not a member of the Academy at the time of his
death, and, under the circumstances, it was her de-

sire and request that all arrangements for a memorial address be discontinued. Dr. Jacobi replied that discontinuance was impossible—the arrangements had gone too far ; and, besides, as the late Dr. Flint had at one time been an honored member of the Academy, and was, moreover, a man conspicuous in the medical profession, he believed it the duty of the Academy to have the memorial meeting as arranged.

When the printed cards giving regular notice of the meeting were circulated, and it was observed that the request of Dr. Flint's widow about the memorial address had been disregarded, the friends of the late doctor and his family, who knew of the circumstances, were very indignant. Some of them stayed away from the meeting. " In making this request," said one physician intimate with the family last night, " I know that Mrs. Flint was governed by what she believed to have been the wishes of her late husband. After what has happened a suggestion of a memorial service by the Academy of Medicine would have been peculiarly distasteful to Dr. Flint, if he had been consulted about it. And for another reason I am sure Mrs. Flint would personally prefer that Dr. Jacobi should not deliver the oration. At the time Dr. Flint resigned Dr. Jacobi was reported as saying that if Dr. Flint could manage to get along without the Academy, the Academy could get along without Dr. Flint."

Dr. Jacobi's memorial address was a continuous flow of eulogy. He traced Dr. Flint's career from its Puritan ancestry through forty years of continuous medical practice in six medical colleges,

and dwelt at length upon the incalculable benefits
of the results of his work to the profession. Particularly did he refer to Dr. Flint's eminent success
as a teacher, his systematic clearness and elegant
simplicity of language in the lecture room, and his
invaluable contributions to medical literature. He
was a model for young men in demonstrating that
a sound preliminary education, systematic work,
and solidity were the only basis for successful
teaching. Dr. Jacobi referred to Dr. Flint's reluctance to see medico-political differences creep into
organizations with which he was connected, and
said that he knew from personal information that
the demoralization growing out of party lines on
the code question had caused Dr. Flint much pain.

Inasmuch as Dr. Flint was President of the Academy from 1871 to 1873, the doctors listened with
much interest, and some of them with astonish-
ment, to the portion of Dr. Jacobi's address quoted
verbatim at the outset of this report. Dr. Jacobi
said to a *Times* reporter that he considered it an
honor due him, as President of the Academy, to deliver the memorial address to Dr. Flint. His correspondence with Mrs. Flint and the misunderstand-
ing with some of her friends was, he thought,
based largely upon a mistake.

"The night that Dr. Flint's resignation was acted
upon," said Dr. Jacobi, "no one present spoke in
response to my reading the resignation. I com-
mented on this showing significantly with what
regret the resignation was received, and I said
furthermore that I considered it a very high honor
to belong to this Academy and felt very sorry that

Dr. Flint should have taken a step which would deprive him of the privilege of membership. It was a very great surprise to me to learn that my remarks had been interpreted, and even reported, as saying that the Academy could get along without Dr. Flint if he could get along without the Academy. I certainly never meant to convey any such impression."

DR. AUSTIN FLINT.*

EINER der bekanntesten und achtungswerthesten
Aerzte Amerika's hat am 13. März diesem Jahre
seine lange Laufbahn beschlossen. Dr. Austin
Flint stammte von einer Familie ab, welche im
Jahre 1638 in Massachusetts einwanderte und seit
jener Zeit in demselben Staate ansässig war. Sein
Urgrossvater, Grossvater und Vater waren Aerzte,
alle nahmen eine geachtete Stellung ein. Er besass
somit, was man in diesem jungen Lande eine lange
Reihe von Ahnen nennen kann, und diejenigen
Vortheile, welche eine wohlhabende und gebildete
Umgebung gewähren kann. Seine erste Erziehung
erhielt er auf dem College zu Amherst, später in
Harvard. Hier erwarb er sich sein Doktordiplom
im Jahre 1833. Die nächsten drei Jahre praktizirte
er in Northampton und Boston, und begab sich, zu
dauerndem Aufenthalte, im Jahre 1836 nach Buf-
falo. Während eines einzigen Winters hielt er im
Rush College in Chicago Vorlesungen, ohne seinen
Wohnsitz in Buffalo aufzugeben, gründete 1846 das
Buffalo Medical and Surgical Journal, und 1847 in
Verbindung mit James P. White und Frank H.
Hamilton die medicinische Schule in Buffalo.
Während zweiter Jahre (1852–1854) siedelte er nach
Louisville über, wo er an der medicinischen Schule
Vorlesungen hielt, und der Praxis oblag. Dann

* New Yorker Medicinische Presse, 1886, p. 225.

kehrte er nach Buffalo zurück, brachte mehrere
Winter als Professor der Medicin in New Orleans
zu, und siedelte 1859 nach New York über. Von
hier aus bekleidete er bis zum Jahre 1868 eine Professur am Long Island Hospital College in Brooklyn, und vom Jahre 1861 an, in welchem das Bellevue Hospital Medical College gegründet wurde,
die Professur für innere Medicin an dieser Anstalt.
Einen Tag vor seinem Begräbnisse fand die letzte
Entlassungsfeierlichkeit für die eben Diplomirten
Statt.

In seiner Schule war er die bedeutendste und ein-
flussreichste Persönlichkeit. Es ist daher zu bedauern, dass er seinen grossen Einfluss nicht zu
Gunsten der Verlängerung der Lehrcurse und der
Vertiefung des Unterrichtes angewandt hat. Un-
gewöhnliche Schwierigkeiten müssen dem Manne
in den Weg gelegt worden sein, dessen medici-
nisches Gewissen und reife Einsicht ihm ohne
Zweifel lange klar gemacht hatten, dass der ärztliche Stand Amerika's nur durch bessere Vorbildung und gründlichere Schulung der Studenten
gehoben werden kann. Dies ist um so mehr zu
bedauern, als in mässigem Grade eine andere der
hiesigen Schulen, in viel höherem aber die medicinische Schule der University of Pennsylvania und
des Harvard College, lobenswerthe Schritte in dieser Richtung gethan haben.

Als Lehrer war Flint sehr populär. Seine Dar-
stellungsweise war, ohne beredt zu sein, einfach
und klar. Dem Fassungsvermögen seiner Hörer
wusste er sich genau anzupassen. Aber nicht blos
Studirende, sondern auch Aerzte folgten seinen

Vorträgen gern. In seiner vierzigjährigen Lehrthätigkeit hat er Tausende in das Gebiet der Medicin eingeführt. Als consultirender Arzt war er gesucht. Er war ein anständiger College, von imposanter Figur, und einnehmenden Wesen. In Fällen, welche zu dem Spezialfache gehörten, das er mit Vorliebe gepflegt hatte, wurde sein Rath vorzugsweise gesucht.

Dieses Spezialfach war, die Krankheiten der Brustorgane. Mit Auscultation und Percussion hatte er sich früh und ausgiebig beschäftigt ; eine Reihe von Journalarbeiten und einige Monographien beweisen sein Verständniss und seinen Fleiss. Ohne dass er bahnbrechend gewesen ist, enthalten seine Arbeiten doch manchen anerkennenswerthen Wink. Seine schriftstellerischen Arbeiten zeichnen sich durch System und Ehrlichkeit aus. Seine ersten Arbeiten waren klinische Berichte, dann folgten seine Arbeiten über Auscultation und Percussion, ein Handbuch über die Krankheiten des Herzens, und zuletzt erst sein Lehrbuch, welches in erster Auflage im Jahre 1866 erschien, sieben Auflagen erlebte und in 40,000 Exemplaren verkauft worden sein soll. Die letzten Auflagen haben dadurch, dass er die pathologische Anatomie von Wm. H. Welch bearbeiten liess, bedeutend gewonnen.

Im ärztlichen Stande war er sehr populär. Es giebt kaum eine Ehrenstelle, welche derselbe ihm nicht zugewiesen hat. Er war Präsident der Medicinischen Gesellschaft des County New York, der New Yorker Akademie der Medicin, der Amerikanischen Medicinischen Association. Schliesslich

wurde er zum Präsidenten des Internationalen
Congresses designirt, dessen Zusammentreten in
Washington, im Jahre 1887, er mit Sicherheit erwartete. Auch in Europa war er gern gesehen.
In London und Copenhagen wurde er ausgezeichnet, und die British Medical Association erwartete
von ihm einen Vortrag im kommenden Sommer.
Sein plötzlicher und schmerzloser Tod hat sein
arbeits- und erfolgreiches Leben zu einem glück-
lichen Ende geführt. Seine ruhige und anspruchs-
lose Arbeit sollte ein Vorbild für diejenigen sein,
welche da glauben, durch eine einzige glänzende
oder prahlerische Leistung, durch Zeitungsrekla-
men, sich schnell Ruf und Einkommen sichern zu
können. Unter den amerikanischen Aerzten
nimmt er einen der ersten Plätze ein, obgleich man
an ihm und der Wahrheit ein Unrecht begeht,
wenn man, wie seine Lobhudler gethan haben, ihn
über Laennec, Skoda, oder Stokes erhebt, oder
Trousseau an die Seite stellt.

INSCRIPTION ON TABLET ERECTED IN THE HALL OF BELLEVUE HOSPITAL

IN MEMORY OF

AUSTIN FLINT, M.D., LL.D.,

BORN OCT. 20TH, 1812.   DIED MARCH 13TH, 1886.

Entering his profession with broad culture and thorough education, he remained an active physician to the last day of his life.

As a medical writer he added to the knowledge of the American profession and to medical science.

As a teacher he was loved and respected by thousands of pupils in all parts of the country.

As a physician to Bellevue Hospital for twenty-five years he contributed largely to its reputation, by his character, acquirements, labors, and wise counsels.

Erected by the Commissioners of Public Charities and Correction.

H. H. PORTER, *President,*
THOS. S. BRENNAN,
CHAS. E. SIMMONS.

ANNUAL (NINETY-NINTH ANNIVERSARY) DINNER, COLLEGE OF PHYSICIANS, PHILADELPHIA, APRIL 14TH, 1886.

TOAST.

NEVER *more* than to-night have I appreciated honors conferred on me by the Fellows of the New York Academy of Medicine. For it is to the circumstance that I occupy the place of President of that corporation that I am indebted for the opportunity of appearing before the *élite* of the medical profession of Philadelphia, and to speak to you on a subject dear to us all.

The Academy, composed as it is of practitioners of medicine, has but one great object in view, viz., the cultivation of medical science. No other purpose is contemplated in its constitution. Will you permit me, therefore, to reply to your toast from the point of view of the Academy, whose representative you were kind enough to call here, and whose delegate I consider myself.

What an association of medical men means by medical science is easily told. It comprehends the knowledge and the evolution of the knowledge of the biology of man, no matter whether we have to deal with the normal condition or with its modifications called disease. Now, the progress of science, while it may be the sole object and aim of an individual explorer and expert, has, considered from the standpoint of the profession at large, a practical tendency. If we exclude, as we all do, metaphysics from the domain of science, there is no science, or part of it, ever so abstract, apparently ever so abstruse, but is utilized and useful in the interest of mankind. Here it is where the most abstract medical scientist and the most practical professional man meet on common ground. All science, as it is human in its origin, is raised above the level of mere theory by the service it renders to humanity. Thus the medical profession, with its practical tendency and its claim that all medical science can and must be made serviceable to the physical and mental well-being of man, is the best representative of science, and both science and the profession may well be considered together. Indeed, I believe there is no country in which this principle, that medical science's highest aim and main object are the preservation and restoration of health in the individual and the community, is recognized to a greater extent than in America.

The aim of medical science to preserve or restore health is reached in two ways, and the men who reach it, and form the whole of the profession, are of two classes. Some work as searchers, experimenters, and teachers; some in the ranks in the service of daily practice. But all have the same interest at heart, that of relieving suffering and benefiting mankind. Thus the physician, of whatever grade, has a double responsibility: he shares the duties of a citizen of the Republic with every intelligent man, but he has his own, graver, more responsible duties to perform in behalf of the commonwealth. To be able to do so a great deal of preparation, training, intellectual and moral development are required. I should be willing to say that, not to speak of trades at all compared with a profession, the responsibilities of the medical profession are by far greater than those of any other. The lawyer gives his attention to property questions and those of law; the clergyman is engaged in moral and emotional problems; the teacher has the mental capacities of his pupils to develop, and what he does for physical exercise and culture he does so under the rules laid down and the advice given by the physician. The medical profession only is concerned in the whole man, body and mind, each conditioning, and depending upon, each other. From cradle to grave his advice is required and sought for; the physiological development of period after period of life requires his attention and study; with the changing conditions of the body its marks on mind and soul are examined, the incipient symptoms of physical and mental aberrations known. Public and private hygiene are his domain. The care of the present generation and of those on whom rests the future greatness of the country are the legitimate subjects of his studies. In fact, the professional man is the very one to whom—to use the words of the philosopher—nothing that is human is foreign. I cannot imagine anything connected with human life and interests which would not legitimately belong to the domain of the physician. I foresee the time when his knowledge will be sought

11*

for and consulted, not only by those who are acknowledged to be physically diseased, not only in the regulation and enforcement of private and public hygiene, but in questions involved in the greatest difficulties. I cannot see the possibility of a solution of the most serious questions of criminal law without the physician. The solution of the moral insanity question, it is true, has been sought for without the necessary scientific premises, but still the great questions of insanity and crime, and brain and insanity, cannot be answered except by medical research, and there will be a time when the physical history of a criminal, and the study of his skull and face and teeth, the symmetry or asymmetry of his body, will form the basis of a judicial procedure.

This is an ideal condition and aim, but not so ideal as to preclude its realization. The changes in the political condition of the old world, and those in the social of the old and new, are so rapid that much that was considered impossible but a little while ago is looked upon to-day as the coming necessity.

If such be the future rights and expectations of the profession, if it mean to be the protector and adviser of the commonwealth, what has it to offer to-day as an offset to so much honor, and as its legal claim for the performance of such onerous duties ?

Many of those who at present study medicine and are admitted to the profession—for instance, the farmhand who obtains a diploma after two or three so-called courses, or ten or twelve months altogether, of what he and his chums are pleased to call study; the clerk who was unfit for his trade because he was at war with orthography and was not victorious; the recipe writer who abbreviates because he is at a loss to know the genitivus of the nominativus, which is equally unknown to him ; the drummer who heaps negative on negative, not because he desires to make a stronger affirmative, but because his village schoolmaster was not given time to teach him the mysteries of grammar—all these legitimate members of the party rolls and fire companies cannot be expected to put into practice an exalted ideal which it takes a higher degree of education and a high standard of morality only to understand and appreciate. If I say, therefore, that these persons ought to be excluded from the vestibule which leads into the accesses to the profession, I repeat only what many have said before me, what the University of Pennsylvania tried to enforce forty years ago, and finally after scores of years succeeded in realizing. If there be anything that has convinced me at an early time that Philadelphia had a right to the name of a medical centre, it was the fact that it has first, not laid down in verbose pronunciamentos, but actually tried to raise medical education, and finally been successful. I have recently read an editorial in a journal which claims that a Western city, known for its many grain elevators, cable railways, and anarchists, is a medical centre because of the bacteria-like increase in the number of its medical students and graduates. A medical centre, however, is not formed by numbers of bodies : it is a matter of soul and mind and intellect. If Philadelphia and Boston are medical centres, they are so because they require schooling and intellect before they admit to their schools, and because they reduce the number of their students rather than encourage their locust-like increase. If on *that* basis we were to have not only Philadelphia, New York, and Boston, but every large city of the Union, as medical centres, so much the better for the profession at large, and medical science in the States and everywhere. Until we have, however, accomplished that, let us be modest and acknowledge the fact that we are far below our aims and away from the realization of our hopes. It appears to me that we speak a little too much of the claims of this or that city as a medical centre. If the results equalled the local ambitions, we should hear less of claims. Whoever is on the top does not decry the climbers. If many were on the top there would be no envy. So let us all arrive at the top and work in parallel lines, each proud of and encouraging the other.

And now, Mr. President and gentlemen, I think I might safely conclude my remarks, which you have listened to with courteous attention. You have been good enough to invite a New Yorker to reply to the toast on the profession. I can assure you that the New York profession tries to be as advanced as that of other cities, both in knowledge and morals, and that there are very many amongst us who strive to share in the highest intellectual and moral efforts of the profession of any country. Whatever the country may have been told of the Gothamization of the profession in the commercial metropolis, let me assure you that the reports are based on mistakes, if on nothing worse. Nor is it true that anything has occurred in the ranks of the profession of New York City or State which has seriously interrupted, for more than a very short time, the cordial mutual relations of its medical men. There have been dissensions—where have they not been? Even Philadelphia has had its semi-occasional unpleasantness—but the heart and soul of the New York profession are far above the small interests of a few petrified souls or cunning politicians. Greater differences are met with everywhere, and the ideal of the medical man is still the same. When the physicians in America, like all citizens, are divided into two great political parties to such an extent that they could fight on two opposite battlefields; when in Germany they call themselves agnostics and humanists, to the exclusion of positive religion altogether; when in Russia they are indifferent in religion and nihilistic in politics, good Roman Catholics in Spain and Ireland, liberal in Brazil and atheist in France, or Catholic, as the case may be—there is one great aim and principle underlying medicine, both in science and practice. There is no faith concerned in a biological process; no creed in the action of a medicine; no political differences in the moans of human sufferings; no territorial hues and taints of scientific results. If there is a cosmopolitan and humanitarian science and man, that science is medicine, and that man is the scientific and humane physician. As that is your platform, so it is ours; so it is that of all enlightened and progressive medical men through all generations. In the ancient world the priest was the doctor, erudite in both metaphysics and physics. That has changed. Not in a literal sense of the

word is the doctor a priest, but everything attributed
to the priest and his high calling, intellect, erudition,
general culture, sobriety, earnestness of purpose,
conscientiousness, purity of heart, and self-sacrifice
in the interests of his calling—all the qualities, indeed, which raised him above the ranks and made
him qualified to be priest, physician, and judge—
have been, and will forever be, the honor and the
recognition mark of the true physician.

Let us all work for that end as well as we can,
singly and together. Let that aim be inscribed on
the flag of the profession, and let it be visible far
and wide. By keeping our eye on the great future,
let us not forget that the roads are many while the
ideal is one. We can always prove that we belong
to the great family of idealist physicians, scorning
low motives, despising mean measures, to our honor
and that of the profession and of the country.

And now I *shall* close. I give the floor to my
betters, and return to my seat and to New York. In
regard to Philadelphia I have added to my knowledge to-night. I remember but very few occasions
on which I was in this city. Once I had the pleasure
of meeting some of you over the remains of the
Siamese brothers. Otherwise I know but little of
the city, except that I had to read, and did read
gladly, your books and journals. I knew that this
was the city in which the Declaration of our Independence was signed, and the greatest American
lived, Benjamin Franklin ; that there were several
hospitals here, and two illustrious colleges, and a
museum of natural history. I was also once in a
medical study, that of Alfred Stillé. Thus I came

to the conclusion that every Philadelphian study looked like his, and every Philadelphian medical man was an Alfred Stillé. I was also told that Philadelphia was a very, very quiet place, and I sometimes felt that the whole city must be hushed, like a laboratory or a library. In how many of these beliefs or impressions I may have been mistaken, I cannot judge from this place. But I shall tell the New York friends that I have learned a good deal to-night—namely, how strangers are made to feel comfortable ; and that all the good and great men of Philadelphia's profession can be brought together in a single festive hall without strife, dissension, and hesitation; and that the College of Physicians of Philadelphia has thus accomplished what the New York Academy of Medicine is aiming at and laboring for. If, at last, *I* were to pronounce a toast, it would be no other but this: the College of Physicians of Philadelphia, *vivat, floreat, crescat.*

WACHSTHUM.

EIN IM DEUTSCHEN GESELLIG-WISSENSCHAFTLICHEN VEREIN AM 28. APRIL 1886 GEHALTENER VORTRAG.*

WIE "wächs't" ein Krystall? Dadurch, dass aus der Lauge eine Anzahl gleichartiger und gleichgestalteter Körpertheile eines nach dem andern sich anlegen. Jedes Einzelne dieser Theilchen ist schon an und für sich ein Krystall. Der grössere Körper, welcher sich aus einer Unzahl derselben bildet, ist nur an Masse, nicht an Wesen und Würdigkeit von der kleinsten Daseinsform verschieden. Die Krystallmasse lässt sich in unendlich viele Theilchen zertrümmern, doch dadurch geht der Begriff des Krystalls nicht verloren.

Hierin liegt der Unterschied zwischen der unorganischen Existenz und dem Organismus. Ich sage mit Absicht nicht, zwischen dem unorganischen und dem organischen Wesen. Denn es gibt organische Formen, welche Vermehrung und Theilung vertragen, ohne in ihrem eigenen Wesen zu gewinnen oder zu verlieren.

Solche niederste Form, in welcher sich organisches Leben zeigt, ist das Protoplasma. Es ist dies eine gleichförmige, kaum mit mikroskopischen Körnchen versehene schleimige Masse, welche als organische Materie sich nur mit Mühe erkennen

---

* Sonntagsblatt der N. Y. Staats-Zeitung.

lässt. Die sog. Amoeben sind solche Protoplasmakügelchen von nur mikroskopischer Kleinheit. Sie
sind rundlich, verändern aber auf Reize ihre Gestalt,
sie sind beweglich, bestehen aus gleichmässiger
Masse, haben keine Organe irgend welcher Art,
Nahrungsmittel verschmelzen sie einfach mit ihrer
ganzen Substanz, aber—wie gesagt—sie empfinden,
sie bewegen sich, sie sind belebt. Ihre Vermehrung geschieht dadurch, dass, wenn sie an Masse zu-
nehmen, sie sich theilen, und die glückliche un-
schuldige Existenz von früher fortführen.

Die nächste Stufe aufwärts im Reiche des Organischen ist die Zelle. Vor dem Protoplasmakügelchen
zeichnet sie sich dadurch aus, dass sie einen mehr so-
liden Kern, und weniger veränderliche Form besitzt,
bis zu dem Grade, dass man ihr eine Umgebungshaut zugeschrieben hat, in welcher die Zellenmasse
eingeschlossen gedacht wurde. Die rothen Blutkörperchen sind ein gutes Beispiel dieser Zellen, während die weissen Blutkörperchen den Amoeben noch
näher stehen.

Auch die Zelle vermehrt sich durch Theilung.
Dies ist aber nicht die einzige Veränderung, welche
sie eingeht. Sie verändert ihre Gestalt, sie verlän-
gert sich, bildet Fäden, und die Vervielfältigung
desselben Vorganges gibt zur Bildung von Geweben
Veranlassung. Unterdessen kann sich auch, neben
der vergrösserten Zahl, die Eigenschaft der Zelle
verändern, und zwar geschieht dies ohne allen Zweifel durch eine natürlich innewohnende erbliche Anlage des Protoplasma oder der Zelle selber. Mit der
veränderten Eigenschaft und Gestalt entwickeln
die Zellen Funktionen verschiedener Art. Von den

rothen Blutzellen habe ich soeben gesprochen, sie
haben die Eigenschaft, den Sauerstoff der athmo-
sphärischen Luft zu binden. Daher kommt es,
dass Leute, welche viel Blut verloren haben, oder
kein genügendes Blut erzeugen, wie bleichsüchtige
Mädchen oder Blutende, trotz frischer Luft, und
gesunder Lungen an Athemnoth leiden, gerade wie
Menschen vor gedecktem Tisch und ohne Verdau-
ungskraft an Hunger und Entbehrung zu Grunde
gehen. Die Zellen der aus dem Speisebrei gebildeten Lymphe dienen direkt der Ernährung, die der
Drüsen sondern Stoffe ab oder nehmen solche auf,
diejenigen der Nervenfasern dienen als Leiter von
Empfindungen nach dem Gehirn zu, oder von Be-
wegungsanstössen vom Gehirn nach den Muskeln ;
die Zellen der Gehirncentralpartien, Ganglien, besorgen den Denkprozess.

Nachdem nun diese Differenzirung der Zellen in
andere Formen und der Umwandlung der Zellen in
Fasern stattgefunden und die Bildung von Geweben
ermöglicht wurde, ist der nächste Schritt derjenige
des Zusammenwirkens verschiedener Gewebe zu
Organen, von Organen zu Apparaten, von Apparaten zum Organismus. Die Stufenleiter der Entwicklung ist einfach genug. Das Wunderbare,
wenn der Ausdruck gebraucht werden soll, liegt in
dem Dasein der Amoebe und dem Lebendigsein der
Zelle, nicht aber in der legitimen und der Beobachtung zugänglichen Aufwärtsentwicklung organischer Materie zu einem Aristoteles oder Virchow.

Das Wachsen organischer Materie, wie ich es in
wenigen Worten skizzirt habe. ist das gleiche in
allen organischen Wesen von den niedersten

Fischen aufwärts bis zum Wirbelthierreiche. Der Vorgang ist an dem ungeborenen Thierchen mit Vorliebe studirt worden. Tausend Forscher haben sich mit dem Gegenstand um so lieber beschäftigt, als die Lösung der betreffenden Fragen eine schwierige ist. Vor allen Dingen hat die Entstehung des Hühnchens im Ei aus der Keimschicht, welche der Oberfläche des Dotters in einer Breite von nur 2.5–3.5 Mm. und eine Dicke von 0.27–0.35 Mm. aufliegt, zahlreiche und wichtige Aufklärungen gegeben. In die Einzelheiten hier einzugehen ist unmöglich. Nur auf eine Thatsache will ich aufmerksam machen, welche darin besteht, dass das Wachsthum, sobald Gewebe und Organe gebildet sind, zweifacher Natur geworden ist. So lange der Embryo des Huhnes und jedes andern Wesens aus Zellen besteht, ist das Embryonalwachsthum das Resultat der Saftströmung von Zelle zu Zelle, der sog. Osmose ; sobald aber im Laufe weniger Stunden oder Tage eine Gewebs- und Organbildung stattgefunden hat, kommt zu der Zellsaftströmung die Ernährung durch Blutgefässe von einem entfernten Kreislaufsmittelpunkt hinzu, den wir Herz nennen. Diese zwei Arten von Saftströmung und Ernährung gibt es in jedem neugeborenen Wesen. Durch sie wird das Wachsthum vor und nach der Geburt bestimmt. Ohne mich weiter zu verweilen, will ich daher mich zu dem Wachsthum desjenigen Körpers wenden, für den wir Egoisten uns noch immer am meisten interessiren.

Einige Thatsachen mögen Ihnen veranschaulichen, in wie verschiedenartiger Weise je nach Alter und Geschlecht das Wachsthum des Neugebornen vor sich geht. Dabei sind einzelne namhafte Faktoren nicht einmal in Rechnung gezogen, nämlich Ernährungsweise, erbliche Anlage, Wohlhabenheit. Die Kinder der Armuth bleiben an Mass und Gewicht, wie auch an Lebensenergie zurück. Brustkinder gedeihen besser als diejenigen, welche mit gemischter Kost aufgezogen werden ; diese noch viel besser als diejenigen, welche nur künstliche Nahrung geniessen. Dies ist ein Missverhältniss, welches nicht blos für die jungen Kinder gilt, sondern auch für das ganze Leben nachhält.

Das Neugeborne misst ungefähr 50 Centimeter, der Erwachsene $3\frac{1}{3}$–$3\frac{1}{2}$mal so viel. Bis zum Abschluss des Wachsens gewinnt zu den genannten 50 Cm. der Mann 118, das Weib 100. Das Längenwachsthum vertheilt sich nicht gleichmässig auf die einzelnen Jahre, denn die Hälfte der späteren Grösse wird schon vor Ablauf des dritten Jahres erreicht, nach vierzehn Jahren fehlt nur noch $\frac{1}{12}$ der ganzen Länge, bei Mädchen noch weniger. Der absolut grösste Werth des Längenwachsthums fällt in das erste Jahr. Nachher, bis zum achten, ist der jährliche Gewinn 6 Cm., nach dem achten $5\frac{1}{2}$ Cm. Das siebenjährige Mädchen steht der ausgewachsenen Durchschnittslänge näher als der achtjährige Knabe ; Mädchen wachsen mehr im zwölften und dreizehnten, auch im vierzehnten Jahre, als Knaben, so dass sogar ihre Durchschnittslänge grösser ist. Erst nach Abschluss des eigentlichen Knabenalters wachsen Knaben in rascherem Schritte.

Bei dem Neugebornen ist die Entfernung vom Scheitel bis zum Hüftbeinkamm so gross wie die von diesem bis zur Sohle. Bis zum dreizehnten

Jahre bleibt nun der Unterkörper zurück. Aber vom sechszehnten Jahre an wächst derselbe so, dass das Verhältniss von Oberkörper zu Unterkörper nach manchen Rechnungen wie 382 : 618 beträgt. Mit dem siebenten Jahre ist der Oberkopf fast vollendet, vom zwölften bis zum fünfzehnten Jahre wachsen die Kiefer bedeutend, bis zum sechsten wächst der Kehlkopf, um bis zum dreizehnten bis fünfzehnten zu ruhen und sich nachher, besonders beim Knaben, um so rascher zu entwickeln. Um dieselbe Zeit, besonders vom fünfzehnten bis zwanzigsten Jahre wachsen die Knochen und der Bart ; vom zwanzigsten bis fünfundzwanzigsten schreiten Knochen, Muskeln und Brustkorb in der Entwicklung rasch fort, der Kehlkopf beginnt schon zu verknöchern, während ein Organ, die Thymusdrüse, ganz verschwindet. Das Herz wächst von 120-140 Ccm. auf 215-290 Ccm. in dem kurzen Zeitraume vom dreizehnten bis vierzehnten Jahre.

Nicht blos Mediciner vom Fach, sondern auch Künstler haben sich mit dem genauen Messen des Körpers und seiner Theile befasst. Schadow hat die folgenden Zahlen : die Länge des Neugebornen beträgt 18 Zoll, die des Erwachsenen 66. Die Zunahme beträgt im ersten Jahre 10, im zweiten 4, im dritten 4, im vierten 3, im fünften 3, im sechsten 2, im siebenten, achten, neunten und zehnten je 1 Zoll. Mit dem vollendeten siebenten Jahre tritt also eine Verlangsamung des Wachsthums ein. Das Verhältniss der oberen Rumpfportion (Brust) zu der unteren beträgt im Neugebornen 1 : 2, im Erwachsenen 1 : 1,618. Diese normale Proportion wird mit dem achten Jahre erreicht.

Die Lendenportion des Körpers wächst vorzugsweise bis zum neunten Jahre, dann wieder vom
zwölften bis fünfzehnten. Ganz gewiss soll gerade
dieser Theil des Körpers mässig entwickelt sein,
bevor Kinder zu anhaltendem Sitzen gezwungen
werden. Ueber die Folgerungen, welche sich hier-
aus in Bezug auf das Schulalter ergeben, werde ich
mich später auslassen, wenn ich Gelegenheit habe,
über die sonderbar ungleichmässige und sprung-
weise Entwicklung des Schädels und seines Inhaltes
zu reden.

Die Gewichtszunahme des Neugebornen, welcher
3.25 Kilogramm wiegt, ist im ersten Jahre erstaunlich. Sie ist so gross, dass das einjährige Kind 8.9
Kilogramm wiegt. Von der Zeit an ist die Zunahme gleichmässiger. Allein die Gewichtszunahme einzelner Theile des Körpers steht in sonderbar verschiedenartigem Verhältniss zu derjenigen
des ganzen Körpers in den jeweiligen Lebensaltern.
Der Neugeborne wiegt ein Neunzehntel von dem,
was der Ausgewachsene wiegt, also 1 : 19. Die Ge-
wichtsverhältnisse einzelner Organe stellen sich
aber folgendermassen, wenn wir die neugebornen
Theile ein für alle Mal als 1 bezeichnen. Dann
wiegen bei dem Erwachsenen die Augen 1.7, das
Gehirn 3.7, die Schildrüsen 4.5, das Rückenmark 7,
die Speicheldrüsen, 10.7, die Nieren 12, die Haut 12,
die Leber 13.6, das Herz 15, die Milz 18, Magen und
Darm 20, Lungen 20, das Skelett 26, die Bauchspeicheldrüsen 28, die Muskulatur 48. Somit gehen bei
dem Erwachsenen die Gewichte von Magen und
Darm, Lungen, Skelett, Bauchspeicheldrüsen und
Muskulatur über das Durchschnittsverhältniss hinaus.

Noch in anderer Weise lässt sich die Ungleich-
heit des Wachsthums klar machen. Die Hälfte
des schliesslichen Gewichts erreicht das Gehirn im
ersten Jahr, die Leber im achten bis neunten,
Herz, Nieren und Milz im zehnten, die Lungen im
elften Jahre. Die Reihe der Zahlen und Gewichte, welche sich
auf den ganzen Körper beziehen, will ich hier
unterbrechen, um mich zur Betrachtung einzelner
Organe zu wenden. Nur wenige kann ich zu dem
Zwecke auswählen ; sobald ich an die Behandlung
des gewählten Themas gehe, zeigt es sich, dass
ich ihm im ganzen Umfange nicht kann Gerechtigkeit widerfahren lassen. Nehmen Sie vorlieb mit
dem, was ich im Laufe der nothwendiger Weise
beschränkten Zeit und bei naturgemäss limitirter
menschlicher Geduld, zum Theil an Thatsachen, zum
Theil an Nutzanwendungen, werde bieten können.
Lassen Sie mich mit dem *Gehirn* beginnen, dessen
Wachsthumsperioden zu eigenthümlichen Erschein-
ungen Veranlassung geben. Die Verrichtungen des
Gehirns hängen von seiner anatomischen, physikalischen und chemischen Beschaffenheit ab. Die
Quantität und Qualität der Hirnarbeit beruht,
neben manchen andern Dingen, vorzugsweise auf
der Menge des in der Hirnsubstanz enthaltenen
Fettes und Phosphors. Beide finden sich bei dem
Erwachsenen zumeist in der weissen Hirnsubstanz,
bei dem Neugebornen im verlängerten Mark. So
erklärt sich das Ueberwiegen der Arbeit des verlängerten Marks bei dem jungen Kinde vorzugsweise aus seinem grossen Gehalt an Fett und Phosphor.

Auch die Menge des in der Hirnsubstanz enthaltenen Wassers ist von grosser Bedeutung. Je
mehr Wasser, desto weniger Normalarbeit. Im
Neugebornen ist es das verlängerte Mark, welches
am wenigsten Wasser enthält (84.38 Procent), und
auch dadurch zu grösseren Leistungen befähigt ist.
Die Varolsbrücke in der unmittelbaren Nachbarschaft des verlängerten Marks, welche ein wichtiges
Bewegungscentrum ist und welche am wenigsten
Wasser von allen Hirntheilen des Erwachsenen
besitzt, hat auch beim Neugebornen nur wenig
Wasser (86.77 Procent) und ist dadurch zur Ausführung kräftiger und nachhaltiger Bewegungen besonders befähigt. Sie wissen, wie bedeutend dieselben die intellektuellen Leistungen der Säuglinge
überwiegen. Die letzteren hängen von der grauen
und weissen Substanz des Hirns ab. Bei dem Neugebornen ist nun die weisse Substanz, welche beim
Erwachsenen viel härter ist, sehr wasserreich (89.83
Procent). Dieser Wassergehalt, welcher durch das
mittlere Alter abnimmt, steigt erst wieder im
höchsten Alter. Somit nähert sich das Gehirn des
Greises in dieser einen Hinsicht dem des Kindes,
und von diesem anatomischen Standpunkte aus
lässt sich wohl von einer "zweiten Kindheit"
reden.

Die Unterschiede zwischen grauer und weisser
Substanz sind im Gehirn des Neugebornen nur wenig
markirt. Die ganze Masse des Gehirns ist weich,
gleichmässig, graulich, die Höhlen sind glatt, die
Windungen nicht zahlreich und gross.

Die Heranbildung weisser Masse geht Hand in
Hand mit der Ausbildung der Verrichtungen des

12*

Gehirns. Lassen Sie mich das nur an einem einzigen Beispiele illustriren. Reil's Insel, das Sprachcentrum, ist vollständig violett bei der Geburt. Am Ende des ersten Monats finden sich einzelne weisse Streifen. Nach neun Monaten ist die weisse Substanz vollständig entwickelt. Um die Zeit bildet sich das unartikulirte Gegröhle des Baby allmählig in das beredte Papa und Mama um, und mit welchem Erfolg die Fähigkeiten weisser Hirnsubstanz in das unaufhörliche Geplapper kindlicher Redefertigkeit umgesetzt werden, ist allen Denjenigen bekannt, die es angeht. Um die Zeit bilden sich dann auch die Unterschiede grauer und weisser Substanz in dem Vorderhirn stärker aus, die oberflächlichen Windungen vertiefen sich und werden unregelmässiger, die Höhlen zeigen die Anfänge späterer Mannigfaltigkeit, und, was man Geist nennt, entwickelt sich in gleichem Schritt.

Die Nervenzweige des Körpers sind im Kinde verhältnissmässig viel grösser als die Centralorgane, d. h. als Gehirn und Rückenmark. Von diesen zweiten ist das Rückenmark das grössere. Im Rückenmark wieder überwiegen die vorderen Hörner, nämlich diejenigen Partien, welche Bewegung und Blutlauf kontrolliren. Daher kommt es, dass die unfreiwillige Muskelthätigkeit (die s. g. Reflexe) und die Gefässarbeit bei dem Kinde überwiegend ausgebildet sind, mit Ausnahme der allerersten Tage, an welchen die Reflexe noch wenig entwickelt sind.

Die Anfänge und das Wachsen geistigen Lebens hängen vorzugsweise, neben der chemischen und physikalischen Zusammensetzung der Hirnsubstanz, von seiner Masse, mehr aber noch von dem Verhältnisse ab, in welchem einzelne Theile zu einander stehen. Der Kopf des Neugebornen beträgt an Länge ein Viertel, an Gewicht ein Fünftel des ganzen Körpers. Seine Basis ist kurz, und daher ist das Hinterhauptsbein flach. Die grösste Weite hat der kindliche Schädel zwischen den Scheitelbeinhöckern, daher ist er rundlich und fällt zu Anfang nach vorn ab. Die Schädelhöhle des Neugebornen ist drei- oder viermal kleiner als diejenige des Erwachsenen, wächst aber in einem Jahre von 482 Ccm. bis zu 999 Ccm. Das Wachsthum ihrer einzelnen Theile ist aber nicht gleichmässig. Die Hinterhauptshöhle beträgt 5 Procent, die Scheitelbeinportion 81.11 Procent und die Stirnportion 13.8 Procent des ganzen Inhalts. Die erste wächst sehr schnell, die dritte nur mässig, die zweite bleibt zurück. Dem entsprechen die Gewichte der eingeschlossenen Hirnmassen. Das kleine Gehirn wiegt 25.0 Gramm bei dem Neugebornen, d. h. 6.7 Procent des ganzen Gehirns ; nach zwei Monaten schon 9.1 Procent, mit zehn oder fünfzehn Jahren schon 12 oder 13 Procent ; im Erwachsenen auch nur 12 oder 14 Procent. Ebenso interessant—dies sind alles Zahlen, welche wir den genauen Messungen E. Huschke's, in seinem Buche über Schädel, Hirn und Seele, Jena, 1854, verdanken—sind die vergleichenden Zahlen, welche das Gewichtsverhältniss einzelner Hirntheile feststellen. Das Gewicht der grossen Hirnhemisphären des Neugebornen beträgt 300.0 Gramm, d. h. ein Viertel oder ein Fünftel des Gewichtes der erwachsenen Hemisphären, die Vorderlappen 60-70.0, also ein Fünftel, die

Seitenlappen 250.0, also ein Viertel, das Kleinhirn 25.0, also ein Achtel von dem Gewicht derselben Theile im Erwachsenen. Im Neugebornen steht des Verhältniss des Oberkopfes (Schädels) zum Unterkopfe wie 1:1, bei Erwachsenen wie 1:1,618. Dieses Verhältniss wird schon mit dem achten Jahre erreicht. Schon vor dieser Zeit, zwischen dem fünften und sechsten Jahre, ist die Basis des Gehirns schnell gewachsen, und das Stirnbein hat sich nach oben und vorn entwickelt. Vor einigen Tagen habe ich ein achtjähriges Kind gesehen, das einer bald nach der Geburt vorgenommenen Operation eine Narbe auf die Stirn verdankt. Zu jener Zeit war die Narbe einundeinhalb Zoll von der Nasenwurzel entfernt, heute beträgt die Entfernung fast drei Zoll. Auch die vordere Gehirnportion wächst beträchtlich, doch ist die Ausbildung der eigentlich denkenden grauen Hirnsubstanz noch im Rückstande, und die weisse Substanz und das Mittelgehirn überwiegen noch. Daher sind die Fähigkeiten der Reception und des Gedächtnisses erstaunlich ausgebildet. Was daher um diese Lebenszeit an Lehrmaterial geboten wird, sollte Receptivität und Gedächtniss vorzugsweise in Anspruch nehmen. Ausgedehntere und komplicirtere Arbeit sollte erst später gefordert werden. Alles Dasjenige, was ich über die Ausbildung der Knochen des Lendentheils des Körpers und die Herstellung des schliesslichen Verhältnisses zwischen Ober- und Unterkopf (Schädel und Gesicht) gesagt habe—welches Beides um das siebente und achte Lebensjahr stattfindet—bestimmt dieses genannte Alter, und kein früheres, als das eigent

liche Schulalter. Diese Schlussfolgerung aus anatomischen und physiologischen Thatsachen stimmt
mit der praktischen und intuitiven Erfahrung
von Friedrich Froebel überein, welcher das achte
Jahr als Schulalter feststellte. Bis dahin sollen
Erziehung und Unterricht in Kindergärten geleitet
werden ; man soll die Kinder nicht zwingen, sondern unterhalten und spielend entwickeln. Ihr
Thätigkeitstrieb wird benützt—wie schon Fourier
es wollte und in seiner Sucht, zu übertreiben, in's
Lächerliche zog : er wollte den Thätigkeitstrieb der
Kleinen zum Gossenkehren und Schmutzsammeln
benutzen—und geübt, ihre Aufmerksamkeit erregt,
ihre Muskeln und Sinne geübt durch Modelliren,
Flechten, Figurenmachen, Stäbchenlegen, Bewe-
gungsspiele, Gesang, Blumenpflegen ; Gedächtniss
und Phantasie werden geübt durch Erzählen,
Fragen und Antworten, und zwar ohne Zwangs-
massregeln in Bezug auf Stellung und Benehmen.
Um dieselbe Zeit ist übrigens auch die graue Substanz in lebhafter Entwicklung begriffen ; sie soll
deshalb geübt, aber nicht überangestrengt werden.
In mässiger Weise sollen daher sämmtliche Gehirn-
funktionen in Anspruch genommen werden. Das
Gedächtniss ist schon vorgeübt, das Gefühl und die
Phantasie sind leicht erregbar, das Denken bedarf
zuletzt langsamer Pflege. Neben der Körperübung,
welche an und für sich wichtig und für einen normalen und lebhaften Blutkreislauf unumgänglich
ist, sollen Musik, Auswendiglernen und Reflektiren
in nur langsam zunehmendem Grade an die Reihe
kommen. Neben der zu frühen und zu eifrigen Hirnarbeit besteht die grösste Gefahr darin,

dass einzelne Hirnfunktionen übermässig und einseitig angestrengt werden. Einseitige Uebung ist in keiner Weise Schonung, sondern hat Erschöpfung und Verkümmerung zur Folge. Die unglücklichen Geschöpfe, welche von Kindheit an in eine *einzige* Bahn der Ausbildung gepfercht werden, mit Vernachlässigung gleichmässiger Entwicklung, bieten die Schauspiele des glänzenden Virtuosenthums, mag dieses dasjenige der Bayadere und des Seiltänzers sein oder sich auf andere Gebiete verirren. Ich will Niemandem etwas Böses nachsagen, aber ich kann es nicht ändern, dass ich mich einiger brillant geschriebener Artikel in Karl Heinzen's "Pionier" erinnere, welche die Ueberschrift trugen : "Kann und muss ein Musiker Verstand haben ?"

Die complicirten Actionen des Gehens ermüden viel weniger, als das einförmige Stehen ; so erschöpft die wechselvolle Uebung sämmtlicher Hirntheile und Verrichtungen weniger, als einseitige Arbeit und Ausbildung. So ist Auswendiglernen ohne Verständniss ebenso schwierig, wie erfolglos. Verschlingen ist nicht Verdauen, Auswendiglernen nicht Lernen, Recitiren nicht Denken, Einpauken (*cramming*) nicht Wissen. Die schlechte Schulmethode, welche erst jetzt die entschiedene Aufmerksamkeit und Reformarbeit guter Schulmänner auf sich zieht, und welche in einem öden Frage- und Antwortspiel während der Lectionen besteht, und darin, dass sogar die Schulbücher in Catechismusform abgefasst sind, mag wohl einen Theil der Schuld an der Thatsache tragen, dass bei uns so lange krasser Empirismus im praktischen Leben,

und gedankenlose Sektirerei auf religiösem Gebiet
das Scepter geführt haben. Die Wichtigkeit des Gegenstandes muss mir eine
Entschuldigung dafür abgeben, dass ich auf das
vorhin besprochene Thema des Schulalters noch
einmal zurückkomme. Nicht blos leidet das Gehirn von der Verfrühung peinigend systematischen
Unterrichts, sondern mit ihr stellen sich auch die
sogenannten Schulkrankheiten ein. Zu hohe oder
zu niedere Temperaturen in den Schulzimmern,
schlechte Luft, Zug, Staub, Ansteckungen, unzu-
reichende Athembewegung, ungenügende Muskel-
übung, Druck auf die Unterleibsorgane machen
ihren verderblichen Einfluss leicht geltend. Nasen-
bluten, Kopfschmerzen, Blutleere und Schiefheit
sind häufig. Die letztere bildet sich oft früh
aus, in Folge unzureichender Wachsthumsent-
wicklung in den Muskeln. Unpassende Haltung,
welche durch Ermüdung bedingt wird—in ähnlicher Weise wie die auf einem Arm der Wärterin
ausschliesslich getragenen Babies schief werden—
die einseitige Anstrengung, welche durch das
Heben der rechten Schulter beim Schreiben bedingt wird, das Schiefhalten des Kopfes beim auf-
merksamen Schauen auf die Feder, der unpassende
Bau der Schultische und Bänke, das Zusammen-
schieben der Mädchenkleider unter einer Seite und
das dadurch bedingte Schiefsitzen sind eben so viele
Ursachen der Wirbelsäuleverschiebung, welche be
nicht ausgebildeten Knochen und Muskeln am
leichtesten zu Stande kommt. Von der Ermüdung
des Gehirns, seiner Ueberreizung, von der Möglichkeit, die Neigung zu Krampfkrankheiten zu ver-

schlimmern, Veitstanz und Hirnhautentzündung
direkt hervorzurufen, will ich gar nicht reden.
Erst vor einigen Tagen habe ich ein sechszenjähriges
Schulmädchen an Hirnentzündung sterben sehen.
Sie ist nur ein Beispiel von vielen Dutzend, welche
in meiner eigenen Erinnerung dem Minotaurus der
Schulüberbürdung zum Opfer gefallen sind.
Für die Einhaltung des siebenten oder achten
Jahres als Schulalters spricht noch mehr, nämlich
der Umstand, dass um jene Zeit die Gefahr an-
steckender Krankheiten und Hirnaffectionen merklich vermindert ist. Die Sterblichkeit ist gross
während der ersten sechs Lebensjahre ; die Hälfte
aller Todesfälle kommt auf diese Periode. Von 100
Todesfällen in New York fallen 29.63 in das erste,
10.03 in das zweite, 4.37 in das dritte, 2.40 in das
vierte, 1.64 in das fünfte, 3.20 in das sechste, also
51.28 in die ersten sechs Jahre. Die ganze Zeit vom
Ende des sechsten bis zum elften Lebensjahre liefert nur 1.50 Procent sämmtlicher Todesfälle. Somit ergibt sich für den bis zum siebenten oder
achten Jahre entwickelten menschlichen Organismus eine bedeutende Widerstandskraft. Es ist
auch die alltägliche Erfahrung sämmtlicher Wai-
senhäuser und Anstalten, in welchen Kinder vom
siebenten bis fünfzehnten Jahre aufgenommen
werden, dass trotz aller gesundheitlichen Nach-
theile, welchen diese jungen modernen Troglodyten
in ihren Höhlen ausgesetzt sind, ihre Sterblichkeit
eine geringe ist. Nach allem nun, was ich in kurzem Umrisse Ihnen vorgeführt habe, werden Sie
mir zugeben, dass das Schulalter von der Wachs-
thumsstufe der Kinder, und das Wohl und Wehe

des künftigen Staatsbürgers nicht von der Eitelkeit,
oder Bequemlichkeit, oder Unwissenheit der Eltern
abhängen sollte. Lassen Sie mich nun gefälligst noch einmal zu
meinem Ausgangspunkte zurückkehren. Was ich
Ihnen an Massen und Gewichten von Schädel und
Hirn mitgetheilt habe, liefert den vorläufigen Beweis dafür, dass die beiden in gewisser Wechsel-
beziehung zu einander stehen.

Im Allgemeinen lässt sich als Thatsache aufstellen, dass beide sich zu gleicher Zeit und gleichmässig im Vorgange der Körperbildung, ohne Missverhältniss, entwickeln. Indessen sehen Sie ein,
dass besonders zu einer Zeit, in welcher die Schädelknochen noch nicht ihre starre Unbeweglichkeit
erlangt haben, Zufälligkeiten, welche das Gehirn,
oder solche, welche den Schädel allein treffen, das
Gleichgewicht bedeutend stören können. Daher
kommt es, dass bei Gehirnen, deren Höhlen in früher Kindheit, oder gar vor der Geburt, mit einer
wässerigen Flüssigkeit angefüllt sind, und deshalb
eine aussergewöhnliche Grösse erreichen, der
Schädel die Folgen der innern Entwicklung in seinem Aeussern zeigen muss; daher aber auch, dass
frühzeitige oder auch in späterem Leben erworbene
Veränderungen der Schädelknochen ihre Spuren am
Gehirn zurücklassen.

Sie wissen, dass der Schädel eines neugeborenen
oder jungen Kindes keine harte, unbewegliche
Kapsel darstellt, wie im höheren Alter. Die einzelnen Schädelknochen sind nicht durch Knochen-
masse, sondern durch eine mehr oder weniger
straffe oder nachgiebige Haut miteinander zu einem

Ganzen verbunden. Die häutigen Verbindungen
heissen Nähte, diejenigen Stellen, an welchen
Nähte aneinander stossen, Fontanellen. So unter-
scheidet man eine Naht, welche der Länge nach
auf der Oberfläche des Schädels verläuft, die Pfeilnaht, und zwei andere, welche die eine, Kranznaht,
auf der Höhe des Vorderkopfes, die andere Hinterhauptsnaht, auf dem Hinterkopfe, der Quere nach
verlaufen. Die Fontanelle, welche die Verbin-
dungsstelle der Pfeilnaht und Kranznaht ist, auf
der Höhe des Vorderkopfes, heisst die grosse, diejenige welche durch das Zusammentreffen der Pfeil-
und Hinterhauptsnaht auf der Höhe des Hinter-
kopfes gebildet wird, die kleine Fontanelle. Die
grosse Fontanelle ist diejenige, welche die meiste
Aufmerksamkeit in Anspruch genommen hat ;
denn sie entgeht auch den Blicken oberflächlicher
Beobachter nicht. Sie fühlt sich weich an, lässt
sogar die Pulsation der tief darunter liegenden
Schlagadern erkennen, wölbt sich hervor bei Blutandrang nach dem Kopfe, bei Wasserergüssen in
der Schädelhöhle, sinkt unter das Niveau der umgebenden Schädelknochen bei Abmagerungs- und
Schwächezuständen kleiner Kinder, und bildet
somit in vielen Fällen, da sie an manchen Veränderungen des Blutlebens und der Blutvertheilung
Theil nimmt, häufig einen guten Massstab für die
Beurtheilung des allgemeinen Zustandes.

    Unter normalen Verhältnissen schliessen sich die
Nähte und die grosse Fontanelle, nachdem das
Kind eine Reihe von Zähnen formirt, und seine
Knochen hinreichend mit Kalksalzen durchsetzt
sind, um das Gehen zu gestatten, im Beginn des

zweiten Lebensjahres. Um diese Zeit ist das Hauptwachsthum des Gehirns beendet, und findet nachher nur noch in beschränktem Masse statt; um so mehr, als die hartgewordene Schädelkapsel keine bedeutende Entwicklung des Gehirns mehr gestattet. Oft jedoch bleibt der Schädel für längere Zeit offen, niemals aber ohne einige Störung der allgemeinen Gesundheit oder wenigstens Gefahr für dieselbe. Das Gehirn leidet darunter häufig genug, Blutandrang und Wasserausschwitzung werden bisweilen beobachtet; aber die Gehirnmasse wird wenigstens nicht durch Druck von Aussen genirt. Von grosser Bedeutung aber ist der zu frühzeitige Verschluss; sowohl für die Gestalt des Schädels als die Entwicklung des Gehirns.

Die Fontanelle ist ein specifisches Merkmal des Menschen. Einige Affen zeigen freilich eine kleine Oeffnung auf der Höhe des Vorderkopfes, aber sie schliesst sich sehr bald nach der Geburt, so dass weder Schädel noch Gehirn sich merklich weiter entwickeln können. Somit stehen anatomisch die Affen und Thiere überhaupt auf der Stufe mancher blödsinnigen Kinder, welche mit vollständig verknöchertem und fürderhin nur einer unbedeutenden Entwicklung mehr fähigem Schädel zur Welt kommen. Von diesem Gesichtspunkte aus kann man daher sagen, dass der Blödsinn der Menschen der Weisheit der Thiere gleich steht.

Unter den Völkern und Racen der Menschen ist die Fontanelle nicht gleich gross, noch schliesst sie sich im selben Alter, in England später als in Ungarn, in Ungarn später als in der Slovakei. Grade die grosse Fontanelle ist von besonderer Wichtig-

keit für die Ausbildung des Stirntheils des Schädels
und der grossen Vorderhälften des Gehirns, von
denen unter sonst gleichen Bedingungen die Summe
der individuellen Geistesfähigkeiten abhängt. Im
Allgemeinen kann man sagen, dass, je später im
Verhältniss zu den übrigen Nähten die vordere
Quer- oder Kranznaht verknöchert, desto mehr
Möglichkeit für die Ausbildung der denkenden
Hirntheile gegeben ist. In dem bevorzugten
Weissen verknöchert sie zuletzt, und erlaubt daher
eine passende Wölbung des Vorderkopfes, in dem
Neger mit seiner niedrigen zurückliegenden Stirn
und nach rückwärts mehr entwickeltem Hirn ist
sie die erste von allen, welche sich schliesst.
Schläfenbein und Scheitelbein finden sich oft bei
Negern, sogar bei Mongolen, ohne Scheide und
Grenze ; und in Dahomey hat Duncan öfters
Schädel beobachtet, welche gar keine Nähte
hatten.

Aehnliche Verschiedenheiten finden sich nun
nicht allein typisch in Völkern und Racen, sondern
auch individuell. Das längere Offenbleiben der
Kranznaht erlaubt, wie ich schon bemerkt habe,
eine Hervorwölbung des Vorderkopfes, wodurch
entweder die Entwicklung des Vorderhirns unterstützt, oder nur der schönheitliche Schein derselben
gewährt wird. Ist dieselbe Kranznaht die erste in
der Reihe der verknöchernden Verbindungen, so
verliert die Stirn die Fähigkeit, sich zu entwickeln,
und im besten Falle wird die grössere Masse des Gehirns in die nachgiebigeren Theile der Schädelhöhle
gedrängt, ohne gerade an Masse und Schärfe der
Funktion zu verlieren. Solch einen Schädel hatte

Mirabeau. Verknöchert die Pfeilnaht zuerst, so
nimmt der Schädel eine von oben nach unten breit-
gedrückte und von hinten nach vorn in die Länge
gezogene Gestalt an. Wird hingegen der Hinterkopf in seiner Entwicklung durch die frühzeitige
Verknöcherung der Lambdanaht gehemmt, so wird
die Hirnmasse mechanisch nach vorn gedrängt,
und im Gegensatz zu dem flachen Hinterkopf erscheint der Kopf nach vorn und oben zuckerhut-
förmig verschoben. Solch einen Kopf hatte unser
Freund Karl Heinzen, der auf seinen Mangel an
Hinterkopf eben so stolz war, wie auf die Dünnheit
seines Haares
In mässig entwickelten Fällen frühzeitiger Verknöcherung kann die Intelligenz vollständig unge-
stört erscheinen ; was ohne diese Verknöcherung
aus den geistigen Anlagen des betreffenden Individuums geworden wäre, sind wir immerhin nicht
im Stande zu beurtheilen. Dieser Art mögen die
Fälle sein, in welchen Kinder mit dem zehnten
oder zwölften Monate eine vollständig geschlossene
Schädelkapsel besitzen, wie sie sonst erst bei fünf-
zehn-monatlichen gefunden wird. So auch mögen
die Verunstaltungen beurtheilt werden, welche
viele Ureinwohner Südamerika's und Vorderasiens
mit den Schädeln ihrer neugeborenen Kinder vor-
nehmen. Anders indessen gestaltet sich die Sache,
wo die Nähte und Fontanellen des Schädels, alle
oder zum grössten Theil, viel zu früh verknöchern.
Da mit der Verknöcherung des Schädels sein
Wachsthum fast ganz aufhört, das Hirn aber fort-
dauernd in dieser frühen Lebensperiode sich rasch
entwickelt, so ist es dem steten Druck der vor der

Zeit solid gewordenen Knochen ausgesetzt. Abgesehen von den Reizungs- und Krankheitserschein-
ungen, welche durch dieses Missverhältniss ver-
stärkt oder hervorgebracht werden können, ist eine
regelmässige Folge desselben die Beschränkung der
geistigen und moralischen Fähigkeiten des Leidenden, in Uebereinstimmung mit dem Grade des
Druckes auf die gesammte Gehirnmasse und speziell mit der Abplattung der oberflächlichen Windungen. Vielleicht blos der moralischen Eigenschaften. Viele der Verbrecherschädel, welche ich
in Abbildungen und Beschreibungen zu dem Zweck
ihrer Würdigung vom naturgeschichtlichen Stand-
punkt verglichen habe, zeigen einen mässigen Grad
von frühzeitiger Verknöcherung einer oder mehrerer Nähte. Viele Fälle ferner von Convulsionen,
Epilepsie, Taubheit, mangelnder Empfindung, Bewegung und Intelligenz, sehr viele Fälle von ausge-
sprochenem Blödsinn sind auf keine andere Weise
erklärbar. In der Reisebeschreibung von Fritsche
finde ich eine Notiz, welche beweis't, dass auch die
unbefangensten und von Kenntnissen nicht strotz-
enden Völker diese Beobachtungen gemacht haben,
die Notiz nämlich, dass die neugeborenen Kinder in
einigen Völkerschaften Innerafrikas, welche einen
knochenverschlossenen Schädel auf die Welt bringen, von den vorsorglichen Angehörigen kurzer
Hand umgebracht werden. Idioten und Ver-
brecher brauchen sich nicht zu melden.

Lassen sie mich nun vom ganzen Schädel zu
einem seiner Theile übergehen. Das Wachsthum
der Zähne hängt von einer grossen Anzahl von Bedingungen ab, welche gelegentlich schon vor der

Geburt erfüllt sein müssen. Von einer Löwin im zoologischen Garten in London weiss man, dass sie mehrere Male Junge warf, welche einen gespaltenen Gaumen, also unvollständige Knochen und Zahnbildung, hatte. Als man ihr später neben dem Fleisch auch Knochen zu verzehren gab, hatten die nachkommenden Jungen einen *geschlossenen* Gaumen. Somit hängt für die Zähne des Jungen sehr viel von der Gesundheit und ausreichenden Ernährung der Eltern ab, speziell der Mutter, deren Knochensystem sich ja überhaupt im Jungen wieder erzeugt. Gewisse konstitutionelle Krankheiten der Eltern haben auf die Zähne der Kinder einen ebenso bedeutenden Einfluss, wie auf manche angeborenen Krankheiten oder frühzeitig erworbenen Uebel.

Obendrein sind die Zähne junger Kinder, wie auch ihre Knochen, weicher; auch ist der Schmelz dünner. Dieser Umstand macht sich in verschiedener Weise geltend. Erstens wirken Krankheiten in eigenthümlicher Weise nicht blos auf die schon sichtbaren, sondern mehr noch auf die sich eben bildenden Zähne ein. Mit der Knochenerweichung, welche bei der sogenannten englischen Krankheit eintritt, die sich gern als Knochenkrümmung kenntlich macht, werden oder bleiben auch die Zähnchen weich, sie sind daher leicht beschädigt, werden grau und schwarz, und zerbröckeln. Diejenigen Kinder aber, welche die Krankheit in kurzer Zeit durchmachen, zeigen hinterher Veränderungen an den Zähnen, welche mit den an den Knochen wahrnehmbaren identisch sind; d. h. sie werden solider und härter, dabei gelber, aber gleichmässig gelb. Es gibt Zähne, in welchen die gleichmässige Farbe von weissen Inseln unterbrochen ist; diese bestehen sehr häufig aus kohlensaurem Kalk und machen die Zähne brüchiger; sie sind wohl in den meisten Fällen die Folgen von Verletzungen; oder wo der Wechsel der Farben ein ausgiebiger ist, handelt es sich um das Resultat von häufigem Kranksein. Ehemalige Krankheiten lassen sich nicht sehr selten an den Zähnen ablesen, gerade wie Sie an Menschen, welche schwere Krankheiten, wie z. B. Typhus, durchgemacht haben, die Spuren der grossen Störungen an den Nägeln der Finger und Zehen ablesen können, bis sich im Laufe mehrerer Monate der Nagel ganz erneuert hat. So deuten Fehler, besonders Furchen, auf den Schneide- und ersten Backzähnen auf eine schwere Erkrankung um das Ende des ersten oder den Anfang des zweiten Jahres, Furchen auf den zweiten bleibenden Backzähnen auf eine Krankheit des vierten oder fünften Jahres. Auch entzündliche Krankheiten haben gelegentlich denselben Einfluss; zumeist aber schwere Fieber, wie Typhus oder Pocken.

Das Wachsthum der Zähne hängt aber nicht blos von erblichen oder erworbenen schweren Krankheiten ab, sondern noch häufiger von Einflüssen milderer Art, aber längerer Dauer. Wenn das nicht so wäre, so würden, da die schwersten Formen fieberhafter Krankheiten die kleinsten Kinder nicht oft treffen, schlechte Zähne nicht sehr häufig sein. Die Zähne, zum Verdauungs-Apparat gehörig, leiden von Störungen dieser Organe im Allgemeinen. Mundhöhle und Magen stehen bei kleinen und grossen Kindern im allerintimsten Zusammenhange. Zunächst wohl bleiben Speisereste leicht in der Mundhöhle, sie werden ranzig, Bakterien vermehren sich mit Geschwindigkeit, Katarrhe der Schleimhaut und allmähliges Erkranken der Zähne sind eine naturgemässe Folge. Dazu kommt die Leichtigkeit, mit welcher kleine Kinder erbrechen. Wenn das Mündchen nicht grundsätzlich so appetitlich wäre, so wäre es sehr unappetitlich. . Das Erbrochene ist sehr häufig sauer, denn der Milchzucker der genossenen Milch zersetzt sich gern und schnell in Milchsäure und verwandte, noch gefährlichere Produkte, und der Schaden für die exponirten Zähnchen bleibt nicht aus. Das ist um so sicherer, als die Speichelbildung vom dritten bis zum vierten Monate an sehr kopiös ist und die Zahnköpfchen fortwährend von einer Flüssigkeit umfluthet sind, welche, wenn sie säuerlich ist, Schaden bringen muss. Den besten Beweis für diese Behauptung liefert Ihnen das unbehagliche Gefühl und der direkte Nachtheil, welcher Ihren Zähnen aus dem Genuss selbst mässiger Quantitäten von Fruchtsäuren erwächst.

Der unmittelbare Nachtheil des Zuckers für die Zähne, der alten und der jungen—entschuldigen Sie, unter den alten meinte ich blos die nicht ganz jungen, die siebzehnjährigen und aufwärts—ist wohl übertrieben, vorausgesetzt, dass es sich um reinen Zucker handelt. Die Neger der Zuckerplantagen haben gute, weisse Zähne. Indessen ist es richtig. dass sie Zuckersaft kauen, und nicht Zucker, der mit Kalk geklärt ist ; es ist auch wahrscheinlich, dass sie entsprechend den härteren

13*

Schädeln solidere Zähne besitzen. Ferner ist es wahr, dass Zahnschmelz, wochenlang in Zuckerlösung gelegen, nicht verdirbt. Aber Zuckerlösung im Munde wird sicherlich früh säuern, da sie dem beständigen Durchzug der Luft ausgesetzt ist, und Candies, meine Herren und Damen, ich wollte sagen meine Damen, sind noch lange kein Zucker. Das Mindeste, was man ihnen—abgesehen von Beimengungen und schädlichen Färbungen—nachsagen kann, ist, dass dieselben die Verdauung verderben, den Magen säuern, den Mund mit ätzendem Gas und brennender Flüssigkeit füllen und auf diese Weise den Zähnen schaden. Mit diesen Bemerkungen will ich natürlich nichts Anzügliches gesagt haben; ich will nicht einmal Huyler und Costello boycotten, ich rede ja nur von ganz kleinen Babies, und für diese gelten, um ein gesundheitliches Wachsthum zu erzielen, die folgenden paar Regeln :

Der Mund muss rein gehalten, nach jeder Mahlzeit, nach jedem Erbrechen gewaschen werden. Wasser reicht hin, ein leichter Zusatz von Alcohol ist gut, Alkalien sollen nur bei stärkerer Säurebildung gelegentlich gebraucht werden. Dazu reicht ein Theelöffel voll doppelt-kohlensaurer Soda in einem Pint Wasser hin. Seifen, welche noch Aetznatron enthalten, sind schädlich. Tabaksasche ist schädlich, auch wenn sie aus der Nähe des schönsten Schnurrbartes kommt. Harte Zahnpulver, deren Zusammensetzung unbekannt ist, sollen vermieden werden. Bei Kindern ist ein rauhes Tuch der Zahnbürste vorzuziehen. Temperaturwechsel beim Essen sind gefährlich ; es gibt

nichts Schädlicheres als das Trinken von kaltem
Wasser, zumal Eiswasser, während des Geniessens
heisser Speisen. Das gesunde Wachsthum der bleibenden Zähne
hängt von dem Schicksal der Milchzähne zum
grossen Theil ab. Was man also für die Milchzähne thut, kommt den späteren zugute. Nichts
ist nachtheiliger, als zu glauben, dass auf jene
nichts ankomme, weil doch die bleibenden Zähne
nachkommen müssen. Wenn also die Milchzähne
brüchig oder krank werden, soll man nicht ohne
Weiteres ausreissen. Zeitweiliges Plombiren ist
entschieden vorzuziehen. Wenn man zu früh aus-
reisst, so fällt der Krochenrand ein, wie das bei
zahnlosen Alten so deutlich ist, der Kiefer entwickelt sich nicht, und es bleibt kein genügender
Raum für die bleibenden Zähne (von denen die mittleren unteren Schneidezähne in sechsten oder siebenten-
ten, die mittleren oberen im siebenten, die seit-
lichen unteren und oberen im achten, die unteren
und oberen zwei ersten Backzähne im neunten und
zehnten, die Eckzähne im zehnten und elften, die
dritten Backzähne im elften und zwölften, die vierten Backzähne im dreizehnten und vierzehnten
Lebensjahre fällig sind). Dass solche Zähne,
welche ihres Raumes beraubt sind, schief oder
quer oder hinter einander wachsen, kommt recht
häufig vor. Gelegentlich bleibt eine Anzahl ganz
aus, und der Kiefer wird unförmig. Es gibt nur
einen stichhaltigen Grund für das Ausreissen der
Milchzähne, nämlich Entzündung des Knochens
und der Knochenhaut des Kiefers.

Sonst wissen Sie wohl, dass die Zähne von der

Vielgeschäftigkeit Berufener und Unberufener viel
zu leiden gehabt haben, und noch haben. Bevor
ich indessen diese Bemerkung weiter verfolge, lassen Sie mich einige interessante Abweichungen in
dem Erscheinen und dem Bau der Zähne hier berühren. Ich thue das um so lieber, als ich seit
meinem vorjährigen Vortrag, in welchem ich des
Zahnens und der Zähne nur in einigen Worten ge-
dachte, wiederholt aufgefordert worden bin, dem
Gegenstande mehr öffentliche Aufmerksamkeit zu
schenken.

Der jüngere Plinius berichtet, dass Marcus Curius,
der um 270 A.c. Konsul der römischen Republik
war, Zähne auf die Welt brachte und daher Denta-
tus genannt wurde. Papyrius und eine Dame, Na-
mens Valeria, hatten auch Zähne bei der Geburt,
wie derselbe Autor berichtet. Zoroaster soll nach
alten Historikern, wie Weinrich anführt, alle seine
Zähne auf die Welt gebracht haben ; diese Früh-
reife entspräche dann der gewaltigen Entwicklung,
welche der grosse Moralist und Gesetzgeber während seines späteren Lebens durchmachte. Ludwig
XIV., wie auch sein Kardinal Mazarin, hatte Zähne
bei der Geburt ; in seinem Fall wird dem Hugo
Grotius die Prophezeiung in den Mund gelegt, dass,
wie er als Säugling seine Amme blutig riss, er im
späteren Leben seine Nachbarn zerreissen würde.
Ist natürlich eingetroffen, obwohl man nicht wissen
kann, ob die Prophezeiung der Erfüllung vorher-
ging, oder umgekehrt. Richard III. und Mirabeau
ging es ebenso. Scottus berichtet den Fall eines
spanischen Zwerges, der bei der Geburt Zähne, mit
sieben Jahren einen Bart, mit zehn Jahren einen

Sohn hatte. Uebrigens sind nicht alle solche Fälle sagenhaft oder alt. Viele Autoren beschreiben ähnliche Fälle. Ich habe eine ganze Reihe solcher Anomalien gesehen. Doch ist es charakteristisch für die meisten gut beobachteten Fälle, dass die Zähne, welche den Neugebornen verunzieren, kleiner und weicher sind als die normal entwickelten, dass sie nicht in der Knochenfalte, sondern im Zahnfleisch eingebettet sind, dass sie leicht ausfallen oder ausgezogen und späterhin nicht selten durch andere hinfällige Zähne ersetzt werden.

Eine andere Anomalie besteht darin, dass die Zähne, statt in einer, in zwei oder gar drei Reihen gepflanzt sind. Ein Sohn des Mithridates soll zwei, Herkules drei solcher Zahnreihen besessen haben. Arnold kannte ein Kind von vierzehn Jahren, das zweiundsiebzig Zähne hatte. Von ihnen staken sechsunddreissig in jedem Kiefer und zwar in je zwei Reihen. Bartholin erzählt von Ludwig XIII. von Frankreich, dass derselbe drei Reihen von Zähnen besessen habe.

Statt zu früh, oder zur rechten Zeit zu erscheinen, kommen die ersten Zähne bisweilen spät. Gewöhnlich ist das so bei krankhafter oder zurückbleibender Entwicklung ; die Kinder, welche an der englischen Krankheit (Rhachitis, doppelten Gliedern) leiden, zeichnen sich in der Regel durch Verspätung des Zahndurchbruchs aus. Dass solche Kinder den ersten Zahn mit zehn oder vierzehn Monaten bekommen, ist häufig. Doch kannte Van Swieten ein Kind, das bei sonst gut ausgebildeter Knochenform, den ersten Zahn im Alter von neunzehn Monaten bekam. Rayger erzählte den

Fall eines Mädchens, das im Alter von dreizehn Jahren seine ersten Eckzähne hatte; Fauchard beobachtete ein Kind, das nur einige wenige Schneidezähne hatte, als es fünf oder sechs Jahre alt war. Brouzet berichtet von einem Kinde, das im Alter von zwölf Jahren nur die Hälfte seiner Normalzahl an Zähnen hatte und dessen halber Kieferrand so hart war wie bei alten Leuten. Dugès sah den ersten Zahn im elften, Smellie im einundzwanzigsten Jahr durchbrechen. Solcher ausnahmsweiser Verspätungen gibt es noch manche in der Literatur, ich habe viele davon in einem Kursus von Vorlesungen vor fünfundzwanzig Jahren veröffentlicht. Zu jener Zeit hatte ich ein Kind in Beobachtung, welches im Alter von zwei Jahren und zehn Monaten noch keinen Zahn und keine Andeutung eines solchen hatte. Ein anderes Kind von zwei Jahren ist mir unter ähnlichen Verhältnissen im Jahre 1859 oder 1860 vorgekommen. Sein Fall ist im Register des Deutschen Dispensary aus jener Zeit verzeichnet.

Die Verspätung des Zahndurchbruchs kann am besten durch ungenügende Keimbildung oder durch Entzündung und Verhärtung des Kieferrandes erklärt werden. Diese Ursachen können zu vollständiger Abwesenheit der Zähne führen. Botallus kannte eine Frau von sechzig Jahren, welche nie Zähne hatte. Auch Valla und Baumès haben solche Fälle verzeichnet.

Ungenügende Zahl der Zähne ist wohl öfter beobachtet, abgesehen von Fällen, in welchen zu frühes Ausziehen der Milchzähne den Kieferraum beengte, nämlich wo von Anfang an die Zahl der

Zähne zu klein war. Gelegentlich fehlen die Eckzähne, gelegentlich einige der mittleren Schneidezähne.

Im Zusammenhange damit lassen Sie mich einer
Anomalie Erwähnung thun, welche freilich ziemlich zweifelhaften Charakters ist. Charakteristisch
für viele Erzählungen von wunderbaren Naturereig-
nissen ist im Allgemeinen, dass sie aus frühen Jahrhunderten oder aus fernen Gegenden stammen.
Wenn ein wahrheitsgetreuer Bericht in unseren
Zeitungen über eine Fünfgeburt oder über den bekannten, in einer Nacht auf dem halben Körper
weiss-angelaufenen Neger erscheint, so ist das
immer dreissig Meilen hinter einem entlegenen Post-
office in Nebraska oder in einem Weiler auf der
Grenze von Arkansas und Louisiana passirt. Wie
stark die Tendenz der Wunderbarkeiten, Monstrosi-
täten und Halb- oder Ganzunmöglichkeiten ist,
vor einigen hundert Jahren passirt zu sein, davon
hätte ich Ihnen gern mündliche und bildliche Beispiele gegeben. Die Kürze der Zeit allein hält mich
davon ab. Aus dem Bereich der Zahnanomalien
berichten Plutarch und Valerius Maximus, dass
Pyrrhus, der König von Epirus, und ein Sohn des
Prusias von Bithynien nur einen Knochen in jedem
Kiefer hatten, statt der richtigen Anzahl ; und Ber-
nard Jengha war, so sagt man, im Besitz eines
Schädels, dessen (allein erhaltener) Oberkiefer statt
der sechzehn Zähne drei Zahnabtheilungen hatte :
die mittlere umfasste die Schneidezähne und Eckzähne. Vielleicht aber handelte es sich in allen
diesen Fällen nur um Inkrustation mit harten Kalk-
massen. Das mag eine prosaische Erklärung sein

und daher nicht gefallen. Ich will daher noch einen wahrheitsgetreuen Bericht mittheilen, den ich einem—allerdings seit einiger Zeit verblichenen —Kollegen verdanke. Derselbe hiess Jacobus Horstius und würde heute Jakob Horst heissen. Er schrieb im Jahre 1595 ein Buch mit dem folgenden Titel : "Ueber den goldenen Kieferzahn eines schlesischen Knaben ; erstens, ob seine Erzeugung mit natürlichen Dingen zuging ; zweitens, ob man im Stande ist, eine würdige Erklärung davon zu geben." Es versteht sich von selber, dass die Erzeugung dieses goldenen Zahnes mit natürlichen Dingen zuging und dass die Erklärung dieser Merkwürdigkeit eine höchst würdige war. Daher schliesst das Buch folgendermassen : "Es ist nun unsere Aufgabe, den Zorn Gottes durch glühende Bitten und ernsthafte Reumüthigkeit zu beugen, die Jahre der Tribulation abzukürzen und also das goldene Reich und die Wirkung des goldenen Zahnes schneller herabzuflehen."

Schon damals, wie Sie sehen, gab es Leute, denen die Zähne, Zahnung und Zahntheorien zu Kopfe stiegen.

Neben der ersten und zweiten Zahnung werden auch Fälle von dritter Zahnung erzählt. Selten wird der Anspruch erhoben, dass diese dritte Zahnung sich auf alle oder die meisten Zähne erstreckt. W. Jackson hat einen Fall bei einem Manne von vierundsechzig und bei einer Frau von achtzig Jahren, in welchem die Schneidezähne sich zum drittenmal erzeugten, und zwar ohne Hülfe des Zahnarztes. Sorgoni erzählt, dass ein Knabe zum drittenmal zahnte, als er zwölf Jahre alt war, und ein Dutzend solcher Vorkommnisse werden von Andral berichtet. Storch, der sich in seinen Schriften Pelargus nennt, erzählt von einer siebzigjährigen Dame, dass sie einen neuen Schneidezahn bekam. Seine eigene Tochter habe in ihrem zwanzigsten Jahre fünf Backenzähne erhalten. Dieselben fielen bald aus und wurden in ihrem achtunddreissigsten Jahre von Neuem ersetzt. An diesem Zahnen litt sie, so wird erzählt, jedesmal und recht lange. Was man aber aus der Beschreibung ihrer Zustände entnehmen kann, waren hysterische Beschwerden und nichts weiter. Paulinus hat den Fall einer Gräfin von Detmond, welche im Jahre 1589 zum drittenmal zahnte und hundertvierzig Jahre alt wurde. Cardanus, der berühmte Mathematiker, soll einen Zahn mit dreiundvierzig Jahren bekommen haben. Aus dem Jahre 1725 wird von einer sechsundsechzigjährigen Frau erzählt, welche einen neuen Zahn bekam und ihr weisses Haar gegen braunes auswechselte. Was Sie aber am meisten überraschen wird, ist die Erzählung von Möllenbroc, der vor 170 Jahren schrieb : '' Eine Leipziger Edeldame hatte fünf Kinder. Mit der Geburt eines jeden Kindes bekam sie einen Backenzahn. Wenn einer der neuen Zähne sich lockerte, wurde das zur Zeit des Durchbruchs des betreffenden Zahnes geborene Kind schwer krank. Wenn der Zahn ausfiel, starb das Kind.'' Der ehrliche Autor fügt hinzu, dass alle Kinder vor der Mutter starben. So sehen Sie also, dass, während man heutzutage den Kindern nachsagt, dass sie an ihrem eigenen Zahnen zu Grunde gehen, es vor einigen hundert Jahren passiren konnte, dass sie an den Zähnen anderer Leute starben.

Viele von diesen Fällen sind ohne Zweifel ausge-
schmückt und erdichtet. Die Phantasie alter Autoren war oft so lebhaft, wie diejenige des heutigen
Publikums. Aber ohne Zweifel ist etwas Wahres
an vielen solcher Geschichten. Das Wahre daran
ist, dass, wenn im hohem Alter ein solcher Zahn
durchbricht, derselbe niemals vorhanden gewesen
ist, oder nur deshalb nicht sichtbar wurde, weil der
Kieferknochen ihn nicht durchliess. Sobald dann
in vorrückendem Alter der Kieferknochen und sein
Rand, dem gewöhnlichen Laufe der Dinge nach,
langsam abschwoll und sich verdünnte, oder an der
entsprechenden Stelle ganz verschwand, kam der
Zahn zum Vorschein.

Das Beispiel der Leipziger Dame gibt uns zu denken. Es erinnert uns an die Häufigkeit, mit welcher dem natürlichen und normalen Durchbruch
der Zähne auch in heutiger Zeit die Verursachung
aller möglichen Krankheiten in die Schuhe gescho-
ben wird. Nicht blos Unregelmässigkeit in der
Mundhöhle, und Krankheiten des Nahrungskanals,
Magen- und Darmkrankheiten, werden dem Zahnen als direkte Folge fälschlich zugeschrieben, sondern Lungenkrankheiten, Hirn- und Nervenkrank-
heiten, Gelenksentzündungen, Blutvergiftungen,
englische Krankheit. Die Kinder, so erzählen sich
die Gevatterinnen aller Geschlechter, zahnen durch
den Kopf, durch die Glieder, durch die Brust,
durch die Haut. Ist ein Kind voll von Ausschlägen—es zahnt; hustet es Monate lang zum Erbar-
men, bis es an Schwindsucht zu Grunde geht—es
zahnt ja; hat es Fieber, das es aufzehrt oder in
Convulsionen versetzt—es zahnt; schwillt ihm der

Bauch auf von Kaffee und Bananen—es zahnt;
werden die Augen starr und zucken die Wangen—
es zahnt; schwellen die Gelenke rheumatisch—es
zahnt. Verdicken sich die Knochenenden, und
werden die Unterschenkel so krumm, dass das
arme Ding wackelt wie eine Ente und das Haus-
hündschen hindurchspringen kann, das Kind zahnt.
Erbricht es, es zahnt. Leidet es an Verstopfung,
es zahnt—an Durchfall, es zahnt. Stirbt es, es ist
am Zahnen gestorben. Es gibt gar keine noch so
schwere Krankheitsepidemien, welche nicht im
Laufe der Zeit sich erschöpfen. Der schwarze Tod
und die Pest, Cholera und Schweissfriesel sind aus-
gestorben; selbst die Epidemien von Scharlach
und Diphtherie mässigen sich und sterben aus.
Was aber nicht sterben will, das ist der epidemi-
sche Glauben an die Gefährlichkeit des Zahnens und
die Häufigkeit schweren Erkrankens und Sterbens
von einem normalen Vorgang, wie das Zahnen ist.
Was vor Jahrhunderten von den Aerzten damaliger
Zeit geglaubt und gelehrt wurde, hat sich als Volks-
glaube bis in unsere Zeit fortgesetzt. Vergessen
wir freilich nicht, dass jene alten Aerzte eine Entschuldigung in der Thatsache hatten, dass das Erkennen der wirklichen Krankheit, an welcher das
Kind litt, sehr schwer war. Leichenöffnungen
hatte man nicht gemacht, und die Hülfsmittel zum
Erkennen des Uebels waren nicht gefunden. Die
Hülfslosigkeit war allgemein, und wenn es kein La-
tein gegeben hätte, und keine Allongenperücken,
und keine Stöcke mit silbernen Knöpfen, so hätte
sich der Doktor schwerlich von Seinesgleichen im
Publikum unterschieden. Heute ist das ein wenig

anders geworden. Der Doktor putzt sich nicht
mehr heraus wie ein Feldmarschall, oder ein Kardinal, oder ein Freimaurer, oder ein Milizneger mit
dem Limonadekessel, er macht aber eine Diagnose,
und das ist auch etwas werth—oder man kann
es doch von ihm verlangen. Ich wünschte sehr,
Sie, die Sie Gelegenheit haben werden, würden es
immer von ihm verlangen. Als einer von der Brü-
derschaft gebe ich Ihnen den ganz bestimmten
Rath, dass, wenn Ihnen Jemand einmal sagt, in
Uebereinstimmung mit Ihrer Nachbarin, dass Ihr
Kind am Zahnen erkrankt ist, Sie sich einen andern
Heilkünstler suchen ; es gibt wirklich schon viele
Aerzte, welche sich ihre Diagnose nicht mehr von
den Hausfreundinnen machen lassen, sondern ihre
eignen Augen und Ohren zur Verwerthung ihrer
Kenntnisse gebrauchen ; und wenn Sie so einen
treffen—und das ist glücklicherweise nicht mehr so
schwer—so kann es allerdings vorkommen, dass gelegentlich auch ein entzündetes Zahnfleisch Beschwerden macht, oder dass besagter Doktor in
seiner ganzen Praxis alle fünf Jahr einmal ein
Zahnfleisch *schneidet*, aber es kann doch nicht passiren, dass der Herr die Kinder an den Zähnen zu
sich nimmt, wie ich das in Zeitungsanzeigen wohl
gelesen habe. Vor allen Dingen wird Ihnen der
Arzt sagen können, dass das Zahnen ein langsam
fortschreitender natürlicher Vorgang ist, welcher
wegen seiner Langsamkeit die Aufsaugung des über
dem Zahn gelegenen festen Gewebes schmerzlos
und gefahrlos besorgt. Was möglich ist, ist ein
mässiger Reiz und ein Jucken, das vom Kleinen mit
Drücken und Fingerkauen beantwortet wird. Der

dauernde Speichelfluss ist nicht die Folge des Zahnens, sondern die Folge der schnellen Entwicklung der Drüsen, die unter dem Einfluss des regen Blutlaufes vor sich geht, welcher zu gleicher Zeit Drüsen, Schädel, Hirn und Zähne mit reichlichem Ernährungsmaterial versieht. Was gegen die Theorie des gefährlichen Drucks von vorn herein spricht, ist die Thatsache, dass das Zahnfleisch über dem wachsenden Zahn nicht von unten herauf eingedrückt wird, sondern schliesslich von oben her zerfällt, wie Sie sich oft leicht an der kleinen länglichen Rinne oberhalb des noch begrabenen Zahnes überzeugen können; und ferner die glücklicherweise sehr gewöhnliche Thatsache, dass die Zähne ohne alle Beschwerden zu Tage treten und dadurch Ueberraschung bereiten. Allerdings gibt es einzelne Kinder, wie es Erwachsene gibt, bei denen das Nervensystem durch die geringste Abweichung oder Störung in krankhafte Spannung versetzt wird. Ausnahmen stossen aber niemals eine Regel um.

Das Längenwachsthum des Körpers hängt vom Wachsthum der Knochen ab. Nach ihnen richten sich die Weichtheile, welche der Längenausdehnung der Knochen wohl oder übel zu folgen haben. Die Weise des Knochenwachsthums glaube ich in einigen wenigen Worten deutlich machen zu können. Jeder Knochen steckt in einer Haut, der sog. Knochenhaut, welche sich demselben mehr oder weniger fest anlegt. In ihr verlaufen die grosse Mehrzahl der Blut- und Lymphgefässe. Im Kinde ist sie weicher und blutreicher, im Erwachsenen ist sie härter und straffer. Immer aber gibt sie das Ernährungsmaterial für den Knochen. Dieser bil-

det sich von seiner Umgebungshaut aus, neues Material wird von aussen gebildet und auf dem
Knochen abgelagert, das alte Knochenmaterial wird
in der Markhöhle aufgesogen und aus dem Körper
entfernt. So wird die Markhöhle bei dem zunehmenden Wachsthum allmählig grösser; wenn
man einem jungen Thiere um den dünnen Knochen
einen Metallring legt, findet sich derselbe in späterem Alter, nachdem der Knochen dicker geworden,
in der Markhöhle lose liegend wieder. Die Fähigkeit der Knochenhaut, Knochen zu bilden, ist recht
auffallend. Wenn auf operativem Wege oder durch
Krankheiten Knochen verloren gehen, ist man vor-
sichtig darauf bedacht, die Knochenhaut zu scho-
den, damit neuer Knochen von ihr aus gebildet
werde. Ganze Knochen werden auf diese Weise
wieder gebildet. Nach dem, was ich gesagt habe,
begreift man also leicht, wie der Knochen an Dicke
zunimmt.

Anderes verhält es sich mit dem Längenwachsthum. Die langen Gliederknochen werden anatomisch in mehrere Theile zerlegt, in zwei Endstücke und ein Mittelstück. Die Endstücke sind
rundlich, aufgewulstet und in die Gelenke einge-
passt, die Mittelstücke sind lang. Zwischen End-
stück und Mittelstück liegt eine Knorpelschicht, die
sich langsam in Knochen umwandelt, und zwar an
dem Ende des Mittelstücks. Während also neues
Material sich an das Mittelstück anlegt und dieses
dadurch länger wird, bildet sich die Knorpelschicht
an der Endstückseite immer wieder von neuem, und
dieser Vorgang wiederholt sich, bis nach fünfzehn,
zwanzig oder fünfundzwanzig Jahren alle den lan-

gen Knochen bildenden Theile hart geworden, ver-
knöchert sind und den gleichförmig gefügten
Knochen ausmachen. Von der Regsamkeit der
Knorpelbildung und dem Umsatz der Knorpelschicht
in Knochen hängt also das Längenwachsthum des
Knochens und das Längenwachsthum des ganzen
Körpers ab.

Natürlich hängt dieser Vorgang mit der Ausbildung der Blutgefässe in den betreffenden Theilen
zusammen. Die grössere oder geringere Ernährung hängt von der Blutzufuhr ab, deren Arbeit
unter gewöhnlichen Verhältnissen nicht bemerkt
wird. Die Normalarbeit aller Gewebe und Organe
geht unbemerkt und ohne Störung vorüber. Ath-
men, Verdauen, Wachsen dürfen, so lange Alles
gesund ist, keinen Misston, keinen Schmerz hervorrufen. Unter normalen Verhältnissen gehen auch
alle Verrichtungen gleichmässig und ohne Sprünge
vor sich.

Doch kommen solche Sprünge und solche Störungen vor. Es gibt gewisse Krankheiten des Körpers
im Allgemeinen, welche die Blutbewegung und besonders die Saftströmung im Zell- und Knorpel-
gewebe besonders beeinflussen. Solche Krankheiten sind vorzugsweise die Ausschlags- und infektiö-
sen Fieber. Die Zunahme der Körperlänge nach
solchen Fiebern ist bisweilen ganz auffallend, sie
ist mehr als Einbildung, sie ist wirklich vorhanden.
Sie ist die Folge davon, dass während und bald nach
diesen Krankheiten, wie Typhus, Scharlach, sogar
Keuchhusten, die Knorpel der langen Knochen mit
übermässig viel Ernährungsmaterial versehen werden. Diese plötzliche Zunahme der Zufuhr gibt sich

häufig durch unangenehme Empfindungen, Schmerzen, sog. Wachsschmerzen zu erkennen.

Dieser Zustand findet sich aber nicht blos nach solchen Krankheiten, sondern nicht selten auch ohne dieselben. Das geht folgendermassen zu. Wenn der Knochen wachsen soll, so ist vermehrte Blutzufuhr nöthig. Diese normale Blutfülle wird nicht selten zu abnormer Blutüberfüllung, in derselben Weise, wie z. B. bei dem in früher Kindheit rasch wachsenden Kopf und Gesicht die nothwendige Blutzufuhr zur Ueberfülle wird und zu dem Auftreten von Ausschlägen Veranlassung gibt. Diese übermässige Blutzufuhr an dem Wachsknorpel der Knochen nun führt gelegentlich zu Schmerz, in sehr seltenen Fällen sogar zu wirklicher Entzündung und gefährlicher Eiterung. Nicht immer also soll man sich darauf verlassen, dass dieser Wachsschmerz etwas Natürliches und Unbedeutendes ist, das vorübergeht. Es ist immer abnorm und soll als solcher betrachtet und behandelt werden.

Vielleicht ist es gut, eine Nebenbemerkung hier einzuschalten, welche manchem oder mancher von Ihnen nützlich werden kann. Die Schmerzen, welche als Wachsschmerzen angesehen werden, sind nicht immer von der beschriebenen Art. Es gibt in der Gegend der Gelenke noch andere Schmerzen und anderer Natur. Es kommen wirkliche Neuralgien in der Gegend der Gelenke auch bei Kindern vor, mit oder ohne leichte Geschwulst, welche mit den sog. Wachsschmerzen oft verwechselt werden. Von viel grösserer Wichtigkeit aber ist das Vorkommen von wirklichem Gelenkrheumatismus bei ganz kleinen oder grösseren Kindern. Diese Fälle sind häufig und gefährlich. Selbst der leichteste Gelenkrheumatismus eines Kindes, kaum oder gar nicht durch heftigen Schmerz oder Geschwulst kenntlich, vielleicht kaum zu gelindem zeitweiligem Hinken Veranlassung gebend, gibt zu Herzerkrankung und lebenslänglichem Siechthum Veranlassung. Somit ist das, was als Wachsschmerz betrachtet, gering geschätzt und vernachlässigt wird, durchaus nichts Gleichgültiges. Jeder Schmerz der Art soll der Mutter so wichtig sein, wie dem Seemann das geringste Schwanken des Barometerstandes.

Das Blutgefässsystem macht einen eigenthümlichen Entwicklungsgang durch. Sie wissen, dass es aus verschiedenen Theilen zusammengesetzt ist. Sein Mittelpunkt ist in allen Menschen, nicht blos bei jungen Mädchen, das Herz. Von ihm aus wird das Blut durch grosse und allmählig sich verzweigende, kleinere und kleinste Schlagadern in den Körper geführt, um von dort aus in tausend Kanälchen und Kanälen zum Herzen zurückzukehren; diese letzteren nennt man Venen, oder Blutadern. Zwischen den Schlagadern und Blutadern liegen die endlosen Netze dünnwandiger Haargefässe, durch welche sämmtliches Blut zu laufen hat, um in direkte Verbindung mit allen Organtheilen und Geweben des Körpers zu kommen; auf diese Weise werden die letzteren ernährt. Somit ist die gesammte Ernährung des Körpers in gleich wichtiger Weise, sowohl von der Beschaffenheit des Blutes, wie auch derjenigen seiner Kanäle abhängig. Nun verändert sich der Bau der Gefässe im Laufe ihres

14*

Wachsthums ganz ausserordentlich. Die Blutgefässe des Neugebornen und ganz kleiner Kinder
sind sehr dünn und zerreisslich, die drei oder mehr
Schichten, aus denen ihre Wände bestehen, sind
schwach entwickelt und daher sind Blutungen zum
Theil gefährlicher Art, auch in lebenswichtigen
Organen, wie Gehirn und Rückenmark, gar nicht
selten. Allmählig setzen sich die locker gefügten
Zellen der Gefässwand in Fasern um, die Fasern
vermehren und verdichten sich, die Wände werden
widerstandsfähiger. Aber dieser Vorgang hat nicht
blos Segensreiches, sondern auch Nachtheiliges im
Gefolge. Wie wachsen nämlich die Wände der
Blutgefässe?

Wie Sie an dem Gefässmittelpunkte, dem Herzen, wahrnehmen, dass seine Oberfläche von zahlreichen Gefässen bedeckt ist und sein Fleisch von
Kreuz- und Querlagen von Gefässen durchzogen
ist, so ist das auch in kleinerem Masse bei den
Blutgefässen der Fall. Wie in Ihrer Haut und
Ihrer Muskulatur, wie in Ihrem Hirn und Ihren
Gliedern, so hängt das Wachsthum und die Entwicklung Ihres Herzens und Ihrer Blutgefässver-
änderungen von dem Blutlauf in Gefässen ab, welche
das Herz und die Blutgefässe selber ernähren
müssen. Diese sehr kleinen Aederchen in den
Wandungen der Gefässröhren werden nun einfach
Gefässe der Gefässe genannt. Nun denken Sie
sich die folgende Thatsache: Die kindlichen Blutgefässe, locker gebaut, lose gefügt, werden durch ihre
eigenen Gefässe ernährt. Diese Ernährung ist er-
folgreich. Das lockere Gefüge wird kräftiger,
dichter, härter. Durch diese zunehmende Ver-

dichtung werden allmählig im Laufe der Jahre jene
in der Wand laufenden Ernährungs-Gefässchen zu-
sammengedrückt, und der Dienst, welchen dieselben der Entwicklung und Verdichtung der Gefässwand geleistet haben, wird dadurch belohnt,
dass sie von der festen Wand allmählig strangulirt
werden. Undank ist der Welt Lohn, aber die
Rache ist süss. Wenn nun diese Ernährungsge-
fässe strangulirt sind, oder allmählig strangulirt
werden, so werden sie dadurch gerächt, dass sie
ihre frühere Thätigkeit nicht mehr ganz besorgen
können, also die Wände der Gefässe leiden Schaden.
Von da an wird das Wachsthum zum Fluch. Die
Wände der Blutgefässe sind, vom Ende des normalen Wachsthums angefangen, Veränderungen
ausgesetzt, welche, anfangs unbemerkt, schliesslich
sehr gefährlich werden können, werden müssen.
Man kann sagen, dass nach vollendeter normaler
aufsteigender Entwicklung die niedersteigende
Entwicklung beginnt. Um die Mitte der Dreis-
siger Jahre schon ist ihr Anfang. Wie der
Wanderer langsam und stetig die Höhe erreicht,
eine kurze Zeit auf der Kuppe hinwandelt, und
seine Reise ihn unaufhaltsam abwärts führt, so
führt der normale Gang der Entwicklung der Blutgefässe erst zur allmähligen Reife und nothwendig
zur Ueberreife und zum endlichen Verfall. Das
letzte Resultat dieser Veränderungen in den Blutgefässen der Alten ist höchst charakteristisch. Sie
werden straffer, härter, steifer, sie verknöchern an
einzelnen Stellen ; die kleinsten Schlagadern, wenn
so der allmähligen Altersentwicklung unterliegend,
sind die Ursachen von lebensgefährlichen Krank-

heiten. Schon in den Vierziger Jahren entwickeln
sich Störungen von gewaltiger Tragweite. Die
s. g. Bright'sche Entartung der Nieren ist oft um
diese Lebenszeit die Folge der Veränderungen,
welche sich normal in der Richtung des Krankhaften in den Blutgefässen ergeben. Die häufigen
Apoplexien des vorgerückten Lebensalters sind die
Folge der zunehmenden Verhärtung und Brüchig-
keit der Gefässe. So ist es derselbe Entwicklungsgang, dasselbe Wachsthum in den Gefässwänden,
welches in derselben Weise erst zur Bethätigung
der regsten Lebensentfaltung, und schliesslich zur
Vernichtung des Einzellebens führt. Derselbe Entwicklungsgang, welcher die Spannkraft des Knaben
erhöht, die Jugendblüthe auf die Wangen der Jung-
frau zaubert, die Federkraft in die Muskeln des
jungen Helden giesst, und die gestählte Mannes-
kraft des mittleren Alters schafft, führt langsam
aber sicher zur schliesslichen Abnahme der Kraft,
zur gradweisen Auflösung der Organe, oder zur
plötzlichen Zerstörung des Individuums. So ist die
letzte Entwicklung der Lebensenergie, von mittleren Lebensalter angefangen, das endliche Sterben,
der Tod.

Die Weitschichtigkeit des Thema's, über welches
ich die Ehre gehabt habe zu Ihnen zu reden, verhin-
derte mich—ich weiss das wohl—demselben in genügender Weise gerecht zu werden. Die Nothwendigkeit, mancherlei in die Spanne einer Stunde
zu drängen, lässt obendrein manches Gesagte frag-
mentarisch erscheinen. Aber ich habe mir gedacht, dass Sie über einen höchst interessanten
Gegenstand gern einmal so viel hören würden, als

sich in aller Kürze mittheilen lässt. Ueberdies lassen sich an denselben so viele Nutzanwendungen knüpfen, dass gerade dieser Gegenstand augenfällig einer von denjenigen vielen ist, in dessen Betrachtung sich Theorie und Praxis, Wissen und Anwendung, unmittelbar vereinigen.

FEUILLETON

I.

Um dem deutschen Arzte das Verständniss der
Ursachen, welche die Verwirrung in den Angelegenheiten des Internationalen Congresses hervorgebracht haben, zu ermöglichen, erlaube ich mir
zunächst das Wort zu einigen einleitenden Bemerkungen über das Wesen amerikanischer ärztlicher
Gesellschaften. Dieselben sind in zwei verschiedenen Weisen zusammengesetzt. Es giebt eine
Klasse, welche streng ärztlich, eine zweite, welche
ärztlich politisch ist.
Die erste Klasse trägt den Charakter der ärztlichen Gesellschaften der ganzen Welt. Aerzte
finden sich zum Zweck wissenschaftlicher Discussionen, Mittheilungen, Vorträge zusammen und or-
ganisiren sich zu dem Zwecke zu loseren oder festeren Verbänden. Vereinigungen dieser Art sind
bei uns sehr zahlreich. In den grossen Städten
giebt es eine stattliche Liste von grösseren und
kleineren Gesellschaften der Art ; die letzteren
sind meist spezialistischer Natur, wie die geburts-
hülfliche, laryngologische, orthopädische, ophthalmologische, dermatologische u. s. w. Gesellschaft.
In New York hat auch die Academie der Medicin,

eine ausschliesslich wissenschaftliche Vereinigung,
denselben Zwecken durch die Gründung von Sec-
tionen Rechnung getragen. Die zweite Klasse von ärztlichen Verbänden sind
nur zum Theil wissenschaftlicher Natur. Bis zu
einem gewissen Grade sind sie politisch und stehen
in einem festeren oder lockereren Verhältniss zum
politischen Leben, zu den Legislaturen der einzelnen Staaten. Die Vereinigten Staaten sind ein
Staatenbund, der erst seit zwei Jahrzehnten sich zu
einem Bundesstaat langsam umgestaltet hat. In
diesem Staatenbunde sind die einzelnen Staaten
souverän, aber ihre Gliederung, Verwaltung und
ihre ärztlichen Angelegenheiten sind in allen ziemlich gleich. Ich will daher an dem Staate New
York ein Paradigma dessen aufstellen, was mehr
oder weniger genau sich in jedem anderen Staate
wiederholt.

Bis lange nach der Annahme der Constitution,
vor beinahe einem Jahrhundert, gab es keine medicinischen Schulen. Die Aerzte waren in kleiner
Zahl Schüler englischer Anstalten, oder älterer
Aerzte, oder Autodidacten, oder Schwindler. Die
besseren Kräfte fanden sich in Vereinen zusammen, zu gegenseitiger Belehrung, zu gegenseitigem
Schutz und demjenigen des Publikums. Bei den
Legislaturen ihrer Staaten kamen sie um die Ge-
nehmigung ihrer Statuten ein und wurden sofort
mit gewissen Gerechtsamen versehen, welche vorzugsweise darin bestanden, dass der Mann, welcher
Medicin zu practisiren beabsichtigte, von dieser
staatlich gewordenen "State Medical Society" eine
Licenz durch abgelegte Prüfung erwerben musste.

Im Laufe der Jahrzehnte sind in allen Staaten
diese Gerechtsame verändert, erweitert, oder be-
schränkt worden ; in vielen Staaten ist die Erlaubniss zur Ausübung der Praxis nicht mehr von einer
Licenz der State Society abhängig, sondern ist mit
der Erwerbung eines Diploms von einer der ent-
setzlich vielen gesetzlich befugten medicinischen
Schulen identisch. Aber der Charakter der State
Society als politisch-ärztlicher Körper ist nicht verändert. Die erste staatliche Gesellschaft wurde in
dieser Weise in New Jersey gegründet, die zweite
in Massachusetts. Ihnen folgte Pennsylvania und
New York (1806).

Die "Medical Society of the State of New York"
war also eine freie Vereinigung, welche legalisirt
wurde und politische Gerechtsame erhielt. Ihre
Versammlungen waren jährlich, mit manchen Un-
terbrechungen. Denn das Reisen war schwer, die
Entfernungen gross, die Aerzte zum Theil arm.
Aber die Verhältnisse wurden besser, die Bevölkerung dichter, die Zahl der Praktiker grösser. In
den bevölkerten Counties (Districten) bildeten sich
lokale Gesellschaften, auf welche manche der Gerechtsame der State Society, unter der Oberhoheit
dieser letzteren, übergingen. Schliesslich bildete
sich eine County Medical Society in jedem County des
Staates, und die State Medical Society bildete sich
allmählig in eine jährliche Versammlung von Delegirten der zahlreichen County Medical Societies
um, welche in einem gewissen Abhängigkeitsver-
hältnisse zu der ersten standen. Erst nach längerer Dienstzeit wird ein Delegirter möglicherweise
—durch Wahl—permanentes Mitglied der ersteren.

Aus diesen permanenten Mitgliedern werden ihre
Beamten gewählt. Die County Societies versam-
meln sich meist monatlich, in den dünnbevölkerten
Districten in längeren Zwischenräumen, die State
Society hat eine jährliche Sitzung von drei Tagen
im Februar im Regierungssitze, Albany. Diese
drei Tage sind wissenschaftlichen Arbeiten und der
Politik der Standesinteressen und Standespolizei
gewidmet. Gesetzesvorlagen werden direkt der
Legislatur des Staates, welche zu gleicher Zeit ihre
Sitzungen hält, übermacht. Diese Gliederung,
diese hierarchische Abstufung zwischen State
Society und County Societies wiederholt sich in
jedem Staate, in den meisten Staaten auch die ge-
setzliche Bestimmung, welche im Staate New York
noch vor ganz kurzer Zeit gültig war, dass nämlich
kein Arzt zu practisiren berechtigt war, der nicht
Mitglied der Medical Society seines County und damit Angehöriger (nicht Mitglied) der Staatsgesellschaft geworden war. Somit gab (giebt) es allerdings eine Gesellschaft, welche als der wirkliche
Repräsentant des ärztlichen Standes aufgefasst
werden musste, und zwar aus dem Grunde, weil
jeder Arzt gesetzlich zu ihr oder einer der unterge-
benen Gesellschaften gehören musste, nämlich die
Staatsgesellschaft (Medical Society of the State of
New York). Und dasselbe gilt, oder galt, für jeden
einzelnen Staat.

Allmählig wuchs die Zahl der Aerzte, der
Staaten, der Schulen und Anstalten. In New York
und Philadelphia regte sich das Bedürfniss einer
grösseren Vereinigung. So entstand im Jahre 1846
und 1847 die American Medical Association. Die-

selbe konnte und kann nicht dasselbe Verhältniss
zu der Regierung der Vereinigten Staaten haben,
welches die State Societies in ihren Staaten einnehmen. Denn die Centralisirung und Oberhoheit,
welche ein Staat für sein spezielles Gebiet besitzt,
existirt nicht in der Unionsregierung für die Union.
Die Staaten sind souverän, jeder in seiner Weise,
und die Unionsregierung kümmerte und kümmert
sich nicht um die ärztlichen Angelegenheiten,
welche von jedem Staate für seine Staatsangehöri-
gen geregelt werden. Daher war von vorn herein
von einer gezwungenen Mitgliedschaft, von einer
Oberherrlichkeit in der Association nicht die Rede,
und ist es heute noch weniger. Sie besteht aus
Delegirten von Gesellschaften (staatlich anerkannten und losen wissenschaftlichen) und Schulen, und
aus Privaten. Jeder Anwesende ist von dem Mo-
mente an "permanentes" Mitglied und wird, willig
oder nicht, todt oder lebendig, in den Listen weiterge-
führt. Vor einiger Zeit erschien so eine Liste von
über vier tausend Namen. Weshalb ihre Wort-
führer nun von fünfzig bis sechszig Tausend reden,
wäre unerfindlich, wenn es nicht seinen guten
Grund hätte, der später klar werden wird. Bis zu
einem gewissen Grade hat die Association ihren
politischen Charakter beibehalten; d. h. Comités
werden am liebsten territorial zusammengesetzt,
das Präsidium wechselt geographisch, der Versammlungsort ebenso, so dass San Francisco, New
Orleans, St. Paul, Boston, Atlanta u. s. w. die
jährlichen Versammlungen beherbergen mussten.
Die grossen Entfernungen machen nun eine rege
Betheiligung von allen Gegenden unmöglich;

Aerzte reisen nicht immer tausende von Meilen und wenden Wochen ihrer Zeit auf, um geringfügiger Resultate willen. So wechselt das Personal der American Medical Association aus territorialen Gründen. Vor einigen Monaten waren daher in New Orleans die Theilnehmer aus Texas und dem Mississippi- und Ohiothal in der Majorität. Nur Eines ist sich in diesen fast vierzig Jahren gleichgeblieben, nämlich das regelmässige jährliche Erscheinen einiger weniger alter Herren auf der Tribüne. Aber noch Eines ist unverändert, wovon sich Jeder überzeugen kann, welcher alte und neue Journale vergleichen will. Klagen über Rangstreitigkeiten, Personalien, ethische Punkte, füllen die alten wie die neuen. Dieselben Musiker und dieselbe Musik. Daher ist es gekommen, dass im Laufe der Jahre der Besuch der jährlichen Wanderversammlungen abgenommen hat, sich eine grosse Anzahl von Spezialwanderversammlungen (chirurgische, augenärztliche und ohrenärztliche, hautärztliche, weiberärztliche u. s. w.) gebildet haben, und die Bedeutung der gedruckten Verhandlungen der Association der Dickleibigkeit der Bände nicht das Gleichgewicht hält. Soviel steht nach dem Obengesagten fest, dass die American Medical Association in keiner Weise die allumfassende Repräsentation des ärztlichen Standes der Vereinigten Staaten ist oder war ; weder gesetzlich, noch factisch.

Natürlich kann nicht geleugnet werden, dass die American Medical Association einen Theil des Guten, dass jede Wanderversammlung schafft, auch hier hervorgebracht hat ; aber abgesehen von den durch Entfernungen u. s. w. erzeugten Schwie-

rigkeiten hat sie zu vielerlei thun wollen, und ist
dabei zu viel menagirt worden, hat keine weiten
einfachen Ziele gehabt, und ihre Zusammensetzung
war zu bunt. Daran zerbröckelt sie.

An dieser Stelle kann ich nicht auf Einzelheiten
eingehen. Aber die Aufgabe, welche ich mir gestellt habe, verlangt die Beleuchtung eines Gegenstandes, welcher in der Congressfrage allen Staub
aufgeworfen hat, oder haben soll. Ich rede vom
Code of Ethics, dem ethischen Codex.

"The Code of Ethics of the American Medical
Association" ist eine Nachbildung von "Thomas
Percival, M.D., Medical Ethics, or, a Code of Institutes and Precepts, adapted to the professional conduct of physicians and surgeons, etc. Manchester,
1803." Mit diesem Codex hat sich die Association
zu jener Zeit ein grosses Verdienst erworben.
Deutsche Aerzte in Deutschland dürfen nicht vergessen, dass sie keiner Regel des Anstandes und
der Pflichterfüllung gegen einander und ihre Kranken bedürfen. Sie leben unter mehr geordneten,
mehr beaufsichtigten, mehr *gleichmässig* gesitteten
Zustände, sie alle sind mit einem für hinreichend
gehaltenen Vorrathe von klassischen und anderen,
neben ihren medicinischen, Kenntnissen ausge-
stattet. Diese Gleichmässigkeit der sittlichen und
intellektuellen Ausstattung konnte, und kann, in
Amerika noch nicht existiren. Wir haben Harvard
und Johns Hopkins, aber auch die Schulenlosig-
keit des Hinterwalds und der Prairie; wir haben
Emerson und Holmes, aber auch den Goldgräber
und den Cowboy. Diesen verschiedensten Klassen
der Bevölkerung in dem sich immer ausdehnenden

Gebiete der Union entsprechen gar viele Stufen der Heilkünstler. Gesetze, welche sich dem Einen von selber verstehen, sind dem Anderen eine Nothwendigkeit, oder doch eine Mahnung. Genug, der ethische Codex wurde, trotz mancher Ungereimtheiten (worunter z. B. die Regeln, nach welchen der Patient sich zu verhalten habe) vor fast vierzig Jahren mit Dank angenommen und hat wahrscheinlich Manches dazu beigetragen, gelegentlich den Achtlosen, vielleicht auch einmal den Gewissenlosen in den Regeln des Anstandes zu unterrichten. Doch dreissig oder vierzig Jahre machen einen grossen Unterschied. Damals war noch ein grosser Theil von New York Hinterwald, und Ohio klang uns mehr "westlich," als heute Puget Sound.

Einer der wesentlichen Punkte in dem ethischen Codex ist die Kriegserklärung gegen die Homöopathie und die Homöopathen. Er sagt: "Eine regelmässige medicinische Ausbildung liefert den einzigen Wahrscheinlichkeitsbeweis für ärztliche Fähigkeiten und sollte den einzigen Anspruch auf die Ausübung des Berufes und die Ehrenstellung im Stande ausmachen. Doch, da es sich bei einer Consultation um das Wohl des Kranken allein handelt, und dieses oft von persönlichem Vertrauen bedingt ist, so sollte kein intelligenter regelmässiger Praktiker, welcher zur Ausübung der Praxis von einer ärztlichen Behörde autorisirt ist, welche anerkannt befähigt, und auch von dieser Association anerkannt ist, und welcher in gutem bürgerlichen und ärztlichen Ruf steht, mit übergrosser Bedenklichkeit ('fastidiously') von der Kameradschaft ausgeschlossen, und seine Hülfe in einer Con-

sultation abgewiesen werden, wenn der Kranke
dieselbe verlangt. Jedoch kann Niemand als regu-
lärer Praktiker oder als ein passender Consiliarius
betrachtet werden, dessen Praxis auf einem exclu-
siven Dogma basirt und auf Verwerfung der ange-
sammelten Erfahrung des ärztlichen Standes und
derjenigen Hülfsmittel, welche von der Anatomie,
Physiologie, Pathologie, und organischen Chemie
geliefert werden."

Dieser Paragraph, vor vierzig Jahren geschrieben,
ist die Folge und zu gleicher Zeit der Grund der
feindseligen Stellung gegen die Homöopathie, aber
auch die Ursache der Blüthe der Homöopathen in
den Vereinigten Staaten. In jener Zeit wurden die
paar Homöopathen aus den ärztlichen Vereinen
ausgewiesen, sogar aus der legalen County Medical
Society, und jede Kameradschaft verweigert. Die
Folge war ein schrofferes Auftreten der Ausge-
wiesenen und die Theilnahme des Publikums für
diejenigen, welche man verfolgte oder zu verfolgen
schien und zu Märtyrern machte. Das amerikanische Publikum nimmt immer Partei für "the
under dog," d. h. für den schwächeren und unter-
liegenden Theil. So ist die Homöopathie gewachsen
und zu einem Glaubensartikel geworden, speziell
bei "Geistlichen" und Weibern aller Klassen; so
haben diese Sectirer es zu Schulen, Hospitälern,
Journalen und reicher Praxis gebracht. Und dieser
zelotische Eifer für die Homöopathie hat um Nichts
bei dem Publikum nachgelassen, während die sogen.
"Homöopathie" alles andere, aber nicht mehr die
Homöopathie von 1840 und 1850 geworden ist.

Thatsache ist, dass die "homöopathischen"

Schulen "Anatomie, Physiologie, Pathologie und
organische Chemie" als regelmässige Lehrzweige
betreiben, dass viele homöopathische Vereine ihren
sektionellen Namen haben fallen lassen, dass die
befähigtesten homöopathischen Praktiker, speziell
in New York, der Homöopathie öffentlich entsagt,
und manche um Aufnahme in regelmässigen Vereinigungen nachgesucht haben. Gewiss hatte der
Präsident der New Yorker Academy of Medicine
Recht, wenn er kürzlich öffentlich erklärte, dass,
wenn es keine besseren Gründe für ihre Abweisung
gäbe, der oben citirte Paragraph keine Verweige-
rung der Mitgliedschaft in der Amerikanischen
Medicinischen Association für die Homöopathen
mehr rechtfertige.

Das Hauptdogma für den "regulären" Arzt ist
die Weigerung, mit einem Homöopathen zu consultiren. Ueber die Unmöglichkeit, in Durchschnitts-
fällen mit einem wirklichen Hahnemannianer, oder
einem Menschen, der den fashionablen Homöo-
pathentitel als blosses Aushängeschild benutzt,
nutzbringend für den Kranken zusammen zu arbeiten, brauche ich mich hier nicht auszulassen. Sie
versteht sich von selbst. Dass aber jede Consultation, jedes gelegentliche Zusammenarbeiten mit einem Sektirer oder Dogmatiker ein Verbrechen ist,
davon werden sich wenige überzeugen. Es war
auch gar wohl bekannt, dass gemischte Consulta-
tionen im Lande häufig und in den grossen Städten
nicht unerhört waren. Man wusste auch wohl,
dass manche Spitzen des ärztlichen Standes, welche
späterhin von Moralität übertrieften, häufig mit
homöopathischen "Collegen" ärztlich verkehrten.

Obendrein dürfen unsere deutschen Collegen nicht
vergessen, dass die " Homöopathen " und die " Ek-
lektiker " staatlich anerkannt, " legal practitioners "
sind, dass sie ihre eignen legalen Organisationen besitzen, und dass wir oft genug zu unserm Schaden
die Erfahrung gemacht haben, dass wir auf medici-
nisch-politischem Gebiete mit ihnen rechnen müssen.

Die Medicinische Gesellschaft des Staates New
York modificirte auf den Bericht eines im vorhergehenden Jahre eingesetzten Comités hin, den
obigen Paragraphen in seiner Sitzung zu Albany,
im Februar 1882, so dass er folgendermassen lautete:
" Mitglieder der Medicinischen Gesellschaft des
Staates New York und der mit ihr in amtlicher
Verbindung stehenden Gesellschaften *dürfen* (may)
mit staatlich anerkannten Praktikern consultiren.
Es können Nothfälle eintreten, in welchen es dem
Urtheil des Arztes überlassen werden muss zu be-
stimmen, ob irgend welche Restriction der Anfor-
derung der Menschlichkeit zu weichen habe."

Dass ist der vielverschriene " neue Codex." In
dem folgenden Jahre verlief Alles ziemlich ruhig.
Nur wurden die Delegaten der New Yorker Medicinischen Gesellschaft von der Amerikanischen Medicinischen Association, welche im Mai 1882 in St.
Paul tagte, unter Getümmel hinausgewiesen. Als
aber die nächste Versammlung der Medical Society
of the State of New York, in Albany, 1883, ihre
alten Beschlüsse nach heftigem Kampfe aufrecht
erhielt, brach die " moralische Entrüstung," welche
sich ein Jahr Zeit genommen hatte, sich als Ueberraschung zu geriren, los. Die " New Coders " wur-

15*

den mündlich und schriftlich als irregulär, abgefallen, geldgierig, consultationssüchtig bezeichnet, und kein entehrendes Beiwort war zu schlecht. Die Verfolgung und Hetzereien waren so übertrieben und überkomisch, dass sie über das Ziel hinausschossen, und die persönlichen und Parteiinteressen der bekanntesten Führer der "Old Coders" wohl gewürdigt wurden. Diese Hetzereien werden noch jetzt fortgesetzt, aber die grosse Masse der Aerzte wird indifferent gegen den Kampf, der sich um eine Kleinigkeit dreht, und der sehr einseitig geführt worden ist. Thatsache ist, dass er von einem halben Dutzend Führern jetzt noch allein weitergesponnen wird, und gelegentlich in so plumper Weise, dass z. B. die editoriellen Angriffe des *Philadelphia Medical Bulletin* (J. V. Shoemaker) gegen den Präsidenten der New Yorker Academy of Medicine auch seine eigenen Anhänger unbehaglich stimmen. Eine fernere Thatsache ist auch die, dass die diesjährige (1885) Versammlung der Amerikanischen Medicinischen Association in der Sitzung zu New Orleans eine Zusatzerklärung zu ihrem Codex annahm, welcher im Wesentlichen den Animus des New Yorker "New Code" wiedergiebt. Diese von dem öffentlichen Bewusstsein erzwungene Zusatzerklärung hat aber die moralische Entrüstung der Führer gegen die "New Coders" nur gesteigert. Dieselbe wird vielleicht auch noch dadurch gesteigert, dass old und new coders in New York einträchtig neben einander wohnen, einander nicht zerfleischen, mit einander consultiren, und sich (mit wenigen Ausnahmen) als Gentlemen benehmen, und dass die New York Academy of Medicine, welche sich

einen neutralen Boden erkämpft hat, an Mitgliederzahl und Bedeutung schnell zunimmt.

In dem Vorhergehenden haben Sie, in möglichst
engem Rahmen, ein Bild der hiesigen ärztlichen
"politischen" Zustände zur Zeit des Copenhagener
Congresses und im verflossenen Jahre.

II.

Die Amerikanische Medicinische Association hielt
vom 6. bis 9. Mai 1884 eine denkwürdige Sitzung
in Washington. Der damalige Präsident, Austin
Flint der Aeltere von New York, betonte in seiner
Rede die Nothwendigkeit, den Codex durch gewisse
Erläuterungen zu der Consultationsfrage dahin zu
ergänzen, dass den gelegentlichen Anforderungen
der Humanität in etwaigen schwierigen Fällen
Gerechtigkeit geschehen möge. Die Folge dieser
Ermahnung war die Einsetzung eines Comité's,
welches die in meinem vorigen Briefe erwähnte
Zusatzerklärung in der New Orleans Sitzung vom
April 1885 vorlegte und zur Annahme brachte.
Trotzdem ist seit dem 1882 in New York eingeführ-
ten "New Code" für die Zulassung zu der Sitzung
der Association bis zum heutigen Tage eine "eisen-
gepanzerte" Erklärung für nöthig erachtet, welche
besagt, dass der Betreffende an dem Codex der
Amerikanischen Medicinischen Association unver-
brüchlich festhält.

In derselben Sitzung, am 8. Mai 1884, wurde beschlossen, ein Comité zu ernennen, welches den
Internationalen Congress *im Namen des ärztlichen
Standes von Amerika* (on behalf of the American
medical profession) einzuladen habe, seine nächste

Zusammenkunft in Washington zu halten. Zu
gleicher Zeit wurde beschlossen, *das Comité zu er-
mächtigen, seine eigenen Beamten zu wählen und,
im Fall der Annahme der Einladung, als Executiv-
Ausschuss zu fungiren, alle nothwendigen und spe-
ziellen Vorkehrungen für die Versammlungen zu
treffen, Fonds zu sammeln und auf die Kasse der
Amerikanischen Medicinischen Association bis zur
Höhe von 500 Dollars für die vorläufigen Ausgaben
zu ziehen.* Das Comité sollte aus den Herren A.
Flint d. A. und L. A. Sayre, New York ; J. Minis
Hays, Philadelphia ; Chr. Johnson, Baltimore ; G. J.
Engelmann, St. Louis : H. F. Campbell, Augusta ;
J. S. Billings von der Armee, und J. M. Browne
von der Marine bestehen. Mit Ausnahme von
Campbell waren alle Genannten in Copenhagen.
Die Einladung nach Amerika wurde genau in der
Form angenommen, in welcher sie angeboten
wurde ; vom Comité der Amerikanischen Medicinischen Association im Namen des ärztlichen Standes Amerika's. Es schien nicht nöthig, dass der
Congress das amerikanische Comité als sein Executiv-Comité ausdrücklich ernenne oder anerkenne
—in den Beschlüssen vom 8. Mai war diese Vollmacht ausdrücklich gegeben—denn der Usus war
immer der gewesen, wie J. Paget das in einem ausdrücklich zu dem Zwecke geschriebenen Briefe
betont—dass die zuerst mit der Einladung oder
Ausführung betrauten Comités oder Personen ein
für alle Mal als Executiv-Comité fungirten. Paget
legt vor allen Dingen Gewicht darauf, dass die
Congresse niemals anders, als von dem gesammten
ärztlichen Stande Einladungen erwarten oder an-

nehmen, und dass, wenn man in Copenhagen den
Verdacht gehabt habe, oder hätte haben können,
dass eine einzige Gesellschaft oder Association die
Führung des Congresses usurpiren wollte, die Einladung nach Amerika nimmermehr wäre angenommen worden.

Manche der in Copenhagen anwesenden New
Yorker sahen den Vorbereitungen zu der Einladung
mit Missbehagen zu. Sie fürchteten das Hinein-
tragen von lokal amerikanischen Differenzen in den
Internationalen Congress, und, bei der feindseligen
Old Code Stimmung unter einigen der Comitémitglieder, die Ausschliessung der New Yorker
New Coders. Diese Befürchtung wurde aber durch
die ausdrückliche Versicherung speziell der Herren
A. Flint sr. (New Yorker Old Coder) und Billings
beseitigt, welche erklärten, dass unter keinen Umständen ethische und politische Streitfragen die
Theilnahme am Congress beeinträchtigen würden,
dass der Internationale Congress ein wissenschaft-
liches Institut der Welt und von den Lokalfragen
eines Landes unabhängig sei. Niemand zweifelte
dann an der Verwicklichung dieses Grunsatzes, obgleich es lautbar wurde, dass in einer Comitésitzung nur fünf für jenen Grundsatz, und zwei sich
gegen denselben ausgesprochen hatten. Mit diesem
Gefühl der Sicherheit, dass der amerikanische ärztliche Stand wieder einmal ein gemeinschaftliches
Ziel habe, und dass die albernen Streitigkeiten um
des Kaisers Bart an den Thoren des Internationalen
Congresses ein Ende finden würden, kehrten die
New Yorker in ihre Heimath zurück.

Das Achter-Comité begann alsbald seine Arbeit

und ergänzte sich, wie ihm aufgetragen war. Es ist eine Unwahrheit, wenn das *Journal der Amerikanischen Medicinischen Association* noch bis auf den heutigen Tag behauptet, dass die hohen Aemter aus wenigen Lokalitäten besetzt seien; eine Unwahrheit, welche dadurch nicht geringer wird, dass man sie wöchentlich einmal wiederholt. Die sieben Vicepräsidenten, welche in dem zu Anfang des Jahres 1885 bekannt gemachten Organisationsplan genannt wurden, wohnen in sieben verschiedenen Städten, die achtundzwanzig Mitglieder des General-Comité's (acht ursprünglich, und zwanzig Ergänzungen) in zwölf. Das engere Executiv-Comité, aus jenem gewählt, bestand aus acht Mitgliedern, bei deren Wahl wohl mit darauf gesehen wurde, dass sie sich in nicht zu grosser Entfernung von einander befinden sollten. Die acht Mitglieder des Executiv-Comités wurden aus den Städten Washington, Baltimore, Philadelphia und New York genommen. Die neunzehn Sektionen wurden mit Präsidenten, Vicepräsidenten, Secretären und berathenden Ausschüssen aus allen Theilen der Staaten versehen, freilich mit grösserer Rücksicht auf die Fähigkeit und literarische Bedeutung der Männer, als auf die Quadratmeilenzahl der Territorien und Staaten, in denen sie sich aufhalten. Auch in dem einen fraglichen Punkte kam das ursprüngliche Achter-Comité seinem feierlichen Versprechen nach, und das ergänzte General-Comité folgte bona fide der vorgezeichneten Politik; nicht nur wurde A. Jacobi von New York zum Mitglied des General-Comité's cooptirt, sondern auch in den Executiv-Ausschuss des Congresses gewählt. Seine Wahl beruhigte die Gemüther der New Yorker "New Coder" vollkommen über die Absichten und Pläne der Leiter des Congresses. Denn obwohl der Genannte sich niemals auffällig an dem Codekriege— den die Zukunft bald als Froschmäusekrieg belächeln wird—betheiligt hatte, so war doch der neue Codex in der New Yorker Staatsgesellschaft unter seinem Präsidium zur Berathung und Annahme gekommen, und er wurde mit der ganzen Bewegung und Richtung—mit Recht—identificirt.

Die Arbeit der vorläufigen Organisation war in vier Monaten vollbracht. Gegen dreihundert und fünfzig Erlesene waren in Reih' und Glied. Alle nahmen die Plätze bereitwillig an, welche man ihnen bot, einerlei ob sie Arbeit verlangten, oder blos viel Ehre brachten. Niemand lehnte Arbeit oder Ehre ab, die Besten des Landes sind in den Listen der fertigen Organisation, welche vom 24. März 1885 datirt ist, verzeichnet, und mit Genugthuung überfliegt mein Auge noch heute die lange Reihe ehrenwerther und geehrter Namen, von denen viele auch Ihnen drüben geläufig sind. Allein es fehlten Einige darunter, es ist wahr. Für Manche wäre es leicht geworden, Arbeit und Ehre zu schaffen, und das war die Absicht. Es fehlten auch Solche, welche Jeder geflissentlich übersah; sogar Einer, der sich erboten hatte, eine grosse Summe Geldes zu den Fonds des Congresses zu sammeln, wenn er einen Platz in dem General-Comité erhalten würde.

Es kam die Zeit für die Sitzung der Amerikanischen Medicinischen Association, Ende April 1885. Sie fand in New Orleans statt. Eines der bakann-

testen Mitglieder des ursprünglichen Achter-Comité's sprach die Ansicht aus, dass man der
Association keinen Bericht schulde, da die Selbst-
ständigkeit und Unabhängigkeit der Congressbe-
hörde selbstverständlich sei. Ein Anderer war der
Meinung, die Höflichkeit erfordere Berichterstat-
tung. Der General-Secretär John S. Billings las seinen
Bericht. Derselbe wurde auf dem Tisch niederge-
legt, und seine Besprechung auf die Tagesordnung
für den nächsten Tag gesetzt. Die Scene, welche
sich dann am 29. April 1885 abspielte, spottet nach
Aussage aller anständigen Augenzeugen jeder Beschreibung. J. V. Shoemaker von Philadelphia
brachte den Ball ins Rollen mit einem Protest gegen
den ganzen Bericht. Denn das Achter-Comité habe
seine Befugnisse überschritten ; es habe den Drohungen der New-Codexleute nachgegeben, welche in
Copenhagen erklärt hätten, dass, wenn man ihnen
nicht Aemter gäbe (unless they were recognized),
sie ihren Einfluss aufbieten würden, um die Annahme der Einladung nach Amerika zu verhindern;
dass er, Shoemaker, bei diesen Drohungen gegenwärtig gewesen sei ; dass die Männer, welche diese
Drohungen ausgestossen hätten, jetzt'hohe Stellen
in der geplanten Organisation bekleideten ; dass ein
Handel abgeschlossen sei u. s. w.

Diese Behauptungen wurden von J. S. Billings,
der allein der tobenden Menge Widerstand leistete.
für durchaus unwahr erklärt. Das Achter-Comité
habe sich innerhalb der Grenzen des im vorigen
Jahre gegebenen Auftrags gehalten, seine Befugnisse nicht überschritten, und das erweiterte Gene-

ral-Comité bestehe aus ehrenhaften und allgemein
geachteten Männern. Die Discussion wurde von da
an ein Bedlam von moralischer Entrüstung und
Gesinnungstüchtigkeit. So schloss King von Mis-
souri seine Rede mit dem Satze, man solle "die
Spezialisten vom Neu-Codexglauben beim Schopf
nehmen und ihnen die Hälse abschneiden." Einer
der milderen Herren, aus Arkansas, stellte den An-
trag, das Verfahren des Achter-Comité's gut zu
heissen, vorausgesetzt, dass die Namen der Anhänger
des neuen Codex ausgelassen würden. Ein Texa-
ner sprach gelassen das Orakel aus, es scheine ihm,
"es sei irgendwo im Schiff eine Wanze." Es wurde
der Vorwurf ausgesprochen, dass das General-Comité vielen seiner eigenen Mitglieder Aemter gegeben und auf einzelne zu viele Aemter vereinigt
habe ; dass Philadelphia und der Osten gegenüber
dem Süden und dem Westen zu reichlich bedacht
worden, und dass New Coders als Mitglieder und
Beamte des Congresses in Aussicht genommen
seien. Thatsache ist allerdings, dass einzelne der
Comitémitglieder so hervorragend waren, dass man
ihnen Sektions-Präsidien zumuthen musste. Später
wurde besonders namhaft gemacht, dass sogar ein
Mitglied des Executiv-Comité's an die Spitze der
Kindersektion gestellt wurde, wobei die Thatsache
unbekannt war oder übersehen wurde, dass der Betreffende gegen seinen Willen und gegen seine
Ueberzeugung mit diesem Amte betraut wurde.
Dass viele hohe Aemter auf die grossen Städte
fielen, versteht sich übrigens bei denjenigen von
selbst, welche im Congress wissenschaftliche Bedeu-

tung, und nicht geographische Lage vertreten sehen wollen. Gegen die New Coder wurde von allen Seiten Protest erhoben. Dem neu ernannten Comité wurde zur Pflicht gemacht, Niemand zum "Internationalen Congress" auch nur zuzulassen, der nicht zum Verband der Amerikanischen Medicinischen Association gehöre. Dies Comité wurde so zusammengesetzt, dass alle vom Achter-Comité Cooptirten abgethan wurden. Das Achter-Comité wurde belassen und ergänzt durch je ein Mitglied von jedem Staat oder Territorium, von der Armee, von der Marine, vom Marinespitaldienst und vom District Columbia. Diese achtunddreissig neuen Mitglieder wurden in derselben Sitzung am selben Tage vom Vicepräsidenten ernannt. So bestand das Comité aus sechsundvierzig Mitgliedern. Es wurde sofort beschlossen, im Juni in Chicago eine Comitésitzung zu halten.

Aber es erschien nöthig, noch etwas Anderes zu thun, oder vielmehr es war schon gethan, ehe die Versammlung in New Orleans zusammentrat. Sam Randall, ein bekannter Jurist und ehemals Sprecher des Repräsentantenhauses, wurde um ein Gutachten darüber angegangen, ob, oder dass, die Association jeder Zeit das Recht habe, etwaige Aufträge zu revociren oder zu annulliren. Wie die Anfrage gestellt war, so fiel die Antwort aus, nämlich, dass dieses Recht unzweifelhaft sei. Es wurde bei der Anfrage und Antwort nur die Kleinigkeit übersehen, dass die Rechte des Internationalen Congresses, welcher die Einladung des *ärztlichen Standes* Amerikas angenommen hatte, keines Wortes

gewürdigt wurden. Der Internationale Congress
sollte eben dazu dienen, der Association zu einer
glänzenden Extraversammlung zu verhelfen, von
welcher Missliebige auszuschliessen seien.
Eine andere Massregel, welche im Interesse der
" guten Sache " beschlossen wurde, war diejenige,
dass die nächste Sitzung in St. Louis stattfinden
solle. Der Regel nach war Washington für 1886
der Versammlungsort. Aber in New Orleans waren die Süd- und Mittelstaaten vertreten gewesen
und hatten Geographie und Ethik getrieben. In
St. Louis konnte man dieselben Elemente in grosser
Uebermacht erwarten. Washington lag den Ost-
staaten bequem—also St. Louis durch besonderen
Beschluss.
Ueber die Verhandlungen der Sitzung in Chicago
sind wunderbare Berichte laut geworden. Mitglieder, welche nicht gegenwärtig waren, wurden
in dem Protokoll aufgeführt und protestiren nachher dagegen und gegen das ganze Verfahren. Von
New York wurde ein Stellvertreter geschickt, der—
weil genehm—ohne Weiteres Sitz und Stimme bekam und sich dann recht gefällig erwies. Die Aufträge der New Orleans Versammlung wurden ausgeführt. Die Organisation und Beamtenliste
wurden nach geographischen Rücksichten revidirt.
Die New Yorker New Coders wurden von ihren
Stellen entfernt und von der Mitgliedschaft am
Congress ausgeschlossen. Dies Schicksal betraf
Loomis, Curtis, Weir, Vander Poel, Emmet, Lef-
ferts, Roosa, Agnew, Keyes, McLane Hamilton,
Otis, Sexton, R. W. Taylor, L. Johnson, Buck,
Ripley, Draper, Noeggerath, Mundé, Prudden,

Knapp, A. H. Smith, Jacobi.* Auch Bosworth und Bulkley wurden fallen gelassen. Sie waren "Old Coders," aber dem oben erwähnten "Stellvertreter" aus New York persönlich unangenehm. Als Secretär fungirte noch für lange Zeit derselbe Herr, welcher in New Orleans die Stichworte vertheilte, von Billings und Jacobi öffentlich der Lüge überführt war und nicht einmal im Privatleben eines unangefochtenen Rufes sich erfreute. An dieser Stelle mag übrigens der Irrthum berichtigt werden, welcher sich in einige europäische Blätter eingeschlichen hat, der nämlich, dass J. V. Shoemaker jemals das offizielle "Präsidium" geführt habe. Diese Kleinigkeit ist von der gesinnungstüchtigen Masse als grobe Missdeutung und übelwollende Darstellung proklamirt worden.

Die Beschlüsse des New-Orleans-Chicago-Comité's riefen eine grosse Aufregung hervor. Billings,

---

* Der letztere nimmt die eigenthümliche Stellung ein, dass ihm der Eintritt in den "Congress" der Amerikanischen Medicinischen Association versagt ist, obgleich er zum Beamten des Internationalen Congresses—zu Copenhagen—ernannt worden ist. Er ist das Amerikanische Mitglied des Ausschusses für Collectiv-Untersuchung. Als er von den Herren Paget, Gull, Bernhardt u. s. w. um die Ernennung eines zweiten Comitémitgliedes angegangen wurde, wählte er—N. S. Davis von Chicago, den ehemaligen Präsidenten der Amerikanischen Medicinischen Association, Redacteur des Journals derselben und das Haupt der Kämpfer gegen den neuen Codex. Weisheit? Thorheit? Er ist übrigens in derselben Lage, wie viele seiner Collegen, welche, wenn sie nach Europa zum "Congress" reisten, mit Achtung und Ehrenbeweisen empfangen wurden, sich aber im selben "Congress," wenn derselbe im eigenen Lande zusammenzukommen bestimmt ist, nicht sehen lassen dürfen.

Hays, Johnson, Engelmann und Browne von dem
ursprünglichen Achter-Comité resignirten sofort.
Ihnen folgten, in Haufen oder einzeln, fast sämmtliche der ernannten Beamten des Congresses über
die ganze Union. Absagen liefen ein von Philadelphia, Washington, Baltimore, New York, Provi-
dence, Portland, Boston, Buffalo, Cincinnati, St.
Louis, Louisville, Montreal und andern Plätzen.
Was in Amerika einen geehrten Namen trägt, alle
in Europa bekannten medicinischen Schriftsteller
und Lehrer des Landes, wollten mit dem neuen Comité und dem von ihm auf seine Bedingungen ge-
leiteten "Internationalen" Congress nichts zu thun
haben. Der einzige Flint, auch von dem neuen
Comité zum Präsidenten ausersehen, hat noch
keinen Absagebrief geschrieben. Agnew, Stillé,
Pepper, Weir Mitchell, Bartholow, Gross, H. C.
Wood, Chadwick, White, Busey, Engelmann,
Howard, J. Leydy, Yandell, J. N. Mackenzie,
Derby, Blake, im Ganzen etwa hundertundsechzig
berühmte und geachtete Männer, ausser den ausgestossenen New Yorkern, überlassen den usurpirten
Congress seinem Schicksale. Wenn man die Behauptung aufstellt, dass unter dem ganzen Personal
der jetzigen Administration und ihrer Beamten
höchstens ein halbes Dutzend Namen sich befinden,
welche in den Vereinigten Staaten eine verdiente
Reputation haben und in Europa nur gekannt sind,
so sagt man nicht zu viel. Die grössten Journale
des Landes (achtzehn wurden kürzlich namhaft gemacht) sind in der entschiedensten Opposition ;
andere, wie das berühmte *American Journal of the
Medical Sciences* und das *American Journal of*

Obstetrics, nehmen von der ganzen Angelegenheit, als ausserhalb ihres Bereiches liegend, überhaupt keine Notiz. Das erste wird von Hays, das zweite von Mundé, redigirt. Die Gründe, welche die Resignationen begleiten und von den Journalen befürwortet werden, sind, einfach wieder dargestellt, die folgenden :

1. Die Organisation des Congresses war nach der ursprünglichen Vollmacht und unter der Billigung des Internationalen Congresses vollendet, wurde, mit ganz geringen Ausstellungen, allgemein gebilligt, nahm einen ruhigen und viel versprechenden Verlauf. Sie wurde muthwillig unterbrochen.

2. Die Amerikanische Medicinische Association betrachtete den Congress nicht als internationale, nicht einmal als nationale Angelegenheit, sondern als Sache ihrer Vereinigung.

3. Sie versuchte den Internationalen Congress in lokale ethisch-politische Streitigkeiten zu verwickeln, obgleich von vornherein jede solche Absicht abgeleugnet war. Das Versprechen ihres eigenen Comité's wurde gebrochen, auf den Vorwand hin, dass die Association jeden gegebenen Auftrag widerrufen könne.

4. Die Verwerfung der Arbeit des ersten Comité's war in Wahrheit das Resultat der Bemühungen einiger Unzufriedenen, welche sich den Umstand zu Nutze machten, dass die Versammlung zu New Orleans meist von Aerzten der Mittelstaaten besucht war.

5. Die Beschlüsse zu New Orleans und Chicago berauben den Congress der Mitwirkung mancher

der bekanntesten amerikanischen Mediciner, und
ostraciren den grössten Theil des grossen Staates
New York.

6. Der Charakter einiger der Männer, welche in
der neuen Organisation eine Hauptrolle spielen,
macht die Erfolglosigkeit des unter solcher Leitung
zu haltenden Congresses nicht zweifelhaft und
stellt die Sympathie und Mitwirkung des ärztlichen
Standes ausser Frage.

III.

Weshalb blieb das alte Achter-Comité und das
von ihm gebildete General-Comité nicht in Thätigkeit? wird man fragen. Wenn die besten und bekanntesten Männer der Union an ihren Plätzen
blieben, erklärten, dass sie trotz aller Hindernisse
weiterarbeiten würden, hätten sie nicht allen
Widerstand überwinden, die Sympathie des Standes
erringen und sich bewahren und den Congress sieg-
reich zu Ende führen können? Vielleicht, sogar
wahrscheinlich. Aber der Rücktritt war nicht
ganz allgemein, und die Zwietracht im ärztlichen
Stande war zu offenbar. Die Ausscheidenden,
einerlei welches ihre Bedeutung und ihr Einfluss,
wollten die Verantwortung nicht übernehmen, den
Internationalen Congress in ein zwieträchtig ge-
theiltes Haus einzuladen und an einer lokalen Fehde
Theil nehmen zu lassen. Dabei darf man sich aber
nicht einbilden, dass die Ausscheidenden jemals
dem "Neuen Codex" das Wort redeten; im Gegen-
theil beharrten sie bei der Erklärung der Anhänglichkeit an den Codex, immer wieder betonend, dass
es eine Unwürdigkeit sei, die Codexfrage überhaupt

in irgend welche Beziehung zum Internationalen
Congress zu bringen. Gelegentlich nur machten
einige bedeutende Journale (auch canadische) darauf
aufmerksam, dass dem " Neuen Codex " dadurch,
dass man seine Vertreter zu Märtyrern mache, be-
deutender Vorschub geleistet werde—in derselben
Weise, wie man durch kurzsichtige Ausschliessung
und Verfolgung die Homöopathen zu einer Macht
umgeschaffen habe. Man wollte eben nicht zanken
und streiten, weil man der unausbleiblichen
Schmach und Erniedrigung vor dem Urtheil der
ganzen medicinischen Welt sich wohl bewusst war.
Damals war auch der Ueberdruss an der ganzen
Existenz der Amerikanischen Medicinischen Association noch nicht so verbreitet, wie seit einigen
Monaten, wo unter den besten Geistern der Nation
das Bedürfniss einer wirklich wissenschaftlichen
allgemeinen Vereinigung, ohne Rücksicht auf Brei-
ten- und Längengrade und politischen Einfluss,
immer lauter ausgesprochen wird.

Soweit schien das neue New-Orleans-Chicago-
Comité gewonnenes Spiel zu haben. Aber wie
wenig behaglich es sich bei seinem Pyrrhussiege
fühlte, geht aus dem Ton seiner Presse hervor.
Ein einziger Leitartikel, in dem *Journal . of the
American Medical Association*, welcher sich über
die massenweisen Austritte auslässt, enthält aus
der Feder von N. S. Davis (dem jetzigen "General-
Secretär"!) die folgenden Auslassungen über die
Ausgetretenen : " Halb erwachsene Schuljungen—
heterogene Mischung von Arroganz, Bitterkeit und
Fälschung—engherzige Impulse—Inconsequenzen
und Fälschungen—Getobe und Bravado der Opposi-

tion—abgekartetes Spiel (*preconcerted game of bluff*)—keine Männlichkeit—die üblichen "*ruts*"*) und die Gesellschaften für gegenseitige Bewunderung, welche bei einem Theil der Aerzte der Quäkerstadt wohl bekannt sind—Rücksichtslosigkeit und Thorheit—die rücksichtslose und verzweifelte Nothlage jener egoistischen Führer, welche vergebens sich abmühen, das abgekartete Spiel durchzuführen."

Die Juni-Conferenz in Chicago hielt sich für so sicher, dass die nächste Comitésitzung für St. Louis, während der Jahressitzung der Am. Med. Assoc., Mai 1886 anberaumt wurde. Als es aber offenbar wurde, dass binnen kurzem weder Offiziere noch Soldaten mehr vorhanden sein würden, berief man eiligst—mitten im Sommer ist in den Vereinigten Staaten keine Sitzung zu versammeln—das Comité für den dritten September nach New York. Die Sitzungen wurden bei verschlossenen Thüren gehalten; erst nach langer Zeit verlautete etwas von dem Geschehenen, und zwar durch einen offenen Brief eines der Mitglieder, welchem das *Journal of the Am. Med. Assoc.* die Veröffentlichung versagt hatte. Nach dem Verfasser, Dr. Kinloch aus Charleston, war der Druck der öffentlichen Meinung so empfindlich geworden, dass man beschloss, den " regulären Aerzten " ohne Ausnahme (wahrscheinlich schloss man die New Coders vom Staate New York ein, obgleich das offiziell niemals ausgesprochen ist) die Mitgliedschaft am Congress zu gestatten. Kinloch opponirte auf den Grund hin, dass man mit einer solchen Anordnung dem Befehl der Amer. Med.

* Ich wage den gemeinen Ausdruck nicht zu übersetzen.

16*

Assoc. und der Chicagositzung ungehorsam sei, und
sprach sich männlicherweise dahin aus, dass er be-
reit sei, wie früher, für Ausschliessung der New
Coders zu stimmen, dass er aber consequent genug
sei, darauf zu bestehen, dass, wenn man sie überhaupt zulassen wolle, man ihnen auch gleiche Stellung und Aemter geben müsse. Die Weise, wie
man ihn zurückwies, veranlasste ihn, seinen Austritt zu erklären.

Der Brocken, welchen man den New Coders auf
diese Weise hinwarf, wurde von Niemandem aufgehoben, weder von den New Coders selber,
welche seit der Sitzung in New Orleans sich mit
keinem Worte an dem Streite betheiligt haben,
noch von denjenigen, welche im Interesse der In-
tegrität des Internationalen Congresses und seiner
ausschliesslich wissenschaftlichen Natur den Hand-
schuh aufgenommen hatten. Die Resignationen
nahmen ihren Fortgang. Neu ernannte Beamte,
wie der greise geniale Dichter und Arzt, Oliver
Wendell Holmes, versagten ihre Dienste, Noyes
von New York und Bowditch von Boston schrieben
ausführliche und missbilligende Absagebriefe. Um
jene Zeit versuchte es das *Journal of the Amer. Med.
Assoc.* einmal für eine kurze Zeit mit Sanftmuth.
Es (N. S. Davis) flüsterte von Frieden und Harmonie, sprach von dem hergestellten guten Verhältniss, von der Bereitwilligkeit des Comité's,
jedem Wunsche nachzukommen, wie die Satzungen
für den Congress bewiesen (!), appellirte auch an
den amerikanischen Patriotismus ; kurz und gut, es
waren das Leitartikel, welche sich für die Verbrei-
tung in Europa, wo die Journale an amerikanischen

Breiten und Längen, an Politik und Ostracismus keinen Gefallen fanden, vortrefflich eigneten. Sie haben freilich weder in Europa noch in Amerika durchgeschlagen. Wieder erklärten einige berühmte Namen ihren Austritt (Dalton und Delafield von New York u. s. w.), und die Zerbröckelung machte Fortschritte. Natürlich musste wieder eine Comitésitzung nach New York berufen werden.

Sie fand am 18. November statt, und nach einiger Zeit wurde (ein Theil von dem) bekannt gemacht, was beschlossen war. Das *Journal* vom 28. November theilt mit, dass nun alle Hindernisse zur Wiederherstellung der Harmonie geschwunden seien. Denn man habe beschlossen, nicht blos Mitglieder der Association, sondern auch die nationalen Organisationen der Spezialisten (Ophthalmologen, Otologen, Gynäkologen u. s. w.) zuzulassen. Grossherzig wurde hinzugesetzt: Ihre Ausschliessung "wurde von allen Parteien für unnöthig und unzweckmässig erklärt." Es wurde wieder einmal ein neues Executiv-Comité eingesetzt, welches aus den Oberbeamten und den Präsidenten der Sektionen bestehen sollte. Aber eingestandenermassen waren viele Präsidien unbesetzt, der in Chicago ernannte General-Secretär, Packard von Philadelphia, hatte nicht angenommen, und N. S. Davis musste auch das General-Secretariat übernehmen, Kopf und Hand zu gleicher Zeit sein. Die Codexfrage wurde geflissentlich ignorirt, es blieb beim Alten. Aber Eines blieb nicht beim Alten. Man erinnert sich, das Sam. Randall's juristisches Gutachten, welches der Amer. Med. Assoc. das

Recht zuspricht, jeden Augenblick Aufträge zu
ändern, oder zu widerrufen, zu dem Zwecke einge-
fordert und benutzt wurde, das ursprüngliche
Achter-Comité mit Beleidigungen zu überhäufen,
und die Organisation des Congresses zu stürzen.
In New York, im November, beschloss nun das
Executiv-Comité einstimmig, *dass es von der Association unabhängig und ihr keine Rechenschaft
schuldig sei!!*
In dem Journal des General-Secretärs heisst es
dann weiter: "Jetzt bleibt dem Executiv-Comité
Nichts weiter übrig, als *ohne Reserve einige* Aemter
so vielen der Hervorragendsten unter denjenigen,
welche früher resignirt haben, anzubieten *wie die
vorhandenen Stellen es erlauben*, bevor es irgend
welche andere wichtige Vacanzen besetzt (?).
Wenn sie annehmen, werden die Discussionen über
den Congress aufhören, ohne dass die Grundsätze
irgend einer Partei verletzt werden." Wo die
Grundsätze der zweihundert Ausgetretenen und
Ausgestossenen bleiben würden, wird nicht gesagt;
wird wohl als bekannt vorausgesetzt. Es wird
wohl auch als bekannt vorausgesetzt, dass es sich
von selbst versteht, dass die "einigen" neuen Beamten in einer hoffnungslosen Minorität sein würden. So schafft man keine Harmonie, so will man
auch keine Harmonie, so wahrt man nicht einmal
den Schein.
Der Theorie folgte die Praxis. Man versuchte,
einzelne der Ausgetretenen heimlich zum Wieder-
eintritt zu bewegen, indem man ihnen hohe Aemter
anbot. N. und L. in New York wurden Sektions-
präsidien zugesagt. Die Präsidien waren feil, die

Männer nicht. Ich glaube nicht, dass ich ihre Namen nennen darf, denn die Verhandlungen wurden confidentiell gepflogen. Ich habe Stösse von Briefen gesehen, welche sich auf diese Angelegenheit bezogen. Dr. I., auch von Chicago, reiste als Emissär im Lande herum, um persönlich die Reihen derjenigen zu durchbrechen, deren Grundsätze nicht zu kaufen waren. Von einem einzigen der Herren in Cincinnati habe ich gehört, dass er zu der Fahne des New-Orleans-Chicago-Comité zurückgekehrt sei.

Auch offiziell wurde vorgegangen. Von dem Achter-Comité hatten fünf resignirt, Hays, Billings, Browne, Johnson und Engelmann! Den vier letzteren schlug man vor, wieder einzutreten, ausserdem Pepper und Da Costa von Philadelphia. Dass Hays unter keinen Umständen für das Executiv-Comité wieder zu gewinnen sei, wusste man nach der Haltung seiner *Medical News* gut genug; die andern vier hätten dem Achter-Comité wieder die Männer zugeführt, welche früher aus Ueberdruss und Verachtung resignirten. War es wirklich Ernst mit der Einladung? oder glaubte man auf diese plumpe Weise den Schein wahren zu können?

Und doch beriefen die Philadelphier eine grosse Versammlung, zu welcher Männer aus Boston, New York (nicht New Coders), Baltimore, Washington, Cincinnati u. s. w. eingeladen wurden. Die Fremden erschienen nicht, aber viele ausführliche Briefe liefen ein. Es wurde unterdessen bekannt, dass die sechs Herren das besagte Anerbieten nicht angenommen hatten. Und da geschah fast Unglaubliches.

Die Philadelphier Versammlung vom 4. December 1885 und ihre Correspondenten waren der einstimmigen Meinung, man solle im Interesse des Internationalen Congresses Gewaltstreiche, Usurpation, Inconsequenzen, Beleidigungen gering achten, und noch einmal die Hand zu gemeinsamer Aktion bieten. Zu dem Zwecke wurde der Vorschlag gemacht, neben dem vollen Achter-Comité der Am. Med. Association, die beiden Comité's, nämlich das vom Achter-Comité cooptirte General-Comité der ursprünglichen Organisation, und das jetzt existirende Executiv-Comité zu verschmelzen, und den Aufbau schnell von Neuem zu beginnen.

Keine Antwort.

Oder doch. Der Ton der Leitartikel des Herrn N. S. Davis (Redacteur des *Journal of the Am. Med. Association* und General-Secretär dessen, was die Herren unter "Internationalem Congress" verstehen) änderte sich wieder einmal. Während er immer noch behauptet (für die Europäer?), dass die medicinisch-politischen Fragen mit dem Congress nichts mehr zu thun haben, spricht er von dem "schimpflichen" Aufgeben seiner Verpflichtungen seitens des ärztlichen Standes. Unterdessen werden die Erlasse und Berichte über Angelegenheiten des Congresses unter der Ueberschrift : "Associationsangelegenheiten" bis in die neueren Nummern des officiellen Journals behandelt. Trotz alles editoriellen Ableugnens spielt die Codexfrage die Hauptrolle. Editoriell wird dem alten Comité auf S. 101 der Vorwurf gemacht, dass es Einem, der den nationalen Codex verworfen habe, hohe Ehrenstellen gegeben habe. Der permanente Secretär

der Am. Med. Association und vier andere Herren
verbreiteten am und nach dem 17. August ein aus
abgedruckten Leitartikeln des offiziellen Journals
bestehendes Circular über die ganzen Vereinigten
Staaten, in dessen Eingang es heisst : "Es kann
über die Pflicht der Freunde der Association und
die Gesinnung ihrer Feinde kein Zweifel bestehen.
Wir halten uns versichert, dass Ihre Gesellschaft
die Handlung der Association billigen und in der
Unterstützung des ethischen Codex feststehen
wird." Von Zeit zu Zeit werden die Beschlüsse
lokaler Gesellschaften, welche ihre Anhänglichkeit
an Association und Codex glaubenstreu documen-
tiren, in dem *Journal* veröffentlicht, während natürlich gegensätzliche Kundgebungen todtgeschwie-
gen werden. Als vor einigen Wochen die Med.
Ges. von Lackawanna County, Pa., Beschlüsse
im Interesse des Original-Comité's gefasst hatte,
drängte Shoemaker von Philadelphia telegraphisch
auf Widerruf, fand aber natürlich kein Gehör.
Auch das *Journal* erwähnt der Thatsache mit
keiner Silbe. Dagegen bringt es, noch am 19. December 1885 unter der Ueberschrift "Interna-
tionaler Congress" die folgende Erklärung der
Columbia (Pa.) County Medical Society : "In Er-
wägung der Thatsache, dass im ärztlichen Stande
in Bezug auf die Beschlüsse der Amer. Med. Assoc.
—in ihrer Sitzung zu New Orleans—und des von
ihr creirten Arrangements-Comité's, soweit es die
Ausführung seiner dort erhaltenen Instruktionen
betrifft, Meinungsverschiedenheiten bestehen, wird
hiermit beschlossen, dass wir unsere Unterwürfig-
keit (*allegiance*) unter den ethischen Codex der

Amer. Med. Assoc. von Neuem erklären, und unsere unzweideutige Zustimmung zu ihrer Hand-
lungsweise geben, als sie das Original-Comité ver-
änderte. Es wird ferner beschlossen, dass diese
Gesellschaft den Beschluss des Arrangements-Comité's zu Chicago billigt, nach welchem im Internationalen Congress nur diejenigen, welche der
Amer. Med. Assoc. verantwortlich sind, amtliche
Stellungen einnehmen dürfen."

Wie weit nun der neue Organisationsversuch es
in den Angelegenheiten des "Internationalen"
Associationscongresses in diesen acht Monaten, seit
der New Orleans Sitzung, gebracht hat, ergiebt sich
am Besten aus dem folgenden Leitartikel des *Journals der Amer. Med. Assoc.* vom 26. December
1885. Man wolle nicht vergessen, dass der Schrei-
ber des Leitartikels, N. S. Davis, zu gleicher Zeit
der alleinige Redacteur des Journals und General-
Secretär des "Congresses" ist. "Der General-
Secretär hat auf Veranlassung des Executiv-Comité's ein offizielles Circular mit der Ankündigung
der vorläufigen Organisation des Congresses ergehen lassen. Es enthält die Liste der obersten Beamten, welche man dem Congress zur Bestätigung
vorlegen wird, die Namen der Mitglieder des Executiv-Comité's und des Arrangements-Comité's in
Washington, und die von dem Organisations Comité
angenommenen Satzungen in den drei offiziellen
Sprachen, Englisch, Französisch und Deutsch. Es
wird augenblicklich in Europa und Amerika weit
verbreitet."

Die Schlussparagraphen lauten folgendermassen:
"Eine Liste der Präsidenten, Vicepräsidenten,

Secretäre und Berathungsausschüsse für jede Sektion wird in dem vollen Programm gegeben werden, welches während des Fortschrittes der Arbeit zu einer spätern Zeit veröffentlicht werden wird (schlechte Aussicht für die Sektionen nach so langer Zeit!) u. s. w." Am Schluss des Leitartikels heisst es ferner : "Wir sind informirt" (wir, d. h. der Redacteur, welcher zu gleicher Zeit General-Secretär ist), "dass die Organisation der Sektionen schon weit vorgeschritten ist, und dass die Arbeit, welche darin besteht, das volle Programm für den Congress zu arrangiren, vom Executiv-Comité so eifrig wie möglich in Angriff genommen werden wird."

In acht Monaten hat die "Association," welche Congress spielen will, es schon zu Versprechungen gebracht.

Dieses Resultat ist genau dasjenige, welches vorhergesagt werden konnte und vorhergesagt worden ist. Dass die Amer. Med. Assoc. mit dem Versuche, den Internationalen Congress zu ihrer eigenen Verherrlichung zu benutzen, den Internationalen Congress in den Wirrwarr lokaler Politik hinunterzuzerren, fanatische " Ethik " statt Wissenschaft zu treiben, und das in Copenhagen gegebene Versprechen dadurch zu brechen, dass der Congress, welcher die Einladung des amerikanischen ärztlichen Standes hoffnungsvoll annahm, der Gast einer Association werden soll, welche Zwietracht gesät und Sturm geerntet hat—dass die Amer. Med. Assoc. ihr eigenes Grab gräbt, ist kein Unglück. Jedermann fühlt, dass sie niemals einer grossen Aufgabe gerecht geworden, und ihr Ende nahe ist. Aber was sie angestiftet hat, wird ihr der ärztliche

Stand, so weit er in den Besten der Nationen vertreten ist, niemals verzeihen. Der Fluch der
Lächerlichkeit und Unfähigkeit, welcher uns, den
amerikanischen Aerzten insgesammt, durch das
zerstörende Treiben der Wenigen, welche die zufällig versammelte " Association " in New Orleans
gängelten, anhängt, wird von uns allen bitter em-
pfunden. Diejenigen, deren Namen man in Europa kennt, fühlen, dass man sie, und nicht die grosse
Menge der Namenlosen, für das Fiasco des nächsten
Congresses, falls er sich in Washington nominell
zusammenfinden sollte, verantwortlich machen
könnte, vielleicht verantwortlich machen wird.
Sollten Europäer die Versammlung in Washington
besuchen wollen, so werden sie freilich diejenigen
Amerikaner nicht treffen, deren Gegenwart ihnen
am meisten erwünscht wäre. Mögen unsere euro-
päischen Collegen überzeugt sein, dass die Mediciner von Philadelphia, welche ihrer Entrüstung
über das Zerstörungswerk der Association zuerst
Worte gaben, von Boston und Baltimore, New
York und Washington, und ihre zahlreichen Ge-
sinnungsgenossen Nichts mehr bedauern, als den
Umstand, dass particularistische Selbstsucht, und
nicht die Aerzte Amerika's den Congress zu einem
totalen Misserfolg machten.

Die Ueberzeugung, dass es sowohl für uns, die
wir mit Beschämung auf unser Fiasco schauen, als
auch für den Congress besser sei, wenn derselbe
noch zu dieser Stunde nach irgend einer Stadt
Europa's berufen werde, ist seit Monaten in den
Journalen laut geworden. Ich kenne die öffentliche Stimmung genau ; aus den amerikanischen

Journalen können meine Leser sich ihr eigenes Urtheil darüber bilden. Wenn nun irgend einer unter ihnen ist, welcher dieser Erzählung unserer Fehler und Misserfolge Parteilichkeit beimisst, dem antworte ich getrost mit der Thatsache, dass in dieser Angelegenheit Jeder von uns auf einer oder der anderen Seite steht. Ich habe die grosse Genugthuung, mit den Männern, deren Namen in Europa einen gutem Klang haben, in einem Lager zu sein. Wer aber zu einer Partei gehört, ist darum noch nicht parteiisch. Nicht zu einer Partei sich zu bekennen, ist in der staatlichen und internationalen Politik möglich, aber unrecht; in den Angelegenheiten der Wissenschaft und Standesehre aber unmöglich und schimpflich.

IV.

Die Wirren in den Angelegenheiten des "Internationalen Congresses," dessen nächste Sitzung, wie man sagt, im September 1887 in Washington gehalten werden soll, sind zu Ende. Friede, Harmonie, die Ruhe des Kirchhofs, sind das Losungswort. "L'ordre regne à Varsovie." Das Geschick des Congresses ist besiegelt. Sollte er wirklich abgehalten werden, so wird er eine Enttäuschung für etwaige europäische Besucher, während er für uns Amerikaner eine unausbleibliche und unauslöschliche Blamage sein wird.

Es war meine Absicht, Herr Redacteur, als ich Ihnen vor Monaten meinen letzten Brief schickte, sofort nach Beendigung der Sitzungen der Amerikanischen Medicinischen Association zu St. Louis, d. h. also zu Anfang des Monats Mai, Ihnen wieder zu schreiben. Aber unsere Zustände sind so unerbaulich, und die Aussichten so trübe, dass erst Ihre Mahnung mich veranlasst hat, den Faden meiner Erzählung hiermit wieder aufzunehmen. Im Grunde ist auch wenig zu berichten ; ich wiederhole nach einem meiner früheren Briefe, dass der Redseligkeit des Herausgebers des *Journals der Amerikanischen Medicinischen Association*, als es sich um die Beantwortung von Vorschlägen handelte, welche im Interesse des etwaigen Internationalen Congresses von Seiten der Ausgetretenen gemacht wurden, ein absolutes Schweigen folgte. Unterdessen geschah nichts. Resignationen kamen nur noch in kleiner Zahl vor, denn die Män. ner, welche eine Vergangenheit und einen Ruf haben, waren schon ausgetreten. Der Mann, welcher durch seine Stellung und Bedeutung der Amerikanischen Medicinischen Association und ihrem Congresse noch einen gewissen Halt bot, Austin Flint der Aeltere, starb ; und eingestandenermassen war Niemand da, auf dessen Schultern sein Mantel fallen konnte. Man sprach von Da Costa als seinem Nachfolger, aber nach wie vor blieb derselbe bei seinem Entschlusse, mit dem Internationalen Congress, wie er in Aussicht stand und steht, Nichts zu thun haben zu wollen. Unterdessen suchten aber doch sowohl er, wie seine Philadelphiaer Collegen, noch einmal in praktischer Weise vorzugehen, um den Congress vielleicht noch zu retten. Es handelte sich um die Wahl der Delegirten für die diesjährige Sitzung der Association zu St. Louis. Shoemaker und Genossen brüsteten sich noch immer damit, dass sie in der Philadelphia

County Medical Society bestimmenden Einfluss
hätten, und dass die Resignationen der Philadelphiaer Gelehrten Nichts bedeuteten gegenüber der
grossen Mehrzahl der Aerzte der Gesellschaft, welche unter der Aegide Shoemaker's zu der Amerikanischen Medicinischen Association ständen. Am
Abend der Wahl waren etwa 200 Mitglieder anwe-
send; von diesen Stimmen bekamen Shoemaker
und Genossen nicht ein Fünftel. Die besten Männer der Stadt liessen sich zu Delegirten wählen,
um die Möglichkeit zu haben, in St. Louis die Ge-
schicke des Standes in würdigere Bahnen zu len-
ken. Die geschlagene Fraktion erhob den Vorwurf
ungesetzlichen Verfahrens bei der Nomination und
Wahl, enthielt sich aber jeden gerichtlichen Schrit-
tes, um ihre vorgeblichen Rechte zu wahren.
Als die Philadelphiaer Delegirten aber nach St.
Louis kamen, wurden sie einfach nicht zugelassen.
Wie New York gegangen war, so wurde Philadelphia hinausgestossen. Als die Philadelphiaer heim-
kehrten, wurde eine Versammlung der County
Society berufen, in welcher das Verhalten des Delegirten gebilligt, dasjenige der Association gemiss-
billigt wurde, mit 137 Stimmen gegen 24. Die
Nachwirkungen bleiben natürlich nicht aus. In
diesem Augenblicke tagt die Medicinische Gesellschaft des Staates Pennsylvanien; die in der Stadt
Philadelphia in der kläglichen Minderzahl Begriffe-
nen sehnen sich auch hier nach einem ephemeren
Siege und bestehen auf der Ausschliessung von
Philadelphia. In einem oder zwei Tagen werden
wir erfahren, ob ihnen der selbstmörderische Sieg
zu Theil wird.

Die Kurzsichtigkeit und Engherzigkeit der Amerikanischen Medicinischen Association war aber mit der Ausschliessung der Philadelphiaer nicht erschöpft. Welcher Ton dort herrschte, geht vielleicht am besten daraus hervor, dass der Vorsitzende (Dr. Wm. Brodie aus Michigan) in seiner offiziellen Präsidialrede einige medicinische Journale wegen ihrer angeblichen Feindseligkeit gegen die Association namhaft machte und ihnen rieth, ihre Redacteure zu wechseln, "wenn sie die Absicht hätten, die Patronage der Mitglieder der Association zu behalten." Er war es auch, der in derselben Rede dem Redacteur des offiziellen Journals wieder einmal das Stichwort der Geldgier entgegenhielt, welche die Ursache zu der Aufstellung des "Neuen Codex" geliefert habe.

In dieser Versammlung der Association zu St. Louis wurde Alles gut geheissen, was das jetzige "Executivcomité des Internationalen Congresses" beschlossen hatte, Massregeln sowohl wie Ernennungen. Soweit ist Alles besorgt und aufgehoben, und Sie können sich aus veröffentlichten Listen die Namen derjenigen heraussuchen, denen Sie in der Fachliteratur schon etwa begegnet sind.

Bevor man sich aber vertagte, that man einen grossen Schritt vorwärts. Man beschloss, den Congress der Vereinigten Staaten um Geldmittel zur Abhaltung des Congresses anzugehen und ermahnte jeden Anwesenden, seinen territorialen Congressrepräsentanten in dem Sinne zu bearbeiten. Das *Boston Medical and Surgical Journal*, ein ausgezeichnet redigirtes Wochenblatt, sagt über diesen Beschluss in seiner Nummer vom 13. Mai : "Solch ein Ersuchen, so scheint es uns, steht einer Versammlung von Männern ausserordentlich schlecht an, wenn sie auf irgend Etwas bestehen, und darauf Werth legen, dass der Internationale Congress die Amerikanische Medicinische Association repräsentirt. Wenn diese Association den beabsichtigten Congress in ihrem eigenen Interesse zu halten gedenkt, so sollte sie auch die Kosten decken, und nicht verlangen, dass die Steuerzahler des ganzen Landes ihre Rechnungen bezahlen. Wir glauben nicht, dass solch ein Vorschlag in ausgedehntem Masse annehmbar erscheinen wird." Auch ich glaube das nicht nur nicht, sondern ich weiss aus ganz massgebender Quelle, dass die Behörden in Washington und die höchsten Beamten des Landes sich nicht für berechtigt halten, Concessionen zu machen, wenn sie nicht vom ganzen ärztlichen Stande gewünscht werden.

Das Facit bis dahin ist wohl folgendes : Die grosse Zahl der bekannten Mediciner des Landes stehen ausserhalb des Congresses. Männer sind wenige. Dahingegen Mittel—noch weniger.

Aber ich habe fast die grosse Errungenschaft der letzten Wochen zu melden vergessen. Da Austin Flint todt ist, musste ein neuer Präsident für den Internationalen Congress nominirt werden. Der neue Präsident ist Dr. N. S. Davis von Chicago, dessen Namen ich in meinen früheren Correspondenzen genannt habe, der einzige überlebende Gründer und permanente Amtsinhaber in der Amerikanischen Medicinischen Association, Redacteur des offiziellen Journals, aus welchem ich Ihnen früher Auszüge geliefert habe, und seit der Resig-

nation von John S. Billings und der Ablehnung
Packard's (Philadelphia) General - Secretär des
"Congresses."

Wer ist nun aber Dr. N. S. Davis, der die Verwe-
genheit hat seinen Lesern, den Mitgliedern der
Amerikanischen Medicinischen Association die
Zumuthung zu machen, zu glauben, dass die New
Yorker, welche sich der Zuchtruthe des Herrn Davis
und Consorten entschlagen zu können meinen,
"aus Geldrücksichten" den Codex abgeworfen
haben.* Ein ethischer Codex, welcher seine vor-
nehmsten Fürsprecher in die Versuchung führt,
sich in so thörichten Verleumdungen zu ergehen,
sollte recht schnell in's Meer versenkt werden, wo
es am tiefsten ist. Wer ist nun Dr. N. S. Davis?
Im Subject Catalogue of the Surgeon-General's
Library ist er mit elf Nummern verzeichnet;
darunter sind eine Anzahl von Gelegenheitsreden
und kurze Geschichten der Amerikanischen Medicinischen Association und der Versuche, der ärztlichen Erziehung in den Vereinigten Staaten aufzu-
helfen, schliesslich eine kleine Sammlung von Vor-

* Im Journal der Amerikanischen Medicinischen Association vom 8. Mai 1886 steht Folgendes zu lesen, und zwar aus
der Feder des Herausgebers, Dr. N. S. Davis: "Gewisse Mitglieder des ärztlichen Standes, welche, aus Geldrücksichten,
sich gegen die klar definirten Pflichten des Arztes aufgelehnt
haben, suchen sich damit herauszuhelfen, dass sie sagen, dass
Gentlemen keine geschriebenen Regeln für ihr Benehmen
nöthig haben, und wollen ihre Stellung damit befestigen, dass
sie sagen, dass es in England keinen ethischen Codex gebe."
Es wird auch wieder behauptet, dass es eine "Minoritäts-
Versammlung" war, welche im Staate New York den ethischen Codex "unserer Väter" verwarf.

lesungen, vor Studenten gehalten. Ausserdem hat
er zu verschiedenen Zeiten sechs Journale herausgegeben, von der leider bei uns zu gewöhnlichen
Sorte, welche darauf basirt ist, dass jeder Arzt,
welcher bekannt zu werden wünscht, die Ueberzeugung vertritt, dass der betreffende Staat noch
nicht die entsprechende Anzahl von medicinischen
Journalen besitzt. Uebrigens hat N. S. Davis kaum
in einer der vierzig Jahresversammlungen der
Amerikanischen Medicinischen Association gefehlt,
ist persönlich mit Jedermann bekannt, sitzt jährlich in einem der Haupt-Comités und hat durch das
Alles einen nationalen Ruf im ärztlichen Stande.
In Europa ist er schwerlich durch irgend etwas bekannt geworden, es sei denn dadurch, dass A.
Jacobi denselben zum Mitglied des Comité's für
Collectiv-Untersuchungen in Copenhagen vor-
schlug. Und dieser Dr. N. S. Davis wird jetzt der
wissenschaftlichen Welt, wird den Paget's, den Virchow's, den Charcot's, als Präsident des "Internationalen Congresses" vorgeschlagen, von dem
man um den Mississippi herum noch immer sagt,
dass er sich im September 1887 in Washington versammeln werde.

Wer lacht da? Erlauben Sie mir, an dieser Stelle
zum Schluss noch einen kurzen Leitartikel des *Medical Record* vom 15. Mai 1886 zu citiren :

"Viele, vielleicht die meisten ausländischen
Standesgenossen sind in Unkenntniss darüber, was
der Streit über den nächsten Internationalen Congress bedeutet. Ganz gewiss, während sie nicht in
der Lage sind zu wissen oder zu bezweifeln, ob es
hier einen Internationalen Congress oder einen

17*

nationalen Zank geben wird, tragen Sie ein natürliches Bedenken, sich für ihre nächstjährige Reise
hierher zu rüsten.

" Diesen Herren wollen wir Folgendes sagen: Wir
haben in unserem Lande gewisse Streitigkeiten er-
lebt. Diese betrafen hauptsächlich die Frage, ob
der Internationale Congress durch die Amerikanische Medicinische Association, eine Gesellschaft
von etwa drei Tausend Mitgliedern, oder durch den
ärztlichen Stand, welcher sechzig Tausend zählt,
controllirt werden soll. In diesem Streite hat die
Association gesiegt, aber nur mit Anwendung von
solchen Mitteln, welche den Austritt der Mehrzahl
derjenigen amerikanischen Aerzte veranlasst haben,
die hier und in der übrigen Welt am besten bekannt
sind. Es wird einen Internationalen Congress geben, aber, wie die Dinge jetzt liegen, einen Congress, in welchem viele der besten Aerzte Amerikas
fehlen werden.

" Immerhin sagen wir den fremden Delegirten, sie
werden eine grosse Zahl fähiger und gastfreier
Herren bei dem Congress treffen, alle Amerikaner
werden Ihnen ein herzliches Willkommen bieten,
und Sie werden während Ihres Aufenthalts in den
Staaten keinen Zank vernehmen. Wir wissen, dass
viele Aerzte in New York, Philadelphia, Boston
und anderen medicinischen Centren, welche verhin-
dert worden sind, Gäste in offizieller Eigenschaft zu
empfangen, sich freuen werden, alle ausländischen
Besucher unoffiziell zu empfangen und ihnen jede
gastfreundliche Aufmerksamkeit zu erweisen."

Nach allen den unbehaglichen und bedenklichen
Mittheilungen, Herr Redacteur, welche ich Ihnen

in meinen Briefen zu machen hatte, will ich mir indessen die Freude nicht versagen, Ihnen von Erfolgen zu berichten, welche theils erreicht sind und theils ihrer Vervollständigung entgegen gehen. Es handelt sich um die Wahrscheinlichkeit der Schaffung eines *Nationalen* Medicinischen Congresses auf wissenschaftlicher Grundlage, ohne Rücksicht auf Länge, Breite, Quadratmeilen, Territorien, Eitelkeit, und " Codex."

Thatsache ist, dass von Anfang an viele Mitglieder des ärztlichen Standes mit den Leistungen der Amerikanischen Medicinischen Association unzufrieden waren. Territoriale Streitigkeiten, persönliche Drahtzieherei und Standespolitik nahmen den besten Theil der jährlichen Versammlungen in Anspruch. Diese lagen von Jahr zu Jahr viele hunderte, gar tausende von Meilenauseinander und wurden daher den wissenschaftlichen Arbeitern oft unzugänglich. So kam es, dass seit einer Reihe von Jahren sich eine Anzahl von Spezielgesellschaften bildeten, welche naturgemäss sich *meist* aus den östlichen und mittleren Staaten rekrutirten. Diese sind : die Amerikanische Chirurgische Association, die A. Ophthalmologische A., die A. Otologische A., die A. Neurologische A., die A. Laryngologische A., die A. Gynäkologische A., die A. Dermatologische A., und die A. Klimatologische A. Jede von Ihnen hat ihre eigne Organisation, ihren ständigen oder wechselnden jährlichen Versammlungsort zu fester oder wechselnder Zeit und ist wählerisch in der Aufnahme ihrer Mitglieder. Es ist natürlich, dass diese Associationen und ihre Mitglieder, während sie für ihr eignes wissenschaft-

liches Gedeihen gearbeitet haben, der "Amerika"
nischen Medicinischen Association" mehr oder weniger fremd geworden sind. Schliesslich hat sich im
Laufe der letzten Monate nach langen Vorbereitungen der Plan verwirklichen lassen, eine "Association von Aerzten," zu gründen, deren erste Sitzungen am 17. und 18. Juni in Washington stattfinden werden. Die Mitgliederzahl dieser Association
ist auf Hundert festgestellt. Sie werden nicht fehl-
gehen, wenn sie jeden Kliniker Amerikas, dessen
Name Ihnen bekannt ist, als Mitglied betrachten
wollen.

Der Anblick des Verfalls, in welchem die Amerikanische Medicinische Association begriffen ist, und
der Verdruss über die mörderische und selbstmörderische Politik derselben in der Angelegenheit des
Internationalen Congresses hat den Plan, die sämmt-
lichen speziellen Associationen zu einem "Congress
amerikanischer Aerzte und Wundärzte" zu vereinigen, zur Reife gebracht. Angeregt wurde derselbe
im letzten Jahre in der Amerikanischen Chirurgi-
schen Association, in diesem Jahre wieder berathen,
und ist auf die Tagesordnung des nächsten Jahres
gesetzt. Die Grundzüge der Constitution des Nationalen Congresses werden ohne Zweifel folgende
sein: Jede Association behält ihre eigne Verwaltung
und controllirt die Aufnahme ihrer Mitglieder.
Jedes Mitglied einer Association wird dadurch Mitglied des Congresses. Die Associationen geben ihre
separaten Versammlungszeiten auf und kommen
zu einer und derselben Zeit unter dem Vorsitze eines
nach noch zu bestimmenden Modalitäten zu ernen-
nenden Präsidenten zu einer (oder mehreren) ge-

meinschaftlichen Sitzungen zusammen, um sodann ihren Spezielarbeiten nachzugehen. Die Präsidenten der einzelnen Associationen sind Vicepräsidenten des Congresses. Der Ort des Congresses ist Washington.

Die Spezielassociationen haben in ihren Versammlungen seit Jahren Bedeutendes geleistet. Die neu gebildete Association von Aerzten wird ihnen hoffentlich würdig zur Seite stehen. Die Verschmelzung aller schon gebildeten, oder noch zu gründenden Associationen zu einem Ganzen, auf ähnlichen Grundlagen, wie diejenigen der einzelnen Gesellschaften sind, wird für Mittheilung, Ausgleichung, und Einheitsgefühl Erspriessliches leisten. Was uns fehlt, soll der ausgedehnte Plan schaffen: Vereinigung der arbeitenden und strebenden amerikanischen Mediciner zu selbstlosen, wissenschaftlichen, unpolitischen Zwecken. Quod bonum, felix faustumque sit!

RESOLUTIONS

PASSED BY THE NEW YORK ACADEMY OF MEDICINE
IN REFERENCE TO THE TENTH INTERNATIONAL
MEDICAL CONGRESS, INTENDED TO BE HELD
IN WASHINGTON IN 1887.

WHEREAS, A Committee was appointed by the American Medical Association in its session of 1884 to invite, *on behalf of the medical profession of the United States*, the International Medical Congress, then assembled in Copenhagen, to hold its next meeting, in 1887, in Washington; and

Whereas, That Committee was authorized at the time of its appointment, in case of the acceptance of that invitation by the International Medical Congress, to enlarge its numbers and make all proper preparations for the Congress; and

Whereas, The International Medical Congress accepted the invitation tendered on behalf of the medical profession of the United States, and recognized the Committee of invitation as its own Congressional Committee; and

Whereas, The International Medical Congress is, and always has been, a scientific body, never called or controlled by any medical society, association, or school, and not swayed or divided by ethical questions or local politics, but assembling solely for scientific purposes; and

Whereas, The original Committee of invitation enlarged its numbers, according to the authority conveyed in its appointment and confirmed by the International Medical Congress, completed its organization, and made full and mainly satisfactory preparations for the next meeting to be held in Washington; and

Whereas, The American Medical Association in its session held in New Orleans in April, 1885, usurped the powers of the Organizing Committee of the International Medical Congress, insisted upon none but members of the Association, or societies in affiliation therewith, to be admissible as officers or members of the Congress, and thus carried local politics into a purely scientific international body; and

Whereas, The new Committee appointed by the American Medical Association in New Orleans carried out the resolutions passed in New Orleans, and were compelled by the universal opposition of the profession of the United States to its usurpation only to consent to the admission to mere membership in the Congress those who were not affiliated with the American Medical Association, displacing from posts of trust and honor all those who do not belong to its number or hold certain ethical opinions not entirely sanctioned by it; therefore be it

Resolved, That the New York Academy of Medicine expresses its appreciation and thanks to the large number of distinguished men of Philadelphia, Boston, Baltimore, Washington, Cincinnati, Louisville, St. Louis, Chicago, New York, and other places, who decline to sanction this usurpation by participating in the Congress, or holding office, under a

Committee appointed for the purpose of dragging, in the mistaken interest of the American Medical Association, the International Medical Congress into strifes and disputes of a merely local character.

2. *Resolved*, That the New York Academy of Medicine recognizes in the action of those honored men who have made the American name a power in legitimate medicine, the true scientific spirit which has always been that of the International Medical Congress.

3. *Resolved*, That the New York Academy, though its Fellows do not pretend to be unanimous in all questions of medical politics, acknowledges and recognizes the International Congress as a scientific body only, and declines to participate in any international medical assembly of a personal, sectional, or political character.

4. *Resolved*, That any International Medical Congress held on American soil without the co-operation of the great and deserving men who have declined to hold offices or accept membership in the same, under the present management, cannot by any means be representative of American medicine, and will prove an utter failure.

5. *Resolved*, That therefore, under the present circumstances, though feeling deeply the disappointment and humiliation involved in taking this step, but profoundly impressed with its responsibility to the profession of Europe, which knows so well how to bury political or ethical differences on account of the common scientific interests, the New York Academy of Medicine requests the Executive Committee of the International Medical Congress, now

in Europe, to postpone the gathering of the International Medical Congress, thus far intended for Washington, until a more propitious time when the whole and undivided profession of the United States shall be prepared to receive it, delivered from the spirit of local dissensions, unanimous and harmonious.

INAUGURATION OF A NEW PAVILION, IN THE COUNTRY BRANCH OF FORDHAM HEIGHTS, OF THE NEW YORK SKIN AND CANCER HOSPITAL.

Ladies and Gentlemen :

To Mr. Napper, of Cranleigh, England, is attributed the credit of being the first to recommend the erection of cottage hospitals. It was he who wrote in 1855 on the advantages accruing through them to both the medical profession and the public. His plans were so in accordance with the public needs that what they call cottage hospitals in Great Britain were built in large numbers all over the Islands. Indeed, in 1880, when Burdett wrote his book on the subject, every county but five had its cottage hospital, and these five had no hospital accommodation whatsoever. Altogether they counted two hundred and fifty all over the land ; it is stated one hundred and eighty of them were in working order as cottage, and a number had developed into general hospitals. This last notice, and the hope expressed by Burdett that there will be in future one bed for every one thousand inhabitants, appear to prove that what we prefer to call a cottage hospital is by no means carried out by institutions called by that name in England. What they are is amply characterized by the pious wish expressed

by Dr. G. Derby in the report of the Massachusetts
State Board of Health in 1874, who says : " There
are many reasons for believing that at the present
time small and well-arranged hospitals in at least
twenty of our busy towns would be the means of
saving life and of preventing useless suffering both
to the sick and well."

A genuine cottage hospital plan for the *insane*
was favored and partly realized by Bucknill, who,
in 1865, transferred a number of patients to the
country, into smaller houses, under the supervision
of a nurse and his wife, so that they enjoyed something like a family life, more quiet and freedom,
pure air, and a moderate amount of work at the same
time. In Belgium, Parigot—whom some of the
older men in the profession of New York will remember; a paper of his on " Moral Insanity in
Criminal Cases " was read by him in 1861, and published in the first volume of the Bulletin of the
New York Academy of Medicine—introduced the
country cottage, together with the farming-out system, on a large scale. It has often been imitated
on the Continent of Europe. What the State Board
of Charities of the State of New York intends to do
with the sixteen hundred acres lately purchased in
Long Island for the relief of the overcrowded institutions of Blackwell's and Ward's Islands appears
to be in the nature of the same laudable enterprises.
Still, while giving credit to Bucknill, Parigot, and
whosoever else deserves it, we ought not to forget
where the real cottage system originated. Our
eagle, which knows how to screech, always, as we
believe, on proper occasions only and at proper

times, ought not to be silent on this occasion. For
the cottage hospital system is an indigenous American plant. If we were to forget it, Europeans remember it very well, for the pavilion and barrack
system, initiated by the skill and knowledge and
humanity developed and exhibited in our Civil
War, is acknowledged to have been the origin and
model of everything that has since been established
in that line. We require no words of praise of our
own. I am satisfied with what Rudolf Virchow,
whose name has been a household word in both
hemispheres for decades, says of "the critical and
thoroughly scientific spirit, the clear perception,
the sound and practical common sense, which pene-
trated gradually every part of the American military organization, and which, with the astounding
co-operation of an entire nation, accomplished more
humane results than any great war ever produced
before."

In the institution of the cottage system—that is, a
conglomerate of small hospitals in place of a large and
bulky institution—the combination of common sense
and science has obtained a great triumph. Still,
there is a point we might here consider, just *because it* appears to render the cottage system less
indispensable in our days than it was formerly. It
was, and is, deemed superior in part for the greater
facility of protecting the relatively healthy from
contagious and infectious diseases. There are so
many reasons for this, and they are so well understood, that it is not necessary to enumerate them
here. That was and *is* true, but it is no longer true
to such a degree as it was formerly. I will give

you instances. It is not much more than a dozen years ago that the whole medical profession and the knowing part of the public were fully convinced that there was but one way in which to deal with Bellevue Hospital. It was believed that whoever entered had to leave hope behind. Infectious diseases were fatal, inflammatory diseases became complicated with infectious fevers contracted on the premises, there was erysipelas all the time, and surgical operations terminated fatally in large percentages. Bellevue had to be torn down, and rebuilt there or in a better place. And at present? Having known it for many a long year, and appreciating the peculiar difficulties connected with the institutions filled with the poorest, and often most abject, criminal, and neglected part of the population, and depending on too scanty appropriations of money, Bellevue is in a fair, though improvable, hygienic condition. Erysipelas does not grow on our own ground; almost every case we treat there is brought in from outside. Hospital gangrene is not known, surgical operations terminate favorably, and infectious fevers are apt to get well. And still Bellevue has *not* been torn down and holds six hundred beds and more. The reasons for these enjoyable changes have been set forth impliedly by the late Dr. Van Buren when he delivered the introductory address at the opening of the new New York Hospital. His principal point was this, that the pavilion system and the very large grounds were no longer required; that the New York Hospital had a right to pile story upon story without risks, because of the new light shed

upon the nature of morbid processes and the antiseptic methods of treating diseases and wounds.
Into the merits of that assertion I shall not go here.
Medical men and a goodly part of the public know
that the last ten years have supported his opinions
and expressions to a great extent.

But nobody claims that, though large hospitals at
the present time can be so arranged and the treatment has been so perfected as to give unprecedented
results to such a degree as to render the best statistics of olden times absolutely worthless and mean-
ingless, large institutions are again to take the
place of cottage hospitals. What we have learned
is that large hospitals are no longer the curses and
man-traps that they often proved to be, that they
have been made comparatively safe, and no longer
so injurious, in spite of all the good they did, as
they necessarily were in former times. But the
increase in knowledge, which has worked such
changes in hospitals, favors cottages as well, and
the relative value of the two classes of institutions
is still the same. Our main sources of rejoicing are
the fact that all classes of institutions can be kept
in a healthier condition.

The advantages of the cottage system are, in a
few words, as follows :

Small wards offer more comfort to the patients
than large ones. They are not so easily disturbed
by each other, make themselves acquainted more
readily, and feel more at home.

Nuisances, excrements, soiled and soiling material, are less, and more easily removed.

The air can be more easily renewed with simpler
methods of ventilation.

Patients with nauseating diseases in a large ward are a source of suffering to a great number; in small ones the isolation of bad cases is more readily assured. A uniform plan of building permits of expansion from time to time, as necessity commands and means permit, and such changes in the additional cottages as prove desirable, at a proportionately low expense. Altogether the cost of building and furnishing is but trifling in comparison with that of large institutions. Within seventy miles from this place of yours there is a great hospital in which every bed cost eight thousand dollars, or as much as two or three of your pavilions. The money which founded a single bed in that institution would have been sufficient to start twenty of yours. In the former it was the State which exhibited the meagre results of clumsy, perhaps corrupt or negligent, efforts. In the latter the enthusiasm of intelligent and painstaking private benevolence has accomplished great results. Unfortunately, with us, the State does not appear to be able to do better. Its aid has thus far been mostly perfunctory. At best it recognizes aid or protection for its citizens as a painful duty. They are offered through hospitals and schools, in the same spirit in which State prisons and gallows are erected and sustained. As the State is now constituted, it finds means, more or less appropriate, to perform its cool, naked duty. When will it begin to take care of its own through sympathy and love? It will be a period of rejoicing when the conscience of the State will be raised to the standard of conscious sympathy, instead of matter-of-fact and unpleasant necessity. That time will come, for mankind is perfectible and on the road to moral and intellectual progress. To-day, however, it appears that that big conglomerate has to learn from its constituent parts.

A further advantage of cottage hospitals is the possession of large grounds such as you have here, and which can never be obtained in the heart of the city. On them you can manage to find employment for those of your patients who are not confined to bed. The question of employment becomes more important with the numerical increase of the institutions destined to take care of the poor or helpless. Prisons, almshouses, and hospitals are the dangers to society mainly through the enforced idleness of those who are supported in them. Those who are healthy and free have no idea of how time wears upon the unoccupied. What are they to do? You may be able to supply them with books or newspapers; there never are too many of them. The mouths of the station boxes for the benefit of the hospitals are always open and are filled to overflowing. Papers and journals and books will instruct the hospital inmates and aid them in passing their time. Still, they cannot always read. They require occupation, which as an exercise is useful to them, and at the same time leads to a visible result. It is in a cottage hospital only that you can accomplish these two ends.

No country under the sun has so proved the superiority of individual and collective efforts over those emanating from the political commonwealth than America. Its citizens have had the privilege of not being provided for and directed by a ubiquitous

18*

government, but of learning to help themselves and each other. This good humanitarian citizenship we see the evidence of here. Those whose hands and hearts we behold in the existence of these buildings have done better than the State ever could have done. They have performed the duty they felt in their hearts equally well or better, and at low cost. Indeed, for those who can afford the luxury of proving beneficent, that luxury is comparatively within easy reach. May those who have the means spend some of it in imitating the benevolent examples before them and in showing their power! For as power may be, and is, shown in doing harm, destroying peace and subverting the harmony of communities or countries, so there are those, in ever-swelling numbers, who experience in themselves the blissful consciousness of spending and exhibiting their power by doing good. They are the very ones who prove through their own experience that beneficence has its twofold blessings. For while it relieves the sufferer, it elevates the benefactor into the heights of the aristocracy of both intellect and heart. And a higher aristocracy there is not. No feudal or money aristocracy will ever be so enduring and, let me say that also, appreciated. For we are undergoing great changes in our public sentiment. We have arrived at that state of private and public culture that no millions command respect any more by themselves, but by what they do for humanitarian and scientific objects. Riches are covered by oblivion; no song and no history tells of a man because he gloated over barrels of gold; history is the tale of progressive development, and songs immortalize the names

of those who by brave and humane acts aided their
fellow-brothers and sisters. The heroes of antiquity
relieved the world of dragons and wild animals; the
dragons of the modern world are physical and moral
sufferings, which clamor for relief.

This relief is offered by those who contribute to
such a charity as that to which you give the support of your presence to-day. For the well-to-do,
the erection of a pavilion, or an ample donation for
its support, is but a trifling sacrifice compared with
the good it is doing for all times and the immor-
tality it secures for the kind donor. It relieves
suffering for an indefinite period; by aggregating a
number of cases of the same class, it accumulates
not only patients but also experience, and thus aids
in the accomplishment of the ends of medical research, which works to relieve and cure by new
thoughts and methods, and finally to reduce the
number of so-called incurable diseases.

What I wish to emphasize once more is the relative facility with which those great results are
obtained. To accomplish those ends, however, earnest co-operation is required, and submission to a
common sacred purpose. The secret of success lies
in the centralization of means and efforts. A few
thousand dollars will accomplish nothing when by
themselves; joined to the rest, free of personal
vanity and sterile rivalry, they are a great power
for good for all time to come, and benefit equally
those who receive and those who give. I wish I
had the eloquence to prove to all that the practice
of benevolence ought to be dictated by a sense of
duty: not that duty which directs your steps annu-

ally to the tax office or the jury box, because the law of the land enforces it, but that which is impelled by the laws interwoven with the folds of your hearts. That is the sense of duty which bids you to speak kindly to a weeping child in the street, to climb the rickety stairs of a dark tenement to hunt up the indigent, to distribute flowers amongst the beds of the poverty-stricken, forsaken, hungry-looking sisters in the hospitals—hungry for bread and hungry for a look of sympathy; or, if your means permit, to give of these means—both a permanent benefit to the suffering poor and a lasting blissful gratification to your own hearts.

INTRODUCTORY REMARKS

AT THE ANNIVERSARY MEETING OF THE NEW YORK
ACADEMY OF MEDICINE, NOVEMBER 18TH, 1886.

THE New York Academy of Medicine is of about the same age as modern medicine, as anæsthesia in America, and as Virchow's *Archiv* and his cellular pathology in Germany. During these forty years scientific medicine has progressed all over the globe in steady evolution. This Academy has not only followed this progress, but has contributed to it very largely. Of this assertion its historian would find many and irrefutable proofs. Indeed, very many of the names connected with the Academy would be bright lights in any country's literature ; to mention them here, however, would call the blush of pride to many a modest man's cheek, for there is many a Fellow in this hall, at this moment, who is both admired in our country and blessed in foreign parts for his contributions to the science and art of medicine.

Still, justice requires me to say that the Academy owes its position and efficiency to more than the efforts and genius of its best and most powerful minds alone. The political and the scientific republic thrive on the co-operation of the great capacities and the democratic masses. The bi-weekly stated meetings, with their papers and discussions, have kept the interest in scientific pursuits awake, more or less, all these decades ; the vigorous life of the newly established sections proves the zeal of the many participants ; the rapid increase of the library, which is accessible to both the whole profession and the public, speaks as well for the Academy's success as for its generosity ; the absence of ethical codes from the requirements of admission, and of ethical wrangling from its gatherings, for its scientific spirit ; and the unencumbered possession of this large building, for the Academy's perpetuity and lasting influence. In its name I am directed to extend to all of you a hearty welcome to this hall. Still, while so doing I cannot abstain from expressing the hope that my successor may, in the near future, have the honor of receiving you in a larger hall, and one more worthy of being the centre of the profession of this metropolitan commonwealth and the representative of American medicine.

American medicine has always exhibited a peculiar feature, mostly in common with the rest of the Anglo-Saxons on the other side of the Atlantic. It is eminently practical. In this I do not wish to be misunderstood. Science need not have, *ea ipsa*, an exclusively practical aim ; its value is not its weight in bread or butter. Mental efforts must not always be directly changeable into coin. The very branches of philosophical and exact sciences which have contributed most to increase the growth of human powers carry their reward less in money than in their intellectual results.

Indeed, for a long time American medicine has suffered from the very fact that we had no class of men who studied for study's sake, and found their aims reached in the cultivation of a pure science. We had no institutions to aid them, no citizens—though they would have fain done so—rich enough and interested enough to endow the institutions, no scientific men independent enough to allow themselves to be absorbed in their intellectual labors. All this is being changed. The number of strictly scientific workers among us is still small, but it is increasing constantly, and the men and women outside of the profession who are interested in, and willing and anxious to aid, the cultivation of medical science, begin to make themselves known. The American family who but lately enriched a medical school and thus, let us hope, rendered the prospects for a vast improvement in medical teaching and an elevated standard of professional merit more promising than ever; the large bequest to this Academy, due within a few months, by a lady connected with one of the most illustrious medical families of the city ; the munificent donation, a few weeks ago, by another lady who desired to lend an expression of her husband's and her own admiration for medical science and the medical profession—all of them prove the interest the public is beginning to take in medicine and medical progress.

Well it may, for if there be a science, or a complex of sciences, pure and at the same time practical, it is medicine. The medical professions of all countries, and medical science in every land, have but one aim and end—that is, the preservation of the health of the commonwealth and the individual, and the saving of life. The very results of the most abstruse investigations, the very highest intellectual efforts, are always directed to the accomplishment of these practical ends.

If there were no other tie between the public and the profession, there it is. Its existence is proven by the interest you have exhibited and the readiness with which you have kindly yielded to our invitation. As for the profession, it has felt it always ; certainly, since the time when its adepts ceased to wear wigs wherewith to cover the occasional emptiness of heads, and discarded the gold-headed canes from which the oracularly sealed lips liked to suck wisdom, the thoughtful and progressive professional man has always understood his connection with, and his responsibility to, the community, and known this also, that the more intimate the public became with the foundations and tendencies of his science—not to be gathered, however, from the cheap publications and advertising sheets which they steal into your houses, or sell to you in the garb of a religious or secular newspaper—the easier and more successful was his own task, viz., to protect or save his individual charge, and to benefit the community at large. In this spirit, dictated by the feeling, more or less conscious, of the existence of interests common to the public and to the profession, once, nearly thirty years ago, an anniversary discourse was delivered to which the public was invited. What at that time appeared to be merely desirable has at present become a necessity. The revised constitution of the Academy ordains that the anniversary discourse must be delivered in November of each year, and must be public. To me personally it is a source of intense gratification that the new rule should be inaugurated during my presidency. Thus was granted to me, what I hardly had the courage ever to hope, to witness the realization of what often was considered an ideal future. Thus there is one ideal at least that has become a fact.

The participation of the most intellectual class of the lay public in what formerly would have been, and was, the exclusive domain of the profession, proves that the conviction is gaining ground that medicine is the most humane and the most practical of sciences. Indeed, science and practice are not divergent. Their aims are identical, they serve each other, and both joined serve mankind.

Learning and practical tendency go very well with each other. That is what I shall prove by the discourse of a gentleman who is known to erudite men of all classes as a scholar, to his professional brethren as a learned physician, and to his numerous admirers among the public at large as a consummate practitioner—Dr. William H. Draper.

INTRODUCTORY REMARKS

AT THE ANNIVERSARY MEETING OF THE NEW YORK ACADEMY OF MEDICINE, NOVEMBER 17TH, 1887.

IN its last meeting the Council of the Academy directed its President to present to the audience, previous to the anniversary discourse, a short report of the life of the Academy during the current year. Thus it becomes my pleasing privilege to appear before you, as I did a year ago, with a few brief statements. Altogether this twelvemonth has been a period of successful work and increasing prosperity. We have a great many gains to record, but also sad losses. Eight Fellows have been removed by death. All of them filled their places well. Their names and memories will not be forgotten. May the Academy, the profession, the public have more like them!

Fortunately, the life of a great institution, like that of a nation of free men, does not cling to, or depend on, that of individuals. While the Academy lost eight Fellows by death, and one by resignation because of removal, sixty-two joined our ranks, so that the roll of Fellows contains at present five hundred and eleven names, the largest number at any time since its incorporation.

One of the principal features of the Academy is its reading rooms and library. The reading rooms are filled with most of the medical and scientific periodicals of the world. These form a stock of volumes increasing in number and value from year to year, and swell the library.

Besides, the latter has added to its shelves during one year eleven hundred and twenty volumes and four hundred pamphlets. Works begin to come in from foreign parts in exchange for our Transactions, two more volumes of which have been printed and sent abroad. With the encouragement we now have, we may hope that within a reasonable time we shall gather a large and influential collection of books, such as will supply all the intellectual food the profession will want. A special donation of five thousand dollars, and the application of another five thousand to the same purpose, have begun to yield an income which enables us to purchase regularly some of the latest works.

To what extent the profession sympathizes with our efforts is proved by occasional gifts and bequests. The will of Dr. A. Flint ordered his whole library to be given to the Academy, with the exception of such books as the family might wish to retain. A medical gentleman of a neighboring State has seized an opportunity to purchase for us a collection of four hundred books on the special subject of congenital malformations, and within a few weeks we shall be in possession of a library of four thousand volumes, collected during a long lifetime by a medical man ripe in years, rich in merits, and long retired from his vocation and public life. When his name will become known in connection with this welcome gift, many of the older members of the profession will gladly recollect him as a former townsman, in large practice, a public-spirited gentleman, and one of the founders of the Pathological and other societies—Middleton Goldsmith. He prefers to part with his library to being parted from it, and to enjoy our enjoyment while he is still alive ; thus teaching a lesson to those who defer, until they are gone forever, their acts of goodwill and beneficence. But, after all, the future of every library is firmly secured *by funds only.* When our nearest and most urgent wants will have been supplied, it will be our duty to see to it that, instead of our present library fund of ten, there will be one of a hundred thousand dollars. Then only can the profession know that all the intellectual food required is within reach. To the erudite man a large library hall is what a church is to the religious.

The account of the work of the Academy includes brief information in regard to its scientific proceedings. The nine Sections held each its regular monthly meetings with but a few occasional interruptions. Their number is about to be increased by one which will occupy itself exclusively with the diseases of children as special studies. The stated meetings of the Academy were occupied with topics of great importance and general interest. The selection of chloroform or ether as an anaesthetic— a question the merits of which have often been curtly, if not correctly, decided by a coroner and his jury, guided by accumulated ignorance—was made the subject of a careful and protracted discussion. There were several other surgical papers, too technical, however, to be mentioned on this occasion. But it will interest the audience to learn that the electric instrument which failed to indicate the location of the bullet in President Garfield's body, was presented here in an improved shape and performed what it was announced to do—viz., to detect and locate metallic substances in the human body.

The diseases of the nervous system have been studied from different aspects. Epilepsy and the combination of spastic and paralytic symptoms in spinal diseases have aroused much interest. The antiseptic treatment of summer diarrhœa was eagerly discussed, and the respiratory organs came in for a full share of attention. Besides a number of purely technical papers, there were others whose themes commend them to the public at large. Men who knew from personal experience whereof they spoke entertained us on the climatic and sanitary conditions of Southern California, and the comparative value of Colorado Springs and Davos Platz, as winter resorts for those suffering from pulmonary ailments. There was, finally, a discussion on intubation—a proceeding to relieve the strangulation of children dying with membranous croup, by introducing into the larynx a hollow cylinder instead of opening the windpipe below it by tracheotomy (which many of us did in many hundreds of cases, since we had been taught to do so by our late Fellows in olden times—Waldemar von Roth, Gurdon Buck, and Ernst Krackowizer). To that meeting of last June I look back with great satisfaction, for it will be a memorable one in the history of the Academy. Not only was a large amount of new information brought out, but, in the shape in which it has been collected and distributed, it will not fail to instruct men and save lives here and in Europe. Besides, the whole proceeding is the discovery of a Fellow of the Academy, who, after years of careful and painful labor, succeeded in enriching medical art and adding to the reputation of the American profession.

The latest proof of the methods pursued in the public interest by this New York Academy of Medicine, whose object is " the promotion of the science and art of medicine," is found in the readiness with which the present Health Department and the profession as represented in the Academy have joined hands. Jealousy and rivalry have sometimes existed between them, for reasons at present well understood. They have been substituted by hearty good-will and close co-operation. A fortnight ago to-day, in the presence of the president and other officers of the Health Department, its medical member addressed us with a paper on the question, " How can the Medical Profession aid the Board of Health ?" Let me say only this, that this anxiety on the part of the Health Department to bring the message, and the profession to receive it, resulted in the appointment, at the suggestion of the Health Department, of a conference committee of five to co-operate with the constituted authorities.

Exactly a year ago, on this very platform, I expressed the hope that within a reasonable time I, or my successor, should have the glorious opportunity of greeting you in a larger hall and with nobler sur-

roundings. The circular I hold in my hand, which
is to be distributed shortly among our friends, has
reference to that subject. It is signed by a committee of thirty, and reads as follows :

"The New York Academy of Medicine is an incorporated institution forty years old. Its object is
the cultivation of medical science. This is accomplished by lectures and discussions in the
stated meetings of the Academy and its numerous
Sections ; by sustaining reading rooms which furnish nearly all the medical journals of the world ;
and by collecting a library containing at present
35,000 volumes and 20,000 pamphlets, which are
free both to the profession and the public. The
growth of the library is secured by donations of
books, annual appropriations of the Academy, and
special library funds, which, we hope, will increase.

"The number of its Fellows is at present about
five hundred. They are elected from among the
professional men who have practised medicine in
New York City or its vicinity three or more years.

"By careful management and voluntary contributions of its Fellows the Academy has accumulated
some property. It owns its building, No. 12 West
31st street, free of debt. That, however, is too
small for its membership, its many and various
meetings, and its steadily increasing library. The
house not being fireproof, the library is in constant
danger.

"A large fireproof building is, therefore, an immediate necessity. In recognition of this fact, Mrs.
Anna Woerishoffer gave to the Academy the sum
of $25,000, Mrs. Celine B. Hosack bequeathed

$70,000, and Dr. Beadle $5,000 for the purpose of erecting a new building. More funds, however, are required, and therefore we appeal to both the profession and the public to aid us.

"Some of the grounds on which we base this request are the following:

"The Academy is not connected with any school or college. It is self-supporting, and carried on in the interest of the whole profession. There are no fees or emoluments of a private or individual nature. It is a democratic commonwealth with equal duties and rights. It is not supported or subsidized by the State or municipal corporation. Its aims are the elevation of the profession to a higher scientific standard for increased public usefulness. These aims concern the public as much as the profession. Increased scientific attainments on the part of the medical men of the country secure to the public great advantages and more effective services. Here it is that the interests of the public and the profession meet.

"Thus we appeal to the wise generosity of the public, and request contributions large enough to enable us to accomplish the purposes for which the Academy was founded. The sum required is $200,000. It will not be the first time for the well-directed liberality of American citizens to do what some in the old countries still believe to be the prerogatives of the centralized means of powerful governments."

You perceive we are not afraid to beg, or, rather, to announce now that we shall go a-begging shortly. We trust the time is opportune and we shall be

19*

welcome. For New York has undergone great changes. After trying hard to become the centre of industry and commerce, and having succeeded ; after breeding millionaires by the hundreds, and riches untold ; after raising itself to the front rank of the cities of the globe in money power and commercial dignity, the consciousness of accomplished results has taken possession of the minds who were chasing after their aims, and reached them. The stupendous generosity of wealthy Americans has been a byword in Europe this quarter of a century. But, indeed, of the variety and size of the gifts bestowed in the service of religion, charity, and science but few have a correct idea. Our sentiments have so changed that no longer do millions enforce respect and position for their own sake amongst cultured men and women, except in exactly the relation to what they accomplish in the service of mankind. Among the public institutions which profited by this sentiment, the majority were religious and charitable. Of late the scientific have commenced to share the blessings conveyed by well-spent money. Medicine has been the last to enjoy the sympathy of the rich, and still the few remarks I have had the privilege to make before you ought to convince you that what you do for medical institutions you do for yourself and the commonwealth. Moved by *such* considerations, and from *that grand and sublime* business point of view, a single wealthy man and his family spent nearly a million and a half in building a solid foundation for the now best-equipped medical school in the land, *one* of the best-equipped in the world.

Their hope is, among others, that the one hundred or one hundred and fifty young men who graduate from that school annually will go forth with better preparation for their work and increased enthusiasm for the continuation of their studies, and that this school, together with the two other large and prosperous similar institutions of the city, will yield an example to those in other States, make them look to New York for inspiration, and their graduates come to New York to complete their studies.

We, the New York Academy of Medicine, apply to the public to add the crowning dome to the edifice. New York must have a medical profession worthy of the city. To centralize the profession, to elevate it socially and intellectually, to enhance its opportunities for development, to evolve a future most worthy of its past and in keeping with the proud position of the metropolis, a seventh part of the immense gift alluded to will prove competent. One-fifth of a million added to what we now possess will erect a home worthy of the profession of this great city; accommodate a large library such as we require and *will* possess; give a home to all the medical and scientific gatherings; become more than it has already begun to be, the head centre of the ever-changing, ever-developing and improving medical brotherhood ; and form the centre of gravitation for the medical world of the whole land, and a welcome refuge to those coming from beyond the seas. It will suffice for thrice our number, rouse the enthusiasm for liberal studies which ought to begin, indeed does begin, in earnest, when the college doors close behind us, and aid in raising

New York to be the city of learning, erudition, and culture, as it has become that of industry, commerce, and wealth.

It will have still another influence interesting to every one of you, not so much indeed as proud citizens of this much-berated and much-beloved New York, but as individuals. In behalf of your own domestic circle, of your children, and those who come next in your affections, it will aid in creating that being whose nature will be discussed to-night by a gentleman who is known among us as one of the most honorable, sturdy, philosophical, and learned physicians of the *present*, and whom I now have the great honor to introduce with his discourse on *The Family Physician of the Future*—Dr. Andrew H. Smith.

RULES OF THE NEW YORK STATE BOARD OF EXAMINERS.*

To the Editor of the Medical Record.

Sir:—A law of 1874 established for the State of New York a State Board of Medical Examiners. Frequent deaths and occasional resignations changed its original membership several times, until, upon the recommendation of the undersigned (who, therefore, objected repeatedly to his own appointment), and for reasons easily understood, all the members of the present Board, with one exception, were selected, by the Honorable the Board of Regents of the University of the State of New York, from among the medical men of Albany, the seat of the Government and the Board of Regents.

The profession never expected the law, as it was passed in 1874, to be efficient. It was believed by many that some of the medical colleges objected to the establishment of a State Board altogether, though others were known to favor it. It was certain that sectarian influences succeeded in undermining the passage of the original bill and emasculating it. *It is certain* that no State Board of Examiners will ever benefit either the profession or the public—both of which stand in equal need of it—before the license to practise medicine will de-

* The Medical Record, August 6th, 1887.

pend on the *compulsory* passing of a successful examination before the State Board. As the law stood, nobody ever applied for examination and the degree of M.D. of the University of the State of New York who was in the possession of a diploma from a college in good standing. Such few as volunteered to come forward were men who had previously failed in their college examination, or "practised medicine" without study, knowledge, or any title whatsoever. There being no rules and regulations referring to a minimum of accomplishments or requirements, a few of these were let loose upon the unsuspecting public with a diploma ; the majority, however, failed.

When the new Board was appointed in the beginning of this year, its members accepted their positions upon the condition that the Board of Regents would authorize a number of rules and principles which were to regulate the examinations. As such have been approved by the Regents, I am directed by the Board of Examiners to present them to you for your information and, if you deem proper, for publication and comment. We know quite well that, as long as the examination by the State Board is not made *compulsory*, any number of rules and principles will prove their inadequacy and inefficacy again and again. But the present Board hopes that its earnest recognition of the rights and dignity of medical science, art, and practice will be admitted by, and found acceptable to, the profession, and that the latter, after a minimum of requirements for the admission into the ranks of the profession has been officially accepted by the

Regents, will feel encouraged to continue its exertions in behalf of both the elevation of the standard of medical education and the protection of the public.

Not one of the recent applicants for a degree has proved successful. One of them had failed in his college examination a few weeks previously, and now threatens to swell the number of graduates of the "university" of a neighboring State. Similar occurrences are not rare at all. Candidates failing in one college will obtain their degrees from other colleges in the same or other States. Will not that suggest the necessity, instead of a "State Board," of a United States Board of Examination?

Very respectfully,

A. JACOBI, M. D.

110 WEST 34TH STREET,
NEW YORK, July 25th, 1887.

STATE BOARD OF MEDICAL EXAMINERS.

The members of the State Board of Medical Examiners accept their positions with this understanding :

A candidate for the degree of Doctor of Medicine, to be given by the Board of Regents, either desires an additional degree after he has received a diploma from a chartered medical college, or he has no diploma from any chartered medical college and desires or prefers one from the Board of Regents. The degree given by the Board of Regents is to be, or become, an honorable distinction. It must be the object of the law to protect the people and to ennoble the medical profession, and not to facilitate the entrance into it of persons unfit or unqualified. The profession does not require larger numbers, but does insist upon an elevated standard. Therefore the examination must be strict, and must be conducted according to the following rules:

1. The examinations before this Board shall be conducted in the English language exclusively.

2. The candidate shall be allowed two and a half hours for each examination. The examination shall be in writing. The candidate must not consult books, extracts, notes, or persons, and must not communicate with any one during the two and a half hours allotted to him. To do so is to be considered a failure to pass.

3. The examination in clinical medicine and in clinical surgery shall consist in the actual examination of patients by the candidate, and a discussion in regard to the diagnosis, prognosis, and treatment of the cases.

4. The examination in chemistry shall include the actual testing of a specimen of urine, in regard to its reaction, specific gravity, and the presence or absence of albumin and sugar.

5. Each examiner shall have the privilege, if he so desire, of supplementing his written examination by an oral one, in the presence of two other members of the Examining Board.

6. The scale of marks shall be from zero to ten; ten being perfection, and anything below six being a failure to pass the examination.

7. The questions and answers, with their marks, shall remain in the possession of the Board of Regents, and shall be open to inspection.

8. When the candidate will have completed all his examinations the Board of Examiners shall meet and hear the result of the examination in each branch. And within ten days thereafter each member of the Board shall make a written report as to the merits and acquirements of the candidate; being guided in this report, not alone by the result of the examination in his particular branch, but also by the result of the examinations in the other branches. And each member of the Board shall send his report, together with the questions and their answers and their marks in his branch, to the secretary of the Board of Examiners, to be by him transmitted to the secretary of the Board of Regents.

And, furthermore, it is the opinion of the Board of Examiners that, in order to receive the degree of Doctor of Medicine, the candidate should successfully pass in every branch, or at least in every branch but one.

STATE BOARD OF MEDICAL EXAMINERS.

ABRAHAM JACOBI, M.D., President, Examiner in Pathology.

ALBERT VANDER VEER, M.D., Vice-President, Examiner in Surgery and in Clinical Surgery.

HENRY HUN, M.D., Secretary, Examiner in Clinical Medicine and in Materia Medica and Therapeutics.

JAMES P. BOYD, M.D., Examiner in Obstetrics.

FRANKLIN TOWNSEND, M.D., Examiner in Physiology.

SAMUEL R. MORROW, M.D., Examiner in Anatomy.

WILLIAM HAILES, JR., M.D., Examiner in Histology.

WILLIS G. TUCKER, M.D., Examiner in Chemistry.

RESOLUTIONS

OF THE MEDICAL SOCIETY OF THE STATE OF NEW YORK
REFERRING TO THE STATE CARE OF THE INSANE.

THE Committee of the Medical Society of the State of New York, to whom was committed that portion of the President's opening address relating to the treatment of the insane, would respectfully report :

1. That until comparatively recent times the insane were considered and treated as criminals and confined in dungeons or prisons.

2. Their subsequent retention in poor-houses was but a remnant and mitigation of the old system.

3. The treatment of the insane has improved with the progress of civilization.

4. Therefore special hospitals were supplied for them, and their welfare was entrusted to scientific and humane experts.

5. To return to anything like the old system of treating the insane in poor-houses or relegating them to the custody of county officials would be a grave mistake.

As early as 1855, at a meeting of the county superintendents of the poor, held at Utica, the following, among other resolutions, was passed :

"*Resolved*, That no insane person should be treated or in any way taken care of in any county poor- or almshouse, or other receptacles provided for, and in which paupers are maintained and supported " ("Fifty-fifth Annual Report, State Asylum at Utica ").

6. For the proper classification and treatment of the insane more means are required than for the patients of general or even other special hospitals. Institutions for the insane therefore demand medical experts as superintendents, nurses trained in the general care of the sick, and then in the special care of the insane, schools for the physical and intellectual training of the insane, for the practice of outdoor and indoor industries, and many other appliances.

7. The Medical Society of the State of New York expresses, therefore, its objections to any plan or law which in any way looks to the return of the insane to the county poor-houses, as being unscientific and inhumane, and expresses its conviction that those institutions which, like the State Asylum, have Boards of Managers accountable to the State Government and also to the public, are best adapted for the care of the insane poor of the State.

All of which is respectfully submitted.

A. JACOBI,
C. R. AGNEW.

RESOLUTIONS

OF THE NEW YORK ACADEMY OF MEDICINE.

" *Resolved*, That the New York Academy of Medicine heartily indorses the action of the managers of the State Charities Aid Association, having in charge the bill pending for the better accommodation of pauper lunatics in this State, and recommends it to the favorable consideration of the Legislature of the State of New York."

The New York Academy having been informed of a special bill, passed February 21st last, authorizing Madison County to withdraw its indigent insane from the State Insane Hospitals, and to care for them in a so-called county asylum—poor-house—cannot but deplore this step taken by the Assembly of the State.

As medical men the Fellows of the Academy object to the principle embodied in the bill alluded to. The insane require more care, attendance, and special knowledge than they can find in a small community or in connection with poor-houses. The attendance on them and their cure require more than the means and the scientific opportunities of a small community can afford to furnish, no matter how good the intentions and how high the intellectual standing and humane instincts of the present authorities of Madison County.

The New York Academy of Medicine, the Neurological Society, the Medical Society of the County of New York, the Medical Society of the State of New York, in their meetings of 1888 and 1889, have therefore expressed their approval of the bill prepared by the State Charities Aid Association, which is now before both houses of the State Legislature. That bill provides that the indigent insane shall be cared for in State institutions, such care being the only one which can effectually lead to the fulfilment of the requirements of both science and humanity.

Therefore the New York Academy of Medicine begs to protest against the special bill (exempting Madison County from the general laws of the State) becoming a law of the land, and again recommends the bill introduced into the Legislature, on behalf of the State Charities Aid Association, to every well-meaning and humane legislator, and calls upon the medical profession of the State to enlist the sympathies of the people in favor of the indigent insane, and resolves to offer the opinions here stated to the consideration of the Legislature by a committee appointed for the purpose.

INTRODUCTORY REMARKS

AT THE ANNIVERSARY MEETING OF THE NEW YORK
ACADEMY OF MEDICINE, NOVEMBER 15TH, 1888.

As on several previous occasions, I again enjoy the
privilege of introducing, in this medical hall, to a
mixed audience, the orator of the evening. A dozen
times during the course of every month these rooms
are occupied by scientific meetings held under the
auspices of the New York Academy of Medicine.
Upon this one annual occasion, however, the public
are invited to participate in the exercises of an official assembly. The respectful request extended to
the public to join us is dictated by our desire that
the aims and objects of the Academy, and through
it of the medical profession, should be more fully
understood by the community at large.

The object of the New York Academy of Medicine is the promotion of medical science and art. In
the words of a circular lately published in behalf of
a building fund—for the purpose of erecting a new
edifice—"this is accomplished by lectures and discussions in the stated meetings of the Academy and
its numerous Sections ; by maintaining reading
rooms which furnish nearly all the medical journals
of the world; and by collecting a library containing
at present about sixty thousand books and pamphlets, which are free both to the medical profession
and the public." The number of its Fellows is ever

five hundred. They have been elected from among
those who have practised medicine in New York
City or its vicinity three or more years. But lately
Fellowship has been extended to those residing in
the State.

In its composition the Academy participates in
many of the peculiar features of our political organization, which means to benefit all through the
co-operation, if not of all, still of the best. In Europe an academy of medicine means a small body
comprising a few select men only, appointed by the
body itself, or by the political rulers. Thus the academies form an aristocracy of the mind parallel to
the aristocracy of birth, with all its exclusiveness
and real or assumed superiority. They are representative bodies only in this, that the best minds and
most efficient scientific workers are expected or believed to fill the chairs.

The New York Academy of Medicine is a more
democratic institution. Forty-one years ago it was
founded by a number of medical gentlemen, but
few of whom are still with us. Since that time,
with the changes for good and bad appertaining to
everything organic, it has developed and prospered.
Its prosperity has been growing constantly, in spite
of, or, as I am more inclined to say, in consequence
of, its very constitution as an independent and democratic body. In the words of the same circular alluded to before, " the Academy is not connected with
any school or college. It is self-supporting and carried on in the interest of the whole profession. It
is not supported nor subsidized by the State or municipality." Whatever has been accomplished by it—

its scientific labors, most of which are laid down in its Bulletins and Transactions, and in the medical journals of the country; the hall you fill, the library and reading rooms in the upper stories, the wealth of books and journals at the disposal of those eager to learn, and so numerous that they alone compel us to look for more appropriate quarters—all of it has been created, with but few exceptions, by the exertions and pecuniary sacrifices of the medical men themselves.

The election of Fellows takes place after a close scrutiny of their attainments and respectability. Beyond the condition of a three years' practice, we know of no claim on Fellowship except worth : age or worldly position do not count. The democratic spirit of the country, as represented in every one of the great political parties and those independent of official platforms, is exhibited in our organization. In the last years it has even been the special object of those at the helm to see to it that the younger and young men, those on whose shoulders the interests and dignity of the profession have to rest for the future, were given ample encouragement to work, to co-operate, and to teach. We claim that in so doing we have fulfilled the duties of citizens loyal to the spirit of the country and to the scientific exigencies of this time and that to come ; secured the aid of all, roused a justifiable ambition, and awakened the sense of professional and moral fraternity and solidarity.

Thus the New York Academy of Medicine represents for you the choice of those interested and active in the promotion of medical science and art ;

20*

such as have earned an international reputation,
such as deserved well of the community by a life
filled with services rendered to the public, and those
who look forward for the accomplishment of their
dreams and aims through coming years of honest
labor spent on theoretical study and practical work.
In this co-operation of the old and young, the illustrious and those, unknown, promising or anxious
to become so, the mature and maturing, you have
one of the features of a unity of the profession.

Another feature of unity, which, moreover, ties
the profession indissolubly to the community at
large, is the labors performed in the interest of
one and all. It is in these and their results that
the community at large ought to have, and has, a
deep interest. The more medicine has been founded on the study of the exact sciences—chemistry,
physics, and physiology—the more its field of usefulness has enlarged. The more theoretical it
appeared to become the more did it develop practical usefulness. Indeed, the dignity of a science or
study rises with its ability of being utilized in the
service of mankind. Nor is there any study so
abstruse, any scientific hypothesis so apparently
vague, but must and can be rendered profitable to
the best interests of the race. No field has been
more profitable than that of medical and scientific
research. Thus the promotion of medical science
and art does not mean only the improvement of
diagnosis and of the administration of drugs and
remedies, but that of the best means of placing the
human being in the best possible condition. The
labor of the physician is not exhausted by carrying

you through a severe case of illness; his duty and anxiety is to render you the, to him, less remunerative service of preventing you from falling sick. While it is his duty to save you from the consequences of your transgressions, his knowledge of their consequences leads him to protect you against committing them.

The peculiar relations of the individual physician to his patient or the family entrusted to his care are widened in the relations of the profession to the public. Great epidemics take the place of a single case, the protection of a community that of the guarding an individual, the hygiene of the schools that of the dwelling, the sanitation of a large city that of inspecting a suspected trap or sewer in a private domicile. The hygiene of the whole population, the superintendence of public buildings in which many people, young or old, are gathered, public hospitals, quarantine stations, the question of physical and mental elevation, of legal responsibility, are just so many parts of the domain of the medical profession. To legislate in reference to the pauper insane without consulting medical experience and knowledge; to pass a law according to which the president of the Board of Health of a city of a million and a half of inhabitants must not be a medical man; to refuse to abolish the usage according to which the medical expert even in a criminal case before a court of justice must not be a medical officer, appointed because of his special knowledge, but the paid aid of the contesting parties, reminds us of past semi-barbarism. If a salutary change will be accomplished, that result will

be due to the influence attained by the medical
profession over the minds of men. The Academy
has been instrumental in producing such a change
to a certain extent. From the Fellows of the Academy the Health Department has selected its consulting board of all its institutions ; the Academy
furnished to the same department a special committee to inspect and report on the condition of
Quarantine, and it is to the report of that committee, as finally compiled by the late Dr. Agnew,
that the exact condition of the Quarantine Islands
was fully known and appreciated in all its mediæval recklessness and futility, and that the
appropriations for improvement are largely due.
Thus the profession, as gathered in, and represented by, the New York Academy of Medicine, is
beginning to be recognized and known as both a
proper authority in matters of public concern and
the natural guardian of public health.

Why is it that I remind you of this? It is because it is never too often that we recognize the
connection of the links with the chain, the member
with the body, of the parts with the whole. Human society is an organism. It has so evolved as
to consist of parts closely necessitating and depending upon each other. Men, trades, professions require each other for maintenance and development.
Not that all are equivalent as to dignity and result;
still there is nobody and nothing but is indispensable in the economy of nature or society. This
knowledge of intimate correlation of all is the
source of the conviction of the unity of the race, of
uniform though slow progress, and the fountain

head of republican institutions. In the medical
profession, which like all sciences is a republic, this
correlationship means a great deal. Medicine, both
as a science and a profession, is an organism, the
branches of which, after leaving the common stem,
appear to start away from each other and get lost
in increasing distance. The special studies which
lead into the investigation of narrow paths and by-
ways, and the specialistic practices which obscure
the general view while throwing concentrated light
on a special point, may appear to contract the scientific conscience and split the body medical into dis-
jected splinters. But what seems unavoidable in
an individual soul less endowed with breadth and
depth, does not affect the comprehensive nature of
science or the profession at large.

The really great specialist, the man who had no
trade, but a calling; no cunning, but force; no itching for money or temporary popularity, but an eye
upward to the sky in which he beheld inscribed the
future of his science and its shaping and ennobling
influence on mankind in general—that specialist was
always a good physician, thoroughly well informed,
comprehending the intercommunication between
the separate branches, and appreciating, as well in
science as in art, both diversity and unity.

Involuntarily, when I made this remark, my
thought turned to the gentleman whom I am to introduce to you to-night. The Council of the Academy has been peculiarly fortunate in year after
year securing representative and prominent men as
the orators on these occasions. During my terms of
service I have had the distinguished honor to preside

over meetings addressed by Drs. Noyes, Wm. H. Draper, and A. H. Smith. To-night it is a great satisfaction to be able to present a gentleman of equal and unquestionable worth, on whom I have always looked as one of the most representative men in the best of professions; a specialist with thorough general information on medicine, a medical man with the ideals prompted by conscientious habit and scientific spirit, he is amongst those best fitted to speak on the unity of the profession and the means of effecting it. A professional man with the best instincts of the citizen, disproving the narrow impression that a professional man must needs keep aloof even from the discussion of public affairs or the turmoil of political life, he might well be called upon to deliver a discourse on the means of effecting the unity of all party interests, both in science and life. Whatever he will say on his chosen subject, whether in accordance with the preconceived ideas of every one of his listeners, no one doubts two things—namely, that he knows exactly what he is going to say, and will exactly say what he knows or believes to be the truth, the whole truth, and nothing but the truth.

Ladies and gentlemen, I have the honor of presenting the orator of the evening—Dr. D. B. St. John Roosa.

VALEDICTORY ADDRESS OF DR. JACOBI, AND INTRODUCTION OF DR. LOOMIS AS PRESIDENT.

Fellows of the Academy :

THE annual reports submitted to you during the four years of my presidency exhibit the gradual growth of the New York Academy of Medicine in many of its most important points. The library has increased in books, both old and new, the hundreds of journals you possess fill your shelves to overflowing, and the several library funds have accumulated so as to become available for regular purchases.

Your permanent fund is larger by more than a hundred thousand dollars than it was a few years ago, and your expectations of having a new and suitable Academy building are approaching their fulfilment. Though it may appear long since the movement in favor of erecting a new Academy was started, the delay was not due to procrastination. Protracted preparations made, and dozens of committee meetings held during the last two years have finally smoothed your path. They have given ample opportunities for exchanging opinions, removing doubts, spurring hesitations, controlling haste.

There never was in your Council and Committee a dissenting voice in regard to the question of the necessity of obtaining an appropriate building, nor was there a doubt as to the possibility of accomplishing the end. If there were any differences of opinion at any time, they referred to the selection of the best means of rendering you, and through you the whole profession, the best service. It is a source of great satisfaction to the retiring president to be able to announce that your Council and your Committee are unanimous, that they believe in, and are assured of, the near perfection of their plans, that there is no doubt as to the acquiring of the means, that the locality of our future home has been determined upon, and that we shall have a home for ourselves, our journals, library, and the medical and other learned societies of the city, before the term of service of my distinguished successor will have expired.

In the early period of my first term of service a few changes were made in the by-laws which have worked quite well. The only object of the Academy has ever been declared to be the promotion of the science and art of medicine. That article will never give rise to strife and dissension. Nor has the dropping of the Committee on Ethics produced the evil results which were feared by some. Indeed, the belief that the Council would prove a better Ethical Committee than one appointed *ad hoc* has been borne out by a valuable experience in a few cases where transgressors, by admonitions of a private nature, got easily convinced of the advisability of mending their ways. I allude, of course, mainly to the practice of advertising glaring reports of glorious deeds committed on other people's limbs and bones. Now, it is well understood that all of us live in glass houses, that the newspaper reporter is as ubiquitous as a police spy in an absolute monarchy, and that now and then even the most honorable physician has the misfortune to be shown up at the pillory of a penny-a-liner craving to satisfy the prurient appetite of the omnivorous part of the credulous public. But it is just as well understood by the smiling profession that the mishap of getting into print with unheard-of cures falls mostly upon the same gentlemen, of number one in *Main Puff* street, who are acrobatic experts in the art of balancing on the line fence which parts sheep and bucks. *

Such things have always taken place and will continue to do so. For ambition and egotism are not always directed by moral self-control and intense regard for the public good. If the latter prevail no hampering written laws are required in a society of the educated and free. But public opinion, as represented in the Council of the Academy, will always, we hope, direct sufficient influence in supporting the morally weak or unstable. The Council, however, looks for its own authority and support amongst the Fellows who elected it. It is for the latter to direct this *Council*, as it is for the people to control their servants in the public offices in the municipal and political commonwealth. It is your lookout to have in your Council not only the oldest, or those who enjoy a personal following, or even those who have made a deserved reputation by scientific labors, or those who are acquainted with the pecuniary and business affairs of the Academy, but those also who are known for

the morality of their professional life, for their ab-
horrence of cheap and nasty notoriety, and their
respect for the dignity and purity of the medical
profession.

The number of Fellows has increased considerably. Nearly three hundred certificates were
signed during the last four years. I wish, however, we had to report gains only ; it often appeared to me that some of the losses we had to submit to could never be repaired. We shall long miss
the persuasive earnestness, the unselfish bearing,
the sound counsel, and the moral strength of C. R.
Agnew, one of the nineteen we had to give up during the past single year, to say nothing here of the
death of Sabine, Loring, and so many others who
were ornaments and staffs of the profession.

Amongst our accessions there are many young
men. It has been my object, since the Academy
placed me at its head, to interest the best element
of the young members in the welfare of the profession. Our Academy is, as I said four years ago, a
democratic institution. It is not limited in numbers ;
on the contrary, it is desirable that the many respectable physicians should gather around its flag.
Like our political commonwealth, it looks for its
development and success in the co-operation of the
competent and cultured masses. Like the Union,
it is a voluntary confederation of peers, who make
their own laws, and obey them because these *are* of
their own making. All the Fellows have the same
interests, both scientific and professional. Thus, in
the Academy, the mixture of the best brains of the
profession and the modest practitioners is capable of

raising the standard of the average professional man far above the level of the European medical man. Anglo-Saxon medicine has always had the peculiar feature of being practical in the best sense of the word. For, indeed, the aim and end of all medical science is the prevention and cure of disease, and every special study is but a means of obtaining that end. In this respect also we are fortunate, for the number of those who are given to special theoretical studies is growing amongst us from year to year ; the scientific spirit displayed by many of our young colleagues compares favorably with the ambitions and efforts of their European peers, and I look forward to the elevation of the standard, both of the Academy and American medicine, through the labors of the young, to whom belongs the future, and whom I was anxious to bid here a hearty welcome. Nor will it be else but a gain to the Academy that the *Council* will not exclusively consist of older men only. Modern methods of study may and do mature in a proportionately shorter time those who embark in them, provided they be amply prepared. Science, though old, is always young ; and the organism of the profession requires the proliferation and co-operation of young cells.

In my inaugural address delivered four years ago I remarked that our natural position was that of advisers of the community in all matters concerning sanitation and health. The more we represent the best minds of all ages in the profession, the more readily will the public and its legislators be inclined to listen to us. When they will have learned that they can rely on our knowledge and public spirit, they will, as they call on the bar for legal advice, consult the medical profession for their hygiene and sanitary necessities. I expressed the hope that, in this way, some time or other the President of the Board of Health would be nominated or appointed by the profession ; that no Board of Education or of Charities would be considered complete without a prominent medical member ; that medical bills, when supported by the whole power of the profession, would pass the Legislature without either delay or mutilation ; that the supervising officers of factories, nurseries, streets, baths, gas houses, would be physicians ; ay, that the most improbable thing would happen, which, in the opinion of men who are self-made in all their conservative ignorance and ignorant conservatism, has seemed a crime against Nature—that the governments of hospitals ought not to be without the presence of medical advisers in their boards. I speak of that simply to point out what *has* occurred. The Health Department of the city has, as you all remember, when Quarantine was found incompetent and dangerous, requested the sending by this Academy of a committee to examine and recommend plans for improvements. It is mainly in the line of the propositions of that committee, as collated by our late Fellow, C. R. Agnew, that the work of improvement has now been inaugurated. The same Health Department has requested the appointment by the Academy of a standing committee to co-operate, when wanted, with the health authorities, and selected the board of the consultants for all its institutions from amongst our Fellows.

The scientific work of the Academy during the last year compares favorably with previous periods. Many of the papers submitted to the stated meetings were of superior value and will last. They deserve, after having been published in the current literature, this preservation in a permanent form. Two volumes of Transactions have been printed during my presidency, and a large amount of material awaits the publication of at least as many more. Scarcity of funds must be no excuse for the neglect of what I consider a public duty. There is no large learned body without its Transactions. They never are expected to become a source of income ; they are the proofs of existence, the connecting links between comrade bodies in all countries. To them, as well as to ourselves, do we owe the exhibits of our labors. I have no doubt that with the co-operation of the Council the energy of my successor will find the means of adding to our accumulated scientific treasures.

Besides the stated meetings you have worked in ten sections. My fondest hopes in regard to them have been excelled by many of them. If I allude mainly to that on Practice of Medicine, of Surgery, of Obstetrics, of Pediatrics, I mention but a part of those which have been eminently successful. They have brought out many papers and discussions of the first rank, given encouragement and opportunities to many who formerly had none, induced the young men in the profession to join in the general work, fostered scientific ambition, and by their publications aided in drawing the eyes of the medical world more than ever before to New York as a medical centre. Those who have aided in the labors of the sections may well be proud of their achievement. It is only by active co-operation that in the commonwealth both of politics and of science genuine citizenship is established. If the sections will enhance their work as heretofore, if they will see to it that only those fully competent and anxious to perform this duty, various and onerous often, be elected chairmen and secretaries, they will thrive as hitherto. Indeed, the scientific work of a large body like ours ought to be done mostly in the sections. The stated meetings of the Academy are in part given up to business. I should not think it a loss to the general welfare if even less than before the Academy itself would give its attention to scientific discourses. Perhaps a single meeting a month might suffice, provided that the sections contrive to increase their usefulness.

[After some further remarks regarding the work of the sections on Hygiene and on Therapeutics, the President concluded as follows:]

Fellows of the Academy, you must not believe that I have forgotten why I am here to-night—I am to introduce my successor. But before so doing I meant to express a few thoughts, both scientific and practical, connected with the welfare and the purposes of the Academy. Of the latter I have a high opinion. It is, and is to be, the head-centre of medicine in New York; by its labors and example it is to become the leader, we hope, of American medicine; it is the means of making many great, conscientious, truthful physicians. How high my opinion is of, and how profound my gratitude for, the advances accomplished by the arduous labors of specialists and specialties, I need not repeat here, after I have done so on many previous occasions and taken particular pains in establishing and facilitating the work of the sections. But what is uppermost in my mind is the love of my profession as an undivided one. Upon the general practitioner with his arduous, often unpaid labors, with his mind bent in different directions and instructed through many channels; upon the great physician with his keen intellect, sympathizing criticism, vast knowledge, and moral tone, I look as the shrine of the many flowers, the pivot of the many wheels in the great machinery. He is, and is to be, the true representative of the whole medical profession, the adviser of both the public and the specialist, the centre of the medical household, the statesman amongst the scientific ministers of the community. If the Academy will succeed in always, for the future, showing one of them as its official leader, I am certain it will not miss its high destination.

Therefore I am also certain of this, that you will thrive more than ever under the leadership of my successor. As my predecessor combined with his great practical experience a well-deserved reputation as a scholar, an unsurpassed renown as a medical writer, and the most exquisite urbanity of manners of the gentleman and leader, thus my successor is known to you and the whole country for his scientific attainments, literary labors, success in administration, and force of character. When you permitted me to nominate him personally for the high office he is to occupy, I looked upon that opportunity as a joyful privilege. After I have enjoyed these four years the highest honor the profession can confer, and your unvaried and kind support in the pursuit of our common interests, I now express my appreciation of the same, and my sincere thanks in introducing your President — Dr. Alfred L. Loomis.

PRESENTATION SPEECH BY AUGUSTUS CAILLÉ, M.D.,

AT THE NEW YORK ACADEMY OF MEDICINE, APRIL 4TH, 1889.

Mr. President and Fellows of the Academy:

The natural and spontaneous impulse which leads us to admire the greatness of others is one of the most gratifying features in human nature.

Now, it appears to me that of all the busy men and women who make up a well-regulated community, the busy physicians are more apt than any other class to turn their thoughts in leisure moments to the contemplation of the higher aims of life, and to sympathize with those who devote their energies to the advancement of all matters pertaining to the common welfare. Thus it is that thoughtful and appreciative men have placed upon these walls and within this Hall the portraits and images of many of our most distinguished leaders who have aided in shaping the course of medical progress, and thus it is that we are the recipients to-night of the portrait of a colleague whose honorable life and high scientific attainments will perpetuate his name and memory without the use of canvas or marble.

Any attempt, at the present time, to review in detail the brilliant career of Dr. Jacobi as a skilled physician, wise sanitarian, lucid teacher, and most

21*

accomplished writer, would be out of place. Nor is
it necessary to remind this audience of the fact of
his having been called frequently, and at an early
date, to assume duties of great responsibility.
In 1857, just three years after his arrival in this
country, Dr. Jacobi was Lecturer on Infantile Pathology at the College of Physicians and Surgeons,
and from 1860 to 1864 he was Professor of Diseases
of Children in the New York Medical College, now
extinct.

From 1864 to 1870 he held a professorship in the
University Medical College, and from 1870 up to the
present day pupils from all parts of the Continent
have listened to his words as Clinical Professor of
Diseases of Children at the College of Physicians
and Surgeons.

In 1871 and 1872 he was President of the County
Medical Society; in 1882 he was President of the
State Medical Society. The New York Academy of
Medicine flourished as never before under his leadership of four years, and on many other occasions
he has been one of the guiding minds in national
and international gatherings of medical men.

In what other country would the most accomplished foreigner have received such recognition except in the United States, in which the medical fraternity is just as liberal as the country itself?

I shall not attempt to outline the scientific attainments of Dr. Jacobi. He is among us in the prime
of life, his work is not yet finished, and we all hope
to see him carry his great knowledge and experience
far into the beginning of the next century. Endowed with a wonderful and retentive memory and

rare powers of observation, he has been able to accumulate that vast amount of positive knowledge which has stamped him an authority of the first rank in all the departments of medicine to which he has given serious and special attention. When the medical history of our times is accessible to future generations, the name of ABRAHAM JACOBI will shine upon its pages.

And whosoever shall present such claims to public recognition will not deem it empty flattery to receive the sincere congratulations of his colleagues for his honorable and useful life, which was shaped not for self-enjoyment, and devoted solely to the public good.

Let us all unite in our expressions of esteem ; let the younger men in the profession echo the sentiment and rejoice in the opportunity of discharging a debt of gratitude to one whose kindness and accessibility have become proverbial, and let us remind our colleagues who have come to us from overflowing Europe that to him, more than to any other man, belongs the credit of having established an international goodfellowship among the medical practitioners of this great city.

With these few words, Mr. President, I have the honor to present to the New York Academy of Medicine, in behalf of a number of colleagues whose names are inscribed upon this roll, the portrait of a great physician and good citizen—ABRAHAM JACOBI.

DONORS OF THE PORTRAIT OF ABRAHAM JACOBI TO THE NEW
YORK ACADEMY OF MEDICINE.

J. RUDISCH, M.D.,
B. SCHARLAU, M.D.,
H. KNAPP, M.D.,
P. F. MUNDÉ, M.D.,
E. GRUENING, M.D.,
A. GERSTER, M.D.,
W. MEYER, M.D.,
G. W. JACOBY, M.D.,
H. BALSER, M.D.,
WM. BALSER, M.D.,
N. H. HEINEMANN, M.D.,
A. CAILLÉ, M.D.,
L. WEBER, M.D.,
C. DENHARDT, M.D.,
W. H. DRAPER, M.D.,

G. FRAUENSTEIN, M.D.,
D. FROEHLICH, M.D.,
H. GULEKE, M.D.,
ED. JANEWAY, M.D.,
F. LILIENTHAL, M.D.,
A. L. LOOMIS, M.D.,
J. H. RIPLEY, M.D.,
E. C. SEGUIN, M.D.,
D. STIMSON, M.D.,
F. HUBER, M.D.,
A. BROTHERS, M.D.,
L. A. SAYRE, M.D.,
F. W. KRETZSCHMAR, M.D.,
W. H. KRETZSCHMAR, M.D.,
ALEX. SKENE, M.D.

DAS BACKEN DER TUBERKELBACILLEN.

BEMERKUNGEN VOR DER NEW YORKER AKADEMIE DER
MEDICIN, AM 20. JUNI 1889.*

HERR PRÄSIDENT :—Sie haben mir gütigst gestattet, heute Abend einige Bemerkungen über die Behandlung der Lungenphthise mittelst Einathmung trocken-heisser Luft zu machen, trotzdem der Abend schon für einen anderen Zweck vergeben war.

Robert Koch's Entdeckung des Tuberkelbacillus hat nicht allein eine Umwälzung unseres pathologischen Denkens bewerkstelligt, sondern ist auch die Quelle, aus welcher vielfältige Versuche zur Verbesserung der Phthisiotherapie seither entsprangen. Da ich mich kurz fassen muss, sollen diese Versuche nicht weiter erwähnt werden. Sie denken wohl noch an das durch Bergeon's Methode hervorgerufene Interesse ; Beelzebub sollte da unfehlbar durch den Teufel ausgetrieben werden, durch Ersticken des arglosen, wohlverwahrten Bacillus. Nur Diejenigen, welche nicht an die Wirksamkeit der Injektionen von Schwefelwasserstoff glauben konnten, wurden vor späterer Enttäuschung bewahrt.

Der neueste Zuwachs unserer Therapie besteht in

* Autorisirte Uebersetzung der Redaction der Medicinischen Monatsschrift 1889.

dem Backen der Microorganismen. Es wird behauptet, dass heisse Luft die Bacillen in der Lunge nicht allein unschädlich machen kann, sondern, dass das auch bestimmt geschähe. Besteht aber nur die leiseste Möglichkeit eines Erfolges durch solche Therapie, so kann die Akademie ihre Zeit kaum besser verwenden, als indem sie sich durch Untersuchung und klinische Beobachtung einen klaren Einblick in derartige Methoden zu verschaffen sucht. Theils in diesem Sinne bat ich für heute Abend um Ihr geneigtes Gehör ; theils aber bat ich aus persönlichen Gründen um Ihre Aufmerksamkeit, benöthigt durch die Nothwendigkeit individuellen Schutzes, welche in jeder parlamentarischen Körperschaft demjenigen das Wort ertheilt, der in seiner persönlichen Ehre und in seiner Würde verletzt wurde. Es handelt sich darum, dass seit ein gewisser patentirter Apparat zum Inhaliren heisser Luft bei Schwindsüchtigen in den Handel gebracht wurde, die Anzeigen und der Agent dieses Artikels vielfach hier und in anderen Staaten angegeben haben, dass ich den Apparat gekauft und rückhaltlos empfohlen habe. Viele an mich gerichtete Briefe beweisen diese Angabe. Deshalb möchte ich hier erklären, dass ich keinerlei patentirte medicinische und chirurgische Artikel und Apparate je empfohlen habe, noch je empfehlen werde. Wenn der in Rede stehende Apparat der einzige seiner Art wäre, der gewissen Indicationen entsprechen könnte und brauchbar zur Linderung oder Heilung von Krankheit, ich würde mir denselben zweifellos im Interesse meiner Kranken anschaffen, aber selbst dann würde ich denselben nicht ''öffentlich empfehlen''

oder für denselben Reclame machen, namentlich
aber dann nicht, wenn der Fabrikant und Patentinhaber desselben dem ärztlichen Stande angehört.
Kein Arzt, der von seinen Verpflichtungen gegen
die Menschheit durchdrungen ist und die Würde
seines Berufes als über Handel und Handwerk
stehend hochhält, selbst wenn er aufgehört hat
diesem Stande anzugehören, annoncirt noch ver-
käuft irgend welchen patentirten Gegenstand, der
armen oder reichen Kranken scheinbaren oder
wirklichen Nutzen bringen könnte. Ausserhalb
der Union scheint ein Arzt, der sich als Praktiker,
als Specialist oder gar als Patentinhaber annoncirt
wenig von seiner Reputation einzubüssen. Die
ganze Geschichte aber des ärztlichen Standes in
Amerika im Allgemeinen, sowie die dieser Akademie insbesondere, unterstützt mich in meinem
Protest dagegen, dass mein oder der Name irgend
eines Collegen mit einem Stück "Waare" in Verbindung gebracht werde. Ein Handelsartikel soll
für sich selbst Propaganda machen und sich selbst
überlassen bleiben. Gestatten Sie mir diesen Theil
meiner Bemerkungen hier gleich zu beendigen.
Dr. Louis Weigert's Apparat ist sehr einfach, ziemlich unvollkommen und sehr theuer. Heisse Luft
ist nicht patentirt, die Lunge ist auch nicht patentirt und das mechanische Genie irgend eines
Yankee ist genügend einen Apparat, wenn nöthig
und nützlich, herzustellen, um der Lunge heisse
Luft zuzuführen, und zwar reichlich vier or fünf
mal billiger als der in Rede stehende Mechanis-
mus.
Zum besseren Verständniss dieser einleitenden

Bemerkungen gestatten Sie mir folgende Angaben zu machen: In den Nummern 36-38 der *Berliner klinischen Wochenschrift*, 1888 (September 3.-17.), veröffentlichte Dr. L. Halter eine Reihe von Beobachtungen über "die Immunität der Kalkofenarbeiter nebst therapeutischen Vorschlägen." Die von diesem Autor gemachten Angaben sind sehr beachtenswerth und sein Apparat ist in obigem Blatt vom 17. September bildlich dargestellt. In der Provinz des Verfassers, Westphalen, ist die Tuberkulose sehr häufig anzutreffen. In den Kalköfen seiner Nachbarschaft waren fünfzig Personen angestellt, von welchen trotz der schweren Arbeit keine Einzige an Phthise erkrankte. Die Beobachtungsdauer erstreckte sich auf einen Zeitraum von fünfzehn Jahren.

Thatsächlich haben die Gegenden, welche als "immun" gelten, und wo Tuberkulose verhältnissmässig selten zur Beobachtung gelangt, nach August Hirsch (der grössten Autorität in der geographischen Pathologie) eine merklich trockene Atmosphäre. Die Luft vor den Kalköfen ist sehr trocken. Die Arbeiter verbringen dort einen grossen Theil ihrer Lebenszeit. Zugleich ist nun diese Luft sehr heiss, zwischen 50° und 70° Celsius (122°-158° Fahrenheit). Die Hitze bewerkstelligt, 1, dass diese Luft frei von Tuberkelbacillen ist, denn diese gehen nach Sormani durch einen einstündlichen Aufenthalt in einer Temperatur von 60°-65° Celsius (140°-149° F.) zu Grunde; 2, dass die Luft sehr verdünnt wird und so die Lunge, analog der Hochgebirgsluft, gründlich ventilirt wird.

Die Körpertemperatur der neuen Arbeiter an den Kalköfen ist stets 1°-1.5° C. über der Norm. Die acclimatisirten Arbeiter behalten die normale Eigenwärme, es sei denn, dass die Ofentemperatur 65°-70° C. erreicht, in Folge dessen auch bei ihnen eine gelinde Steigerung beobachtet wird. Demnach sind die Tuberkelbacillen, welche am besten in normaler Körpertemperatur gedeihen, solchen Einwirkungen ausgesetzt, welche ihre Existenz leicht gefährden. Der Puls steigt auf 120-160, die Athmungsfrequenz auf 24-30; neue Arbeiter beschweren sich sehr über die grosse Hitze und schwitzen dabei nur mässig, während die Eingewöhnten viel schwitzen und sich dabei wohl fühlen. Die Leute arbeiten angestrengt, essen reichlich und nahrhafte Speisen, trinken zehn bis fünfzehn Quart Wasser täglich und werden dünn, bleiben aber dabei gesund.

In den Nummern 39 und 40 der *Berliner klinischen Wochenschrift*, 1888, veröffentlicht Dr. Edward Krüll zwei Artikel über "die Behandlung der Lungenschwindsucht mittelst Einathmung feuchter Luft von gleichmässig-warmer Temperatur." Er benutzt feuchte Luft von 42°-46° C. (108°-115° F.), welche stundenlang inhalirt wird. Dergestalt führt er der Lunge eine grössere Blutmenge zu, zum Zweck regerer physiologischer Metamorphose, und um die Bacillen zu zerstören, welche sich noch in der Nähe der Schleimhautoberfläche befinden. Monate lang hat dieser Autor seine Methode bei Gesunden angewandt, ohne weitere Resultate als die vermehrter Metamorphose. Die bei Phthisikern erlangten Resultate sind noch frag-

würdig. Die Abbildung seines Apparates findet
sich in der *Berliner klinischen Wochenschrift* vom
24. September 1888. Feuchtigkeit als Zugabe mag sich als vortheilhaft
erweisen. Wer sein mechanisches Talent bei der
Erfindung neuer und billiger Apparate verwenden
will, kann die Angabe Halter's beachtenswerth
finden, welche er in einem Schreiben an obiges
Journal vom 24. September machte, in der er be-
zweifelt, dass es ihm je gelungen sei die Expirationsluft auf 43° C. (110° F.) zu erwärmen; und be-
zweifelt er darin seine eigene diesbezügliche einzige
Beobachtung. Er nimmt jedoch an, dass es leichter sei die Expirationsluft durch feuchtwarme Inhalationen auf einen Wärmepunkt zu erhitzen,
welcher den Bacillen schädlich werden könnte. Er
benützte feuchtwarme Inhalationen von 50°–100°
C. (122°–212° F.), mit folgenden Resultaten :

	Temperatur			
Dauer.	der Inhalation.	der Expirationsluft.	des Zimmers.	des Mundes.
15 Minuten	50°– 95° C.	42.0° C.	38.0° C.	37.4° C.
10 Minuten	50°– 90° C.	41.6° C.	37.5° C.	37.5 C.
16 Minuten	40°– 93° C.	41.8° C.	38.0° C.	37.5° C.
15 Minuten	50°–100° C.	42.0° C.	38.5° C.	37.5° C.
15 Minuten	50°–100° C.	42.1° C.	38.5° C.	37.5° C.

Die erste Mittheilung Dr. Louis Weigert's über
seinen Apparat zur Einathmung heisser Luft erschien im *Medical Record*, December 15. 1888,.

drei Monate nach den Publicationen Halter's und Krüll's. Letztere Autoren werden von Weigert überhaupt nicht erwähnt, trotzdem er mit jenen zusammen in einer Stadt wohnt. Es ist mir nicht bekannt, dass Weigert sich die Mühe gab die ärztliche Welt von seiner angeblichen Entdeckung vor oder nachher in Kenntniss zu setzen, thatsächlich aber annoncirte die Tagespresse Berlin's und anderer Orte dieselbe schon im September 1888. Halter gibt diese Thatsache selbst zu, betont aber auch, dass Weigert erst dann mit Untersuchungen anfing, nachdem verschiedene prominente Collegen (wie Schüller und Landois) schon mit seinen eigenen (Halter's) Arbeiten bekannt waren. Es steht zweifellos fest, dass die ärztliche Welt Herrn Dr. Halter das zu verdanken haben wird, was in dieser neuen Methode von Werth ist.

Dagegen wendet sich Dr. Louis Weigert (der ein in Amerika promovirter Arzt sein soll) in einer Broschüre, betitelt "Das neue Schwindsuchtsheilverfahren" (1889), an das grosse Publikum, worin er hervorhebt, dass nur Diejenigen seine Methode verwerfen, welche sich mit einer oberflächlichen Kritik derselben begnügten, und dass "welterschütternde Entdeckungen und epochemachende wissenschaftliche Errungenschaften stets gegen Vorurtheil und Gleichgültigkeit zu kämpfen hatten."

Sodann vergleicht sich Dr. Weigert mit Robert Koch, dessen Theorie (nach Weigert) aller Welt durch die Tagespresse bekannt gemacht wurde, welch' letztere nicht erst die Sanction von "Katheterhelden" benöthigt, um der Menschheit das zu

liefern, was sich als gross und gut erwiesen hat.
Seine Theorie hat ihn in Stand gesetzt, ''denjenigen Unglücklichen Gesundheit zu bringen, welche
sich bisher als in den Krallen des Todes befindlich
betrachteten.'' Ferner sagt Weigert : ''Durch
meine Erfolge habe ich bewiesen, dass der Glaube
an die Unheilbarkeit der Phthise unhaltbar ist.
Jeder muss das zugeben, der nicht wissentlich bak-
teriologische Thatsachen und die meiner Methode
negirt.'' Der hervorragendste Förderer der Verdienste und
des Apparates von Dr. Weigert und in Wirklichkeit
der einzige mir bekannte, ist Professor Kohlschütter
in Halle. Am 20. Februar d. J. hielt derselbe in
der dortigen Medicinischen Gesellschaft einen Vortrag, in welchem er bedauert, dass Weigert's
Methode zuerst in der Tagespresse angekündigt und
bisher auch ausschliesslich besprochen wurde und
betont den deletären Eindruck, welcher hierdurch
auf die ärztliche Welt gemacht wurde, trotzdem
der Name des Herrn Professors selbst häufig in den
Anzeigen von Chocolade und anderen guten Dingen
in den politischen Zeitungen zu finden ist.

Nach diesen Bemerkungen, welche ich im Interesse der Gerechtigkeit gegen alle Betheiligten machen musste, erübrigt mir noch über eine Reihe von
experimentellen Versuchen zu berichten, welche
ich mit einem, mir zu dem Zweck nach meiner Abtheilung im Bellevue Hospital überwiesenen Apparat
von Weigert angestellt habe. Die Krankengeschich-
ten der damit behandelten Patienten liegen hier vor
mir. Es soll hier nicht unerwähnt bleiben, dass ich
vor einiger Zeit geneigt war günstig über die an-

geblichen Resultate dieser Methode zu denken.
Doch war es mir von vorn herein klar, dass spätere
Apparate erfunden werden müssten, welche zuver-
lässiger wären als der in meinem Gebrauch, und
dass es ferner gelingen müsste die Temperatur der
Lunge auf mindestens 41° C. zu erhöhen, ehe man
überhaupt auf therapeutische Erfolge hoffen
könnte, denn dieses ist der niedrigste Hitzegrad, in
welchem das Wachsthum der Bacillen allmählig
behindert wird.

Die horizontale Röhre an diesem Apparat, welche
die heisse Luft dem Munde zuführt, ist sieben Zoll
lang. Die Röhre selbst ist von Metall ; das einige
Zoll lange Mundstück ist aus Hartgummi. An dem
der Flamme nahen Ende, sowie in der Mitte der
Röhre sind Thermometer angebracht, so dass dieselben dreiundeinhalb Zoll von einander entfernt sind.
Die Temperatur der Einathmungsluft betrug :

Nahe der Flamme:		3½ Zoll näher dem Munde:
220 Fahr.	und	blos 87° Fahr.
250° " nach einigen Inhalationen, "		" 110° "
250° " bei gerollter Zunge und		
nasaler Athmung, "		" 117° "
304 " nach forcirter Inspiration, "		" 171° "

Demnach kühlen sich Luft und Röhre zwischen
den zwei Thermometern sehr schnell ab, und demnach auch zwischen zweitem Thermometer und dem
Mund, und so fort. Es gelang mir heute Nachmit-
tag nicht die Temperatur meines Mundes zu messen,
da mein Thermometer in demselben zerbrach.

In dem Mund, dem Larynx und der Trachea ist
die eingeathmete Luft schon wesentlich abgekühlt,
namentlich auch durch die dort stattfindende Aus-

dünstung von Wasser. Etwas von der inspirirten
Luft gelangt wohl in die Alveolen, aber verhältnissmässig wenig, indem ein grösseres Quantum in der
Trachea und den grösseren Bronchien stagnirt.
Das verhältnissmässig kleine Volumen heisser Luft
trifft in der Lunge einen grossen See von Blut,
welch' letzteres stets erneuert wird, und dessen
Temperatur nicht merklich über 38.0° C. beträgt.
Die abkühlende Oberfläche der Lunge würde, wenn
ausgebreitet, einen Raum von zwei Tausend Quad-
ratfuss bedecken, und sind somit dort alle Bedingungen zum raschen Abkühlen eingeführter heisser
Luft vorhanden. Der Einfluss der letzteren ist aber
so minimal, dass selbst die Körpertemperatur der
neuen Arbeiter vor den Kalköfen nicht über 1.0°–
1.5° C. erhöht wird. Weigert nimmt an, dass die
Ausathmungsluft eine Temperatur von 45.0° C.
habe, gibt aber dabei selbst an, dass es ihm bisher
nie gelungen sei die exacte Zahl zu constatiren.
Ferner nimmt er an, dass die Luft sowohl beim
Ausathmen wie beim Einathmen Wärme abgebe,
und sei man bisher voll berechtigt zu glauben, dass
die ausgeathmete Luft vor dem Verlassen der Alveolen eine Temperatur über 45.0° C. habe. Das ist
eine ganz falsche Annahme, denn der bei weitem
grösste Theil der Ausathmungsluft stammt nicht
aus den Alveolen (wo sie gründlich abgekühlt worden wäre), sondern besteht aus der stationären Luft
der oberen Athmungswege. Diese ausgeathmete
Luft ist sicherlich wesentlich wärmer als die, welche
bis in die Nachbarschaft des Bacillenaufenthaltes
gelangt ist.

Wo befindet sich nun mittlerweile der Bacil-

lus? Vor einiger Zeit muss er durch die Blut- oder
Lymphgefässe oder direkt durch die arrodirte Respi-
rationsschleimhaut der feinsten Bronchien in's Lun-
gengewebe eingedrungen sein. Auf der wunden
Schleimhaut könnte ihn die heisse Luft erreichen,
wenn er noch da wäre. Die Eintrittsstelle hat sich
jedoch geschlossen, der Bacillus hat sich im Gewebe
vermehrt und lebt dort ruhig weiter, in ihm be-
hagender Wärme, unbekümmert um irgend welche
heisse Luft ausserhalb seines Bezirkes.

Ist es wahrscheinlich, dass sich das weiche Lun-
gengewebe über $38.5°-39.0°$ C. erhitzte, während
weder Puls noch übrige Körpertemperatur, oder
der Einathmende selbst nennenswerth afficirt erscheinen? Denn dem ist wirklich so. Oft habe
ich vor dem Apparat gesessen, den Puls unter dem
Finger; letzterer wurde nur mässig beschleunigt,
wenn nicht viele heftige und schnell wiederholte
In- und Expirationen gemacht wurden.

Es erscheint demnach, dass mehr nöthig ist als
die ruhige Einathmung heisser Luft in gewöhn-
licher Zimmertemperatur. Um eine Wirkung zu
erzielen sollte die Haut überhitzt sein; ein heisses
Bad wird aber von den Kranken schlecht vertragen.
Ein überheiztes Zimmer, trocken oder feucht,
würde zur Erhitzung des Blutes und der Gewebe
beitragen, den Puls, die Respiration und Metamorphose beschleunigen und würde in Wirklichkeit ein künstliches Fieber verursachen. Die Temperatur eines solchen Raumes müsste wenigstens
$41°$ C. ($105\frac{1}{2}°$ F.) betragen, was dadurch zu erlangen
wäre, dass man der Sommerhitze noch Ofenhitze
hinzufügte. Halter's Arbeiter waren täglich ein oder

zwei Mal, während der Dauer von zehn oder dreissig Minuten, einer trockenen Luft von 41°-70° C. (106°-158° F.) ausgesetzt. In einer umgebenden Temperatur von 21° C. (70° F.) und bei einer Inhalationstemperatur von 65°-150° C. (149°-300° F.) erreichte die Ausathmungsluft nicht mehr als 40° C. (Halter). Sowohl die heissen Einathmungen als auch die heisse Umgebung im überhitzten Zimmer finden indessen ihre Contraindicationen in grosser Schwäche, hervorgerufen durch irgend welche Ursache, speziell durch Phthise, sowie in Neigungen zu Lungenblutung und im Fieber.

So erscheint es mir nun bis jetzt (bis ich eines Besseren belehrt bin), dass wir berechtigt sind die Inhalation von trocken-heisser Luft nur im Anfang der Phthise zu versuchen, und dann nur in umgebender heisser Atmosphäre. In der Erkrankung vorgeschrittene Patienten dürften nur selten in einem Zustand sein, der diese Behandlung ertragen könnte. Feucht-heisse Luftinhalation bedarf niederer Temperatur, wird jedoch gerade wegen der Feuchtigkeit schlechter ertragen werden.

Wenn sich einige meiner Patienten unter dieser Behandlung wohler fühlten, so sollte nicht vergessen werden, dass ausser der Einathmung noch die gute Luft der Abtheilung, die temporäre Abwesenheit von der Proletarierwohnung und der Familiensorge, die günstige Jahreszeit und die gymnastische Uebung des Thorax—wesentlich zu dieser Besserung beitrugen. Thatsächlich findet nach der Aufnahme im Bellevue Hospital fast bei allen Phthisikern eine Besserung in allen Jahreszeiten

statt, vorausgesetzt, dass sich dieselben nicht im
letzten Stadium befinden.

Ein Kranker besserte sich sofort vom ersten
Tage an nach Anwendung des Apparates. Dieser
"Erfolg" wurde nach acht Tagen von meinen
Assistenten mit Frohlocken angekündigt. Fieber
und Husten hatten abgenommen, die Kräfte waren
sichtlich gewachsen—ein grosser Triumph für den
Apparat. Als ich der Sache indessen auf den
Grund sah, fand ich, dass der Patient allerdings
mit grosser Gewissenhaftigkeit verschiedene Halb-
stunden vor dem Apparat zugebracht hatte, dass er
aber mit derselben Gewissenhaftigkeit die Zunge
aufrollte und dabei hübsch regelmässig durch die
Nase ein- und ausathmete. Später wurde dann in
allen Fällen die Nase comprimirt.

In einigen Fällen wurde der Husten stärker und
war weniger leicht zu besänftigen, nachdem die
Kranken den Apparat gebraucht hatten. Zwei
Männer litten bedeutend an Erschöpfung und Er-
brechen, und erholten sich, nachdem wir mit den
Inhalationen ausgesetzt hatten.

CORRESPONDENZ.

110 W. 34. Str.,
New York, 8. Juli 1889.

An den Redacteur der Medicinischen Monatsschrift.

WERTHER HERR:—In Verbindung mit den vor-
stehenden Seiten halte ich es für gerecht die Mittheilung zu machen, dass Herr Dr. Med. Louis
Weigert kürzlich unter dem Titel : "Die Heissluft-
Behandlung der Lungentuberkulose" (Berlin 1889),
eine Abhandlung veröffentlichte, welche den ein-

22*

gestandenen Zweck hat, für seine Behandlungs-
weise die "theoretische Grundlage" zu schaffen
und dem Misstrauen, welches die Folge seines unmittelbaren "Appel's an das Publikum" gewesen
ist und—bleiben wird, zu begegnen. Daneben
theilt er "praktische Resultate" mit, für den Fall,
dass es jenen "theoretischen Deduktionen hier und
da an überzeugender Kraft noch fehlen sollte." Es
ist billig anzuerkennen, dass Dr. Weigert "Lücken-
haftigkeit und Mangelhaftigkeit" in seinen früheren
Veröffentlichungen zugiebt, indessen zu bedauern,
dass die marktschreierischen Behauptungen seiner
für das Zeitungspublikum bestimmten Auslassungen nur den ärztlichen Kreisen gegenüber gemildert
werden sollen. In der That, die Anzeigen des Apparates, welcher nach seiner Aussage und derjenigen seiner Agenten von "hunderten von Aerzten
und in einer Reihe von Hospitälern"—darunter
auch Bellevue—"gebraucht" werden, dauern natürlich fort, und das Patent wird weiter verwerthet.
Es ist eine betrübende Thatsache, und spricht
Bände für den niedrigen Stand ärztlichen Bewusst-
seins im alten deutschen Vaterlande, dass es dort
möglich ist, ohne Verlust der ungeschriebenen
Ehrenrechte in politischen Zeitungen zu annonciren,
zu marktschreiern und Prioritätsstreitigkeiten aus-
zufechten. Der einzige Trost, welchen ich kürzlich
in Betreff dieser Angelegenheit gefunden habe,
liegt freilich in einer Stelle des Weigert'schen Bänd-
chens selber, in welcher er sagt, dass "je intensiver
der direkte Appell für eine Heilmethode an das
Publikum zu gehen scheint, desto reservirter sich
die Aerzte ihr gegenüber verhalten." So soll es

sein, und so soll es bleiben ; obendrein kann ich aus
meiner sehr ausgiebigen, und sich über sechsunddreissig Jahre erstreckenden amerikanischen Erfahrung den deutschen Collegen mit Bestimmtheit
sagen, dass noch kein Mediciner, der die Zeitungen
unsicher machte, jemals der Wissenschaft, der
ärztlichen Moral, oder dem Gemeinwohle genützt
hat. Erschwatztes Geld erkauft weder Würde
noch Wohlanständigkeit, und wir hier sind ge-
wohnt, solche Lobredner ihrer selber, Eigenthümer
von Patenten, agents provocateurs von Interviews
gründlich "allein zu lassen." Das hat Herr Dr.
Weigert, trotzdem er ein amerikanischer Arzt sein
soll, nicht gewusst, oder vergessen.

Der flüchtige Ton seiner Arbeit wird durch die
Versuche, seine Zeitungsreclamen zu erklären oder
zu verdecken, nicht gehoben ; und—das Bestreben
den Latinisten neben dem Pathologen zu zeigen,
berührt unbehaglich. Denn auf zwei Seiten exitus,
funditus, Encheirese, Anwendung ad hominem
aegrotum, und quoad therapiam sich in einem deutschen Buche gefallen lassen zu müssen, ist eine
starke Zumuthung.

So viel über das Buch und seine Richtung. Da
indessen nur Wenige geneigt sein werden, eine Arbeit zu lesen, welche nur im Anschluss an Zeitungsreclamen geschrieben und zum Theil nur durch die
Kenntnissnahme derselben verständlich ist, so will
ich nicht verfehlen, einige der Hauptsätze desselben, vom Verfasser selber als solche bezeichnet,
in Kürze hier zu citiren : Seite 22. "Ich will aner-
kennen, dass es ein vergebliches Bemühen ist, auf
tuberkulös infiltrirte Herde, seien sie klein oder

gross, mittelst des Inspirationsstromes einzuwirken.
Ich urgire hier auch ganz besonders, dass es niemals vorwiegend in meiner Absicht lag, derartige
tuberkulöse Infiltrationen und käsige Degeneratio-
nen durch meine Methode zur Ausheilung zu bringen."

"Ich glaube auch, dass Kranke mit ausgedehnten
zerfallenen oder zerfallenden Infiltrationen, Kranke
bei denen kaum noch ein Lobulus frei von der
Tuberkelinvasion ist, nicht mehr die Domäne für
unsere Heilbestrebungen bilden können."

Seite 25. "Die Bekämpfung des Tuberkelbacillus
hat vorzugsweise nicht an den Stellen des Lungen-
gewebes zu geschehen, an denen es bereits zur In-
filtration oder gar zum Vorfall gekommen ist, sondern an den Partien, in die er frisch verschleppt
wird; mit anderen Worten : Die Sterilisation des
Koch'schen Bacillus hat in den bis dahin intacten
Theilen zu erfolgen."

Seite 26 spricht von dem "*Constanten Ergeb-
niss,*" dass die Tuberkelbacillen durch discontinuir-
liche Sterilisation vollständig abgetödtet werden.
*Die eingehende Darlegung der betreffenden Ver-
suche, deren minutiöse Schilderung mich an dieser
Stelle zu weit führen würde, werde ich binnen
Kurzem an geeignetem Orte veröffentlichen.*

Und warum nicht hier, Herr Redacteur? Hier
bei dieser ersten und besten Gelegenheit? Zum
ersten Mal wendet sich der Verfasser, nachdem er
früher sich als unfehlbarer Schwindsuchtsdoktor
von den Zeitungen hat puffen lassen, und als gesetzlich geschützter Apparatbesitzer, Geschäfts-
mann und Agentenoberst sein "Business" in Gang

gebracht hat, an die ärtzliche Welt, um "theoretische Grundlagen" zu schaffen, und vertröstet dieselbe wieder auf unbestimmte spätere Gelegenheit
mit dem Beweise den er postulirt und gewissenhaft
—schuldig bleibt. Wer da will, kann in nächster
Zeit die täglichen Zeitungen von mächtigen Citaten
aus der grossen wissenschaftlichen Arbeit des
berühmten Herrn Verfassers, welche ich Ihnen hier
habe charakterisiren wollen, überfliessen sehen.
Wird das Ding nie aufhören geduldet zu werden?
Achtungsvoll der Ihrige,

A. JACOBI.

ADDRESS

DELIVERED AT THE LAYING OF THE CORNER STONE
OF THE ACADEMY OF MEDICINE, OCTOBER 2D,
1889, AT 19 WEST 43D STREET.*

THE New York Academy of Medicine has called
upon the profession and the public alike to assist it
in this ceremony of laying a corner stone. Where
we are now standing there will be the home of the
Academy, we believe, for generations to come. If
we be mistaken, if this large building should be too
small before long, it will be the pleasant duty of
our successors to provide for their wants. That
this may become necessary is possible, for the Academy has experienced a development rapid beyond
expectation. Forty-three years ago it was founded;
dozens of years it held its meetings in hired quarters; ten years ago it occupied its own building,
No. 12 West 31st street; to-day we are preparing
accommodations such as the profession of New
York, or of any other city of the country, has never
possessed. Meanwhile, however, the spirit and the
aims of the Academy have remained intact. Among
these aims are the cultivation of the science of medicine and the promotion of public health.

In the words of a circular published nearly two
years ago in behalf of our building fund. "these

---

* Transactions, vol. vi.

purposes are accomplished by lectures and discussions in the stated meetings of the Academy and its numerous sections; by maintaining reading rooms which furnish nearly all the medical journals of the world; and by collecting a library containing about sixty thousand books and pamphlets, which are free both to the medical profession and the public." The number of its Fellows is nearly six hundred. They have been selected from among those who have practised medicine in New York City or its vicinity three or more years. Some time ago fellowship was extended to those residing in the State.

In its composition the Academy participates in many of the peculiar features of our political organization, which means to benefit all through co-operation, if not of all, still of the best. In Europe an academy of medicine means a small body comprising a few select men only, appointed by the body itself when there is a vacancy, or by the political rulers. Thus the academies form an aristocracy of the mind parallel to the aristocracy of birth, with all its exclusiveness and real or assumed superiority. They are representative bodies only in this, that the best minds and most scientific workers are expected or believed to fill the seats.

The New York Academy of Medicine, however, is a democratic institution. It is not limited in numbers ; on the contrary, it is desirable that the many respectable physicians should gather round its flag. Like our political commonwealth, it must look for its development and success in the co-operation of the competent and cultured masses. Like the Union, it is a voluntary confederation of peers, who make their own laws, and obey them because they are of their own making.

The members have common interests, both scientific and professional. Since its foundation, with the changes for good and bad appertaining to everything organic, the Academy has prospered constantly, in spite of, or, as I am more inclined to say, in consequence of, its very constitution as an independent and democratic body. In the words of the same circular alluded to before, "the Academy is not connected with any school or college. It is self-supporting, and is carried on in the interest of the whole profession. There are no fees nor emoluments of a private or individual nature. It is not supported nor subsidized by the State or municipality." Whatever has been accomplished by it— its scientific labors, most of which are laid down in its Bulletins and Transactions, and in the medical journals of the country; the hall in West 31st street, the library and reading rooms in the upper stories, the wealth of books and journals at the disposal of those eager to learn, and so numerous that they alone compelled us to look for more appropriate quarters—all of that has been created, with few exceptions, by the exertions and pecuniary sacrifices of the medical men themselves.

All classes of these are represented in the Academy. It shows you the choice of those who are interested and active in the promotion of medical science and art ; those who have earned an international reputation ; those who have deserved well of the community by a life filled with services rendered to the public ; and those who look forward for the

fulfilling of their dreams and the reaching of their
aims through coming years of honest labor spent in
theoretical study and practical work. In this co-
operation of the old and young, the illustrious and
those yet unknown but promising or anxious to
earn renown, the mature and the maturing, you
have one of the features of a unity of the profession.

Another feature of unity, which, moreover, ties
the profession indissolubly to the community at
large, is the labor performed in the service of one
and all. It is in these labors and their results that
the community at large ought to take a deep interest. Modern medicine is probably the greatest
benefactor of mankind. The more medicine has
been founded on the study of the exact sciences—
chemistry, physics, and physiology, with mathema-
tics—the more has its field of usefulness enlarged.
The more theoretical it appeared to become, the more
did it develop practical usefulness and dignity. Indeed, the dignity of a science or study rises with its
ability of being utilized in the service of mankind.
Now, the promotion of medical science and art does
not mean merely the improvement in diagnosis and
in the administration of drugs and remedies, but the
discovery of the best means of placing the human
being in the best possible condition. The labor of
the physician is not exhausted by carrying you
through a severe case of illness; he renders you the
greater service, less remunerative to him though, of
preventing you from falling sick.

The peculiar relations of the individual physician
to his patient or the family entrusted to his care are

widened in the relations of the profession to the public. Great epidemics take the place of a single case, the protection of a community that of the guarding a person, the hygiene of schools that of a dwelling, the sanitation of a large city that of inspecting a suspicious trap or sewer in a private domicile. The more in your Health Department the medical element predominates over the military and political, the more actual benefit will the people derive from it. The hygiene of the whole population; the superintendence of public buildings in which many people, old or young, are gathered: public hospitals, quarantine stations ; the question of physical and mental elevation, of legal responsibility, of the State care of the insane—they all belong to the domain of the profession. This is not theory only.' No grave question of the kind has come up without the gratuitous and spontaneous aid of medical men. The Health Board of the city has long appreciated that. The Academy has furnished a consulting board to all the Health Department's hospitals. A committee of the Academy was entrusted with the inquiry into, and the report on, the condition of Quarantine. It is to its report that the first appropriation for the building of the Quarantine Station was due, and to its recommendations that improvements are being carried out at the present time. In this way the medical profession excludes epidemics and guards both the physical health and the economic interests of the city. Imagine the pecuniary loss to the city if the cholera and the yellow-fever scare of a year or two years ago had not been prevented by the profession, as indeed it was. A week's panic would

have been a pecuniary calamity amounting to the
loss of a good many millions.

These are but a few examples of the value of
medical services, both paid and unpaid ones, to the
public. The health of the city is the foundation of
its prosperity. Let epidemics prevail, and not only
will your children die, your families be decimated,
and the graveyards be filled with places where
flowers and tears mingle, but your commerce will
be drawn to other ports. It is due to increased
knowledge and activity on the part of the profession, both official and unofficial, that, in spite of the
unchanged severity of the epidemics and the rapidly
increasing population of the city, the number of
cases of diphtheria shows an absolute diminution.

Such, among many, are the services of the profession, not to speak of the gratuitous daily work of
hundreds of medical men in the hospitals and dispensaries. Nobody can count or calculate, but
everybody can appreciate how many lives are pre-
served, how many millions are saved for the poor
and rich alike. From that point of view, a whole-
souled, generous woman presented to the Academy
twenty-five thousand dollars in recognition of the
services to the public on the part of the profession,
and in accordance with the esteem her husband
held the profession in while he was alive. To this
consideration we owe the bequest of seventy thousand dollars coming to us under the will of Mrs.
Alexander Hosack, who had spent a large part of
her valuable life with illustrious example of professional worth. It is the same thought that induced
men and women with means, intelligence, and pub-

lic spirit to make donations of five, two, or one thousand dollars. All we require now is fifty thousand dollars to complete this building. There must be many who have that sum, or a part of it, to spare in the interest of the profession ; perhaps to commemorate the name of a dear one who has passed away, or to imprint his or her name—and a legitimate ambition it is—on one of the halls of the new building, or to perpetuate the memory of one who has been saved from a premature grave by the endeavors of one of those who are now striving to erect a home for the most practical and beneficent of all sciences and arts.

It is a home we want, more than merely a house. To make the house of the medical profession a home, it requires a library. This is to the profession what a tool is to the mechanic, an engine to the engineer, a telescope to the astronomer. A complete library represents the thoughts, experience, genius, and discoveries both of all previous centuries and the present time. All of these treasures must be accessible to the profession whose knowledge and skill is to be the safeguard of the public's best interests. To accomplish that end the whole medical literature of all countries must contribute. New York has never been satisfied with anything that is second class ; it cannot afford to trust itself to a profession without the first order of learning and erudition.

Why do we insist upon physicians being erudite ? Do I ask why do you apply to a particular watchmaker, an engineer, an architect, a milliner ? You select him because you believe or know him to be well informed or skilful. And the physician? His practice is the application of knowledge acquired by hard brainwork spent on all the learning and practice which have been evolved out of the labor and efforts of thirty centuries. A learned doctor may happen to be an unsuccessful practitioner for more reasons than one; but among those reasons erudition is not. An uninformed man is never a good practitioner; under equal circumstances, the more learned man is the better man in practice. Practice and learning do not exclude each other; on the contrary, the former depends on the latter. It ought not to suffice for your selection of a doctor that you met him at a bar, or a ball, or at a church meeting, or at whist, in a concert, or on a hotel piazza, or that he be well dressed, pleasant, and tells you he is your "friend"; all these are fine opportunities and agreeable social and personal qualities which may also be considered when you are credibly informed that he burns midnight oil over medical literature, and that his professional brethren speak well of his abilities and achievements. And as far as medical friendships are concerned, your best friend is he who knows best how to protect you and your children and your parents from disease, and to cure them when they are sick.

The erudition we claim for the profession demands a large library of constant growth. A fund of $100,000 will enable us to keep abreast with any similar institution. The library of the Surgeon-General's Office in Washington, which contains at present seventy thousand volumes and one hundred and thirty thousand pamphlets, is the result of industrious and systematic collections. It is not much over twenty years old, but it is the richest and most complete medical library in the world. Still its annual appropriations for the purchase of books have seldom exceeded $5,000. Thus a fund of $100,-000 will enable us to procure nearly everything medical that appears in any land. Of that sum we have only $10,000. One-half of that sum was set aside by the Academy, the other half is a donation separately administered in perpetual honor of a departed one. Such special funds, or additions to our general library fund, are urgently requested. The citizens of New York have developed a metropolis of large size and commercial power; they can well afford to tax themselves in the interest of medical science, than which there is none more cosmopolitan and humanitarian.

But it is not the medical profession only which will be directly benefited by the endowment of a large and complete library. The intimate relations of the medical and legal professions are such that much of what we require is found in law books, and the lawyer has to look for much of his information in medical literature. Indeed, forensic medicine, which originated in law, has its main representatives in medicine. In both the names of Plenck and Ploucquet, Farr and Duncan, and our own Beck, and many others of more modern times, are household words. Moreover, our library is a public one, free to the profession and the public. Now, there is a class of literature which, in a free and public library like ours, ought to be well represented. Laymen intending to avail themselves of it expect to find mental food adapted to their comprehension and taste. That sort of literature is by no means scarce. Much of it is of fair quality, some of it surpassingly good. Books on anatomical and physiological topics, those on subjects connected with natural history, hygiene, and statistics, will always be found interesting and instructive. They ought to be well represented in our library, for they cannot be found in large numbers in the public and circulating libraries. Indeed, the frequenters of the latter differ much from the class of readers consulting ours.

The additional knowledge acquired in this manner will not only improve a man's ability to protect himself and his family, it will also facilitate the work of his doctor. A person who has filled his mind with comprehensive ideas and sound facts will no longer study quack advertisements. He who has learned something about the functions of his body, and been taught to consider the correlation of causes and effects, can appreciate a disease to be the result of either a preventable or an unavoidable cause, and recognize that whatever disease was not the result of faith cannot be cured by faith, not even by faith in panaceas. The business of the quack may thus cease, the nostrum mixers may suffer, but individual and public health will be the gainers. There is less sickness in a man who has some knowledge of his body and its requirements; and when he falls sick he expects relief from natural and intelligible sources only. That man is a better patient, more accessible to reasoning, more obedient to the rules imposed in the interest of recovery. If he knows enough to recognize the superiority or inferiority of his physician, so much the better. To-day most people have not a sufficient knowledge to guide them in their selection; there are many who are so little informed that they do not so much as care. If, in a matter ever so trifling, a medical man is called as a witness before a court of justice, the first question he is asked refers to his membership in a medical society. The uninformed public, however, often select their doctor for reasons known to nobody, least, perhaps, to themselves. All this would be changed if a small part of what is the basis of a physician's thinking and knowing were made accessible and intelligible to every man and woman. A library like that which we intend to establish is destined not only to supply the professional man, but furnish healthy mental food to all those who are thirsty for knowledge. Those who have means to spare in the interest of public education, hygiene, and health, cannot possibly apply them better than by providing for a library fund sufficient for the gradual accumulation, from year to year, under the supervision of experts, of all the good, popular literature on the subjects of anatomy, physiology, hygiene, dietetics, and statistics.

May all this become true! We are preparing this edifice to be the head-centre of medical study in the city, an example to the profession of the country, and a resort for the brethren who come to us from near or distant parts. This building, when completed, will be an ornament to the metropolis. What is still more important is that we mean it to become, and feel assured that it will be, an additional element of intellectual and ethical power, and in its results a blessing to the commonwealth.

Mr. President, Ladies, and Gentlemen :

A circular published by a special committee of
this Academy in January, 1888, contained the statement that the New York Academy of Medicine was
an incorporated institution, then more than forty
years old ; that its object was the cultivation of
medical science and art ; and that this aim was,
among other means, reached by maintaining reading rooms which furnished nearly all the medical
journals of the world, and by collecting a library
which was—and is to-day—free to the Fellows of
the Academy, to the whole medical profession in-
discriminately, and to the public at large. Our
library was steadily increasing, the capacity of its
shelves strained to the utmost, the building not
fireproof, and our accumulated treasures were in
constant danger. For these reasons we appealed to
both the profession and the public for aid in procur-
ing for our meetings and our books a fireproof
building large enough to accommodate two hundred
and fifty thousand volumes, spacious enough to
afford quarters to all the scientific societies of the
city, stately enough to worthily represent the medical profession of the metropolis, and able to testify
both to the unity and earnestness of that profession
and the sympathy of the city, which at the same

time is the largest in size and the greatest commercial power of the continent.

This library of the Academy of Medicine had a slow but steady growth. Thirty-three years ago, when I was admitted to membership, in the presence of the great and good men who then were the guiding stars of the profession, Alexander Stephens, Valentine Mott, Horace Green, Gurdon Buck, Edward Peaslee, Edward Delafield, John Francis, John Watson, Ernst Krackowizer, there was no library at all, not even a medical reading room, in the city. It took many years before the Journal Association was organized, which furnished, in a room fitted up for the purpose in 64 Madison avenue, the current medical journals. Other years elapsed until an amalgamation of the Journal Association and the Academy of Medicine, then in 12 West 31st street. was brought about. The accumulation of the annual volumes, and a valuable collection of American journals and other books presented by two Fellows, were the first stock of the library. The journals were paid for by an appropriation of the Academy, which, being small in the beginning, for many years amounted to from three to four thousand dollars annually. More could not be spared. Thus it was that we could not purchase new books. Occasionally a sum was raised by voluntary contributions for the purpose of buying the collection of a deceased member, certain publishers would present us with their publications, authors donate copies of their writings, Fellows and others give old and new books, and men interested in special branches of literature furnish a shelf-ful of special

works. The largest and most valuable addition of
the kind was bequeathed to us by the great specialist, Dr. Freeman I. Bumstead. That was our library. Thus it grew slowly, but steadily. In the
course of years our stock of journals became more
and more valuable, but what we wanted was a regular supply of new books, for which we had no
funds at all.

On October 2d, 1889, when I had the honor of
addressing you at the laying of the corner stone of
this edifice, I could refer to the fact that at last we
had, for the purchase of new books, a special
library fund of ten thousand dollars, half of which
was a memorial gift. For the same purpose and in
the same spirit the widow of a deceased Fellow and
vice-president has since presented another special
fund of ten thousand dollars, so that one-fifth of
the sum required for the perpetual endowment of
the library is now secured. We are thus approaching the time when New York City will possess a
medical library fully adapted to meet its ends.
What are they? A large library, besides being the
proof of existing culture and accumulated intellectual labor, fulfils its destiny by giving information. Here the medical man with scanty means
will find his text books and monographs to aid him
in unravelling the obscurities of a difficult case on
hand. He with an ample library of his own will
come here to consult rare books, old journals,
expensive works. Here all the journals of the
world may be consulted from day to day ; here
those who are engaged in literary pursuits find
their historical records. But what a library is most

successful in, is the inculcation in a great many of
the habits of study and research. In that result the
public is very much interested. Its safety and
dignity require cultured and erudite physicians.

In the same degree that the ethical and intellectual standard of society is raised, the community will
demand a higher standard of education and culture
on the part of its liberal professions, among them
the medical. A profession is called liberal in this,
that it is generous, charitable, and high-minded ; in
this, that it liberates its members from ignorance
and mental and moral hebetude. But in reality
the medical profession of the country was mostly
liberal in this, that it admitted to its ranks uneducated persons of all colors, sexes, ages, and previous
conditions of servitude and illiteracy. Instead of
being a truly liberal profession, it has merely been
too liberal. In this tendency it has been encouraged, or, rather, this inferior standard has been
forced upon the medical profession, by the public.
He who requires manners in his corn-cutter, and
demands gentleness in his tailor, would often not
object to selecting for his family physician and
public hygienist a medical adviser with the orthography of a village school, the touch of the corner
grocer, and the mental level of a soap peddler.

From this depth the profession has risen spontaneously by study and its indigenous moral development. Not all of you know, however, to what
extent you are under obligation to the medical profession. Fifteen years of incessant agitation were
required to finally pass the bill for the establishment of a State Board of Medical Examiners. If in

future you will be protected against practitioners who have nothing to show besides their diploma, granted by a college no matter of high or low standing; if the license to practise on you, your parents and children, will be made dependent on a second examination, you owe that blessing to the exertions of the medical profession. You might have made the result more striking. If the public had understood its interest you would have worked with us in behalf of making the State Board one, and not three.

Another achievement of the profession which concerns you as much as it does us, is the final passing of the bill requiring some degree of general education on the part of every medical student who expects to obtain his medical diploma. Thus a step is made in the direction of rendering the profession more liberal, more cultured, more effective, more fit to take charge of the most sacred offices that can fall to the lot of men. For the holiest and greatest of the objects of human study and care is man. That is so much a part of the creed of the medical profession that you can imagine the painful and contemptuous surprise at our learning that a medical man, in a public position, but fortunately not one of us, worked all winter to have the law repealed.

Fortunately not one of us. For from its very first days this Academy of Medicine had the elevation of the standard of medical education and culture inscribed on its banner. That object has become such a settled axiom in the mind of every Fellow that years ago it was no longer considered

necessary to retain it in just so many words among
the written laws. In this tendency you can sustain the efforts of the profession. Insist upon this,
that your physician be a gentleman and a scientist,
and do something for that purpose yourself. For
the State does not contribute to that end. The
State is only society organized for certain purposes
of co-operation and protection. But medical education, though ever so indispensable for the pursuit
of health and happiness and the training of erudite
and liberal physicians, has not been recognized
among them. But you who do not say to the
hungry, the cold, and the naked, "Be ye fed, be ye
warmed, be ye clothed," without helping them to
food, fire, or clothing, must not expect a profession
that always works in the private and public interest
of yourself and all those dear to you and yours, to
be at once learned, erudite, and wise, and refuse
aid in its efforts to perfect itself and benefit the
commonwealth, aid by pecuniary support, by your
social influence, and also some occasional gentle
political pressure on our representatives in Albany.

Our greatest drawback has long been that we had
no large class of learned medical men, such as study
for study's sake, irrespectively of pecuniary gain.
Our profession has always consisted of practitioners.
The necessities of life have acted upon the medical
fraternity as on the community at large, which
knew but exceptionally of art, of music, of philosophical refinement as long as the country was still
wrestling with the difficulties of the soil, the insufficiency of commerce, and the hamperings of
poverty. Thus the immense majority of the medi-

cal men of the country gloried in being practical, and that only. That there were architects who never laid a brick, mathematicians who never triangled a mountain, astronomers who never sailed a ship; that no cathedral, no coast survey, no ocean travel could exist without them; that indeed there is no rational practice without an underlying theory, was not considered. The very strongholds of medicine, histology, physiology, the fields of experimental labor and microscopical research, all those branches which you cannot immediately exchange for cash, have been neglected among us until lately. Like special laboratories, it is but a short time since great medical libraries have sprung up in Washington, Philadelphia, Boston, and New York. ' The sooner we admit that we have been far behind Europe in that respect, the better for our scientific future. Indeed, the intellectual maturity of a nation can best be measured by the amount of its original and unpaid research. Europe knows that thoroughly. The intellectual atmosphere of Paris depends greatly on its universities. The universities of Germany, with their independent workers and thinkers, have always been the pride of the nation, even in the distress of national poverty and political humiliation. In all of them the principal means of information through centuries have been their large libraries. And it will be our library round which the scientific interests of the profession will largely centre; but not of the profession only, for the Academy, as it opens its doors to whosoever will attend, without regard to membership, has always held that in order to increase the number of its beneficiaries it must make its library free. This is so well understood and so highly appreciated that the city has released the taxes on its building. A medical library contains of necessity many works and journals of interest to professional men besides medical. The lawyer and physician have many studies in common. There are in the city two societies for the special study of forensic medicine and medical jurisprudence, both of which can be better studied in a medical than a legal collection. Nor is a medical library, such as we have and mean to increase, a forbidden fruit to the intelligent, well-informed non-professional man or woman. Fortunately there are a great many good popular works, besides those compiled for an ephemeral market, which treat of physiology, hygiene, statistics, and other topics of universal interest.

Therefore we hold that the profession has a right to look to the public for appreciation and aid. We are not situated as they are in Europe, where educational institutes, as they are controlled, are also supported by the Government. For the democratic spirit of our social and political institutions is opposed to centralization of that kind, and the generosity of the citizens has often been appealed to, and hardly ever in vain. There was a time when the Church, centralizing all information, beneficence, and social and political influence, was the only legatee of the rich and benevolent. Now there are a hundred opportunities for liberal outlay. To select the proper ones is an art. I suppose it is a great achievement, which only a few select ones can attain, to make money ; but it is a greater art to spend it both generously and profitably in the interest of science and charity. The greatest of all charities, however, is to benefit mankind by levelling the road of science. It is not millions we want. A hundred thousand dollars will clear this temple of science from debt and swell our library fund to a sufficient sum, the interest of which will forever supply us with everything medical and scientific that will appear in any country. Well-to-do ladies and gentlemen will, I hope, not leave this building without making up their minds to contribute their share to the extinction of a debt which the community owes to the profession and to itself through improved educational facilities. "Let your light so shine before men that they may see your good works."

In conclusion, my friends of the profession may permit an additional word or two on the subject of the library, which is so dear to all of us that it was selected as the subject of a special address to-night. In one of its retired nooks I was sitting a few days ago, contemplating its past and future. I sat wondering how long it will take, and whether any of us older men will see the day, when America, after having given the political world the guiding example of a stationary popular government both conservative and perfectible, will lead the world of science, as it does that of politics, and, we hope, of healthful social development; wondering, also, how much this head-centre of the medical profession and this ever-growing library will contribute to that consummation, which you can hasten by industri-

ous, honorable, and modest work—but by work
only.

This library of yours has started from small be-
ginnings, like medicine itself. It comprehends the
labors of thousands of workers assiduously employed
through long centuries. That one of them could be
missed is difficult to say. For the co-operation of
the many, the gradual development of ideas, the
slow changes in experience and doctrines, are of as
much importance as the revolutionary and epoch-
making labors of the greatest. For no single man
can stand alone, a law to himself and others. Even
genius is the child of its time. No Washington or
Lincoln, no Hippocrates or Aristotle, no Virchow or
Pasteur, or even Koch, none of these immortal ones
is a world by himself, and an isolated, self-lit sun
illuminating and warming the universe. Every one
has been raised on the shoulders of his predecessors.
By that knowledge it is that while hope and energy
are aroused, patience is taught to the individual and
the profession. For while life is short, science and
art are unlimited and eternal. And the comparison
of what you furnish yourself with the existing mass
of accumulated knowledge inculcates modesty and
enhances zealousness. Thus good citizens are made
and model scientists. Besides, what to the pupil
the information gathered from the lips of his master, that is for you the collective bequests of all
centuries as represented in your library. Thus an
intellectual kinship is formed between you the living, and the spirit of all eras of history. That is
what the study of the history of medicine teaches
us, which we have so long neglected.

Pondering over the shelves, you behold abstract scientific treatises, works on practical therapeutics, and books on art and appliances—all of them composing our beloved "medicine." Remove the theoretical works on anatomy, histology, and embryology, experimental physiology, physics, and chemistry—what remains? The wreck of the edifice, the foundation of which is torn away.

Look at the shelves holding special literature. There the specialist will comprehend that his doctrine and art are but a minimal trifle when compared with the surrounding wealth, and that the basis and link of all specialties is general medicine. Every one of them evolved from a minute bud of the great tree, and but few have ever been able to grow up with anything like independence. Thus medical science and art is shown to be an organism of slow, consistent, historical growth. Even the very excrescences—call them fallacies, superstitions, theories, schools, or sects—do not disturb the organic economy. In accordance with this, your very library, the representative and exponent of all medicine, is no longer a mere collection, but a vitalized organism.

That is why there is an atmosphere of solemnity in your large library; for you are standing in the presence of the spirit and soul of all previous ages, each evolving from and connected with its neighbor. That is why a library is to the scientist what the church is to the pious; or a museum of a hundred gems, like that which a generous Fellow presented to our reception room, to the artist. No consideration of lucre invites you there. While nourishing your minds, you disconnect yourself from the embarrassments of trivial employment and deliver yourselves from the merely terrestrial. In that way idealism is nurtured, that no feeling and thinking man is to be without ; idealism, without which no nation can expect to live. When she lost it, even Hellas perished, though she had given birth to Solon, Pericles, Aristides, and Sophocles.

Let me suggest this reflection as a platform, my young colleagues. It is not a dream, but a reality, if you will make it so. By so doing, not only will you elevate your august science and the noblest of all callings, but you will also remain in constant and indissoluble intellectual and moral contact with the most cultured elements of society. If you do, this evening, which is both an anniversary and an inauguration, will prove a blessing for all future to both the profession and the community. Look upon this edifice not merely as a new and commodious building, but as the visible portal into a new epoch. If you do so, you will consecrate this solemn occasion as the Fourth of July of American Medicine.

OPENING ADDRESS

Ladies and Gentlemen :

As I have the honor of being the presiding medical officer of the hospital with which the Mount Sinai Training School for Nurses is connected, I look upon the demand that I should open this fair, as a tribute paid to my office and my institution. There are, however, a few persons on whom, rather than on me, I should have desired to see the enjoyable opportunity of addressing you bestowed : these are the President of the Mount Sinai Hospital, or the President of the Training School.

With the hospital I have been connected longer than any of its other officers, having been entrusted with a position on the Medical Board more than twenty-eight years ago. At that time the hospital was in Twenty-eighth street, between Seventh and Eighth avenues. It was what we then thought to be an immense establishment, with a frontage of, I believe, twenty-eight feet. Next door was a tenement house—in the interest of symmetry, there were tenement houses on the other side, and shanties opposite. Inside there were about forty beds, and a small number of doctors—most of them are dead ; amongst them Ernst Krackowizer, whose name must never disappear from your annals. There were also nurses.

Many changes have occurred since that far-off time. The shanty hospital has been turned, fairy-like, into a palace, poverty into riches ; and all this because the spirit of benevolence, which commenced by erecting the shanty, continued to live, and the tree planted by the Touros, Jos. Fatmans, and Nathans has borne and ripened its fruit. And inside the palace the services rendered to the sick are of a higher order, since the successful example of the Bellevue Training School stimulated the private enterprise of clear sighted and noble-hearted women to establish the Mount Sinai Training School for Nurses.

In an address I delivered half a dozen years ago before one of your graduating classes and the public, I drew from memory a picture of the hospital and private nursing before the time of training schools. The comparison was not 'at all favorable to the past. Woman's nature at its best is always sympathetic, pure, and unselfish, but that part of the sex which turned to nursing as a business was, with some rare and excellent exceptions, far from belonging to the sympathetic, pure, and unselfish class. Still, the nursing of the sick in those times was, in principle, superior to that which preceded it.

In ancient Greece, when a poor man was taken sick, he found admission to, and nursing in, the house of a rich fellow-citizen. During the Crusades the nursing order of the Hospital Brothers was

recruited from amongst Italian and German merchants. All the other organizations for the nursing
of the sick, from the Templars and the Order of St.
Elizabeth down to the Protestant Deaconesses, were
founded under the authority and supervision of the
Church. An immense deal of good has been done
by all of them, for, indeed, the most solid foundation
of every religion of civilized and semi-civilized nations is the sum of humanitarian instincts and tendencies embodied in them. Through centuries it
was the Church alone which could provide nursing
on a large scale, though it were ever so insufficient
when compared with the total sum of suffering.
As in our times the physician and priest, who were
long identical, have parted in peace, to the benefit
and satisfaction of both parties and of mankind, so
the profession of nursing must be independent. It
has also been acknowledged *at last* that the nursing
of the sick is a sufficiently important, difficult,
and grateful task to be *learned* before performed.
Moreover, what the occasional generosity of a fellow-citizen would do for a sick person in olden time,
what the Church would order or sanction in the
Middle Ages, that has finally become the outgrowth
of well-understood individualism, in accordance
with the spirit of the time and our social constitution.

It is a characteristic feature of our time that there
need not be a contradiction between the different
interests of the many. In an organization like a
training school you serve at the same time the
nurse, the sick, and the community at large. In
the address alluded to I mentioned the fact, stated

24*

by the census of Berlin in 1872, that two-thirds of all the women of that city had to provide for themselves, and that but one out of every four hundred and seven such women turned to nursing as a regular occupation. In facilitating the obtaining of sufficient knowledge and training you give a woman a profession by which to secure her independence, an occupation which will serve the sick, a position than which there are few—there ought to be none—more appreciated and more honored. At the same time you serve the community. Whoever has feared and grieved at the bedside of a dear one, old or young, or has been exhausted by constant care and physical work, and tormented by the evidence of his or her own insufficient knowledge or training, has appreciated long ago the services a trained nurse alone can render. I believe there is none amongst you in whose household a good trained nurse has not shed light and given confidence and rendered valuable services already. We physicians know the difference between the hospital and private nursing of former times and that of the present. We do not feel as if we could or ought to take the responsibility of a doubtful case without the aid of a trained nurse, and wonder how we could ever get along without her. It is not a matter of fashion, but of necessity. If it were a fashion only, surely the name of the greatest and most blessed woman in the history of womanhood might be Semiramis, or Lucretia, or Roland, or what not ; but you do know that *that* name is Florence Nightingale.

Sickness and suffering are unsectarian. Human-

ity is unsectarian. Your school is unsectarian.
Neither the names nor faces nor creeds of the
pupils remind one of a *single* nationality or church.
They are taught that their home is to be the sick-
room, their church the hospital, and it is expected
that they should use their intellect to learn enough
of knowledge, and practise enough of their art, to
be efficient workers in the chosen field. No brass
band, no clamor, no mob shouts at their presence.
Knowledge adapted to their purpose, educated
common sense, trained hands and minds, distinguish them. It is by these qualities that excel the
humane and humanitarian soldiers of the genuine
army of salvation.

The Mount Sinai Training School—I can say that
with great satisfaction—has obtained a good reputation in the community and the medical profession.
However, as so many of its officers are here, and I
am somewhat of an officer myself, I shall say no
more on this theme. Still, the eagerness with
which the preparations for this fair have been commenced, and the readiness with which the call of
its initiators has been responded to, prove both the
hold the institution has gained on the public and
the feeling that increased means will enhance its
usefulness. To aid in obtaining these substantial
means you were kindly but categorically besought,
invited, told, or ordered, as the case may be, to
attend this fair, and not to leave it before you paid
the ransom. You are prisoners in the chains of
your own good-will, or convictions, or domestic
ties, or affiliations, or love, or curiosity, or fashion

—I do not care which, so the end of this fair be attained. I was selected to tell you so.

When, however, I complacently informed a friend that I was to open this fair, I was bluntly told that I did not even know what a fair was, and certainly did not know how to open one. Becoming doubtful of my knowledge, I consulted Webster (I have the impression that is what books are made for, my own too). There I found that "fair" means "free from spots, specks, imperfection, or hindrance ; cloudless, propitious, favorable, unencumbered ; characterized by frankness, honesty, impartiality, candor." You see I know all about your fair here ; and that I know how to open one I must prove this very moment, for I have been told that my remarks must be brief. Besides, I am used to opening things—I have opened a great many things in my life : I have opened my eyes quite often, though sometimes I was glad to close them quickly ; my heart sometimes, and found it quite unprofitable business mostly ; opened accounts and was soon told I had overdrawn ; college courses, and the doctors continue to increase to an incredible and uncomfortable degree, and the cry is still they come ; hospitals and dispensaries, with such success that they have remained open ever since ; I have opened champagne bottles, very successfully in most cases ; and now I am called upon to crown my work by opening this fair.

I shall do so after having made a single remark. The young ladies who expect to have fun only are greatly mistaken. Their satisfaction must be in serious work. Most of them have spent all their young lives in spending money ; now they are expected to make it. Every one of you is to be a wheel in the big coining machine. If you enjoy your function, so much the better. I do not believe that the end sanctions every means, but when a good cause is advanced and serious work accomplished by frolicking and laughing, teasing and dancing, I wish to encourage laughing and dancing. Life is too much, anyway, like a graveyard, and larks and flower beds are too few. David was dancing and was called pious. You cannot be too pious, or do better than imitate him in his piety, in this cause and in these surroundings. While I behold them and look upon this splendor, full of wealth and promise, I am reminded that "all that glitters is not gold." But I tell you, if Shakspere knew about this fair, he would say, "All that glitters here is gold." Pure gold was the idea that started the plan of this fair, pure gold the enthusiasm which matured that plan into reality, and the humanitarian instinct and practical tact which enlisted the sympathies of old and young ; pure gold the sagacity which taught friends and foes how to look upon the required labor as one of love and fun. Pure gold is the purpose for which this fair was established. I hope the result will be plenty of pure gold. As for myself, I look about, and, seeing that all is " fair," hereby declare this fair of yours open for the good will of a generous public.

ADDRESS

TEN years ago the wards of the Mount Sinai Hospital, particularly those located on its northerly exposure, contained more cases of typhoid fever and dysentery than were carried into it. The fountain-head of these pests was the very place on which this edifice has been erected. Like our great country, which shelters at the same time the choicest development of civilization and the most uncouth barbarism, the building dedicated to scientific charity was separated by the width of a street only from unfathomable mire, the remnant of former cowpens and the uncared-for refuse of the Third Avenue shanties. To-day the place is filled with four public buildings, the juxtaposition of which displays just as many symptoms of modern society—a synagogue, a fire-engine house, a police station, and, lastly, a home dedicated by charitable science to scientific charity, and a school established for the purpose of rendering charity more effective, disease less harassing, death less threatening and more avoidable through the trained efforts of women educated for the purpose.

Thus, what has happened under our eyes, and partly under your hands, is a repetition of the uniform development of human affairs and events. Unless we measure the history of mankind by the duration of a presidential term or a score of years, we come to the conclusion that simplicity, coarseness, inadequateness, and individualism are being slowly substituted by complexity, refinement, appropriateness, and organized efforts. The latter alone have resulted in the realization of the modern wonders of industry, commerce, science, and art, and also in the attempts at rendering the existence of all human beings, rich and poor, well and sick, more enjoyable or bearable. They are mostly an achievement of modern culture. In fact, what the ancients wanted most was organization and co-operation in most branches of knowledge or activity. There was but one thing in which voluntary organization was perfect in its way—that was the organization in the interest of bestiality ; when they had a war on their hands, they knew how to congregate and to destroy. Even then, however, that organization was but temporary : their very battles were apt to be single combats.

The men in those times were individually as wise, brave, pure, and eloquent as any in later centuries. Though we have a Washington, Franklin, Lincoln, Sherman, we have none to excel a Pericles, Aristides, or Cincinnatus and Aurelius Paulus. But the results of their labors were not lasting, and their political edifices broke down in relatively short periods, for they were not held together by the thousand threads composing the texture of modern life.

Every new institution which owes its existence to the organized co-operation of the many is a new proof of the correctness of the statement that, in spite of all the individualism of modern life, there are many purposes in common and a thorough appreciation of mutual indebtedness. It is not even necessary that every one should know why he is drawn into the performance of his duties toward his fellow-men. There is an ethical atmosphere, as there is a physical. As no person can fully escape the effect of the malaria poison while living in a malarial district, or the paralyzing influence of dog-day temperature, or the exhilaration of a glorious May morning, or the refreshing breath of Alpine air, so there are few who breathe the air of a republican commonwealth and live under the flag of a democratic country, the emblem of mutual responsibility, but are getting imbued with the dictates of charity and of tolerance. You may close your ears— you must hear something ; turn your eyes—you will gather some impression of light. It must be a place as dark as Hades which does not admit some trace of the light that abounds all over the universe.

In that way the Mount Sinai has outgrown its original plan and size; thus the Montefiore was established, the German Hospital, Roosevelt, the new building of the New York Academy of Medicine, and the many scientific and charitable institutions which cover the continent, not at the dictation of a personal government, but the outflow of the self-education of a generous people.

I am led into the utterance of these thoughts, regretting though that I have no time for the proper expression of my appreciation of their exalted importance, by the presence here of so many men and women shining in commerce, society, or science. For what is it that called you out in such numbers? I trust it is not curiosity—that might have been satisfied at a more convenient hour or day; no longing for amusement—we have no play, no games, no music; not the thirst of knowledge—for we have no new discovery, doctrine, or facts to impart in a lecture. What drew you here was the impulse of seeing and enjoying, with fellow-men and women, the result of co-operation in the service of an idea—that idea being directed to charity guided by science, and to instruction provided in the interest of both science and charity. You wanted to see to what end and with what result you have been uniting for a great aim; and I know you must feel that your combining your forces has had tangible results of no mean order. It is a pleasing fact in the consciousness of thinking men and women that the same fundamental principles underlie science, society, and political existence. In all of them the basis of existence and the source of development is the intertwining of interests and the combination of energies. It is in this way that many of the demands of socialism have already been solved by the political commonwealth and social custom; and that we may safely hope that the future will find it easy to work out a happier frame of social life, if not in impossible equality, still in the ties of fraternity and solidarity.

When I was first connected with the Mount Sinai Hospital thirty years ago, before some of the present Directors and any of the ladies present were born, it consisted of a large shanty in West 28th street—a tenement-house district. I think we had only thirty beds, but we had Willard Parker and Ernst Krackowizer, we had Beujamin Nathan and Joseph Fatman ; their warm hearts and clear heads must never be forgotten in the history of New York. In accordance with the increase of population, means, and necessity, the present hospital was erected. There have since been added an Isolation House and the ever-growing Dispensary Department, and the service has been enriched by a number of special branches. Finally the inadequacy of the accommodations, and the impropriety and danger connected with the presence of an out-door department within the hospital building, have necessitated the erection of the edifice in which part of the work of this great institution is to be performed.

The Board of Directors must be congratulated upon the consummation of their plans and objects. They have deserved well of the community for which they worked so long and so faithfully. They knew how to communicate the interest they felt themselves to those who had something to contribute, be it brains, money, or labor. They have enlarged the roll of their contributors, and, by making them stockholders in the realm of good citizenship and humanitarianism, have benefited both the institution and the members, whose horizons they have widened and hearts warmed. The thanks of all those are due who can appreciate the task so successfully performed. I know the Directors will consider themselves amply paid if their expectations in reference to the usefulness of this new building be fulfilled.

Besides its destination as the Out-door Department of the Mount Sinai Hospital, it is to be the head-quarters of the Training School for Nurses. Mrs. President, I had the great honor of addressing the first graduating class of your school, seven years ago, on May 12th, 1883. I trust that the difficulties, which must always be overcome in the founding of a new institution, appear slight when compared with your results, and that you have reason to look back to these years of honest and successful exertions with great satisfaction. One thing is certain, namely, that the pupils and graduates of the Training School have enjoyed constant opportunities to serve the institution while being served by it. Another thing is as certain, namely, that the Training School has supplied a want which was sorely felt. For it is just as certain that a modern hospital requires a number of co-ordinate component parts. Besides a public willing to pay and add its blessing, you want a good board of directors, effective administration and officers ; you require also medical men, instruments, and other remedies. Besides, you require the best possible and most scrupulous and conscientious nursing, and that is what your school was meant to contribute to the performance of the common duties.

Seven years ago, after giving an outline of the

history of nursing the sick, from the individual charity of the ancients to the first foundation of hospitals amongst the Buddhists and Arabs, from the original lay brotherhoods to the large nursing organizations of the Catholic Church, I alluded to the period in which, while the influence of the Church was evanescing and no other strong mental or emotional power took its place, intelligent and efficient nursing was on the decline. Nursing the sick —unless it were that performed by the relatives, who are often least fit for the task—was held in practical contempt. In an address I had the honor of delivering at the opening exercises of your fair held in the Brunswick Hotel on December 19th, 1888, I mentioned the fact, stated by the census of Berlin in 1872, that two-thirds of all the women in that city had to provide for themselves, but that only one out of every four hundred and seven turned to nursing as a regular occupation. Whether this quarter of a per cent, however, was efficient, we are not told. I am very much afraid it was not superior to the class of women who undertook nursing the sick as a means of livelihood in our New York. I remember the time quite well, and also the women. They and I did not think well of each other. Many of them were fat, much more than forty, and not fair ; the rocking chairs they sat on, the many cups of coffee they drank with their cake after numerous and copious meals, agreed well with them. After they had gone through that course of self-sacrifice a great many times, they looked upon themselves as oracles and the legitimate critics of the services of the medical man, who had almost as hard a time as the patient. Or they were thin, wiry, and spiry, a terror on the premises, sharp and venomous *noli-me-tangeres*, and, like their more corpulent sisters, the self-sufficient possessors of mountains of accumulated ignorance. They have left the field, as ought to do, because it is a logical consequence of the growing knowledge of the danger they convey, the hundreds of so-called midwives who—I do not exaggerate—carry puerperal fever to the woman and the newly born from tenement to tenement, in their unwashed clothing, unkempt hair, and soiled finger nails, this very day. There, Mrs. President and ladies, is another field on which you can again begin to reform and revolutionize.

I well remember the meeting of the Medical Board of Bellevue Hospital in which it was announced that a number of ladies had formed an association for the purpose of training nurses in behalf of the hospital and the public. While we were unanimous in desiring good nurses, many of us were doubtful as to the possibility of obtaining them by such means. What, however, women are able to do, without stepping beyond their "spheres," has since been demonstrated by the Bellevue, the Charity, the Mount Sinai, New York, and other hospital training schools for nurses, and all those which have since been established all over the country.

The object of these training schools was to utilize the facilities afforded by the wards of the hospital to obtain a better class of nurses by a prolonged course of theoretical and practical instruction for the work required both in public institutions and in private life. By so doing two objects have been accomplished. A large number of young women have found a profession by which to make themselves useful and to benefit the sick. I do not know of any calling which can be made more beneficial and more honored while affording independence and competency. Besides, in most cases the services rendered the sick are thoroughly appreciated, for it is not always true that services rendered make enemies of those you have benefited. The public have been quick in imitating the appreciation bestowed on the trained nurse by the physicians. It is the latter who know, better than anybody else can know, the difference between hospital nursing now and in former times before the inauguration of the present system, and wonder how we could be expected to assume the responsibility of grave private cases without a member of this genuine army of salvation to execute orders intelligently, quickly, and success-fully.

For without the most conscientious and best-informed class of nurses the ideal hospital cannot exist. The ideal hospital is that which surrounds itself with, and claims as its prerogatives, the best possible hygienic measures, the most profound medical learning and greatest skill, and the most intelligent and dexterous nursing.

Your share of the common duties, ladies of the graduating class, you have performed in a creditable manner. It gives me pleasure to publicly bear testimony in your behalf.

From what I have learned from my colleagues, I have reason to believe that you will be better nurses than even a diploma can proclaim you to be. It is knowledge acquired for which you receive a diploma, and the skill of your hands which is certified by your teachers and directors. But I do not forget, nor do I want this assembly and yourselves to forget, that brains and fingers can be trained, but that there is one thing nobody can teach you, but which must be possessed and developed—that is the heart; that is feeling and sympathy with the suffering and powerless. You have heard, and the thoughtless will tell you, that the constant contact with the suffering, the continued beholding of the quiverings of pain, and the listening to the outcries of anguish render the heart obdurate and hard. But whoever, physician or nurse, is found hard after long contact with misery and suffering, has not *learned* to be so—they were always so. Your physicians or nurses who give way to, or feign, overwhelming feeling are unfit for their duties. Whatever you feel, to what degree you sympathize, that feeling and sympathy must not influence the performance of your duties. On the other hand, the nurse who feels indifference or displays levity after years of practice was always indifferent and coarse. She ought to have selected a trade, but not a profession. Treating and nursing the sick and suffering may be made either. Without culture of both heart and mind nursing is lowered into a vulgar business; with it, its humane character raises your work into a sacred calling, a blessed and blessing vocation, similar to that of the most sublime and therefore the most modest of all professions, the medical.

In this spirit I want you to enter upon your independent career. You will be able to render great services in more than one direction. Your skill and watchfulness will benefit the individual under your charge; your trained common sense and acquired knowledge will be able to teach the simple lessons of hygiene to a vast number of people. A single seed you plant may bear fruit a hundredfold. The hundreds of trained nurses now in practice ought to exert a lasting influence on the people at large, on their hygiene and that of their children, by conversational teaching. Thus, every one of you has a great duty to perform. Do not forget that after you have been blessed with great opportunities to learn, you have duties to fulfil to your fellows. Your possibilities to do so are vast without your overstepping the boundaries of your province and the limits of your capabilities. Do not forget that every one of us is but a link in a chain. When I spoke of the public, the directors, the doctors, the officers, the nurses being the component parts of an institution, each one indispensable in his or her appropriate place, you will in a given case never overlook that you are nurses, but not doctors. I speak of an actual danger which lurks in your path, and I have seen many an otherwise useful woman foundering on the cliff of self-sufficient overestimation of her powers and responsibilities. As our good old genius, the poet-doctor Oliver Wendell Holmes, said of himself nearly half a century ago, I want you to bear in mind that your work and your mind must be "too serious for either humility or vanity." So I want you to step out into your independence without either humility or vanity, with the consciousness that you have powers to use and

25*

duties to perform. May that strong but modest feeling, may the enthusiasm for your vocation, the sympathy with the suffering, may the love of learning and of fulfilling the dictates of your conscience, never fail you, forevermore!

AUFRUF.*

DIE unterzeichneten Aerzte sind durch die mannigfaltigen Anforderungen, welche ihr Beruf an ihre Zeit und Arbeitskraft stellt, häufig an der vollen Ausübung ihrer Bürgerpflichten gehindert. Zu den letzteren gehört vor allen Dingen die Betheiligung an der Entscheidung über nationale, staatliche und städtische Angelegenheiten am Stimmkasten und die Bethätigung des Einflusses, welchen der Einzelne auf seine Mitbürger zum Wohle der Gesammtheit auszuüben im Stande ist. Sie fühlen sich indessen heute verpflichtet, aus ihrer zurückhaltenden Stellung herauszutreten und ihre Kollegen und ihre deutsch-amerikanischen Mitbürger an die Nothwendigkeit der Betheiligung am diesmaligen Wahlkampfe zu erinnern.

Denn die Missstände unserer städtischen Verwaltung sind so augenfällig und gefährlich geworden, dass die Fortdauer derselben sich für die gesammte Bevölkerung der Stadt New York als unmöglich erweist. Auch dem Langmüthigsten wird die Nothwendigkeit einer durchgreifenden Aenderung klar. Unsere Strassen sind schmutzig und gesundheitsgefährlich ; unsere Abzugskanäle unzulänglich und die Quelle epidemischer Krankheiten ; viele Hunderte von Wohnhäusern, besonders der

---

* Aufruf zur Betheiligung an der ''People's Municipal League.'' Staats-Zeitung, 31. October 1890.

ärmeren Klassen, sind Pesthöhlen, Gemeinschäden für die Bewohner, und eine Gefahr für die ganze Stadt; die Zahl der Volksschulen ist ungenügend und ein Theil der bestehenden ungesund; unsere Polizei ist nicht immer der beste und annähernd ausreichende Schutz, und unsere Richter sind nicht immer ideal, weil manche von ihnen entschieden politische Augendiener und Parteiklepper sind.

Alle diese Uebelstände und Gefahren sind die Folgen der Gewohnheit, welche sich bei uns eingeschlichen hat, städtische und nationale oder staatliche Angelegenheiten miteinander zu verwechseln. Es ist vergessen worden, dass städtische Verwaltung und nationale Parteifragen nichts miteinander zu thun haben und dass die Sicherheit des Verkehrs in den Strassen, die Gesundheit in den Häusern, die Verwaltung der Krankenanstalten, der Unterricht der Jugend, die Besetzung der Stellen im Gesundheitsrath und die Fähigkeit und Redlichkeit des Richters mit der Frage, ob Demokrat, ob Republikaner, nicht gleichbedeutend sind. Bei uns ist es dahin gekommen, dass ein Richter, ein Schuldirektor, ein Kassenbeamter, ein Strassenkommissär nicht wegen seiner Fähigkeiten und Amtskenntnisse angestellt wird, sondern weil er für den jedesmaligen Präsidenten oder Gouverneur gestimmt, oder weil er—oder vielleicht gar nur ein einflussreicher Freund—in den Parteiversammlungen seines Distrikts die lauteste Stimme und die heftigsten Gestikulationen entwickelt hat.

Unter diesen Umständen hat sich die "People's Municipal League" das grosse Verdienst erworben, eine Anzahl Kandidaten für die vakant werdenden

städtischen Aemter auf Grund ihrer persönlichen
Eigenschaften und Fähigkeiten, ohne Rücksicht
auf ihre politische Parteistellung, dem Volke New
York's zur Wahl zu empfehlen. Schon haben sich
sogar einige Parteiorganisationen der Nothwendigkeit gefügt und, Verzicht leistend auf strikte Par-
teinominationen, die Kandidaten befürwortet, von
denen man weiss, dass sie die Stadt im Interesse
der Stadt ohne Nebenzwecke und politische Hinter-
gedanken verwalten werden. Und unsere deutsch-
amerikanischen Mitbürger, welche einer ehrlichen
und von Parteileidenschaften befreiten Stadtver-
waltung—gegenüber der Verschwendung der ein-
gezahlten Steuern, den schmutzigen Strassen und
gifthauchenden Kanälen, den ungenügenden und
ungesunden Schulen und Wohnungen—den Vorzug
geben, haben es in ihrer Hand, durch die Wahl der
von der "People's Municipal League" vorgeschla-
genen Kandidaten der Misswirthschaft und der
Herrschaft politischer "Bosse" ein Ende zu
machen.

THE AMERICANS AND THE TENTH INTERNATIONAL CONGRESS.*

ON August 4th, 1890, during the first, and largest, general meeting of the Tenth International Congress, there were three universal and spontaneous outbursts of applause. The first and most sympathetic greeted the name of James Paget, and never was there an ovation more deserved. The second rang through the immense building when it was announced that the Government of the French Republic had sent thirty-four official delegates, and that nearly one hundred and fifty more Frenchmen had joined the Congress. They had overcome political enmity and jealousy, disregarded a rather slighting reference to their "national insanity" of twenty years ago, and came with open hearts and friendly feelings, a large number of them men of fame and high rank. The third greeted the announcement of the fact that on the first day of the gathering more than six hundred Americans were inscribed on the rolls. This recognition afforded to our name must have flattered the national pride of every one of us who was present.

* The Medical Record, November 15th, 1890. Being an introduction to special reports of Delegates to the Congress before the New York Academy of Medicine, November 6th, 1890.

This hearty welcome was more than I had mustered the courage to expect. For, indeed, Americans visiting Europe on such occasions as this, labor under certain difficulties. Europeans do not quite understand our country, its political and social configuration or its scientific attainments. If that be so even in Great Britain, both race and language being identical and mutual intercourse more frequent, how much less can we expect it to be known on the Continent! Besides, it is not always the best political, social, and scientific class of our fellow-citizens who travel extensively, and though it be not the crowd of the *"profanum vulgus"* that ought to tell in the estimation of the best spirit of their country, it does so tell. Now, the majority of medical Americans they know in Europe, and particularly in Germany, belong to one of two classes : either they are *bona-fide* students, whom, being mere foreigners, they consent to matriculate even without the preliminary education rigorously insisted upon in their own young countrymen, or they are our young doctors who pass a few months or a year in European laboratories and clinics for the sake of special studies. It is these latter that are also the occasional participants in their national associations, where, nobody else being present, they are naturally considered the representatives of American medicine. Our best men travel little and talk less. Indeed, some of those who were most fit to represent us in the Congress kept in the rear, modest and retiring. Besides, the great opportunity America might have had to present to the view of the world whatever there is great and progressive in American medicine, appears lost. For in the very number of the *German Medical Weekly* which was published in the week of the Congress you could, in the history of previous congresses, read the statement that the Washington Congress was unfortunately a failure, for which all of us, being Americans, are held responsible. Moreover, though English is read by a great many of the best men in Europe, the knowledge of our language is not so general as to insure a wide acquaintance with our literature through anything but the uncertain channels of extracts or translations. Nor are even these well selected. We are all aware that our medical journals are of as unequal rank as our schools, and not infrequently will you find a journal, which is deservedly unknown among us, quoted in Europe under the impression that it is a fair representative of American medical literature. Nor is the treatment Europeans receive at our hands always very courteous or considerate. The editorial remarks of a great New York weekly were quoted as unkind, inasmuch as the efforts to make the Congress international and Berlin a neutral ground for the whole world did not appear to be appreciated by us. It must be admitted, though, they did not deem that Western journal worthy of serious consideration which spoke of the Tenth International Congress as a congress of snobs, and advised every one of the forty thousand practitioners of the Mississippi Valley, "every one superior to the leaders of the Congress," to stay at home.

Public opinion is often made or unmade by trivialities; sometimes, indeed, by personalities of an in-

ferior nature.   It was a source of complaint in Berlin that an American who had been honored with
the request to represent our country by delivering
one of the great addresses, had neglected to see to it
that his refusal reached the Committee of Organization in anything like due time.   The proverbial
courtesy of Americans was found wanting, and that
at a time of feverish excitement and overwork.
Such occasions are the very opportunities for those,
formerly Europeans, who manage to rise, in their
own estimation and that of their former countrymen, by detraction of us.   For there are those who
do not immediately succeed, when they, our guests
and future fellow-citizens, arrive among us, in im-
pressing us with their superiority, or in being appreciated by us as they are by themselves, or in obtaining at once a lucrative practice and professional
positions and honors.   It is they who pay for the
hospitality proffered by our country with shoulder-
shrugging insinuations and pitying remarks upon
our crudeness and inferiority, our " mob rule," our
"civilized barbarism," instead of aiding in the
realizations of the national and cosmopolitan aims
of the medical profession and science.

Nothing is so small as not to have some effect.
Unfortunately there is still so much national jealousy everywhere that faults and shortcomings in
your neighbor beyond the boundary line are easily
believed in, and slanderers and libellers are always
busy.   When I arrived in Germany a newspaper
article was shown me which was concocted by a
sectarian practitioner, formerly in New York, who
detailed the inferiority of American medicine,

schools, and practice to the horrified sanctity of the German public ; and in the very week preceding the Congress, hundreds, or perhaps thousands, of pamphlets were distributed in Berlin for the avowed purpose of insulting us and making us uncomfortable. The pseudonymous author, who appears to have lived, or lives, in Chicago, says, among a great many other things, the following :

"In reference to the transatlantic gentlemen, nothing is more out of place than indulgence. American tolerance, so frequently extolled, exists for Americans only. When about to travel they leave it at home. It is almost always the result of ignorance, indifference, and bad conscience. As the average American never cares for the history of a science, the majority of the transatlantic members of the International Congress are totally unacquainted with European institutions, labors, and scientific methods and their aims. Nevertheless, every one of these gentlemen carries a paper in his pocket, easily compiled, wherewith to resuscitate the obsolete science of Europe."

In the same sheet the man asserts that forty-two per cent of all the doctors in Chicago are professed abortionists and a great many followers of "Christian Science."

Some of the great Germans, with whose names every one of us is perfectly familiar, denied being in any way influenced by such rubbish ; but then, again, it was through them that I was informed of a New York specialist, and a Fellow of this Academy, who was reported to have availed himself of his personal intimacy with the officers of the Asso-

ciated Press for the purpose of having his Congress
paper served at the breakfast tables of a million of
American households on the day of its delivery.
That was a week before the opening.

Thus you see, Mr. President, American medical
gentlemen may meet with difficulties in the face of
such occurrences. Still, though they are as human
on the other side of the Atlantic as we on this, the
facilities of communication between the continents
have become such as to enable those wishing to see
and know the truth that the time when American
medicine was merely receptive and imitative has
long passed by, and that we have entered the arena
as co-operating peers. They were, indeed, anxious
to have us and secure a large American attendance.
In order to accomplish that end the organizing
committee appointed an American committee,
which was to enlist universal sympathy in our
country. No time was to be lost, and the first ten
medical men who expressed their willingness to
serve were appointed. The territorial jealousy, one
of the most marked American littlenesses, which
found its way into print several times, has obliged
me to explain publicly, in the May meeting of the
Association of American Physicians, why that
committee consisted of Stewart, Fitz, Lusk, Draper,
Hun, Pepper, Busey, Osler, and Peyre Porcher.
Will the Western gentlemen who found fault with
the committee, and heaped vituperation on the
mode of its composition, tell us that the names
selected did not deserve the honor conferred upon
them, or that there are better ones among us?
Does American medicine begin at the Alleghanies

or the Sierra? Or will you, gentlemen of Ohio, Mississippi, or Nevada, tell us which of the forty-four stars of the glorious flag is the one you claim as yours? Yours are the forty-four, so are they ours. Are your minds not big enough, your hearts not large enough to embrace the love of, and the pride in, the whole flag of America?

A further proof of the anxiety to secure the co-operation and good-will of the Americans was given by the Berlin committee in this, that they insisted upon one of the public addresses in the general meetings being delivered by an American. Weir Mitchell having declined in time and courteously, and Osler not being within reach, I was telegraphically directed to select an orator. The choice of Horatio C. Wood was heartily approved of in Berlin and elsewhere. Again a few have asked why a New Yorker could not have been honored with that commission. That question is answered by some other queries : Do you know of a better man? Is America bounded by the East and North Rivers? And, lastly, has New York forgotten that she can afford to be courteous and generous?

More, a few weeks only before the meeting of the Congress the American orthopædists expressed the desire that there should be a separate Section of Orthopædics. When I, then already in Europe, was notified of that request by the chairman of the Orthopædic Section of this Academy, and expressed my fear lest it might be too late to make arrangements for that change, I was by returning mail informed by the Secretary-General that the request was at once granted by the Committee of Organization, on the ground that my countrymen must know best what suited them and their scientific labors.

Again, the organization of the Congress was not completed without the election of an American vice-president, John S. Billings, and an American, M. Allen Starr, as one of the two English-speaking secretaries, and a large number of American vice-presidents of sections. And, lastly, when, on the third day of Congress and in the second general meeting, the hour grew late and the audience melted under the hot sun, Dr. Wood's address was, out of consideration for the Americans, postponed so as to be the first topic of the third meeting, though the hour and arrangements and printed preparations had to be changed accordingly.

All this was meant, and believed to suffice, to make every American feel at home. If it did not succeed, it ought to have accomplished that end. But I have been told that disappointments have been keenly felt and complaints been uttered.

When an English paper was read, many have been reported to have left the room. Many essays were not read at all, some were not allowed the time required by the authors, some men would read beyond the legal limits. Such comments are natural, but also their causes. The unprecedented number of papers offered at a late date and too courteously accepted, and some acoustic disadvantages of many of the audience halls, are among the causes of disappointments, which are unavoidable in everything human. The experience of the past may furnish remedies in the future. However, when one man complains that he was not one among the five per cent of members who could be admitted to the court reception in Potsdam ; another, that he had to pay for his share of the section dinner on the evening of Wednesday, the 6th, proclaiming that matters were different in Washington, where no foreigner paid anything—it proves one of two things, either that there were those who went more for the incidental appurtenances of the Congress than the Congress, or that our national failing, which is a highly developed emotional hyperæsthesia, was rather demonstrative. I can assure those who are finding fault with the scantiness of their enjoyments that I know of one at least who neither shared in the entertainment in the City Hall, for which Berlin paid 80,000 marks, nor danced at any of the five balls, nor imbibed the music and songs in eleven languages, and as many beverages, at Kroll's, and—did not feel the worse for it the following mornings. If I have any fault to find, it is with the overflow of entertainments, the excess of generosity, the multiplicity of luncheons, dinners, and receptions, the waste of money in the vast number of public and private social gatherings.

If there ever were hosts spending unstintingly— aye, squandering—money in the service of unlimited hospitality, they were the profession as a whole, and the single medical men, of Berlin.

In connection with this fact let me make a remark, which is dictated by no cavilling spirit, that I have too many reasons to appreciate the universal kindness and untiring hospitality of the great and

gentlemanly members of the Berlin profession, who
were bent on nothing so much as to render the so-
journ of the foreign guests comfortable and pleasant. I must here mention the names of Virchow,
Bergmann, Waldeyer, Gerhardt, Henoch, Martin,
and Leyden, and his accomplished wife, the chairman of the Ladies' Committee, and could name a
host of others. Many of us have found it impossible
to respond at the same time to the requirements of
actual congressional duties and the urgent demands
of hospitable courtesy. In this, also, there is dis-
comfort and loss for the individual member. But
the matter has a very much more important aspect.
An excess of social entertainments on one hand,
and the accomplishment of the end for which the
International Congress is convened on the other, are
incompatible at a certain point. Too many feasts
interfere with legitimate work. The expectation
of a good time may—if I must not say it does—invite the attendance of many, of hundreds, perhaps
of thousands, who would not go for the sake of
work. On the other hand, those who have gone for
the latter are liable to feel sorely disconcerted.
Thus it has happened—at least this disappointment
can be held in part responsible—that the national
associations have suffered from the persistent absence of those who do not wish to lose great opportunities ; and that all over America, Great Britain,
France, Germany, and other countries there have
been formed by dissatisfied men, who place scientific work over any distractions, be they ever so
pleasant, special societies, the objects of all of
which ought to have been accomplished in the sec-

tions of the general bodies. It would be a sad development if the same tendency were to grow up in international congresses. This very moment there are already in existence an international ophthalmological and an otological congress. It would be the fault of the management of international medical congresses if other specialties or doctrines would follow the example, for no other reason than the predominance of the social over the scientific element. If the latter cease to rule, the great men of science will stay away, and the holiday-seekers and a few ambitious office-holders will remain. *Experientia docet.*

It is only a wealthy city and rich professional men who can entertain as Berlin did. For such hospitality as was displayed there you require large and generous hearts, ample and well-filled purses. There are but few communities like her. If the habit of prodigality becomes persistent we shall be received in future with misgivings on the part of our hosts, who must fear lest their efforts fall short both of the results of predecessors and the expectations of the guests. Let these two calamities occur—viz., the absence of the best men of all nations, and, on the part of cities and men, hesitation to request our coming—what will become of the International Congresses?

And where is the prevention of the danger alluded to? Here : Let the social entertainments be reduced to a minimum. Then any city with ample hotel accommodations will be able to receive us, though we be thousands. Then those bent upon pleasure only will seek it elsewhere. Then

26*

the numbers will no longer be unwieldy and shapeless. Then the men looking for work, and for the men who work, will be eager to come and see and be seen, to teach and to be taught.

The unprecedented success of the American Congress of Physicians and Surgeons, the first meeting of which was held in Washington in September, 1888, tells its own tale and exhibits the proof of what I say. In my mind there is no doubt that its second meeting, in September, 1891, will be equally successful ; its three days will be dedicated to work, and the official social entertainment limited to a plain subscription banquet. In that way neither the lawful work of the Congress nor private intercourse and hospitality are interfered with.

It may appear invidious to mention the co-operative services rendered by the members of the different nations represented in the various sections of the Congress. Still, as we generally have a good opinion of ourselves, we are not afraid of looking back at our own contributions to the scientific material that was furnished. When we do so we have to admit, however, that but a small percentage of our seven hundred participated in the general work. It is true there was one who got himself delivered of quintuplets ; fortunately, he had no equals, and he was not, as a medical journal reported, "taken in earnest." Still, there were a number of papers, not compiled, but original. The Orthopædic Section was American to a great extent. The Neurological had a very fair representation from our country. The Gynæcological and Pædiatric Sections were not without American contributions. The Surgical was supplied with papers which were highly appreciated, mostly from the West. Indeed, there were but few sections in which no American took part, though there were some in which no active work at all was furnished by us. The most redeeming feature was the meeting of the combined Laryngological and Pædiatric Sections, in which the ingenuous, painstaking, and successful efforts of O'Dwyer were heartily applauded.

After all, however, the labor performed in the general sessions may be the principal, but is certainly not the only, object in view. An English journal has said that "congresses are not instruments of research"; and still the transactions of all are replete with it. It is true a congress is not so much meant for new discoveries as for the broad dissemination of facts, hints, and ideas. A man, not being ubiquitous, may not take away with him many things new, but what he carries home is a new stimulus, and encouragement.

In the Congress you saw a great many men whom you thought you knew; but since you listened to them, and watched them while you listened, and took their measure, you know better now. You saw and heard the living objects of your admiration, the moulders of professional thought in all countries—discoverers, teachers, laboratory workers, practitioners; those who, after hard work, create books by spontaneous generation out of their brains, and those who compile them out of their pigeonholes; the eagles, the bees, and the moles— also the parrots, and that class of envious cuckoos who transfer other birds' eggs into their own nests. You found there is room in our great army for many men and many classes of men. You gathered encouragement from learning that even truly great men are still men and human ; and that some degree of greatness is within the grasp of any man, in town or village, who will work for it intelligently, bravely, and honorably. All this is what a congress will teach those who consent to learn.

There is another lesson that is taught by a congress : The separation into twenty sections proves the endless and diversified branching of the grand old tree of medical science. Their working under the same roof, however, and under the same administration ; their occasional combination for a common purpose ; their gathering in general meetings, and their listening to the same addresses, with the same interest and profit—all this, in spite of the fact that some of the twenty appear to be threatened with the danger of degenerating into mere handicraft, proclaim louder than steeple bells that medical science is " one and indivisible, now and forever."

The Congress has conveyed to me, like its predecessors in Copenhagen and London, a great lesson, and furnished an elevating spectacle. Imagine, those of you who have not been present, thousands of medical men from all parts of the world, and speaking a dozen different languages, not perhaps endowed with the same erudition or mental or moral power, but moved by the same instincts and interests, and assembling at the same call and for the same special purpose. The great and the lowly, the old and young, meet as brethren on the same platform, if not of equality, still of fraternity and solidarity. National jealousy and prejudice are shelved for at least a week, and a lesson is taught that brethren may live together peaceably under the same roof, an example to the nations both of the present and the future. The man and the man of science are appreciated and loved, though political adversaries. Applause takes the place of hisses. The contest is no longer against each other, but with each other, side by side, arm in arm, with the same weapons of the brain and soul against the common enemy of science and mankind—viz., physical deterioration and social misery. Thus the cosmopolitan spirit of coming centuries is foreshadowed and initiated by the co-operation of the men arrayed in the army of the noblest of all sciences and professions. Therefore may no man who can prove an example to his peers in this or any other country, no man who can teach, none who can learn, none who can worthily represent his country in any capacity and do honor to America among foreigners—may no man, except for valid reasons, ever shirk his duty to attend an International Medical Congress.

THE ACADEMY OF MEDICINE'S DELEGATES TO BERLIN.

110 WEST 34TH STREET,
NEW YORK, November 8th, 1890.

To the Editor of the New York Medical Journal.

SIR :—In to-day's *Journal*, on page 518, you publish a brief editorial in which you say : "The programme for the meeting [of the New York Academy of Medicine] on Thursday evening of this week consisted of reports of so-called 'delegates' to the Tenth International Medical Congress—eleven in number. It is well known that these congresses are not made up of delegates. It was therefore a work of supererogation for the Academy to appoint them, and to devote a meeting to their 'reports' seems to us to argue such a lack of legitimate material as ought not to be encountered at this time of the year."

In order to prove that this criticism is not based on facts, I have the honor of referring you to a circular of the American subcommittee (consisting of Dr. S. C. Busey, Dr. W. H. Draper, Dr. R. H. Fitz, Dr. H. Hun, Dr. A. Jacobi, Dr. W. T. Lusk, Dr. W. Osler, Dr. W. Pepper, Dr. F. Peyre Porcher, and Dr. J. Stewart) which was sent to and printed by a large number of American medical journals, and contained the following sentence : "Delegates of American medical societies and institutions, and individual members of the profession, will be admitted on equal terms."

This notice was based on the contents of an official letter received from the Secretary-General, Dr. O. Lassar, dated February 28th, 1890, part of which reads as follows : "It would please us very much if our invitation were given publicity by your national committee, with your recommendations. We imagine that could be best accomplished by a request directed to all the large societies to participate in the Congress, either *in corpore* or by delegates." This letter, Mr. Editor, I shall take pleasure in submitting to you. Finally, I can assure you that a number of names contained in the official rolls of the central office had the word "delegate" added to them.

A. JACOBI, M.D.

STATEMENT ON TUBERCULIN

BEFORE THE NEW YORK ACADEMY OF MEDICINE,
DECEMBER 4TH, 1890.*

WHEN a medical man's name is paraded in the newspapers as mine has been these ten days, that man must either be suspected of transgressing the written and unwritten laws of the profession, or he must give an account of himself. As I do not wish to be suspected, I shall give an account and request the privilege to be heard on this floor. At the same time it may interest some to hear something about the way in which Koch's lymph is not obtained.

On November 13th the *Deutsche medicinische Wochenschrift*, No. 46a, contained the first and only contribution by Prof. Koch on his inoculations. On the 15th this article appeared in a good translation in the *Medical News* of Philadelphia. On the morning of the same day I cabled to Prof. C. Gerhardt the request to procure some of Koch's lymph for me. His answer came on November 17th and contained the single word "Habebis" (Thou shalt have). On Sunday, November 23d, at 12:30 A.M., a reporter of the *World* showed me a cablegram, which had just arrived from London, which ran about as follows : "Absolutely no lymph to be had in Berlin, with the exception of a

* Commercial Advertiser, December 5th, 1890.

specimen which has been shipped to Dr. A. Jacobi, No. 110 West 34th street, New York." In the Sunday edition of the *World*, a few hours afterward, a little article appeared which was based on the above cablegram.

In the following week I quietly began preparations for the reception of the distinguished foreigner, in arranging with Dr. T. Mitchell Prudden for our co-operation, in reserving a few rooms in the Mount Sinai Hospital, and bespeaking a number of patients in Dr. I. N. Heineman's service and some offered by professional friends.

On November 29th I received a letter from Prof. C. Gerhardt, dated November 18th, in which he refers to the lymph sent me by his good services, and the difficulties in obtaining it, and makes the remark that it must be in my possession at that date. I waited a day, then sent a letter to Mr. Van Cott, postmaster, in which I requested the speedy delivery of the package I expected, if it came by mail. A kind and sympathizing letter was received in reply. A friend went to the Collector of the Port on the same errand, and was assured of his friendly co-operation within the limits of the law. I cannot but express my appreciation and thanks to both officers. At the same time the express offices were searched, but no lymph found.

Yesterday, December 3d, I sent a cablegram to Dr. Einhorn, of No. 120 East 64th street, who is now in Berlin, which read as follows: "Ask Gerhardt immediately to what address, how, and when he sent the lymph." His answer was: "Gerhardt says only Koch sent." Again I inquired: "Then ask Koch to what address, how, and when he sent." Answer by Einhorn this morning : "Koch answered, Sent Jacobi, New York." This being unsatisfactory again, I cabled this afternoon : " Learn what route or express, and when. Hurry." I have not received an answer as yet, and no lymph has made its appearance.

These are the facts of my attempts at, and ill success in, obtaining the coveted article. A few of them had to be communicated to the inquiring gentlemen of the press. They were but few, but I understand that a painfully elaborate literature has been evolved out of a few simple statements made from time to time.

1891.

WHAT I have to offer to-day is but a summary of facts and dates. It is good principle and practice to look about now and then, and view the progress made in any human sphere ; not so much for the purpose of enjoying the sense of having accomplished much, as to behold the height you have to climb, so far above you.

A hundred years ago there was no law regulating the relation of the working people to their employers at all. Seventy-five years ago, and later, babies of three and four years had to work in mines as a matter of course, and died ; little children were employed in sweeping chimneys, and died ; the pauper quarters and poor houses were emptied of their babies and children, who thus proved the cheapest raw material that could be used in the interest of greedy industry. England, being almost the only country in which the industrial and manufacturing interests flourished, was the principal theatre of these abominations. But, having committed the first and greatest sins, she was the first to retrace her steps and legislate in the interest of the helpless creatures. Now, tentative and empirical as all the legislation has been both in England and other countries, it still has accomplished very much.

Restrictions have gradually been found necessary
and possible in regard to the ages of children to be
employed, the number of working hours, the time
of the day, the months of the year, and the character of the work ; and in many parts of the world an
educational test is applied.   All these are as praise-
worthy as they have proved successful.   But the
tentative and empirical nature of all such legislation is perhaps shown by nothing better than by the
fact that the agricultural labors of the very young
have never been included in any of the many acts
provided for the protection of childhood.

Legislation for the purpose of confining child
labor within certain limits will be found parallel
with the advancement of human and social culture
in general.   But to look upon the laboring children
with merely a sympathetic eye and a warm heart
does not cover the case at all.   The question can be
approached both with a sympathetic warm heart
and from a calculating business point of view.   In
America the legislative interference with the old
way of brutally abusing children was first launched
against the manufacturers, to protect the young
against the physical dangers resulting from premature and protracted work, confinement, bad air, and
its consequences ; also deformities, losses of limbs
and lives.   But the study of the discussions of legislative bodies and of the numerous annual reports of
factory inspectors of a dozen States of the Union, and
the provinces of the Canadian Dominion, for the
furnishing of which I am under the greatest obliga-
tions to these gentlemen, has taught me that the
laws enacted, one by one, with progressive improvements in their tendencies and results, were less the

results of warm-hearted impressions than of clear-sighted statesmanship. Early child labor interferes with schooling and education. Child labor means ignorance; ignorance means helplessness and poverty; poverty means, or may mean, and does mean in a hundred thousand cases, shiftlessness and poor-house, crime and prison. Thus human society protects itself, the State secures itself, by setting its face against premature child labor. The dwarfed physical condition may people the hospitals and degenerate the physical state of coming generations— a great misfortune. But, what is more, the results of ignorance and the mental degeneration depending thereon will destroy the life of any nation. We in America are in great danger. In their first report the factory inspectors of the State of New York (1887) make the statement that American-born children were less educated than many foreign-born, to such an extent that many did not know even the name of the State they lived in.

This looks almost impossible with our American public-school system. But it must not be forgotten that the children of the most forlorn and ignorant immigrants are called American-born, and are very numerous; and many of those children who themselves come from foreign parts, Germany for instance, have profited by the system of compulsory education prevailing in their former countries. Now, the very lowest politician amongst us has an interest in the stability of the Republic; the good citizen and the statesman look upon the permanence and perfection of its institutions as the safeguard of its own future, and as an example for, and the future of, mankind. What if the generations of America get drowned in ignorance? Our dangers at this very time are very great. We have to digest and amalgamate the seven millions of negroes, and as many more illiterate foreigners who found a haven on our shores, and help to develop onward their material resources. But while so doing the tornado of the immigration of the scum of Europe, the sunny South, the far Southeast, the mediæval East, is sweeping over our land. Our country gives them citizenship within five years. Many of us are afraid lest the conservative high-mindedness of the united republics will cause the victory of ignorant and uncouth hordes over an established civilization. Education is the only safeguard, but education requires time, and time that must not be spent in manufacturing establishments. Early child labor interferes with child education. That is why most American States have tried to defer the age at which labor in manufacturing establishments is permitted; that is why they insist upon compulsory schooling.

The Commission of the British Parliament appointed in 1875 to consolidate former Acts (those of June 22d, 1802, of July, 1819, of January, 1833, of 1864, 1867, 1874, and many others) reported in February, 1876. Its work resulted in "The Factory and Workshop Act, 1878." English legislation was imitated by Austria-Hungary in 1859, France in 1874, Switzerland in 1877, Germany in 1878. Of the English possessions the Presidency of Bombay enacted laws regulating factories and workshops up to 1882, the province of Ontario in 1884, and that of Quebec in 1885. Some of the United States took

the matter up soon after the British Consolidation
Act—New Hampshire in 1879; Maine, Rhode Island,
Vermont, and Maryland in 1880 ; Massachusetts in
1882 ; New Jersey in 1883 ; Ohio in 1884 ; New York
in 1886 ; Connecticut and Wisconsin in 1887 ; and
Pennsylvania in 1889. It will be noticed that no
Southern States are mentioned ; but it must not be
forgotten that these States, particularly Georgia
and Alabama, are just entering upon their period
of participating in the methods of industry and
commerce of modern civilization. The same may
be said of many Northern, or rather Western,
States.

The "Second Biennial Report of the Bureau of
Labor Statistics of the State of *Minnesota*, 1889-
1890," by John Lamb, Commissioner, contains
much valuable material. Unfortunately, the State
of Minnesota has no laws prohibiting or regulating
child labor.* It is true, however, as I stated before,
that the system of employing children in factories
has not become so prevalent in Minnesota as in
many of the Eastern, Southern, and Central States.
Less than half a dozen establishments are distinc-
tively operated by child's labor. Nothing short of
a census inquiry can reach the bulk of the children
employed, for they are scattered and isolated. Still,
the great manufacturing and mechanical industries
of this State are not of the class wherein child labor
can be, to any extent, profitably employed.

The legislation of the State of *Wisconsin* is about

* Personal letter from Mr. L. G. Powers, Commissioner:
" Minnesota has no laws relating to child's labor: hence there
is no attempt made to place any restriction upon it."

27*

as defective as that of Minnesota, and for the same
reason. Only Section IV., referring to the "Powers
and Duties of the Bureau of Labor and Industrial
Statistics," speaks of the duty of the Commissioner
to examine . . . "the employment of illegal child
labor, the exaction of unlawful hours of labor from
women and children. . . ."

But factory legislation referring to children does
not always depend on external and material conditions, but sometimes on the state of public conscience and social culture, which are not always
identical even in the older commonwealths, and
perhaps even sometimes on mere thoughtless conservatism. Consequently the regulations and stip-
ulations differ very much in different communities;
many resemble the British, many are more advanced, and many lag behind.

Thus, for instance, Mr. James R. Brown, Inspector
of the Central District of the Province of *Ontario*,
Canada, finds fault (1890) with the legislation in
force, and, referring to the State of Ohio, where
nobody less than sixteen years old is allowed to en-
gage in hazardous occupations, insists that fourteen
years should be declared the minimum age for
such employment. Mr. O. A. Roque, of the Eastern District, proposes sixteen years for the same
purpose, and adds, in referring to another topic:
"In my report of 1888 I stated that the inspectors
would be considerably assisted in preventing the
employment of young children in factories by the
putting in force of the school law, compelling them
to attend school, but up to this time I have observed
that no such steps have been taken in any locality

in my district, except, perhaps, in the city of Ottawa. I consider that this object could be more effectually attained by an amendment to the Act preventing the employment of children under fourteen years of age in any saw-mills, and of children in any factory covered by the Act under the age of sixteen, unless such children are able to read and write, and a certificate to that effect be furnished to the inspector whenever required."

From a paper read in New York by Inspector Barber, of the Province of *Toronto*, Canada, before the Fourth Annual Convention of Factory Inspectors, in August, 1890, and from official documents kindly sent me by that gentleman, I present the following statements: The Ontario Factories Act, in force in the Province of Toronto, became law in 1884, but the inspectors, of whom there are three, were not appointed until late in June, 1887. By the definition of a factory (including workshops) no place of employment comes within the jurisdiction of the Act unless there are at least six persons employed ; originally the number was twenty-one persons.

No girl under fourteen years of age, and no boy under twelve, may be employed. Boys between twelve and fourteen years of age must produce a certificate of age from a parent or guardian. This is to prove that such boy is actually of the alleged age. No certificate of age is required for girls, but the inspectors occasionally demand one when they are of opinion that a girl is not fourteen years old. The inspector also has the power to get the opinion of a physician as to a child's age, and such opinion overrules the statement of a certificate, if at variance with it.

The hours of work for boys under fourteen years and females of any age are restricted to sixty a week and ten a day ; but the day's work may exceed ten hours on condition that the number of hours so exceeded be taken off Saturday's working hours.

The Act in no way restricts the working hours of males fourteen years old and upward, nor does it fix the time, day or night, for beginning or ceasing work. So long as sixty hours a week are not exceeded by females and children, they may work by day or by night, as the case may be.

The chief industries in Ontario that utilize the over-time clauses of the Act are confectionery, gloves, hosiery, knitted goods, shirts and collars, ladies' underwear, ivory buttons, fruit-canning factories, flannels, and blankets. The confectionery trade is pressed with orders in November and December. The trade in clothing and textile fabrics increases during the season. Fruit and vegetable canning factories frequently, when the hour for ceasing work approaches, have a quantity of fruit in process. So the law has given considerable latitude to these industries. For the latter industry there is no restriction as to the age of children employed, so long as their work is previous to the cooking process ; after that process the general law applies in any case. Sixty hours are a week's work for all males and females under fourteen years old, except under the over-time permit, when twelve and one-half hours extra may be worked in five nights if it can be done by nine o'clock. Females eighteen years old and upward may work later.

Here are plenty of loopholes for the carelessness of parents and the greediness of trade.

The Province of *Quebec* adopted on December 30th, 1890,* the following:

No male child aged less than fourteen years, and no girl aged less than fifteen years, can be employed in a tobacco or cigar factory. In factories indicated in another list as unhealthy and dangerous, the age of the employed cannot be less than sixteen years for boys and eighteen years for girls.

In all factories other than those above mentioned the age must not be less than twelve years for boys and fourteen for girls.

There is no law that children and women must not work in the night. Under the law, however, the time between midnight of Saturday and midnight of Sunday must not be utilized. Indeed, alternate gangs have been kept at work in many instances.

There is no sort of compulsory education law, and no educational test like that of Great Britain. Therefore one of the inspectors recommends half-time work for children, particularly as it has been found by experience that, though there be evening schools, the overworked children cannot avail themselves of them.

In *New Hampshire* no child under ten is to be employed by any manufacturing corporation. No child under twelve who has not attended the

---

* Not until then was there anything like a classification of dangerous trades.

school of the district the whole time it was kept open. None under fourteen, unless he have attended school six months. None under fifteen, more than ten hours per day, without written consent of parent or guardian. None under sixteen, unless he have attended school for twelve weeks during the preceding year, and no child under said age shall be employed (except in vacation time) who cannot write legibly and read fluently "in the readers of third grade."

The law of *Maryland* prohibits the employment of children under sixteen years of age in factories for more than ten hours per day, but has no limitation of age.

In *Rhode Island* no child under twelve years of age can be employed in any manufacturing establishment. None between twelve and fifteen more than eleven hours in any day, nor before 5 A.M., nor after 7:30 P.M. None under fifteen, unless he have attended school at least three months during the preceding year; and no such child shall be employed for more than nine months in any year.

In *Vermont* children under ten must not be employed at all; between ten and fifteen, not in mill or factory, unless they have received three months' schooling the preceding year; under fifteen, not more than ten hours per day.

The Child Labor Law of the State of *Maine* prohibits the employment of minors under twelve years of age, and fixes ten hours per day as the maximum length of time in which all children between the ages of twelve and fifteen are permitted to work. The "Fourth Annual Report of the Bureau of Industrial and Labor Statistics for the State of Maine, 1890," by Samuel W. Matthews, Commissioner, August, 1891, remarks that a number of large manufacturing establishments do not care to employ children between the ages of twelve and fifteen, for this reason : Under the present law the children between the ages above named are compelled to attend school for a part of the year, and, owing to this fact, many establishments have substituted older help in place of these school children. It also complains that it is more the parents than the manufacturers who openly or stealthily oppose the law ; and also that there is no uniform system as to the issuing of school certificates ; and, lastly, that there is no good compulsory education law. The law in Maine to compel the attendance of truant children is practically a dead letter, and has been so for years, excepting in one or two cities where special officers are provided to enforce it. The manufacturer often complains that he sends the children out of his establishment to go to school, but instead of so doing they spend their time running about the streets. Therefore a law similar to the New Jersey Compulsory Education Law of 1885 is recommended.*

In the State of *New Jersey* no boy under the age

* The New Jersey Compulsory Education Law of 1885 enacts "that in all cities having a duly organized police force, it shall be the duty of the police authority, at the request of the inspectors of factories and workshops, or of the school authority, to detail one or more members of the said force to assist in the enforcement of this Act; and in districts having no regular police force, subject to this Act. it shall be the

of twelve years, nor any girl under fourteen years
of age, shall be employed in any factory, workshop,
mine, or establishment where the manufacture of
any goods whatever is carried on, and no child between the ages of twelve and fifteen years shall be
employed in any factory, workshop, mine, or establishment where the manufacture of any kind of
goods whatever is carried on, unless such child
shall have attended, within twelve months immediately preceding such employment, some public
day or night school, or some well-recognized private
school ; such attendance to be for five days or evenings every week during a period of at least twelve
consecutive weeks, which may be divided into two
terms of six consecutive weeks.

In *Massachusetts* no child under 13 years of age
shall be employed at any time in any factory,
workshop, or mercantile establishment. No such
child shall be employed in any indoor work, performed for wages or other compensation, to whom-
soever payable, during the hours when the public
schools of the city or town in which he resides are
in session, or shall be employed in any manner
during such hours unless during the year next preceding such employment he has attended school for
at least thirty weeks as required by law.

No child under fourteen years of age shall be
employed in any manner before the hour of 6
o'clock in the morning or after the hour of 7

duty of the Board of Education, or the school district officers,
to designate one or more constables of said city, township, or
village, whose duty it shall be to assist in the enforcement of
this Act, as occasion may require."

o'clock in the evening. No such child shall be employed in any factory, workshop, or mercantile establishment, except during the vacation of the public schools in the city or town where he resides.

No child under sixteen years of age shall be employed in any factory, workshop, or mercantile establishment, unless the person or corporation employing him procure and keep on file the certificate of his having obtained a common school education.

No child who has been continuously a resident of a city or town since reaching the age of thirteen years shall be entitled to receive a certificate that he has reached the age of fourteen, unless or until he has attended school according to law in such city or town for at least thirty weeks since reaching the age of thirteen, unless such child can read at sight and write legibly simple sentences in the English language or is exempted by law from such attendance.

In reference to the condition of things in Massachusetts, I quote a few remarks from the report of the Chief of the Massachusetts District Police for the year ending December 31st, 1889. He states that the main objections and obstructions both in regard to education and to age come from the parents of the children to be employed, that the manufacturers have now and then discharged minors who have refused to visit evening schools. It is also complained that the law referring to compulsory education and school certificates is still ambiguous; but it is claimed that eighty per cent o

children between ten and fourteen, formerly at
work, are now receiving an education; and that
there are but few illiterate minors where evening
schools are maintained. Particular stress is laid,
and justly so, on Chapter 348 of the Acts of 1888,
Section 2, which reads, "No child under fourteen
shall be employed in any manner before the hours
of 6 A.M. or after 7 P.M.," and refers to theatres
or other places of amusement.

But under the laws of *Ohio* the employment of
children under twelve years is only forbidden in
manufacturing establishments, while other industries—for instance, the work in mercantile establishments and hotels, and the messenger service—are
entirely unrestricted. This is certainly wrong, inasmuch as in many particulars this labor is as
pernicious as the rest, both physically and morally.
Besides, much of the labor connected therewith has
to be performed in the night, to the detriment of
the general condition, and particularly of the eye-
sight. Indeed, Section 6896 of the Revised Statutes
of Ohio forbids the employment of children under
18 years for a longer period than ten hours per day
or sixty per week, but it matters not when this
employment takes place, whether during the day or
night. This compares unfavorably with New York
and Massachusetts, both of which forbid the employment of children under eighteen and of women
after 9 P.M.

Still, on the 8th day of April the General Assembly of the State of Ohio passed an act to prevent the engagement of children in such employment whereby their lives and limbs might be en-

dangered, or their health injured, or their morals be likely to be impaired.

In order to secure uniform obedience to the law, the Chief Inspector of Workshops and Factories, Mr. William L. McDonald, distributed directions* in reference to very numerous "employments at which children under the age of 16 years shall not be engaged."

In the State of *New York* no child under fourteen years of age can be lawfully employed at any time, or for any period, however short, in any manufacturing establishment.

No child under sixteen shall be employed in any manufacturing establishment who cannot read and write simple sentences in the English language, excepting during the vacations of the public schools in the city or town where the child lives.

The name and age of every child under sixteen years of age must be posted in the room wherein it is employed. A register must be kept of all children under sixteen years of age employed in manufacturing establishments; in such registers must be recorded the name, birthplace, age, and place of residence of such children. This affidavit and the register must be produced on demand made by the factory inspector or any of his deputies.

To violate or omit to comply with any of the foregoing requirements is a misdemeanor punishable by a fine of from twenty to one hundred dollars, or by an imprisonment of from thirty to ninety

---

* Seventh Annual Report of the Department of Inspection of Workshops and Factories to the General Assembly of the State of Ohio for the year 1890. Columbus, 1891.

days, or by both fine and imprisonment. To swear falsely to any affidavit as to age, etc., is perjury, and punishable as such.

In *Connecticut* no child under thirteen years can be employed in mechanical, manufacturing, or mercantile establishments at any time. Children between thirteen and fourteen may be employed if they have attended school for sixty days within the preceding twelve months. Children under thirteen and over eight may be employed if they have attended school for one hundred and twenty days within the previous school year, but not in a mechanical, manufacturing, or mercantile establishment.

In *Pennsylvania* no child under twelve years of age shall be employed in any factory, manufacturing or mercantile establishment. No child under sixteen shall be employed, unless there be first provided an affidavit stating the age, date, and place of birth of said child. No minor under sixteen shall be allowed to clean machinery while in motion. But no person, firm, or corporation employing less than ten persons who are women or children, shall be deemed a factory, manufacturing or mercantile establishment within the meaning of the law.

This latter clause is unfortunately found in the laws of a number of States. Thus it is that under the authority of Society any number of children may be employed and overworked. Besides, the agricultural work, the messenger service, and minor occupations about the houses, restaurants, etc., are not considered at all. The theatrical business is mentioned in the law of Massachusetts only

Thus the working of the laws, such as they are, leaves much to be desired. Still, things are much improved compared with what they were before the enactment of those laws, and compare favorably with the condition of the factory children both in Great Britain and Canada.

How timely legislation in their favor really is, is best proven by the prevailing tendency to coerce them into factory service.

The Census Tables of the United States of 1870 and 1880 exhibit an increase of population of 30.23 per cent. The increase in the number of those actually engaged in gainful occupations was much greater, and a disproportionate share of the increase falls in the class between ten and fifteen years of age. This class was represented in 1870 with 739,164 ; the ratio of increase of this class was 18.65 per cent, and would make the proportionate number 877,018. The actual number employed, however, was 1,118,356, with a relative excess of 241,338.

The object of child-labor laws is to prevent the child from being abused in the interest of production, and from being crippled in its normal development. The final evolution of mankind on the road to culture and humanity must necessarily include the full development of mental and physical forces of the growing individual before the latter is compelled to participate in the labors requiring both. However, for the period of social progress at which we have now arrived, this view may appear utopian. But the very ideas regulating our present intercourse, and the mutual relations of capital and labor, would have appeared utopian centuries ago.

So-called impossibilities have disappeared suddenly, when least expected. Mankind will sometimes adjust long-continued grievances, which appeared to be as firmly settled as the rocks, in sudden explosions. That solemn August night, a hundred years ago, which did away with feudal and class privileges and prejudices in France, and the outbreak of a civil war to wipe the spot of human slavery from the face of the United States, prove the possible proximity of the unexpected, and the perfectibility of the race.

Thus we have reason to hope that child labor will be more and more limited and finally disappear. No hard labor ought to be expected of the individual as long as he is not fully developed. Nor is it required. As early as 1876 the Royal Commission appointed in 1875 reported as follows : "We have no reason to believe that the legislation which has been productive of such marked benefit to the operatives employed has caused any serious loss to the industries to which it has been applied. On the contrary, the progress of manufacture has apparently been entirely unimpeded by the Factory Acts ; and there are but few, even amongst the employers, who would now wish to repeal the main provisions of the Acts, or would deny the benefit which has resulted from them."

I do not care to discount the distant future, when those able to work will by common consent be compelled to contribute their share to the required production of material and intellectual goods ; when the working power of millions of able-bodied men will no longer be spent on the gorgeous display of

alleged preparations for war, and other millions
will no longer waste time and opportunities on dis-
tributing goods by waiting for, and on, customers ;
and when the labor necessary for the accumulation
of products will be no longer demanded from those
who would serve society better by first developing
their physical and intellectual powers. Therefore,
for the time being, we have every reason to greet
with satisfaction the wisdom of additional legislation, as suggested by the Committee on Resolutions of the Fourth Annual Convention of the International Association of Inspectors of Factories
and Workshops of North America, held at New
York City, August 27th–30th, 1890, in the following
words : "To prevent the employment of children
in factories, workshops, and mercantile establishments under fourteen years of age, and compelling
all children of such age, and all unable to read and
write intelligibly the English language under the
age of sixteen years, to attend some public or private school until so qualified. To prevent the employment of any child under sixteen years of age
in any hazardous occupation, or in which its health
is liable to be impaired or its morals corrupted, and
the employment of any minor under eighteen years
of age, or of any woman later than 9 P.M. or earlier
than 6 A.M. of any day, and that no minor under
eighteen years of age, or woman, shall be employed
more than sixty hours in one week ; and we recommend that all legislation for regulating the hours of
labor and the employment of women and minors
be made uniform in the several States, excepting
in the Province of Quebec, where French is spoken

generally, where the same degree of efficiency should
be required in the French or English language, here
represented. That laws be enacted in all States and
Provinces requiring that at least two hundred and
fifty cubic feet of air space be provided for each
person employed in workshops during the day-time,
and four hundred cubic feet during the night-time,
and that adequate means for free ventilation be
provided ; and we deem it advisable that children
in our public schools be taught the importance of
the preservation of health in all conditions of life,
and a knowledge of the laws of hygiene and
sanitation."

"(Signed)   Evan U. Davis (Ohio),
            L. T. Fell (N. J.),
            Jos. M. Dyson (Mass.),
            John Traney (N. Y.),
            Robert Barber (Canada),
            W. S. Simmons (Conn.),
                        Committee."

DINER MÉDICAL À PARIS. AOUT 1891.

MESSIEURS :—Je vous remercie pour l'occasion donnée aux représentants de l'Amérique de faire expression à leur appréciation de votre hospitalité. Quant à eux, ils la considèrent non comme honneur personnel, mais comme compliment payé aux médecins des États-Unis. Nous et nos compatriotes médicaux désirent toujours le contact avec le monde médical en général. Vous aurez observé que dans toutes les publiques occasions scientifiques vous rencontrez les Américains. La cause n'est pas tant dans une curiosité assez naturelle, ni plus dans le seul désir de s'instruire, que dans un motif plus profond et plus philosophique. Il y avait un temps que la médecine—à ne pas dire la science médicale—était la propriété d'individus, un autre (après la civilisation locale s'était accrue) qu'elle devenait locale ou communale, encore un autre qu'elle devenait nationale. Elle était telle jusqu'au dix-neuvième siècle. Par exemple, les Anglais ont été les grands observateurs cliniques de la fin du dernier siècle, la médecine moderne et scientifique doit son existence aux Français des quatre ou cinq premières décades de celui-ci, depuis Bichat jusqu'à Broussais, sans lequel l'école de Vienne, probablement, n'aurait vu la lumière. Après, l'équilibre s'inclina un peu vers l'Allemagne, mais finalement parmi toutes les nationalités civilisées la méthode d'investigation devenait

28*

identique, les résultats plus uniformes et coopératifs, jusqu'à ce qu'il y a maintenant de la coopération parallèle et mutuelle en dépit de montagnes, océans, frontières et différences de langues. Il n'y a plus de science anglo-saxonne, française, autrichienne, allemande, il n'y a qu'une seule science médicale. La science est devenue cosmopolitaine après avoir été individuelle, locale, provincielle, et nationale jusqu'à devenir chauvinistique sous l'influence d'une vanité bornée et excentrique. Nous en avons vu le triste exemple il y a moins d'une année. Ainsi la science cosmopolitaine étant le dévelopement le plus élevé du genre humain, est destinée d'être le précurseur de l'évolution future de la race, après que celle-ci aura vaincu tous les obstacles et préjudices de l'individualisme, provincialisme et nationalisme. Ce n'est ni aujourd'hui ni demain, mais il y aura une période d'union, et de la science et des intérêts de ce qu'ils nomment la politique. Voici les vues des médecins américains concernant et la science en général et la science médicale en particulier, et voici les raisons pour lesquelles ils sont toujours prêts de joindre et les travaux et les sociétés de l'Europe. Certainement, Messieurs les Parisiens, ce n'est pas votre faute s'il n'y a que quinze drapeaux au-dessus du fauteuil du président du Congrès. Mais, pour nous autres Américains, c'était une source de satisfaction de pouvoir participer au Congrès et de voir nos quarante quatre étoiles déployés près des couleurs de la grande république de l'Europe. Encore, les représentants de la médecine de la république la plus grande de l'Amérique répètent l'hommage de leur gratitude et de leurs respects les plus profonds

aux médecins célèbres de la capitale de la plus
grande république de l'Europe, et ajoutent la pro-
messe, tant qu'il est dans leur pouvoir, de leur coopération dans le service d'une république encore
plus sacrée, encore plus éternelle que chacune d'elles
—la république cosmopolitaine de la science.

REMARKS

AT THE CELEBRATION IN THE JOHNS HOPKINS UNI-
VERSITY OF THE SEVENTIETH BIRTHDAY OF PRO-
FESSOR R. VIRCHOW, OCTOBER 13TH, 1891.

You have received more information to-night than I could give, and in choicer words than I can muster. Indeed, to do justice to the subject of our entertainment, I ought to have a degree of eloquence which I do not possess. Thus I beg to apologize for your chairman, whose fault it is—for it is not mine—that I am not permitted to spare you.

What we have to admire in Rudolf Virchow is, beyond everything else, his comprehensive universality of studies and aims. There appears to be nothing that is human to which he is a stranger. He has studied and fathomed a great many things, and has always done not only his best, but the best. In the domain of sciences he has been a varied specialist. His most splendid achievements were from the beginning on the field of pathological anatomy. Indeed, modern pathological anatomy—with all due credit to the French, who created the scientific medicine of the first four decades of this century, and to the Vienna school which followed them—is his work. That is a fact with which medical men who know the history of our science in the last fifty years are well acquainted. His revelations referring to embolism, leucocythæmia, chlorosis, and tumors were but the glorious forerunners of his cellular pathology, which has created a new basis for all of our modern views in pathology and therapeutics. These special studies, however, were always undertaken with a philosophical and humanitarian spirit. When quite a young man his ideas went far beyond the dissecting table. His reports on the typhus epidemics of Siberia and the Rhoen Mountains breathe the spirit which sighs for and loves mankind, and made an immense impression on the people at large. All his studies were directed, beyond eliciting new facts and evolving new theories, to enhancing the welfare of the race in general. Always did he insist upon this—that all science and every scientific effort must be able to be finally utilized for the common good. It is also from this point of view that he was a revolutionist and a leader of revolutionary thought during 1848, and never ceased to take part in the political exertions of the people in the direction of a liberal evolution of the institutions of Germany. Not only did this sense of duty prevail upon him to labor in Parliament for the rights of the masses, in opposition to an absolutistic government and the violence of a tyrannical and self-seeking chancellor, but his time and labor were spent on the duties of an alderman of his city these two dozen years. The sanitary improvements of Berlin, and the impulse given by them to all the cities of Germany and beyond, are mainly the results of his knowledge and his personal efforts. Thus all his theoretical studies were at once fertilized in the practical interest of mankind. He wrote a book on the necessity of unifying the medical sciences, and he lived a life proving the union of all human interests. In his scientific researches, each of which would have been sufficient to make the reputation of a great and gifted man, he did not, however, limit himself to medicine proper; what he has added to our knowledge on archæology and anthropology belongs to the very best any great specialist could have furnished to swell our stock of scientific possessions. Thus the universality of his genius and the immensity of his working faculties are quite unique. Perhaps there is but one man in history whose name is to be mentioned with the same veneration—that is Aristotle, who also was the expert in natural history, philosophy and philosophical history, and politics. But the knowledge of the ancients was limited, and its boundaries more easily reached. At present but few are so gifted as to embrace more than one or a few branches of scientific knowledge or research.

In all Virchow has labored for, there is the tendency of accomplishing a philosophical end, and of establishing a solidarity of all sciences and interests. His is no longer anatomical, or medical, or political science, but science. His aim is man and his improvement. Nor was his work ever national; his science is not German, it is human, humanitarian, international, cosmopolitan. It is greatly through his efforts that the best men of all nations no longer speak of German, or French, or Anglo-Saxon science, but of science only. On that field fraternization has commenced in earnest. The specialism of science finds its final and hoped-for solution in universalism, and less in nationalism than in cosmopolitanism. Thus science, with its broadening influence, will guide the development of cosmopolitanism of the human race ; the latter appears to spend this whole century on gathering and conglomerating nationalities preliminarily to the future, which is fervently expected to evolve into fraternizing cosmopolitan communities. This is the tendency which, up to the present time, finds its best expression in the republican institutions and the hospitable customs of America. Thus it is most fitting that an American University of the first rank should have undertaken to celebrate the seventieth birthday of the very man who has contributed more than any other, first to develop, then to *despecialize* and *denationalize* both scientific and humanitarian efforts. I have to thank your leaders for the invitation to be present, and do so with all my heart. It is becoming that we Americans should celebrate this day. For Virchow has worked persistently, unselfishly, gloriously—never for himself—always in the common interest of all mankind. Thus we pay homage, not to a stranger, but to one of ourselves.

REPORT TO THE MEDICAL SOCIETY OF THE COUNTY OF NEW YORK, 1891.

ACCORDING to the annual report of the Health Department of the City of New York for the year ending December 31st, 1890, there died of croup and diphtheria, between the years 1866–90, forty-three thousand persons, nearly all of whom were infants and children ; and in the twenty years between 1871–90 more than eighteen thousand of scarlatina. The estimate, therefore, of sixty-five thousand deaths from diphtheria and scarlatina within twenty-five years is not too high. As both of these diseases are spread by contagion, and, in the vast majority of cases, by contagion only, and for that very reason are preventable, the loss of life is an injustice committed against the dead and their families and against society.

The dangers of contagion by scarlatina and diphtheria are perfectly well understood. No general hospital must admit them. When a case makes its appearance in the wards it is sent to the isolation house, or, where there is none, to the Willard Parker or North Brothers Island in charge of the Health Department. A hotel keeper who understands his pecuniary advantage does not admit them. When a case breaks out he sends it off. But a week ago, within our personal knowledge, a

child suffering from diphtheritic croup was so dis-
lodged during inclement weather. If a hotel
keeper, however—such instances are quite frequent
—believes it to be to his interest to conceal a case,
it infects his rooms; but he does not believe it to
be to his interest to destroy or disinfect curtains
and carpets and to go, into expenses for washing,
rubbing down, or repapering the walls. Thus the
contagion is perpetuated. We happen to know of
rooms and suites of rooms in big and expensive hotels in which we have met with cases of diphtheria
several years in succession, the patients only being
different, the disease germ, however, the same, and
lodged in the same curtains and carpets.

If hotels mean to do their duty to the travelling
public they must refuse to admit, or must expel,
contagious disease. But what is becoming of the
patients? Where are they to go? There is no
place for them in all New York; even the few private hospitals in existence refuse to, and cannot,
take them. We possess no *maisons de santé*, as
they do in Paris. We ought to have many of them,
for the number of strangers sick in New York is
very great; they would be anxious to pay well for
satisfactory accommodations. And what is becoming of those who are still well in a family in which
scarlatina and diphtheria make its appearance?
There may be no practitioner among you but has
seen such things to occur as these: A family of
strangers have been coming from or are going to
Europe, or arrived from the country to stay here
a few weeks for the sake of a change and of enjoying the great metropolis of the Union. They are

living in a few rooms, and have no accommodations but their bank account. A child is taken with scarlatina or diphtheria ; they must either move, or conceal the nature of the case if they can, while running the risk of infecting their whole flock.

Many have asked you where they can take the child ; where to remove the well to protect them. New York has no answer to give.

It is true we have the Willard Parker Hospital, with its seventy beds, in a remote part of the city.

Seventy beds—and twenty-five hundred cases are permitted to die annually !

The Willard Parker Hospital owes its existence to the initiative steps taken in that direction by the State Medical Society in its session of 1882. The State Society's recommendation of establishing a special hospital for scarlatina and diphtheria was warmly indorsed by both the New York County Medical Society and the profession at large. It was hoped at that time that the Willard Parker would be but the first of a number of similar institutions, for it was believed that the benefit derived from that single one would be an encouragement to establish more like it. The need of them was well understood. In the inaugural address, delivered at the beginning of the session of 1882, the President expressed it in the following words : " It is certain that both scarlatina and diphtheria are contagious ; also that the possibility and probability of contagion extends over the whole duration of the sickness, and is enhanced by the accumulation of the poison brought about by the accumulation of cases. Without thorough disinfection the poison is not destroyed, and remains active. It is also certain that when you enter a room full of healthy and boisterous children playing about the bed of one of them who is stricken with a bad or a mild form of diphtheria or scarlatina, a goodly percentage of the smiling crowd will be dead within a week or two ; it is reasonably certain that the immediate removal of the one who is sick, or of those who are still well, would improve the chances of the first, and probably save them all. It is also certain that a case of diphtheria in comfortable quarters, in a well-to-do family, will infect its clothing, bedding, and all surroundings. The patient may get improved—have another attack more serious—may get well—will be taken again, more seriously than before, and the case will not be checked in its road to destruction except by removal from its quarters, which are replete with comforts, poison, and death. Several such cases we know to have been saved by their removal to a proper isolating room in a public institution. Every one of you has seen those who have been or could have been saved by removal and strict isolation. That holds good both for those who live in infected, unclean, and reeking neighborhoods, and for such as inhabit the better and best parts of the city."

But a few brief months before these remarks were uttered and the State Society took action, an official letter of the Health Department expressed the condition of things at that time as follows :

"Our Reception Hospital is the only place we at present have for the care of such cases. The Reception Hospital was built, not for continuous occupancy, but merely as a place where cases of contagious disease may have shelter and be made comfortable while waiting for the arrival of the boat to convey them to the Island. Within the past year the buildings on the Island were so crowded with cases of small-pox, typhus and typhoid fever, that we have there no room for scarlet fever and diphtheria. Therefore we have been compelled to take such cases as have been forced upon us and give them the best care we could at the Reception Hospital, though always at the risk of their taking some other disease. Our facilities for the care of such cases are so limited that we are often greatly embarrassed, being compelled frequently to refuse patients admission for want of room, greatly to our own annoyance as well as that of the patients' friends."

Nine years have passed since. No improvement has taken place except in the facilities afforded by the Willard Parker Hospital and its seventy beds.

The hope that the Willard Parker would be the first of many has not been fulfilled. It has accomplished all that could be expected, and nobody has had much of a fault to find with it during the few years of its existence. But it was a difficult task to obtain the appropriation to build it; and no Board of Apportionment was ever approached since to build more like it. Still, we require a second Willard Parker near the Battery; a third at West Eleventh or Twelfth streets, on the North River; a fourth between Sixtieth and Seventieth streets, North River; a fifth—one at least—in Harlem. The most serious cases—exactly those which are most in need

of hospital isolation and treatment—cannot be trans-
ported to a distant part of the city. The more
numerous the accommodations will be, the more
will they be appreciated and sought after; indeed,
the Willard Parker is so distant from most habita-
tions that the transfer of a patient is given up by
many a family as a hopeless task, even where the
existence of that charity is well known. This
knowledge, however, is by far not universal. If
there were such an institution in every part of the
city, every householder would be acquainted with
the fact, and the beds would not be vacant except
in the seasons of comparative immunity.

A sad difficulty is that connected with the impossibility of protecting the well against contagion
from a brother or sister sick in bed. The tens of
thousands of families living in two rooms, one of
which is dark, or in two lighted rooms with a few
dark closets between them, or even those who have
a whole floor to themselves, are in a hopeless position. Father and mother, or mostly the mother
alone, takes care of the sick—and the well. No disinfection is of any use where the immediate contact is constant and unrestricted. Similar conditions are found even in better-to-do families that
keep help. Where to send the well children? All
their relatives and friends have children of their
own and refuse to accommodate those who have
been exposed to the infection. So they have to remain until they are taken sick, and pay the penalty
of poverty or of insufficient care on the part of the
family, and on the part of society at large, either
with temporary or permanent suffering or extermination.

The rich must not expect to escape contagion. For many years, and repeatedly, has one of us emphasized the spreading of diphtheria and scarlatina —particularly the former—by adults who have the mild form, and prove daily his old assertion that there is as much diphtheria out of bed and out of doors as in bed. School teachers, business men, factory girls, hair dressers, seamstresses, laundresses, domestics, carry the disease from tenement to mansion, from mansions to burying vaults. The well-to-do classes are endangered by every case occurring in a distant tenement, and the means to relieve the latter protect the former. Thus protection of the poor becomes self-protection to the rich. It is by nothing better than by common danger and misery that the solidarity of fellow-citizenship is proven.

Therefore, besides new hospitals to receive the sick as soon as they are taken, there ought to be stations, refuges—call them what you please— where those children could be housed until the sick at home have either recovered or have been removed, and their residences, bedding, and furniture have become thoroughly disinfected. The number of those thus cared for would easily grow into the hundreds, sometimes into the thousands. Houses arranged for these purposes ought to contain common dormitories, also private rooms for such as can afford to pay for superior accommodations. Fifty cents a day ought to pay fully for the accommodation of those kept in the wards, to be paid for by the families or by the city. Perhaps the appreciation of the blessing procured and of the calamities averted, both from individuals and the communities, by the execution of such a plan, will so impress a wealthy fellow-citizen as to induce him or her to make the experiment with a hundred or two hundred beds. The secular press, which for years has been so anxious to open its columns to the discussion of matters of hygiene and public health, can find no subject more conducive to the public welfare than this. For the subject is no longer one of theoretical meditation, but one of practical citizen- and statesmanship.

After the reading of the report the following resolution was unanimously adopted :

Therefore your Committee on Hygiene begs to move that the Medical Society of the City of New York pass a resolution urging the increase of special hospitals for diphtheria and scarlatina, and expressing its conviction that there is no better protection against the multiplication of contagious diseases over the whole city than by providing temporary homes for the numerous children gathered around a nest of pestilence, from which there is no escape except in flight.

REPORT ON CAPITAL PUNISHMENT.

CAPITAL punishment has engaged the attention of all classes of men, in and out of office—citizens, lawyers, clergymen, legislators, and philanthropists. It has gradually, under ordinary circumstances, been restricted to such persons as have taken the life of a fellow-being. Those in its favor allege the propriety of retaliation, which, among so-called civilized men, becomes the exclusive privilege of the communities, and justify their position by referring to the Bible and the dictates of religion.

Those opposed proclaim their respect for the sacredness of human life under all circumstances. deny the right of the State to destroy it, and protest against the community's imitating in cold blood the example of the very murderer whom it execrates for his brutality and cruel cowardice ; they point to the degrading influence of executions, and also refer, as their justification, to both the Bible and religion. Thus capital punishment is both condemned and authorized by religionists, for the same reason that slavery, but thirty years ago, was both justified and censured.

The questions engaging the attention of this Medical Society of the State of New York are always scientific; they are practical only so far as they are dependent on and based upon science. No matter what any of our members believes or acts

29*

upon as a private citizen outside this hall, and outside the legitimate labors of his professional life ;
no matter what his political party allegiance is, or
his creed and religious belief, here we are neither
lawyers, nor legislators, nor retaliationists, nor religionists. Thus your Committee does not propose
to ventilate the question of capital punishment, or
its perpetuation or abolition, and the subjects connected therewith—viz., the nature of crime, of responsibility or irresponsibility, of the cerebral functions called judgment and will, the existence or
non-existence of a free will and its limitations—
from any other but an anatomical and physiological, that is, scientific, point of view. Your
Committee holds that no questions but those strictly
scientific and conducive to the hygiene of mankind
have any right before your forum. What we must
principally avoid is the reference to metaphysical
speculations, such as that of one of the greatest
minds in history, Spinoza. He maintains that "in
the mind there is no such thing as absolute or free
will, but the mind is determined to will this or that
by a cause which is determined by another cause,
this by yet another, and so on to infinity." Nor
must we allow ourselves to be swayed by an opposite consideration of Huxley's, who contests that
" theft and murder would be none the less objectionable were it possible to prove that they were the
result of activity of special theft and murder cells
in the gray pulp." Objectionable ! That they certainly are, for they are anomalies in themselves
and disturbers of the equilibrium of social and moral
economy. Objectionable they were, both the theft

of a sixpennyworth when it was punished on the gallows as late as this very century, and that which is forgiven or mildly reprimanded by a humane judge of our time. More than merely objectionable is the murder of a fellow-being, whether it is expiated on the gallows, or buried in an insane asylum, or condoned by wire-pulling powers, or justified on the plea of self-defence.

Crime is the result of an evil impulse which ought to have been controlled. The controlling powers are the cerebral functions of judgment and will. Whoever is held responsible for their aberrations and his wrongdoings is termed, and punished as, a criminal. Whoever is considered irresponsible is no longer a criminal to be punished, but a lunatic against whose vagaries society takes pains to protect itself. Indeed, among civilized people, both the punishment of the criminal and the incarceration of the hopelessly insane are, or ought to be, but different modes of self-preservation. By them the theory of revenge and retaliation has been given up long ago. Their minds are more bent upon the preservation of the physical and moral health of the community than on the spiteful annihilation of the rebel against the common welfare.

The question of responsibility or irresponsibility is a very grave one, both theoretically and practically. The assumption of the adage "no free will exists" would explain and excuse and defend everything either friendly or inimical to the interests of society and the rights of the individual. Still, many high in science and literature and philosophy defend it.

Benedict,* one of the best known and deservedly famous physiologists and pathologists of the brain, comes to the following conclusions :

"The brains of criminals exhibit a deviation from the normal type, and criminals are to be viewed as an anthropological variety of their species, at least among cultured races.

"The constitutional criminal is a tainted individual, and has the same relation to crime as his next-of-blood kin, the epileptic, and his cousin, the idiot, have to their encephalopathic conditions.

"The essential ground of abnormal action of the brain is abnormal brain structure.

"The appreciation of these facts is likely to create a veritable revelation in ethics, psychology, and jurisprudence."

So it will, though not every crime be dictated by disease, and because the interests of the commonwealth require protecting and saving.

Responsibility and irresponsibility have but uncertain boundary lines. These cannot always be determined. They depend on a great many factors, which may be fixed or changeable, stationary or transitory. The education of the young, no matter what his cerebral substance or general physical constitution, works only by influencing and changing his brain structure. Disturbances of the health of the body, and particularly of the brain, may either terminate in restitution to the normal estate quickly and easily, or with difficulty and late, or no recovery takes place at all. This difference in the result may depend on the severity of the attack, on

* "On the Brains of Criminals," Vienna, 1879.

a congenital disposition which need not assume the significance of a malformation, but shows itself only in differences in the power of resistance on the part of the cells or organs in the individual bodies ; in the same way in which an infectious fever destroys the one, injures the other, and leaves the third intact and immune.

These varieties of structure, dispositions, and of powers of endurance and resistance are very interesting. There are many anomalies in the nervous system which tend, according to circumstances, either to recovery or to faulty development. Such are the predispositions, recognizable in infancy and childhood, to neuralgia, nervousness, melancholia, misanthropy, eccentricity, dudism, hysteria, hypochondria, inebriety, convulsions ; the tendency to cardiac, vascular, and vaso-motor irregularities, such as palpitations, fainting spells, vertigo, sudden congestions to brain and face. They are neither diseases nor crimes, but they may lead to both. Favorable or untoward influences determine the development of a hypochondriac into either a famous humorist who makes tens of thousands of sturdy men smile through tears, or a homicide who sends a shudder through men and women ; or a boy suffering from congestive headaches may develop either into a heart-moving and soul-stirring poet or a raving maniac. For normal growth and exaggerated overgrowth are but two different results of the same vascular action.

The adult man or woman is the result of hereditary and congenital structure and disposition and a thousand influences of mental or physical nature.

The former are but nominally different from the latter. Education is but the shaping of the brain by impressions, the consequences of which are physical, no matter whether they are permanent or transitory. When the former, they impress even the features of the face ; deep must be the delineations in the nervous centre which are permanently photographed outside. Thus there are educational crimes like social crimes. The formation of the earliest habits is the determination of the character of the man. The dime novel, which spoils the taste and fires the imagination, is as certainly a source of infection as the exhalation of a sewer. Paul Aubry wrote in 1888 on the contagiousness of murder. With him the great factors in inducing it are heredity and degeneration. The latter, according to him, depends largely on education—in its widest sense. He charges the public press with producing crimes by its constant sensational reports which excite the imagination and lead to imitation by the persistent parading of an example. Thus are brought about the acts of cruelty during political upheavals, such as remind one more of insanity than of mere barbarism. His prophylaxis is based upon the same opinions. The prevention of the contagiousness of murder consists in a sound moral, individual hygiene, in the moralization of habits and customs, in proper regulations of the press reports, and in a more logical severity of the courts of justice.

Many of the physical changes which lead, or can lead, to criminality are preventable. The servant girl who lets a baby fall may maim it for life, or may so affect the brain as to change the current of thoughts and feelings into criminality. The development of a syphilitic infant into either a healthy man or an invalid, or the luckless possessor of a cerebral endarteritis or gumma, with their physical or moral consequences, depends on the diagnostic knowledge and the therapeutic agents of the practitioner. It is he who may be the intellectual father of the criminal. The obstetrician's clumsy forceps, or improper use of forceps, has frequently injured both head and brain. The prolongation of asphyxia in the newly born gives rise to thrombosis, hæmorrhages, and secondary encephalitis ; to paralysis, idiocy, epilepsy, or insanity. Thus a few seconds more or less, thus obstetrical knowledge and dexterity more or less, may decide the fate of the newly born, his physical, intellectual, and moral health or invalidism, and his whole future forever. Or, contemplate a few large rachitic heads a few years old, after the disease has run its full course. Their circumference and shape are probably the same ; ossification has been completed for some time, and no great alterations will ever take place. In all of them rachitis was mostly cranial and cerebral. One has attained a normal development : one has developed an unusual amount of brain in the vacant space, and the vascular irritation has added to its vitality and evolution into the growing genius ; the last is a confirmed hydrocephalus with its future semi-paralysis and idiocy. Why these differences? Why—in one case the condition was recognized in time and treated judiciously ; in the other some domestic absurdity of diagnosis—difficult teething—

was furnished by the ignorant mother and meekly accepted by the medical man. Thus the same big head may mean either perfection or incompetence, and it takes more than a jury of fellow-citizens to decide what is going on inside. Psychical diseases or anomalies, both acute and chronic, are frequent under toxic influences. Infectious diseases in their acute stages give rise to acute attacks quite often. Scarlatina, typhoid and puerperal fevers, poison the blood and impair cerebral action by the mere circulation of the ptomaine, though there be no complication with meningitis at all. Even in children, insanity, both maniacal and melancholic, has often been met with in and after infectious fevers. Many of the child murders during the puerperal stage were the results of puerperal infection. Opium and the other narcotics—belladonna, hyoscyamus, stramonium—have similar results of depraving both the judgment and will power. The Chairman knew a woman who took at once a number of doses of cannabis which were given for medicinal purposes, and in her jocose aberration of mind was found dancing and singing round the stove on which she was roasting her baby. Next day the medicinal mania wore off. It took hard work to save her from the gallows. Ergot sometimes, more frequently iodoform, oxide of carbon, and the sulphide of carbon of the india-rubber works, act in the same way. And alcohol? The delirium tremens and its many criminal acts fill the records of both the hospitals and the courts of justice. Still more dangerous, because more numerous, are its chronic effects. Its ethical depravation equals its æsthetical ugliness : mendacity, feebleness of will power as bad as physical tremor, idiotic torpor, and the delirium of jealousy and violence, the habit of idleness and tramping, thieving, and outrages of all kinds, are the mottoes inscribed on its flag. Acute lead poisoning leads often to the same symptoms as that of alcohol—sleeplessness, hallucinations, and violence like those of delirium tremens ; and its chronic influence leads to results resembling those of progressive paralysis. Your Committee merely mentions cocaine, chloroform, chloral, bromides, to remind you of the many external influences which may slowly, silently, and surely so alter the cerebral substance as to result in functional anomalies which, if understood, if recognized through that mute and hard cranial shell, as what they are, would be called diseases ; when they are not they are called crimes.

The anatomy and physiology of the brain are greatly under the influence of the heart. Many chronic and some acute cases of dementia can be explained in this way. It is always the chronic class which is more dangerous, because it is more difficult to notice and guard against. In many of them atrophy, hypertrophy, or congenital smallness; in others, adiposity or fatty degeneration, or stenosis of the aorta with its consecutive cerebral anæmia and ill nutrition, or the obliteration of the pericardium ; in very many the incompetent mitral valve, with its retarding influence on the intracranial circulation, is a cause of insanity or insane actions. The latter precede the recognition of the former a long time. A man whose name was prominently

mentioned in connection with the New York dyna-
mite affair was repeatedly before the courts for
assault and battery and attempts at murder, before
his condition, appreciated and predicted by a
member of your Committee, was finally acknowledged.

The diseases of the brain whose influence on, and
connection with, mental and moral diseases is un-
doubted are either local or general. In many no
other symptoms could be discovered ; in others the
intellectual and moral anomalies were complicated
with other symptoms. To that class belong tuber-
cles, which are quite common in demented persons ;
syphilitic changes ; abcesses, either from emboli or
atheromatous degeneration ; neoplasms of different
nature, and multiple sclerosis. Very frequent is
apoplexy, either from vascular incompetency or
traumatic. A boy of eleven years, under the observation of the Chairman of your Committee, fell
from a tree and had convulsions which lasted for
hours until hemiplegia set in. While his paralysis
was slowly improving he exhibited furibund attacks
of violence with attempts at murder, and finally
epilepsy, all of which improved after several years,
leaving a moderate degree of paralysis.

Of the diffuse affections of the brain we shall only
mention inanition from physical causes and from
overwork and anxiety, and exhaustion from excesses,
insolation, trauma, and other causes of hyperæmia
and meningitis. Here belongs periencephalitis,
which may begin slowly with physical symptoms, or
with mania and hypochondriasis. Senility is a
frequent cause of mental disturbance. Unfortu-

nately the symptoms of most of these conditions
may resemble each other very much ; delirium,
mania of all kinds, mainly persecution mania.
puerility, irascibility. diffidence, misanthropy, are
just as many symptoms of both acute, subacute, and
chronic forms. Epilepsy is a frequent cause of
outbreaks of unexpected violence. This peculiarity
gave it the name of propulsive epilepsy. Many
criminal acts are the positive results of epilepsy,
and many epileptics were cured on the gallows. At
this moment a negro is under trial for a murder.
He is known to have severe attacks of epilepsy.
Experts have sworn he is a criminal. Experts have
sworn he is diseased and not responsible. What
does it teach ? It teaches that there is surely reason
for a doubt as to the causation of the criminal act.
It would also teach that society as represented by
the jury, and society as representing the humane
spirit of the times, ought to keep a sharp lookout to
its own dignity. Man may blunder, but society
cannot afford to be brutally mistaken where it is at
the same time accuser, judge, jury, and executioner.

The malformations of the male sexual organs,
mainly anorchis and diminutive development of the
penis and testicles, predispose to mental degeneration with its consequences. One of your Committee knows a man of thirty-six with infantile organs
and no trace of hair on the pubes. In spite of
repeated warnings not to expose himself to utter
failure, he attempted cohabitation. When alone
with his partner he grew moody and desperate,
becoming more than ever aware of his incompe-
ency. In his rage at rendering himself ridiculous

he attempted to strangle the woman ; she finally succeeded in saving herself and delivering him to the police, which landed him in a penitentiary. Masturbation and emissions produce melancholia and mania ; in milder forms depression, despondency, and moral obliquity. If you wish an example of monomania resulting from masturbation and excessive venery, take that of a man otherwise gifted and in high esteem for many personal qualities— Tolstoï. His *Kreutzer Sonata*, the hero of which is evidently an autophotograph, is the nastiest and most vulgar glorification of male impotence and consequent moral depravity possible. It is again the class of masturbators which furnishes part of the disgusting tribe addicted to sexual perversion, such as pæderasty, sodomy, and homicidal mania. Nymphomania I have not mentioned, because its complication with homicidal mania is but rare. But the influence of the great developmental periods, puberty and the climacteric age, in the production of moral morbidity, is well appreciated.

Great difficulty in deciding the nature of a criminal insult is experienced in cases of periodic insanity. It is these cases which are received in lunatic asylums, retained for a short time, and then discharged cured to exhibit favorable statistics, or are freed by the philanthropoid cranks who mistake a hospital for a dungeon. The dangers of such premature or unauthorized discharges are great indeed ; the daily press reports from time to time homicides and murders committed by men who ought to be protected against themselves and prevented from doing harm to others by being locked up for life. Intervals between acute attacks of mania or melancholia may last years ; particularly, cases connected with epilepsy come suddenly like a flash. Moon and sun, terrestrial magnetism and the electrical condition of the atmosphere, climate, telluric exhalations, intervening disease—be it only influenza, wounds, or other debilitating influences of short duration—are apt to give rise to violent outbreaks. In such cases the decision as to whether the accused was a criminal or a sick man when the murder was committed is very difficult, or even impossible. Years after the occurrence the diagnosis of the case must be attempted. The history of previous cerebral disease, of *petit mal* or full-grown epilepsy, neuroses and fainting spells, eccentricities, hallucinations, possible heredity, will be told with more or less significance. These are the very cases which prove unmistakably that insanity is not always typical and constant in its nature. Doubtful conditions are very frequent. And in the face of these facts a jury is expected, under the spur of one attorney and the derision of the other, to find a verdict of responsibility or irresponsibility. These are also the facts which have induced the Germans to establish the principle of a partial responsibility.

When a crime is made the subject of investigation, the perpetrator ought to be subjected to the closest study. The action of an engine is not estimated or calculated without considering the shafts and wheels and boiler ; but the changes of judgment and will are weighed too often by the so-called common sense of the illiterate or semi-educated. No matter whether Benedict and Lombroso are right or wrong, these facts are incontrovertible. You meet too large heads, too small heads, asymmetrical heads—such as you find so very often in epilepsy and idiocy—asymmetrical faces, disproportion between skull and face and their single parts ; also disproportion between other parts of the body, excessive length of extremities, big mouth, overgrown tongue, the roof of the mouth too much arched or too flat, and the teeth irregular ; the top of the head or the occiput flattened, hare-lip and cleft palate, heavy lower lip, deformed ears, and different colors of iris. There may be the retracted nasal insertion and the shortened base of the skull of the cretin or semi-cretin, or early neurotic symptoms—such as hysteria, chorea, epilepsy, night terrors, and tachycardia.

Suicidal tendency with the result of repeated attempts at self-destruction is but rarely the result of instantaneous despair or despondency. In many cases the actors in that drama had an organic disease—among them leptomeningitis in all its forms, sclerosis, syphilis, embolism, gray degeneration, adhesions, and cysts. Acute and isolated attacks are often the results of fever in pneumonia, pleurisy, meningitis, typhoid fever, or influenza. And these are, in part, the cases which are thought worthy, not of the hospital, but of the penitentiary.

Conclusions.—There are many causes of the perversion of judgment and will.

Those causes which are physical are either congenital or acquired. When acquired, they are so either by the progressive development of hereditary or congenital disposition, or by intervening diseases, or by the impairment of cerebral evolution through bad training, example, and social influences.

The variety of causes, both anatomical and functional, is such as to render an exact diagnosis extremely difficult. The sworn opinions of experts are quite often contradictory. Cerebral anomalies and lesions are very often not accessible to our methods of investigation.

When there is any doubt in an individual case of crime in regard to either responsibility or irresponsibility, it is safer to take the alleged criminal to be diseased and morbid than to declare the sick to be a criminal.

In many cases the innocent and the anatomically sick have been subjected to capital punishment. On the other hand, dubious cases developed full-grown dementia soon after the criminal proceedings.

The knowledge of such occurrences is part of the reasons why juries are averse to rendering the verdict leading to a death penalty, and why but a small percentage of murderers are ever sentenced among us, and why so many are set free to become permanent dangers to the safety of the public.

Human society and the State, while they owe protection and safety to all, must make no mistake, unless it be in the direction of leniency and humanity.

The medical profession must not allow mistakes to be made which can be prevented. This Medical Society of the State of New York—having the advantages of physiological knowledge, and being aware of the difficulties of being always correct and of the absolute impossibility of making a positively safe diagnosis in every case of alleged crime or presumable cerebral disease or anomaly—expresses its opposition to the perpetuation of capital punishment and its hope that means will be found to protect the community by less uncertain and less inhumane methods.

A. JACOBI, M.D., New York,
Chairman of the Committee.
WILLIAM C. WEY, M.D., Elmira.
B. F. SHERMAN, M.D., Ogdensburgh.

[At the meeting of the Society in 1891 a communication regarding the abolition of capital punishment was received from Gen. N. M. Curtis, of Ogdensburgh, which was accepted and referred to this Special Committee ; of their report, presented in 1892, one thousand extra copies were ordered printed and distributed, and the Committee was, on motion, continued for another year.—SECRETARY.]

BRAIN, CRIME, AND CAPITAL PUNISHMENT.
1892.

Ladies and Gentlemen :

Every individual or collective labor derives its justification and dignity from its effect. Unless there be a result, that labor is idle and superfluous, and the vital or intellectual forces bestowed on it have been spent in vain. With the intelligent and thoughtful the effect is not an accident, but a practical aim that is reached after mature forethought and well-directed exertion. The worthiest practical aim of all is the perfection of mankind. I take it that this association was founded with a view of contributing its share to attaining that end. To accomplish such a grand result no one man, society, or complex of societies would ever suffice. Not one drug, unless it be a quack medicine advertised to cure every illness of the index, is expected to meet all the exigencies, anomalies, and disorders of the human frame. Thus the health of mankind, a still more complex organism than even man, requires the co-operation of many specialists. One of them is your Society. But even your Society is a conglomerate or combination of powers. To study the pathology and therapeutics of prison existence, theologians, jurists, administrators, and medical men have combined. The latter class are accustomed to look at things and creatures from the view of their genesis. They are not, *ought* not to

30*

be, satisfied unless they know, or at least try to know, the why and wherefrom. Now, the anomaly of social life which is the subject of your discussions in your annual meetings, has been studied from the most varied aspects. No one aspect, no one man, suffices for that purpose. Thus, what you have consented that I should present here is but a contribution to the common store accumulated for a common end.

What little I shall have to say, fragmentary as it will be under the circumstances, I can characterize in a few words. I shall abstain from presenting any and everything that is not absolute fact. I shall refer to no literature and quote nothing. I must not discuss theories, hypotheses, metaphysics, sociology, or theology. Indeed, there is in other fields so much exact and positive knowledge on the morbid conditions which have long ago conquered your sympathies and controlled your energies, that I can safely limit myself to their sole consideration.

In behalf of those who are not quite familiar with the main points of the structure and the functions of the brain, I here present a few drawings which are destined to refresh the memory. The central nervous system consists of the hemispheres, the cerebellum, the medulla, and the spinal cord. It is composed of two kinds of tissues, the gray and the white. The gray substance is capable of independent action ; it requires no external stimulus ; it is the seat of the psychical functions and connects the sensitive and motory nerves. Its largest mass is accumulated on the surface of the hemispheres, which are the central organ for all mental, motory, and sensitive processes. The most trifling injuries of that part of the brain interfere with the mind, the movements, and the sensations. A slight remnant of a previous inflammation or a temporary congestion, or a small tumor, derange both mental and physical powers. The gray surface of the brain is considerably increased by the formation of so-called convolutions; they are elevations of an apparently irregular shape, which are separated from each other by deep grooves. In their irregular modulations, however, there is a great regularity. In the lower animals and in the fœtus the convolutions are but few; in man they are numerous and elaborate. Brain work develops them, as muscle efforts develop muscle. Each one, and part of one, appears to have a special function. Thus there is a local centre for the mobility of the arms, one for the legs, one for the face, one for speech, and many more. All are joined by fibres which serve the purpose of co-ordination and co-operation. All of the brain, as is also the spinal cord, is covered and protected by two layers of membranes, the so-called meninges. One of them attaches itself more to the skull, one to the brain. Their changes, mostly of an inflammatory character, are so important, and often by their results even worse than fatal, that the mere name of meningitis shakes many a stout heart and pales many a fair cheek in the listener. My remarks of to-night refer principally to the large hemispheres and their gray substance.

Every science has its axioms which require no proof. In biology it is an axiom that the human frame is modelled upon a certain "plan." So is every rose between Shiras and the tiny garden plot of your little daughter ; so is every leaf of all the countless oaks or palm trees of the globe. There is no rose, however, no leaf, that has exactly its equal. So it is with man, with every race of man ; it has a certain type, but no two individuals of the same type are identities. In his structure man comprehends a number of different organs. Every one has two kidneys, a liver, a spleen, five lobes of lungs, a heart : no single one of these organs but has its peculiarities which distinguish it from that of other men. In every teaspoonful of your blood there are two thousand millions of blood cells ; in your ten or twelve pounds of blood you possess almost incalculable billions. No two men have the same number. Fifteen hundred millions of men, women, and children have each a skull and a brain ; not one of them is, or looks, like the other. Here is your second important axiom—viz., that Nature, while evolving her creatures upon a common plan, permits of great latitude within the boundaries of normality.

What now is, with all this variability, the underlying equality—particularly as to the human brain ? And which are the requisites that establish its normality ?

First. There must have been ample building material in its embryonic and fœtal period.

Second. No arrest must have disturbed its development.

Third. It must not have suffered from a disease, either before or after birth, which terminated in persistent changes.

Fourth. The composing parts of the brain must have been developed simultaneously and equally, and essential organs and functions, particularly reasoning power and will, must not be disturbed. Still, these conditions are not fulfilled equally well in all instances ; if they were, there would be more uniformity, perhaps tedious uniformity. If, however, they be not complied with—within the great latitude always afforded by Nature—we have to deal with a morbid condition of either organs or functions, or, what is most common, both. Again, however, though it be ever so difficult to determine the soundness or unsoundness of functions in a given case, the recognition of health or disease of an organ is liable to be still more arduous. Many gross alterations of the brain have been known since autopsies were made, and some before ; but the number of those which have been learned only by late improved methods and instruments is quite large. More accurate knowledge of the anatomy of the brain, and the study of its healthy and diseased structure with high magnifying powers, have revealed abnormalities where formerly no changes were seen at all ; and we have to expect that from decade to decade many a mystery will become unveiled. Still, no matter how great the number of hitherto unrecognized anomalies will become in future, they will belong to two large classes : either arrests of development, or nutritive disorders such as inflammations and tumors.

To these two latter classes belong the local disturbances which have been found in the brains of criminals, such as atypical, supernumerary, or defective convolutions and abnormal grooves between them. By some men of great learning and high standing, such as Benedict and Lombroso, they have been denominated criminal brains. They claim that " the brains of criminals exhibit a deviation from the normal type ; and criminals are to be viewed as an anthropological variety of their species, at least among cultured races. The constitutional criminal is a tainted individual, and has the same relation to crime as the epileptic to convulsions. The essential reason of abnormal brain action is abnormal brain structure. The appreciation of these facts is likely to create a veritable revolution in ethics, psychology, and jurisprudence."

I cannot go so far as to believe in a special type of criminal brains. Crime is not an entity, an absolute and well-defined manifestation of the same kind and tendency ; it is as manifold as human instincts or tendencies in general. The latter are no less manifold in perversity and depravity than they are numerous in the average condition of life and health. Indeed, the same changes which have been claimed for crime are those of insanity. Insanity is the field in which crime may grow ; alleged crime, which landed the perpetrator in the State prison, proclaims itself quite often as insanity after a brief prison life ; crime that was punished by death penalty has been proven to have been insanity in its physical manifestation on the autopsy table. Such facts go very far to intimate that crime is apt to be insanity plus its dangers to society.

Amongst criminals a great many anomalies have

been observed. They refer mostly to the shape and structure of the head and brain, and to the functions of the system of circulation. The head of criminals is more often found brachycephalic than dolichocephalic (more short than long). The prognathic shape is quite frequent. The eyebrows and the underlying arches of the frontal bones are often excessive, the bones in general are thick, the occiput is oblique—symptoms all of which are found in the famous paleontological skull of the Neander valley (and claimed by Lombroso as criminal type). In robbers the head has been found large, in thieves small. That much is certain, that, in criminals, either large heads or very small heads have been met with. The anterior part is poorly developed : asymmetry of the head, and disproportion between head and face, and of single parts of the same and of other parts of the body, are numerous. The occiput is often flat, the hard palate narrow or flattened. The forehead is reclining, wrinkles of the covering soft parts being quite frequent. Hair and beard are often scanty, the nose irregular and inclined to one side, the lips large. The eyelids are in close proximity to the nose, the iris pigmented or defective (coloboma), its color varying in the two eyes, the pupils not centrally located. The nails of the fingers and toes are malformed, so are the genital organs and the feet ; clubfeet are frequent ; goître and rupture are often found. The veins are frequently dilated, and the vascular system is found defective in its function. Thus in many, contrary to lay expectation, blushing is not infrequent ; tobacco is not tolerated, alco-

hol not by some. Irritable heart, neuralgic headache, dizziness, fainting spells, convulsions, partial
paralyses, are frequent occurrences.

Many of these anomalies, however, are met with
among non-criminals. Still, when there are many
of the kind in the same individual, we must not
forget their connection with, and dependence on, the
condition of the nerve centres. Face and head,
their structure and expressions, are under the influence of the brain, even in the adult ; physio-
gnomic doctrines have a certain sound basis in these
facts.

The direct causes of cerebral changes are either
structural and primary, or such secondary alterations of its form and function as are produced by
the effects of distant nerves or complexes of nerves.
I must not, however, weary you with facts which
may appear to you to belong to the sphere of the
medical man only—though, indeed, whoever has
brain himself may well desire to know its structure and its dangers—but my theme demands that
I should at least mention the principal causes of alterations of the brain and of its functions. So I refer to injuries; to inflammations and hæmorrhages;
to tumors, solid and cystic, the latter resulting
from hæmorrhages or from the invasion of certain
worms ; to abscesses ; to diseases of the blood
vessels ; to certain nerve diseases of a severe type,
such as hypochondria, epilepsy, St. Vitus' dance,
and hysteria ; to affections of the senses which result in hallucinations; to changes in the nerves of
the surface which result in insupportable, madden-
ing itching ; to the diseases of the intestinal tract

(the small pinworm has been known to produce
mania) ; to the diseases of the heart that influence
the circulation of the brain ; to the changes in the
life of woman which alter her nature, not only by
raising it to its full perfection, but also by expos-
ing her to the deleterious, because to her too revolutionary, influences of pregnancy and confinement ; and also to the effect of sexual excesses.*

In the interests of intelligibility I shall have to
return to the consideration of a few of these factors
in order to become perfectly clear to those whose
studies lie in different directions, and because what
is to the anatomist and physiologist a subject of
scientific interest only, to the physician an important question referring to the nature, causation,
and preventive and curative treatment, that is to
the jurist a problem of responsibility and irresponsibility for a criminal act, and to the citizen and humanitarian a problem of the preservation and
humanization of society. As far as the jurist is
concerned, his, at least, theoretical points of view
are identical with those of the biologist. A sound
medical jurisprudence inquires into the condition of
the person committing a crime, with the following
questions : Was the criminal, when he committed

* Some of you may have seen one of the nastiest productions of modern literature, the "Kreuzer Sonata," by Tolstoï
—Count Tolstoï they call him. The hero of the plot is
evidently an autophotograph. After ruining his soul, weak-
ening his body, and emasculating his feelings and character
by self-pollution and general excesses, he winds up by marry-
ing, while physically and mentally broken, by killing his
wife, and at the same time justifying and crying over his
deed.

the act, matured both in years and intellect? Was there not an arrest of cerebral and thereby intellectual development, such as idiocy? Were there chronic diseases of brain known to produce psychical diseases? Were there degenerative, mostly hereditary influences affecting the ethical faculties? And, finally, is the criminal person subject to transitory disorders which are apt to make their appearance in long or short intervals, the former sometimes extending over years? On one or several of these factors depends the determination of the presence or absence of the freedom of will, which comprehends two faculties on the part of a person: first, that of recognizing the nature and consequences of his actions, and of the necessities of law and order, and of the consequences of his transgression; and, secondly, that of associating ideas and premeditating a decision.

Disturbances in the nature and the function of any vital organ do not always require grave causes. Slight changes in circulation, particularly when they persist, are sufficient to create an irritation. The higher an organ is in the vital scale—for instance, the brain—the more readily will it submit to essential alterations.

Every cause of brain irritation may lead to permanent changes—mostly of an inflammatory character—and to abnormal cerebral action. That irritation may be due to the effects of poisons floating in the blood or to changes in nutrition. The latter may be defective; lack of blood leads to gradual emaciation and inanition. But the most frequent changes are congestions, mostly chronic.

Every disease of the centre of circulation, the heart, is liable to thus derange the brain. Many of the insane in our institutions have become so in consequence of heart diseases. I knew such a man who was at the head of several kinds of business, changing from one to another, wayward, irritable, and flighty. He often complained of headache and consulted me for it. I found the cause of his headaches and perverted brain action, in a chronic heart disease; at that time he saw spots and sparks, could not lower his head without increasing his symptoms, had to sleep on three or four pillows, and was dizzy. In his business transactions he had been for some time rather incomprehensible, but his relatives were slow in believing that his condition might lead to insanity. There never was such a complaint in the family; why should he develop one? Gradually he became violent; occasionally there was a street fight, now and then unprovoked attacks on friends and strangers, trials for assault and battery, and conviction with penitentiary. From the penitentiary he was sent to the insane asylum, where they soon said they cured him of his now acknowledged insanity. But of the cause of his insanity, his heart disease, he was not cured. When he was discharged "cured"—that is, when he was again forced into the hubbub of daily life—he soon had a relapse. An attempt at murder, which, if it had been successful and the man not formerly been recognized to be insane, would probably or possibly have carried him to the gallows, was again the cause of his isolation in a lunatic asylum.

Injuries to the head, by blow, fall, or otherwise, are frequent causes of mental disturbances and criminal acts. The works on forensic medicine contain plenty of cases in which the gallows cured the diseased brain. Beck relates a case of injury to the head, periodic insanity, and murder. The treatment of the case was a death sentence. He has still another case of injury of the skull for which the man was trephined. He became insane, committed rape and murder, and the surgical treatment was continued by a court of justice—he was executed. In another case, after violent death by the hand of the law, it was found that a whole half of the brain was wanting—the law or the court lacking all of it.

Esquirol reports the case of a child who fell on his head when three years old. Since that accident he suffered from headaches, until, fourteen years afterward, he was taken with mania. In the *Alienist and Neurologist*, 1883, page 646, Brower treats of the question of murders and crimes after-injuries to the head. An injured man was sentenced to be hung in spite of good expert testimony. He was not hung, however, but only because he had an opportunity to commit suicide. Friedreich has a similar case where a man was decapitated because a horse had injured his skull and brain. T. Guder reports eight such cases, six of whom were sentenced to suffer death.

I knew, and treated a part of the time, a boy of eleven years who fell from a tree. He was immediately taken with convulsions depending on hæmorrhages from ruptured blood vessels. After a few hours he was paralyzed on one side. While his paralysis was slowly improving, the inflammation produced by the irritating clot in his brain brought on furibund attacks of mania with attempts at murder, and finally epilepsy. They gradually relaxed under treatment, until nothing was left but a moderate degree of paralysis.

Under the influence of poisons, mostly organic and often medicinal, psychical diseases and anomalies are quite frequent. High temperature of the blood disturbs the nutrition and function of the nervous system, as of the rest of the body. Chills, deliriousness, convulsions, acts of violence, or suicides are but the various expressions of such physical changes. The typhoid-fever patient who jumps from a window or commits a murder is as irresponsible as the one with confirmed melancholia or an acute insanity. A jury would easily be convinced that a fever patient who commits murder must not be sent to the gallows, but what about those whose acute disturbance becomes chronic, with the same ethical and social results? Scarlatina and typhoid fever, even in the child, may lead to permanent insanity. Rheumatic fever is liable to produce inflammation of the brain membranes, on which headaches, paralysis, convulsions, and temporary or permanent insanity may depend. Not only the mental aberration following a clandestine birth, but also the toxic influence of the puerperal state, out of or in wedlock, give rise to child murders. Some of the murderesses are treated for their *crime* and recover in their sick-beds, some are cared for and possibly recover in an insane asylum, others are treated in a court of doubtful justice and may expiate their malady on the gallows or in the State prison.

All medicines which influence circulation in general, and particularly that of the cranial cavity, are liable to seriously disturb the functions of the brain; foremost amongst them memory, judgment, and will power. The doses in which such medicines will have such untoward effects are not always the same. Thus a cautious physician is rather more apt to prescribe, at least in the beginning, too small doses than too large ones. For there are idiosyncrasies in persons who bear but trifles compared with the toleration of others. Opium, and more so nightshade, thorn apple, hyoscyamus, and Indian hemp are apt to excite the brain into perfect irresponsibility. The case of a young woman I have published was one of the kind. She took in one dose a quantity of Indian hemp which had been prescribed for a number of days. When I entered the room she was in high glee, radiant and excited, dancing around her kitchen stove on the top floor of a tenement house. On the stove was her baby, roasted. The medicinal exaltation wore off in a single day; it took prolonged pains, however, to save her from criminal prosecution. Other powerful remedies, when used internally, are ergot, iodoform, oxide of carbon, and the sulphide of carbon of the india-rubber works. Cocaine, chloral, chloroform, excess of bromide, also act by their influence on the nervous system.

Some twenty years ago I was careless enough to attempt an operation on, and give chloroform to, a patient, a man of thirty years, all by myself. We were alone in a third-story room. He was docile enough while beginning to take the anæsthetic;

but during the stage of excitement he jumped up, became violent, and attempted to throw himself out of the window. My efforts to restrain him resulted in a continued struggle, during which I was at a great disadvantage. For days I was laid up, and for weeks exhibited the marks of the combat. If he had murdered me then and there, the probability is that he would have been found, perhaps in a sound sleep, very likely without any trace of chloroform about him. There would have been nothing in that room but a dead man, a live man, and the evidence of a struggle. I have often asked myself whether the man would have had much of a chance to escape the gallows if I had not been muscular enough to protect both myself and him.

The acute effect of the poisons mentioned by me, chloral, chloroform, and cocaine, is but seldom immediately dangerous to society, though it be to the individual. But slowly, silently, and positively they so influence the cerebral substance and the circulation that functional disorders must be, and frequently are, the results. As long as the individual suffers, but individual harm is done. If there be an infringement upon the social equilibrium the condition is called a disease, when the physical changes resulting from the foreign influences are read through the bones in which the brain is concealed; when not so recognized it is called an unmitigated crime. Acute lead poisoning leads to sleeplessness, hallucinations, and acts of violence quite like those of delirium tremens produced by alcohol, which has filled by its many criminal exhibitions the annals both of hospitals and of the

courts of justice. It is only acute alcoholism, however, which is to be considered here, for it is only
its transgressions produced by hallucinations, and
its complications with epilepsy and epileptiform
affections, which come strictly within the limits of
my subject. Still the chronic physical effects of
alcohol predispose to acute outbreaks. The former
are bodily changes, consisting of irritation and
inflammation of the liver, the kidneys, the heart, and
the brain. Socially and physically they show themselves in mental tremor or torpor, in indolence and
idleness, feebleness of will power, mendacity, tramping, and thieving. Thus alcohol is æsthetically as
ugly as socially dangerous. The acute outbreaks,
attended with acute congestion and subacute or
acute inflammation, are frequently the subjects of
investigation before courts of justice and of the
pleadings of lawyers. For the motives of the
alcoholic murderer are weighed in different scales.
Responsibility and irresponsibility are the war cry
of the opposing parties. The fact is agreed upon
that here is a person who has a diseased brain ; here
is an act of violence that cost the life of a better
man, perhaps, than he ; here is the question whether
he is to be killed as he did kill ; also the question
whether society or state, with a *sound* brain, will
have to commit the same act performed by the man
with the *unsound* brain. It is true that the brain
becomes unsound by excesses of its own. These
excesses, however, have various foundations. They
may be the results of whim, vagaries, and levity ;
or of hereditary disposition ; or of habit acquired
in an ill-advised sickness; or in the cares and sorrows

of a man not able to drown or overcome them otherwise. Many of our alcoholics are as much sinned against as they are sinners; and the electrical death-chair is no cure or retribution, any more than Maine liquor laws are preventives. There are very much more efficient prophylactics. There is a story of a liquor dealer who had a theatrical man assaulted because, since he performed, men would not frequent the bar. That story is suggestive of preventives. They are theatres, museums, places of recreation, and exhibitions. In most cases the lack of other stimulation is the incentive to the enjoyment of, and excesses in, alcohol. Permit an honorable stimulation which at the same time is recreation, weekdays or Sundays, and there will be less tedium, less temptation, and less sin. Both the lecture room and the church will be visited more by those who spend part of a holiday in a museum than by those who are allowed no better entertainment than the ginshop.

Syphilis is a frequent cause of diseases of the nerve centres, with all their consequences on motion and sensation, on intellect and will. I speak of it here because it is a calamity, like every other disease, and not always the punishment of excesses or of sin. Indeed, the worst forms we medical men meet with are those in the newly born, or such as are contracted by medical men through a wound in their hands inflicted during the treatment of the sick. The cerebral changes produced by syphilis are frequently quite sudden. Both the membranes and the brain substance with their blood vessels become abnormal. The former becomes thickened and adherent. There are vegetations on the membranes in the ventricles, and in the blood vessels local softenings, indurations, abscesses, and tumors. All these alterations are a permanent danger to mind and to soul, to physical and emotional force ; for treatment is quite often futile. Like the changes in the membranes of the bones and the iris of the eye, which, when they are established, remain perceptible for all time, the material changes in the cranial cavity result in impairment of the memory, depravation of the character, loss of ethical feeling, dizziness and headaches, depression or excitement, deliriousness or stupor, melancholia or mania. Persecution mania is quite frequent under these circumstances, with its tendency to either suicide or homicide, or both ; so is melancholia with remorse and self-accusation. I knew a middle-aged man who had quite a reputation in New York as a street preacher twenty-five years ago. He edified his audience by the public confessions of his own sinfulness and by his tearful implorations for their sympathy and prayers. After these daily exercises he would go to what was called his home and maltreat his wife and children. While so employed he was arrested and sent to Blackwell's Island. His condition was correctly appreciated, and a protracted treatment with mercury and iodine cured him of sinfulness, both alleged and actual, and of his brain syphilis, and of street preaching.

Most of the cases of abnormal brain function, leading to insanity and possibly to crime, which have thus far been enumerated, are those of the adult. There are, however, just as many causes of anomaly which strike at an earlier time. Indeed, while man experiences many things which shape his nature and fate after he is born, so there are as many while he is being born, and still more before he is born.

Let me explain : The day on which a child is born is but the last of a great long number which frame its future existence. Indeed, on the changes which take place in the born infant within the first nine months of his life we are apt to look with awe and wonder ; still they are trifling when compared with the evolution, within the nine previous months, of the specks of combined pseudoplasm which are destined to be shaped into a human being. The organs which give the attributes of superiority to the animal, and particularly to the human animal, develop most rapidly, viz., the nerve centres. Now, wherever rapid development takes place, there is ample opportunity for morbid alterations. We speak of the tendency to pathological variations whenever the physiological development is exceeding its average ; in plain language I should say, where there is rapid growth, there is a tendency to overgrowth ; wherever congestion of blood is required in the interest of development, there is danger of excessive congestion, and inflammation. So daily experience teaches us that exercise of a muscle contributes to its increase, over-exercise destroys its function by injuring its structure. Now, the rapid growth of the several organs of the embryo is not always uniform : the very organs which are mostly nourished and mostly in active demand suffer most. Thus it is that heart diseases in the newly born, depend-

ing either on an arrest of development or on inflammations, are quite frequent; thus also that the
right side of the fœtal heart, which has the principal work to do before birth, is mostly affected,
while in the adult most diseases of the heart are
found on the left. The brain, while growing
rapidly, and because of this, is the subject of many
inflammatory diseases. They either lead to changes
in its substance or to its partial destruction. Thus
it is that many a baby is born that looks absolutely
normal, while inside there is an absence of perhaps
the most important parts. Between the absence of
part or parts of the organs and their perfect formation, however, there are ever so many stages and
forms of development. As there are varieties of
height and looks and faculties in the adult, so there
are thousands of varieties of brain evolution, some
more normal, some more abnormal, all with their
varieties of functions, intellectual, moral, and emotional.

Not in all cases does the fœtal brain work out its
future shape and destiny all by itself in its cranial
capsule. In many, particularly those in which the
abnormal growth begins at a very early period, the
defective evolution is also perceptible in the skull.
Brain and skull grow simultaneously. When the
former remained small, or when, what is more
common, the large hemispheres are but slightly
developed, the skull adapts itself to the brain. It is
quite common that in such cases the bone is quite
thin, evidently because there was a scantiness of
building material all around, like a house with thin
walls and incomplete interior. The result can easily

be estimated, though you never saw a case : a small head, with thin bones, open sutures like those of the normal child, reclining forehead, and the appearance and the soul of an idiot. This class of so-called microcephalics are helplessly doomed to idiocy.

Another anomaly which interferes greatly with the physical, intellectual, and moral condition of the human being is one which shows itself in the preponderance of the bone. Imagine a fœtal or infant brain of normal shape and size ; it requires for its rapid growth plenty of space and support. Now, normally the bones are separated from each other by soft, yielding ligamentous tissues which ossify about the fifteenth or sixteenth month after birth. They sometimes, however, ossify before the child is born ; then the brain is locked up inside, cannot grow, the convolutions of its gray substance are compressed, the blood vessels are hampered, the ventricles encroached upon. The result is, besides difficulties during birth, a hopeless idiot. Or select a case in which the premature ossification takes place a month, or four months, or eight months after birth. The sooner it takes place the worse for the child ; hopeless idiocy, hopeless epilepsy, stupidity, hebetude, gross animality, are the unavoidable changes in the mind and character, parallel with the earlier or later occurrence of premature ossification.

The same forms of disease which are prevalent in the born are found in the unborn. Their results, however, vary with the period in which they occur ; they are the worse, the earlier. As a disease in an embryo cannot be reached, treated, or stopped, it runs its full course. No congenital chronic thickening of the brain membranes, no fixed changes in the brain substance, unless it be syphilitic perhaps, have ever been cured. Thus it is easily understood why there is that legion of absolutely hopeless, or sickly, or incompetent, or irresponsible beings amongst us. They were tainted and doomed six months before they saw the light.

Thus becomes evident what I said, that the path of man is strewn with dangers before he is born. You will see also that it is not necessary to resort to maternal impressions as the cause of physical, intellectual, and moral anomalies in the offspring; that theory may safely be left to the nurses and poets.

The dangers to the body and mind incurred through and during the process of birth are also many. The very means to save mother and child may become a danger to the latter. The application of the obstetrical forceps—one of the most beneficent instruments invented in the service of mankind—is a frequent cause of lasting injury. The blood vessels of the fœtus and infant are very thin and rupture easily; more frequent than hæmorrhages outside the cranium are those inside ; slight traction or pressure is sufficient to burst a blood vessel, with the result of a persistent injury to the functions of the brain ; thus are brought about paralysis, mostly of one side, and incompetency of the intellectual faculties. Thus the very means of saving the new life may, under unfavorable circumstances or in clumsy hands, be the cause of rendering it a burden to itself, its parents, and the community.

Nor is that all. Forceps or no forceps, in the course of natural birth the condition known as asphyxia is a frequent occurrence. With incipient life there is sudden death, or apparent death. The newly born is expected to greet its existence with a cry. That cry is eagerly expected, but not heard ; the lungs do not act; the heart is feeble, perhaps not audible. The absence or retardation of circulation makes itself felt everywhere. Hundreds of small hæmorrhages may be found in the interior of the whole little body; the brain will exhibit them in large numbers; or a large amount of blood will burst through a perforated blood vessel, or the blood will merely clog in small ramifications, and thus a normal nutrition becomes impossible. Again the same result: persistent injury to the brain and its functions; again the possibility of epilepsy, paralysis, idiocy, stupidity, clumsiness, or waywardness, and depravity for a lifetime. Half a minute, more or less, before the baby utters its first cry may forever decide the fate of that baby, body and soul. Now you will find it explainable, too, why it is that serious illness of both body and soul, physique and character, are so frequently the unfortunate gift of the first-born. For it is with the first-born of young parents that both forceps operations and asphyxia will most frequently occur.

Not always will the cases of this kind be absolutely hopeless ; in a number a disposition only will be created to mental feebleness or irritation.

Predisposition is not always, however, the result of primary brain lesion or malformation. For instance, in the adult it accompanies certain occupa-

tions and callings : mental aberrations are frequently met with amongst brain workers, from
over-irritation ; lead workers, from poisoning ;
prisoners, from remorse, dreams, unsanitary surroundings, and such hereditary tendency as landed
them in the prison walls ; prostitutes, from exposure, syphilis, and mostly from alcohol.

Strong predisposition is created by mental contagion. They call it suggestion nowadays. As a
single case of hysterical convulsions in a female
hospital ward may provoke hysterical convulsions
in all or most of the inmates, so in a single family,
where surroundings and influences are the same,
different or like forms of insanity make their
appearance in two or three members of the family
at the same time. The epidemics of insanity and
murderousness of whole populations—the persecutions of the Christians, of the Jews, of witches—
are of that nature.

A few years ago (1888) Paul Aubry wrote on the
contagiousness of murder. With him the great
causative factors are heredity and degeneration.
The latter, according to him, depends largely on
education in its widest sense. He charges the
public press with producing crimes by its constant sensational reports of murders and other
crimes, which excite the imagination and, by the
persistent parading of an example, lead to imitation.
Thus are brought about not only individual murders
immediately after the committal of a single murder
or after the decapitation of a criminal, but also the
acts of cruelty during political revolutions, such as
remind one more of absolute insanity than of mere

barbarism. With Aubry, prevention is based upon the same opinions. It consists of a sound moral individual hygiene, of the moralization of habits and customs, of proper regulations of the press reports, and of more logical consistency in the acts of severity on the part of the courts of justice.

Criminal acts are often committed by persons who were known to be quiet, law-abiding, and industrious. Now, with our notions of right or wrong, of responsibility and irresponsibility, such cases require and meet with the full retaliation of the law. If, however, we look into the merits of such a case, we frequently arrive at unforeseen results. An outbreak leading to crime is as little the outcome of nothing as a sudden lightning or a tornado. On the latter we take no revenge; we only try to protect ourselves against their return. Indeed, if most of the unexpected and unexplainable criminal acts were fully studied, they would be recognized as the consequence of physical changes, and frequently of periodic insanity. Our lunatic asylums are the recipients of many such. Periodic insanity, in which a brief attack may occur after intervals of months or years, is quite common. Many are retained a short term and then reported cured because no symptoms of insanity have made their appearance for some little time. Thus the statistics of the institutions exhibit many alleged recoveries which actually are but temporary interruptions of the mental disorder. The superintendents are to be blamed for it in many instances. They ought to be held responsible for the harm done by the patients whom they restore to civil life with its duties, rights, temptations, and excitements. Still, they are not the only ones to be held responsible. For many of these unfortunates are torn away from their restful seclusion by those who mistake a hospital for a dungeon. I have taken the liberty of calling these people who are constantly attacking the walls of retreats with habeas corpuses and mandamuses, philanthropoid cranks. They appear to suffer from a monomania of their own, and ought to be held responsible for the harm they are doing. The dangers of such premature or unauthorized deliveries are very great; from time to time the daily press reports acts of violence, and murders committed, by men immediately after their forced discharge from an institution which hitherto protected both them and society. Lucid intervals in established melancholia and dementia may last years; particularly is that so in those cases which depend on the peculiar anomaly of the functions of the gray substance of the brain which is called epilepsy. It exhibits itself in sudden attacks, not only of convulsions, but of stupor or of epileptic seizure. It is then diagnosticated in a consultation of twelve citizens, who can afford to swear that they know nothing about the case and have no opinions on it, and is finally treated by the hangman. Not infrequently there is no premonitory symptom and no apparent cause. Sometimes the electrical condition of the atmosphere, the influence of the sun and moon, the changes of the barometer, an intervening disease such as influenza, emotional disturbances, or any other cause, give rise to a crisis. The diagnosis as to either criminality or morbidity is very difficult, particularly when a murder is to be judged, as to its merits, years after the occurrence. It is just such cases as prove to the understanding of everybody that insanity is not a constant, invariable, or typical condition. Doubtful conditions are very frequent. The frequency of such doubts has induced the Germans to establish the principle of a partial responsibility—a very awkward attempt at not solving the problem—while with us the battle of the gallows and the temporary or perpetual restraint is fought by both the exhortations, pathos, and gesticulations of zealous attorneys and the contradictions of opposing and partisan so-called experts.

Nothing is more apt to convince us of our insufficiency and short-sightedness and liability to blunder, and to render us very cautious indeed, than the fact that what is called an act of insanity by some men and some codes of law is called a crime by others. In the State of New York we punish attempts at suicide, perhaps not those which are the immediate results of feverish excitement during brain fever, typhoid fever, pneumonia, or influenza—for in such cases the dependency of mental disturbances or physical disorders is readily recognized; but those in which even the most experienced eye does not always observe the physical foundation of an irresponsible act, and punishment is meted out without stint, are very numerous. Still, in many of them an organic disease can be found ; for instantaneous despair and despondency do not easily get the better of the instinct of self-preservation. Chronic meningitis in all its forms, with adhesions between the membranes or between the membranes and the brain ; chronic induration of the tissue from inflammation, obstruction of blood vessels, changes in the blood vessels or in the brain substance itself, of syphilitic origin, are often found. Our old acquaintance, and new scourge, influenza, yields a number of cases of mild or severe aberration of the mind, from mild melancholia and debility to violent attacks of maniacal fury. Thus we exhibit the brutality of punishing the chronic results of typhoid fever, of previous sunstroke, of heart disease, of vascular changes, of influenza. And we call ourselves children of the nineteenth century, good citizens, Christians, humanitarians, philosophers, and what not.

Physical derangements of distant organs are frequently predisposing causes. The ill-humor and intractable temperament of dyspeptic and costive people are proverbial. Why is it that indigestion and ill-humor are closely connected, though there be no irritating pain? Because gastric disturbance diminishes the introduction into the system of nutrient material, and deprives the brain of its normal amount of food and healthy stimulus ; because it generates gas in the stomach, prevents the normal movements of the diaphragm, and thereby hampers both heart and lungs ; and because it irritates the ramifications of the pneumogastric nerve, which through other branches controls the heart and its functions. A full meal on a healthy stomach renders its possessor more genial, generous, and humane ; a full meal or one hastily swallowed into a dyspeptic organ makes its tenant peevish and morose, and adds another disciple to the school of Schopenhauer. Why is chronic constipation a frequent cause of hypochondriasis, melancholia, and insanity? Because it renders more sluggish the abnormal circulation, not only that of the intestines, but also that of the liver and the stomach and the vast domain of the peritoneum; because it irritates and ill-nourishes the terminations of the splanchnic nerves; and, finally, because it generates noxious gases, which are not expelled, but are absorbed into the circulation and act as systemic poison. That is why a medical ancestor proclaimed that "*Qui bene purgat bene curat.*"

I almost wish, though you may not, that I had six evenings instead of one. For the mutual relations of the body and the soul are more taken for granted than understood, and in the interest of the problem before me I should very much desire to convince every one of the direct and close dependency of intellect, will, and ethics on the shape or misshape of the body. Let me allude to but one example. Why are most hunchbacks ill natured, spiteful, and malicious? Certainly not because they are deformed and ugly and therefore exposed to derision. For persons with grotesquely crooked, rickety limbs or ludicrously ugly features are just as much exposed, and still quite often are placid and good-natured. Nor is it that they are embittered by the long suffering they had to endure before their malformation was finally settled upon them. For, indeed, long-continued pain and intense suffering are more frequently a cause of resigning submissiveness than of malevolent rebelliousness. It is because the abnormal shape of the spine, though not even interfering with the structure and function of the cord, compresses the lungs, interferes with the heart, dislodges liver and spleen, and thus deranges sanguification, circulation, and digestion.

Insanity cannot always be recognized with ease. Particularly those instances which terminate in criminal acts are difficult to fathom. The most extraordinary ones are often those of transitory insanity. It is mostly attended with outbreaks of ferocity. Murders are frequently committed in such attacks; they are quite often, as I have said before, the first symptom, and may look premeditated. For an insane person is not abnormal in all his functions. His will may be absolutely gone, his impulses are no longer controlled by his intellect, and still his reasoning powers may for long periods be quite or nearly intact. The belief that an insane person can be easily recognized as such, and that he is always insane, is a great mistake. Does a consumptive cough and wail without interruption? Are there, or are there not, years or months or days where no symptoms betray him; are there, or not, even in the advanced stage, nights without sweats, days without cough, pain, and anxiety? Are there, or are there not, confirmed rheumatics and gout-stricken men who are well for weeks and months, and still never without their foe always present? Are there, or not, those suffering from diabetes twenty years, until it makes its last call; who once a year, or a few years only, have an attack of boils, or local gangrene, or digestive disorder, and are quite well in the intervals ? Is there, or is there not, malaria in the blood, and sure to break out in a chill, though the sick has uttered no complaint to-day? Not everybody discovers the truth ; it takes a good diagnostician to see a disease when apparently absent ; and the microscope of the mind cannot be read by a jury.

As a person inflicted with insanity is one affected with brain disease, which may or may not be concealed by the solid, immovable, silent skull, the difficulty of its recognition can be understood when you recollect every complexity of the faculties and actions of the brain, and consider, for instance, that even in the abdomen, which is so much more accessible to all sorts of tests and the seat of so much simpler affections, often either the opening of the cavity in the living, or an autopsy, is required to ascertain the nature of the trouble.

Functional disorder always means structural change. Insanity with its results is no fault of the character, no passion, no depravity, any more than typhoid fever or a surgical accident. It is no sin, as which it was maltreated only fifty years ago, but a malady. It strikes the just and the unjust, the religious and the infidel, the rich and the poor, the sinful and the virtuous, those who have spent their time and efforts on their depravation, like those who toiled decades in honorable pursuits in the service of the community.

How long it may take to either appreciate or recognize the insane condition or criminal tendency, and their connection with each other, the following case may elucidate .

Thirty years ago I attended a baby boy for tubercular meningitis. He was one of the few cases I have ever known not to die of the dread disease. In his family there was no instance of either tuberculosis or nerve disorder. Some years afterward, however, a girl was born who developed mild epilepsy when growing up. The boy was apparently healthy in after-years. At school, however, he proved an incompetent scholar, besides being obstinate and occasionally violent. With these traits of character and mind, obstreperousness, laziness, and wilfulness, he grew up, neglected studies and business, behaved quietly enough at times, became now and then violent, and sometimes maliciously so, in the public thoroughfare, and was considered queer and incalculable by his family and friends. My advice to treat him as insane was not heeded, though it was readily admitted that the brain disorder of his early infancy was the cause of his waywardness. The suggestion to confine him in an insane hospital was received with derision and considered an affront. If at those times he had committed a murder, I dare say that the plea of insanity would have been welcome to his attorney, but a jury would hardly have been found willing to accept it. Meanwhile he lived with his family or amongst strangers. One summer afternoon, when in the country, he suddenly seized a heavy missile, after having threatened several times to kill his brother, and, firing it at him, barely missed his head. If the intended victim had been a stranger and been killed, the decision whether the murderer was to go to the lunatic asylum or to the gallows would have been difficult and doubtful. Fortunately it was a member of the family. Then at last they consented that the son and brother was insane. He has been in an asylum since, and will not leave it.

Once, perhaps thirty years ago, I was summoned to call upon a man who was said to be delirious. Was he a drinking man? No. Had he been sick long? No; but he had neglected his work for some weeks. So I went. Upon entering I was attacked by a stalwart man arrayed with an iron poker, but escaped uninjured to the street. I reported the case as one of probable insanity to the police of the district, and was kindly advised not to visit a man who evidently did not want me. A year afterward I learned that after many acts of violence, none fortunately fatal, he had been declared insane. Then also I learned that the man, formerly industrious and mild-mannered, had suffered from an attack of sunstroke years previously; had complained of headaches now and then, but had never been so aggressive as when he selected me for his victim. If he had succeeded in fracturing my skull, without for a month or two giving other proofs of insanity, the possibility at least, aye, the probability, is that an unprejudiced and untaught jury would have sent him to the gallows.

In May, 1891, a man was sentenced to ten years of hard labor in Lübeck, Germany, for seventeen burglaries committed in the course of a number of years. He was known to have been confined in a lunatic asylum several times. The case was referred to two experts, both medical directors of large

32*

insane institutions.   One was certain the man was insane and irresponsible, the other—a man of ripe years and great experience among ever so many thousands of insane—insisted upon absolute sanity and responsibility on the part of the prisoner.   The court sided with the latter testimony, and the man was sent to the State prison ; not for a long time, however, for he had to be transferred to the insane hospital as a hopeless case before many months had elapsed.

You all remember the case of a medical man who, after poisoning a man, killing his wife, stealing a will, forging another in the interest of himself, committed suicide in his cell.   Here was a murderer, plain and simple, a murderer for the sake of personal gain, who moreover appeared to prove his guilt by committing suicide.   Would any jury in the land have thought differently, and was there a possibility of his escaping the gallows ?   I think not, and thousands were grieved when they heard of his self-inflicted death and his escape from proper punishment.   There may be many here who shared that opinion and grief.   A post-mortem examination was made by some of the most competent and most honorable medical men of the country.   Dr. H. M. Lyman, of Chicago, reports in his name and that of others : " At different points the membranes that cover the top of the brain contained patches of inflammatory thickening and exudation.   There was adhesion of these membranes to the cortex of the brain.   These patches were places where the membranes were thickened so they looked as though they were coarse patches sewed on or fastened on

to the natural and healthy portion of the brain.
This denoted inflammation of the membranes, and
would cause derangement of the mind, and, in
many cases, would lead to insanity. It was one of
these cases of slowly developing mental disorder,
produced by sunstroke in India years before." The
dead murderer had been in the East Indies as a
medical missionary.

Many mental diseases—that is, aberrations of the
reasoning and will power—offer much difficulty,
because in most cases they do not arise suddenly,
like lightning, but develop gradually. When you
hear of a person becoming insane from a shock, a
fright, a sudden misfortune or bereavement, the
catastrophe was long prepared by hereditary weakness, exhausting diseases, or protracted cares and
grief. Indeed, we have long accustomed ourselves
to take into consideration the predisposition to a
mental disease as well as the proximate causes. The
former is quite often hereditary ; indeed, what we
call a hereditary disease is by no means the result
of direct transmission of the same form of ailment.
Thus, for instance, tubercular consumption is by
no means liable to be directly transmitted ; cases of
congenital tuberculosis are so rare that one related
by me before the Paris Congress of Tuberculosis
was quite exceptional, and what we call inheritance
of a disease means only a certain feeble condition
of the tissue which predisposes to the invasion and
harboring of germs; or other local causes of disease.
Thus the hereditary taint leading to insanity and
crime need not appear in the same form, but may
take different shapes—for instance, hypochondria,

hysteria, epilepsy, diabetes, or so-called eccentricity. Morel could prove nervous disorders of different types in four successive generations. The first had an ethical defect in the form of inebriety, the second exhibits mania and "*folie de grandeur*," the third mania with murder and suicide, the last idiocy and, happily, extinction of the family. Hereditary influences are liable to show their effects at a very early time of life and on slight provocation, particularly when the education and training of the individual could not, or would not, control the irascibility, peevishness, or maliciousness of the inherited temperament.

In closing my remarks permit me to thank you for your patience and forbearance, for I could not be better than my word. I gave but fragmentary notes on a subject which is as vital as it is vast. Finally, permit me to repeat a few points in the shape of a summary.

The function of an organ depends on its structure and composition, the changes of functions on changes in structure.

The intellect, reasoning power, judgment, and will power are located in and dependent on the condition of the large hemispheres of the brain. They do not exist when there are no hemispheres, are defective when the organ is insufficiently developed, and are apt to be morbid when the hemispheres are diseased.

The anomalies of the hemispheres are either arrests of development or acquired alterations. The first are all prenatal; the latter are either contracted before birth, or during birth, or during life.

The effects of a disease do not show themselves uninterruptedly, just as a malarial fever does not always exhibit its high temperature and its chills. Acquired alterations need not be always evident or perceptible to everybody. As the influence of alcohol on the system may change the structure of the liver, of the heart, of the kidneys and brain, to a dangerous degree, though it cannot yet be recognized, so the influence on the brain which is exerted, for instance, by training and education and by habits, is positive, though it cannot always be calculated or appreciated.

Therefore diseases are not always recognizable.

The effects of structural changes of the brain, from whatsoever cause, are either feebleness or perversion. The many forms of insanity, both intellectual and ethical, are thereby explained. Insanity, as well as that form of aberration which is called criminality, is not possible with a normal brain. Neither form of aberration, insanity and crime, depend on an invariable and identical aberration. Therefore there is no special type of insanity or of criminality. Thus, again, the recognition of either, or of its physical causes, is rendered difficult.

Their dependence on and connection with each other is best proven by the fact that insane persons will often commit crimes, and that criminals often turn insane, or are recognized as such after punishment only, either alive or dead.

This is more or less appreciated by juries, who can often not be induced to render a verdict of guilty. Indeed, not one-tenth part of the murderers of our country suffer the penalty of death prescribed by law. It is better so, for if a mistake must be made it ought to be on the plea of leniency, not of cruelty. Still, society is often endangered by acquittals.

Though the diagnosis of a case of impaired brain function be very difficult, and often impossible, still the morbid condition exists. Explaining is more difficult than hanging; therefore hanging has become less with the increased facilities of explanation.

The word "crime" is not a term which means the same. Centuries ago they persecuted and killed for crimes that did not exist. Many of the alleged crimes were virtues, like the Christian faith fifteen centuries ago. Many are deemed aberrations in one country, crimes in another, like suicide.

With the variability in the definition of "crime" that of responsibility and irresponsibility must vary. There is but one thing fixed, that is the relation of causes and effects, the correlation of physical causes and mental and moral symptoms.

What we have most to fear is that even in our time, while punishment still means retaliation or retribution, we are in constant danger of not recognizing the physical cause of misdirected cerebral action called "crime." The grossest errors have been committed in that respect. If only one mistake were made in a hundred convictions and death sentences, society could not afford to make that mistake. You and I may blunder, but the State cannot afford the brutality of capital punishment as long as the convicted criminal is anomalous. Our civilization, as represented by the law of God and man, has ceased to crucify Christians, burn Jews and witches, torture and violate women and children; it is satisfied with guillotining, axeing, hanging, or electrocuting the anomalous and the diseased. Aye, we are expected not to be surprised if even members of the most humane of all the professions, the medical, could be found to participate in the discussion of the advantages of one mode of official killing over another.

Human society, as represented in the State or the Nation, has the right and the duty to take care of all its members, the sick and the well. The person addicted to suicidal tendency must be protected against himself as surely as the poor sick must be cared for at the public expense. The man with such ethical defects and impaired will and intellect as to prove dangerous to his fellows must be prevented from doing harm or repeating his acts of violence. The well have rights also. No pardoning power of any commission or governor can ever restore a brain to norm or health. The possibility of a complete return to norm or health must not be accepted as proven except after a long time and upon protracted scientific inquiry. Until they be so established, the place for transgressors is in a place of safe-keeping. The murderer has seldom if any chance of being cured, and ought to be isolated forever. But let us have done with killing. Let us see to it that the new century may have no reason to look upon our short-sighted barbarism, as we review with painful awe the centuries of the torturer and the witch-burner.

ANNUAL DINNER

THE PRESIDENT.—I shall next administer to you the favorite remedy of Theodore Turquet de Mayerne, who was a famous physician in England in the seventeenth century, "Raspings of a Human Skull, Unburied," only I shall confine myself to the raspings from the inside of a particular skull, that of our eminent guest, who needs no introduction to insure him an enthusiastic greeting in this city and throughout the length and breadth of our country—Dr. Abraham Jacobi, Professor of Children's Diseases in the College of Physicians and Surgeons, now the Medical Department of Columbia College in New York. [Great applause.]

RESPONSE OF DR. ABRAHAM JACOBI.

Mr. President and Gentlemen :

As long as it is the first object of your Association to advance the cause of medical education, and as you do not tire of seeing it printed at the head of the declaration of your principles, you will not weary to work for it, and will feel pleased with the assurance that fellow medical men from other parts of the country share your convictions and have ever been ready to work for their realization. Perhaps it would be best to close right here with expressing my satisfaction at your successes. Indeed, when the names of the very foremost schools are called, and those who have been among the first to improve medical education, your Harvard will be prominently mentioned, together with Johns Hopkins, Ann Arbor, and, I am proud to say, my own Columbia. [Applause.]

But, while praising the schools for their zeal and success in that line, I must not forget to credit the profession at large with being the most persistent worker in the field of progress. Our very schools, with few exceptions, were the result of private enterprise—an enterprise not always, originally, in the interest of individual self-aggrandizement, but often founded on the appreciation of the necessity of systematic teaching. Now, when finally the schools, or many of them, were slow in keeping up with the progress of science in teaching, it was again the profession at large which insisted upon improved methods and the addition of new branches to the curriculum. New chairs were endowed by alumni, and the democratic spirit of the institutions of the country was often reflected in the unselfish and progressive action of the scientific masses. Again it was the profession at large which year after year appealed to the legislatures of many of the States for the purpose of exacting State examinations after college graduation, and insisted upon a certain degree of preliminary education before matriculation. The persistent and self-sacrificing action of the profession is the more meritorious the more it became known that many of the colleges, some of which were until then highly esteemed by the profession, were bitterly opposed to every movement in favor of raising the standard of matriculants, and of introducing improved methods of teaching or causing legislative enactments which demanded a State examination before the license to practise was to be given. There are on record the stories of some presidents and deans of medical colleges who, after a preliminary education of some kind had been made obligatory by a newly passed bill, applied clandestinely for its repeal. College presidents and deans are expected to know their classics. They know the affecting tale of the Roman woman who, after stabbing herself, handed, dying, the dagger to her hesitating husband, with the words, "Non dolet"—"It does not hurt." Some of our medical educators on cash basis say of the money of the new matriculants—fresh from the plough, the country store, the backwoods—"Non olet"—"It does not stink." [Laughter.]

The colleges are not all like that. We know of some, at least, that have always worked together with the profession in the interest of progress. You will forgive me for always placing the profession foremost. Though I have been a college man almost all my professional life, and though so many of you are leaders and co-operators in a medical school, the democratic spirit of the republic of science makes me always feel proud of knowing that I am one of the file, marching to the same tune in the ranks, to reach a common aim, every fellow an officer himself. [Applause.]

There are some points on which all agree. A preliminary education is considered necessary as the basis of medical study, in behalf both of the student and of the welfare of his future patients. Still, the kind and amount of education required for matriculation are left uncertain. Harvard requires some

Latin; other medical colleges, a common-school
education, whatever that may mean [laughter];
some, none at all. Such was the case formerly in
most of the schools. New York State has passed a
law requiring a moderate, a very moderate, amount
of general knowledge, without which a medical
student must not be granted a medical diploma.
Now, it appears to me reprehensible that any student should ever be permitted to pass a preliminary
examination at any other time than *before* matriculation. If he cannot then pass it, he has not attained the lowest possible degree of mental culture
and habit of application demanded in a medical
student. [Applause.] Besides, his college years
belong to his medical, not to his preparatory, studies.

All those who have the elevation of the medical
profession, through improved medical education, at
heart, are also agreed upon lengthening the lecture
courses, and an increase of the years of study; also,
an extension of clinical instruction, not only as it
is now, but in hospital wards, where the diseases
are best studied, and in private practice among the
poor, where, under competent guides, the necessities of a case are most easily learned, together with
the means of doing the most possible good with
the least possible facilities. Gradually, during decades of first tentative, afterward systematic attempts, clinical instruction has obtained its full
recognition. When I established the first American
children's clinic in 1860 it was looked upon as an
innovation. To-day there is hardly a medical college in the land but claims to teach diseases of

children as a special study. You here have a full professorship, and it is worthily filled. [Applause.]

We have been told that medical education and its improvement is in part a money question; that it was so twenty years ago, when a three years' course was contemplated, and is still more so now that the question is one of four years. This innovation, so we are reminded, will break the backs of some of the best schools, and we must not handicap medical education too heavily. If that remark were meant, not for education, but educators, self-appointed educators, educators depending on and looking for students' fees, it would be more correct. [Applause.] A hundred thousand public schools speak volumes for the average information of the people ; but three hundred medical colleges do not, by their number, prove the satisfactory condition of medical education and a high standard. If a number of medical schools would disappear, no harm would be done to anybody but a few of their professors, perhaps. [Laughter.] We have too many schools, too many doctors, too many students. There is a doctor for every four hundred or six hundred inhabitants of the country. We want more people, and can do with less doctors. [Great laughter and applause.] We can do with less doctors, provided the quality of both the people and the doctors will continue to improve. [Applause.]

We have also been told that the social habits of the nation require consideration, and the doctor must be at something like its level. Thirty years ago a doctor of my most intimate acquaintance was told he was "no *Deutscher Arzt*," "no German doctor," because he drank no beer. [Laughter.] It is said the people do not want or demand well-educated doctors, with heads and hearts equally trained. So we must adapt medical education to their wishes. We need not be told—we know that many popular clergymen and their wives, and novel writers and journalists, also our jurists, favor homœopathy, eclecticism, and run after Christian science and clairvoyance—you know they do. Please adapt your Harvard courses to the wants and demands of the superior intellects and the social habits of that "nation." [Laughter and applause.]

You are, when you consider the question of medical education, no longer advisers of the individual. We are, as a profession and a teaching body, responsible for the condition of things medical and hygienic which concern the State, the people at large, and mankind. We have no longer even to deal with the people of Boston or New York or Oshkosh, or any part of them. The most precious goods of mankind, of all classes, ages, sexes, are in our keeping. We are also responsible, all of us who teach, all of us who practise, to those who learn, to those who practise with us, and to those who will succeed us. The best of us is not too good for the present and future profession, and the best we can give is but what they have a right to demand. [Applause.]

"The social habits of the people." That would mean they must be served according to their own expectations, misguided by the accumulated ignorance of generations. [Laughter.] If it be suggested that the poor, the lonely farmer, the frontiersman must be given up to an inferior practitioner, we have not sunk so low in our democratic country as to publicly proclaim the inferiority of certain classes, as they did in Germany for instance. In Prussia they had a *Wundarzt* (surgeon) "of the first class," different from the second-class surgeon, whose functions consisted in pulling teeth, bleeding, and setting bones. This surgeon of the first class was permitted to practise medicine and surgery in all its branches, but only in such places where there was no physician, the place being too poor and forlorn to tempt a regular doctor. This *Wundarzt* passed his examinations after *three* years of study instead of four, and was admitted to the lectures *without* a classical education. Thus his inferiority was stamped on him officially ; and, being classed inferior, he was permitted to practise on the lowly. In Bavaria it was still worse. Only those graduates who passed their examination with the highest honors were permitted to practise on the military or the jurists or the shopkeepers or the whitewashers in the capital of his sacred majesty the king. The small towns and the farming villages had to be satisfied with the inferior doctor who had just escaped rejection. For them the medical rubbish was good enough. [Laughter.]

We are sometimes told that the population of the interior and our West is well enough off with that class of doctors, the poorly equipped and the uncouth. That is explained by alleged necessities. It strikes me as a sort of medical lynch law. [Applause.]

The fourth year of medical instruction, as it is contemplated, is to be given up mainly to clinical teaching. Besides, there are some branches which may fitly be lectured upon for, and studied by, the advanced students, such as embryology in its various relations not only to malformations, but to diseases which depend on hereditary predisposition, persistence of embryonic conditions, and fœtal diseases. They are very numerous. Another is the history of medicine, which thus far has been sadly neglected by us. While it amplifies our knowledge and reveals the evolution of medical science and of epidemics, it makes us modest. In the latter there is no harm ; for, as a rule, it takes the average graduate, say, five, ten, twenty, or forty years of professional life to become so.

The third is legal medicine and medical jurisprudence, the very doctrine which, while drawing upon all the teachings of biological and medical sciences, connects us most intimately with the public at large, and with its individual and social crises and diseases. In all probability special topics of hygiene would also be treated both in lectures and in the laboratory.

In the present condition both of medicine and of society these subjects cannot be missed ; for the demands on the intellectual faculties, knowledge, and services of the physician are steadily growing. In the last century an erudite physician could at the same time be a learned philologist, or a medical professor would hold the chairs, for instance, of pathology and botany at the same time. Medicine was simpler then. The many component factors of modern medicine cannot possibly be gathered and conquered by a single brain. Still, improved teaching facilitates learning. In most things method is everything. I remember the time quite well when a medical professor would repeat year after year the reading in his lectures of his old manuscript. Now the so-called didactic lectures are giving way more and more to demonstrations and laboratory work. Besides, I firmly believe that all of our immediate successors will learn and think more quickly than I and others perhaps. To-day we adapt our thinking to our facility of reading or writing. In composing, we do not think, try not to think, faster than we can write. If we should all use stenography, we should become accustomed to accelerating our thinking. If our books were printed stenographi cally, we should not be hampered and delayed by the slow pace of our reading. Thus much time would be spared and the mental faculties increased. In that way the all-around doctor, who always was and always will be the philosopher and the statesman of the profession, will be able to cope with the difficulty of mastering, and bind into harmony, the overwhelming material furnished by special investigations.

Let me. after having made some remarks, disconnected and inexhaustive though they be, on medical education, add one on educators. I shall be very brief, not wishing to snub myself, and perhaps offending some who are not here. [Laughter.] Most of us here, I take it, are professors. [Laughter.] There may be a few who are not yet. but cannot escape. In New York we are all professors, nine out of ten ; or, at least, we are instructors or

33*

clinicals, or we are cousins or friends of cousins of college deans, and therefore "in it." [Laughter.] We have to-day paid our respects to the student. He is to know something before he matriculates. He is to study medicine four years. He is even to pass a State examination (except in Massachusetts, where my Harvard friends and celebrities and the Russian peddler who hangs out his shingle are practitioners equally "chartered"). [Laughter.] We expect big laboratories and hospitals to be endowed by citizens or the State for teaching purposes. We insist that society shall hold itself responsible for the health of the people. Boards of health looking after the sources of maladies, many of us claim that the State is responsible for the mental equipment of the practitioner who has to cure disease. Where do the professors come in? How are they to be appointed under a system of improved medical education? There are many ways of becoming or appointing professors, some of which are as follows: Thirty years ago I was offered the place of professor of diseases of children. I replied, I could not think of accepting; I did not know enough. My friend, who was a professor and knew all about it, laughed, and replied, if he were offered a chair of nautics, he would begin lecturing to-morrow. That is, gentlemen, how I became professor of pædiatrics, only because there was no place vacant for a Columbus. [Continued laughter.] Others, as I suggested, are cousins, friends, assistants in private practice. To be rich, well connected, and have relatives among hospital and college trustees is a very good mental equipment. [Laughter.] Have a friend who is wealthy and endows a chair for you. In Germany, be a son-in-law of a leading professor. But lately I read of the death of a German *Privatdocent*, at the ripe age of seventy-four, whom I knew when he was already *Privatdocent*, but proved his incapacity for advancement by refusing to marry the daughter of the full chair. [Laughter.] Write a text book while you are young and fresh. [Laughter.] There are so many that you can extract half a dozen, and make the seventh with the aid of very little brains and much more posteriora. Operate on two alleged lacerations daily, and let no more than fifty per cent die of septicæmia. Prove that the best place for ovaries is in a jar. [Great laughter.] Render yourself a parody of the great Philadelphian, who makes a diagnosis before he cuts babies' skulls, by sawing without diagnosis. The first is seen and heard and heard of : the latter is not. On that line there are many fine possibilities. [Laughter.] There are not so many in thers.

There are men who take things more seriously, at least differently. There are those who, after having been earnest students, bury themselves in a laboratory, or the dissecting room, or the hospitals, intending to finish their education on the day of their death. They will now and then publish an article containing the fruit of their labors, without printing their address or their office hours at the bottom. [Laughter.] They may write a book, text book or monograph, when they are ready, after many years of toil and thought. They will be professors after they have made a reputation, not *vice versa*. Or there is a way they have in Paris, where professor-

ships are awarded after a long, meritorious life or a
searching competitive examination. Thus there are
many ways of becoming a professor, and those who
are bent upon improving medical education will do
well never to cease their efforts and watchfulness in
their selections.

Mr. President, I shall now close at last. My cur-
sory remarks or suggestions have possibly been only
repetitions. If I appeared to display some levity, I
did not mean it. [Laughter.] For, indeed, I feel
very serious always about questions concerning the
elevation of my beloved profession and the safety
of the commonwealth. Both are identical. In
matters of health and hygiene both depend on improved medical education and training. I might
say, if I had time to discuss it, "medical and general education"; for the shortcomings of a one-
sided technical or specific information, lacking general and broad culture, is perhaps best proven by
the many people belonging to other professions who
are taken in by medical sectarianism and down-
right quackery.

Why, now, do I insist upon a medical education
which must appear, and must be, inaccessible to
many? For the reason that the required public
medical work can be done by a smaller number of
men, and there is no ground for lowering the standard in behalf of those who must always be and remain inferior. For science must not be a milch
cow. Medicine is no business : its practice is a
vocation requiring ample brains and no narrow
hearts. For the reason that in your classes of
medical students you speak and teach above the

heads of the less gifted, less prepared, and less industrious. The ideal standard of education must be measured by the capability of the best, not the worst. The perfectibility of the race, of science, and of the profession, and your own individual pride as teachers, go hand-in-hand. What appears impossible and utopian to-day may not be so in ten years or in fifty. Everything changes rapidly. Your very poorest graduate is familiar with many subjects no Boerhaave, no Hunter, no Bichat ever dreamed of ; and in twenty-five years perhaps many of you, and all of your sons, will smile at the feeble inroads of to-day into the knowledge of modern etiological factors and, we hope, of preventive and curative therapeutics, which, after all, is the aim and crowning glory of all medical science. [Applause.]

THE PLACING OUT OF JUVENILE OFFENDERS.

Mr. Chairman :

THE honor of the request to contribute to the dis-cussion of Mr. Carpenter's paper I accepted without hesitation, even with eagerness. I thought I could render a public service by pleading the placing out of children in contradistinction to their institution-izing. Not being aware of the results obtained by the institution (and probably others) superintended by Mr. Carpenter, the lecturer of this morning, I supposed I had still to deal with conditions and practices fought by me nearly a generation ago. At that time I could prove that almost every baby confided to a certain public institution, and remain-ing therein but a few months, had died, and I claimed that placing out was the only method of saving life and complying with the just demands of civiliza-tion.

From Mr. Carpenter's paper, which deals with older children, I learned that the practice of placing out juvenile offenders has been carried out since 1855; that altogether three thousand and fifty-three children have been thus disposed of, and that the results of that practice have been almost universally good. The principles and the methods of their realization have been detailed in a few pages of the pamphlet which bears the title, "General Informa-

tion respecting the New York Juvenile Asylum."
To it I have the honor of referring you. The best
feature of its teachings is this: that the children are
not treated, as far as possible, according to iron-clad
rules. Account is taken of their individualities.
Even the regulation that a child must remain in
the Juvenile Asylum two years before being placed
out, in order to purify him of the spots and crook-
ednesses of his existence, is often modified. Even
the methods of placing out those who do not return
to their homes in New York are variable. Those
who are so placed out are one-fourth part of all who
have been admitted.

Comparing the reports and papers contained in the
fourth volume of the Transactions of the Seventh
International Congress of Hygiene and Demo-
graphy, held at London in 1891, I find that the
system followed in Great Britain with regard to
truants and juvenile offenders of all kinds is not at
all like that described by Mr. Carpenter. It is for
that reason that the results can hardly be the same,
though the same end be aimed at. In 1891 they had
in England 19 truant schools and 55 reform and 141
industrial schools. The former had 3,276 inmates
in 1859 and 5,854 in 1890; the latter, 2,462 in 1866
and 22,735 in 1890. The truant schools received
their inmates for a period of from a few weeks to
the end of the sixteenth year. They were sometimes discharged; when relapses were reported, the
parents were given reminders. When they proved in-
effective, the children were taken away to an industrial school. The proper attachment to it was enforced in the beginning by a few days of solitary

confinement; in 1891 we were told that the London School Board was "now opposed" to this procedure. The reform schools had always a prison system, and left a stigma for life on the inmates, who were old and young, good and bad, in a chaotic mixture. I was present when the statement was made that these schools were rather a success, but at present on the decline. We were not told the nature of the success.

The placing out they speak of in connection with these schools means apprenticeship after the school period. Places were always obtained for the boys, ninety per cent of whom were said to have got on well. It is to be remembered, however, that weakly and deformed children are excluded from the schools; as no disposition is made of them, there can be no doubt that there are but two classes of public institutions in which these deformed waifs will turn up —viz., hospitals and prisons, or both.

The discord produced in the soul of the hearer was lulled only by a remark of Miss Davenport Hill (page 174), who said that "many children sent to an industrial school need only healthy family life to turn them into well-behaved boys and girls."

The importance of institutions for juvenile delinquents of all classes cannot be overestimated. Even such as leave much to be desired are better than none. The starving, dirty, loafing, and criminal boy is better off with a regular meal, a good scrubbing, industry, and watching. Under the proper supervision he can be made to learn order, cleanliness, and the elements. Some may succeed in attaining that in a short time : but certainly those really vicious, having become so by heredity, by acquired physical and psychical defects or diseases, and by the bad examples of the street or home, require strict watching through many years. Indeed, there are creatures so abnormal that they are, and always will be, a constant danger to society ; the time will come when society will, before harm is done by the irrepressible criminal instinct, take charge of such forever, in the interest as well of society as of the faulty individual. This class of inmates Victor Desguin (pages 175–186) wishes to gather in agricultural colonies. There can be no doubt in my mind that, if ever there be a possibility of reclaiming this class of delinquents, no placing out in families only, but strict supervision in an institution of some kind or other is demanded. In every case, however, there are great difficulties. I believe that great superintendents are as scarce as great rulers of nations. A superintendent—as also some of his aids—must be a healthy man in body and soul, active, firm, patient, and self-sacrificing. That is why the experience of a single institution is not conclusive. For while the principles laid down may be the same for all of them, their realization depends on a single man, who may be either ideally competent or fail in his purposes altogether. For be he ever so competent personally, his results depend to the greatest extent on his help. Subordinates are liable to be the reverse of angels. Whoever, for instance, has but watched the promenades of orphan schools and similar institutions, the children perhaps well clad, walking in exemplary order, and attended by adults, mostly females, must have occasionally noticed, as

I have, the frequent outbursts of brutal anger and tyrannical tirades, not couched in choice words, which are more hissed than spoken. All of the children suffer from them ; some are trained to be cowards, some hypocrites, some rebels.

In institutions of the kind with inmates ranging from seven years upward, the danger to health or life—which is unavoidable where infants of tender ages are accumulated—does not exist. Most of the diseases of childhood have been endured or passed by, and the mortality of that age is but trifling. During the first six years of life mortality is so great that one-half of all the deaths occur during that period. Of 100 deaths in New York City, 29.63 take place in the first year, 10.03 in the second, 4.37 in the third, 2.40 in the fourth, 1.64 in the fifth, and 3.20 in the sixth—that is, 51.28 in the first six years. The period from the sixth to the eleventh year furnishes but 1.5 per cent of all the deaths. Thus there is comparative safety as far as life and limb are concerned.

But there are drawbacks which have not escaped the attention of psychologists and wise disciplinarians. After the influences of street and previous home have been overcome, there is the danger of the uniformity of the impressions which must needs dwarf individual development. The number of inmates is too large for individual training and teaching ; the mental and emotional last is apt to be the same for all. It may happen that the same uniform character is developed in all ; if it be not genuine, it may be but varnish, or, in many instances, engender dissimulation.

524 THE PLACING OUT OF JUVENILE OFFENDERS.

The influence of the children, however, upon each other may prove a still more serious danger. If they be kept many years, you have them younger and older, weak and strong, vicious and good. They will learn from each other—bad qualities are more contagious than good ones; indeed, those evil inclined have always a greater influence than those who are well disposed. The latter are more liable to submit to the aggressive boastfulness of those morally inferior. The contagion of vice is greater in all ages than that of virtue. The latter is more negative and unobtrusive. Bad examples, smutty words, loose habits—sexual degeneration being very common in large schools and institutions—create a bad atmosphere. There is a moral atmosphere, as there is a meteorological one. The influence of a bad heart and bad habits is a psychical malaria from which everybody suffers who is within its reach, producing a general deterioration. Though there be no marked criminality, a moderate number of cases with slight moral ailments will spoil the average. A sick-ward with a single typhoid case may not be endangered ; if you accumulate more cases the disease will spread. It is distribution and dissemination that give safety. Thus it is that the general health of a community is thoroughly vitiated by the aggregation of many instances of physical or moral sickness, though the single cases be but mild.

There is another consideration. The institutions are large edifices, no longer houses or shanties. They are big, comparatively luxurious, equipped with much comfort. The meals are always ready at certain hours, bath rooms are handy, the work is done, most of it, invisibly for most of the inmates. They are served even without their asking, and the necessaries of life are furnished without their raising a hand in co-operation. Even if they be called in to help under the rules of the place, everything is on a large scale and under a system of divided labor, and makes them unfit and untrained to adapt themselves to other and smaller surroundings. If they be discharged after many years, they are but little prepared for the battle of life. Every development ought to be gradual; no transition must be sudden and abrupt.

The records of the placing-out system, as carried out under the supervision of the Juvenile Asylum (and the Children's Aid Society also), look more favorable and more encouraging. The placed-out children, after having been carefully trained a year or two and weaned of former impressions and habits, participate in the family life of the people they live with. No stigma need cling to them; personal attachments are formed, at home and at school, with children and adults of different ages and stations in life. If they remain they form part of the growing population. They are accustomed to think for themselves and attend to themselves : there are no halls and dormitories lighted with gas, no dining rooms warmed from an invisible source below, no bath room ready for them, exactly as for those better situated. They learn the difficulties of life and also the satisfaction at conquering them. In this way they grow up men and women of the people, to whom they belong as an integral part.

Meanwhile it is expected that the institution from which they came will take note of their development: change their quarters, if they happen to be badly selected; look out for opportunities of school, church, and trade in proper time; return those evil disposed to the mother institution for months or years; change residence, if the soil prove malarious; select the consumptive for emigration to a State with better climatic facilities; and may aid the pre-eminently gifted to embark in professional studies. I imagine it has been so. If not, or not quite so, the influence of conferences like yours ought to accelerate the realization of these postulates.

This looks almost ideal under the circumstances of the nineteenth century, and practically, I am afraid, it does not always work to entire satisfaction. In the very Juvenile Asylum children are admitted either because of poverty and for a home, or for truancy, disobedience, vagrancy, stealing, etc. There is a mixture of causes for admission which cannot possibly lead to the desired results. From what little I could say in the few minutes allotted to me, it is clear to my mind that these several classes belong to different institutions and ought not to be placed in a position where the leaven of iniquity can work. The *multiplication, not the diminution*, of institutions is a necessity; and in this, as in another point, I differ entirely from some of the opinions expressed during the course of your discussion. Very large institutions are always unwieldy and fail in reaching the individual. We require *many and small* institutions, if we must have them. If that end cannot be reached under the present way of managing institutions, which makes it an object to the trustees to gather in many hundred head-moneys, blindly furnished by the tax-paying community, the system must be changed. The dangers arising from institutionizing in general fall on the community at large. It is human society which suffers from the ailments, iniquities, or incompetency of those who once were its wards, and is held responsible for their shortcomings through life. It is almost incomprehensible that the municipality and the State should furnish large funds to private persons, anxious to act as trustees, who may have plenty of sentiment and good-will, but need not have business competence and logic, to take irresponsible charge of the people's money and hundreds of children, the future citizens of the Republic. It is dangerous, however, to make such statements, or perhaps it was so. When, a generation ago, I directed the attention of those who were concerned to the fact that a so-called private institution to which I was attached, received eleven dollars a month for every inmate from the city, one hundred thousand dollars annually from the State, and six hundred dollars only from private contributions, I was expelled. And here I am with the same heresy, and the claim that the city and State are not only responsible for the funds required for the supporting, training, and directing their neglected and refractory children, but owe it to themselves and to their own safety to see to it that they are compensated for their constant outlays by raising independent, self-supporting, and fair-minded men and women.

There is another point of difference between me and some of those who have expressed the opinion that the number of dependent children in charge of the city (I will add the State, or society) is too large. I urge my point with much hesitation, as I have to dissent even from the lecturer on "Dependent Children in New York," who appeared before you day before yesterday, and whose opinions I have learned to esteem very highly these many years of her searching, fearless, and beneficent labors, both in private and public capacities, in the service of unhappy childhood. What I believe and urge is that the city takes care of *too few* children, instead of too many. First of all, no statistician can ever tell how many cases of waywardness, irregular habits, and criminal propensities and wrong actions on the part of the children are to be laid at the door of the city. It is not long ago that nearly twenty thousand children, more or less, found no place in the public schools. This very day there is no room for school children who seek admission. Thus, much of what we complain of, and what you try to remedy by other measures, is an artefact of our own making. Secondly, we have a large class of people amongst our immigrant population who are unfit to raise their children so as to become valuable citizens. If many of them could be deprived of their offspring it would be a blessing, both for the latter and the community of which they are some day to become members. Meanwhile they grow up in ignorance and, consecutively, vice. But that cannot be done under our laws. Still, many of the inmates of our institutions are just these neglected and unschooled children. Thirdly, those parents whose children have become intractable and perverse because of their own shortcomings or insufficiencies, are forever unfit to deserve being trusted with the bringing-up of their offspring, whom they will raise or allow to develop into criminals. They ought not to be trusted with the sacred office of raising the young. Unless the city or State take charge of them they will grow up enemies of the community. It is preposterous that no fault is ever found with the appropriations for police, penitentiaries, State prisons, and electrical chairs, and for new courts of justice and their various officers, but there is a hue and cry over appropriations when required for preventing the dire necessity. The ounce of prevention is refused with obstinate clamor, the cost of the pound of doubtful cure is meekly submitted to.

The children who at present crowd the dens and sidewalks, grow up without schooling, under the influence and control of illiterate, careless, criminal parents, and of the examples of their neglected, brutal, thieving, depraved neighbors, with soiled souls under their dirty skins and rags, hungry and therefore malicious, not to speak at all of those whose very system is physically predestined to moral deficiency and criminal tendency—they are those whom you have to meet somewhere, either in institutions, not to reform, but to form them; in places you pick out for them where they can be brought up, away from the din and mire of the large city; or in future at the voting places, where they select your masters; or on the highways, or in the hospitals, the

34*

lunacy asylums, the prisons. Is that overdrawn? Or is it that this class must be, after all, looked upon as the benefactors of benevolent society? Is it not ludicrous and farcical, worthy of Mephistophelian philosophy, that the liquor saloons, which aid in feeding vice with all its appurtenances and dangers, furnish the bulk of the money you eagerly receive for your institutions?

The city and State require sober, industrious, and fairly informed citizens. The neglected population can become so only when taken by the hand early. The larger the number you save from the streets, dens, brutality, and bad example, the better. Let your class of dependent children be as large as possible. It *is* large, and is growing. There will never be a stigma attached to those whom the community protects, to save them and itself at the same time. That is the problem, as it must be the programme, of the present and the future. By performing this duty toward ourselves—call it humanitarian, politic, socialistic, what you please—and by accepting the watchword of socialism, love and solidarity, we shall, for we have to deal with multitudes, escape political deterioration and anarchy.

Have we the means? We have ample funds for police and prisons, for capitols, court houses, and cathedrals, for speedways, docks, and asphaltum; we can certainly, if we wish, build school houses for our children, and institutions for the indigent, and can afford to elaborate plans and raise the funds for the improvement of neglected childhood, not only in their interest but that of the community and ourselves : indeed, a slight change of the verse of the New Testament covers it all: What you do unto the lowliest of them, you do unto yourselves.